D1543204

ARISTOTLE

VI

LCL 338

ARISTOTLE

ON THE HEAVENS

WITH AN ENGLISH TRANSLATION BY

W. K. C. GUTHRIE

HARVARD UNIVERSITY PRESS
CAMBRIDGE, MASSACHUSETTS
LONDON, ENGLAND

First published 1939
Reprinted 1945, 1953, 1960, 1971, 1986, 2000

LOEB CLASSICAL LIBRARY® is a registered trademark
of the President and Fellows of Harvard College

ISBN 0-674-99372-1

Printed in Great Britain by St Edmundsbury Press Ltd,
Bury St Edmunds, Suffolk, on acid-free paper.
Bound by Hunter & Foulis Ltd, Edinburgh, Scotland.

CONTENTS

PREFACE

THE text used in this volume is based on Bekker's, but in a sense which may be thought Pickwickian and must be defined. " Based on " means that, to the best of my knowledge, every departure from Bekker has been noted and its authority acknowledged. The departures are many, for Bekker's text is faulty and it would have been contrary to the principles of this series to ignore the improvements introduced in the excellent edition of Mr. D. J. Allan, which appeared most opportunely in the Oxford Classical Texts while this translation was in preparation. I have availed myself extensively of the information contained in his critical apparatus. I have also used the text and German translation of C. Prantl (Leipzig, 1854), but his readings agree to a large extent with those of Bekker, and his own alterations are not always an improvement. I have only occasionally cited him by name.

My greatest debt is to the translation of this treatise by J. L. Stocks in the Oxford translation of Aristotle. This was a pioneer work, and has set an example of true scholarship and philosophic understanding which it is bold indeed to emulate. Others can speak better of the gap which his early death has left in the intellectual life of England, but I would record a sense of

PREFACE

personal loss that this work cannot now benefit by the criticism of his maturer mind. I wish also to acknowledge with gratitude the loan by Miss Wicksteed of her father's text of the treatise with his marginal annotations, which have thrown light in several dark places. In introduction, translation and notes I have tried to make critical use of work which was not available when Stocks published his translation, especially that of Jaeger and von Arnim, and I owe a great and obvious debt to the writings of Sir W. D. Ross. The essay on Aristotle's development has been much improved by the friendly criticism of Mr. R. Hackforth. The Greek commentary of Simplicius has been an invaluable aid, and is referred to by the pagination of Heiberg in the Berlin edition of the Greek commentaries on Aristotle.

Each chapter is preceded by a fairly full summary of its argument. It is hoped that when a passage in the text seems obscure, and no explanatory note is provided, a reference to the summary may remove the difficulty by making clear the relation of the passage to its context.

Finally, since " none of these things moves itself," I should like to thank Professor Cornford, the first mover to whom I owe the opportunity of undertaking this translation. It is dedicated to him above all as one who, through long familiarity with the Greek mind in all its diversity, has learned to understand and to teach others the differences between ancient and modern ways of thinking.

W. K. C. GUTHRIE

INTRODUCTION

I. Contents. Aristotle's World-system

The Greek word οὐρανός, used as a title to describe the subject of this work,[a] bears, as Aristotle himself explains (i. 9. 278 b 11), three different meanings : (i) the sphere which bounds the whole Universe, and contains the fixed stars, (ii) the region between this outermost sphere and the moon, where are the spheres carrying the planets, (iii) the Universe as a whole, i.e. everything enclosed by the outermost sphere, including the earth. Books i. and ii. of the treatise, forming together two thirds of the whole, deal with the first and second regions, which stand in contrast to the sublunary world as being made of the divine and imperishable substance *aither*. The shorter books iii. and iv. discuss the sublunary world, containing the familiar four elements which are the material of the earth and the atmosphere immediately surrounding it. It is conceivable therefore that, as Alexander of Aphrodisias supposed, the title was chosen to indicate the full scope of the work, but more likely that (as Mr. Allan suggests) it was thought of by the ancient editors in its more restricted sense,

---

[a] The name never occurs in A. himself, and seems to have been the invention of his editors. For further details see D. J. Allan, *De caelo* (Oxford Class. Texts), p. iii. n. 1.

and applied to the whole in recognition of the length and importance of the treatment of the heavenly bodies and their substance. If we may accept this, then the only possible English translation (" On the Heavens ") is not so inadequate as might be supposed.

The contents are perhaps best described in the form of a brief outline of the world-system as Aristotle sees it in this work. The Universe is spherical, having the sphere of the fixed stars as its circumference, and the earth at its centre. Between these two are, broadly speaking, successive spherical layers of different kinds of body. (We should more naturally say " matter," but the use of that term to represent σῶμα can only lead to confusion with ὕλη or matter in the technical Aristotelian sense.) Proceeding from circumference to centre, we find bodies of an ever-decreasing degree of divinity, permanence, " form," and all the other attributes believed by Aristotle to endow a substance with worth (τιμή) ; for the concept of value is never absent from his philosophy (i. 2. 269 b 15, iv. 3. 310 b 14 and 4. 312 a 15, *De gen. et corr.* 335 a 18). The outermost sphere, and the stars which it contains (ii. 7), are composed not of fire, as had been supposed, but of the fifth element *aither* in its purest form. This fifth body is described, and the necessity for its existence demonstrated, in the first book. It is distinguished from the other four by its natural motion, which is circular, whereas theirs are rectilinear, either to or from the centre of the Universe. (i. 2.) (These are the only forms of simple motion, and to each simple body is assigned a simple natural motion—268 b 14 ff.) With this goes naturally the fact that the fifth body is eternal and the others are perishable, for alone of motions circular revolution has no contrary and is therefore unceasing. (i. 4. A motion is defined with reference to its goal, and motion around a circle, from whatever starting-point and in whatever direction, is always towards the same goal.) The substance of the fifth body likewise has no contrary by whose action it could be destroyed. (i. 3.)

The Universe being spherical is finite. An infinite body is on general grounds an impossibility (i. 5-7), and in fact our own spherical world contains all the body in existence and there is no possibility of even a finite plurality of worlds. (i. 8 and 9.) Beyond this all-embracing sphere is neither body nor place nor void nor time. Therefore anything that may exist outside it must be incorporeal, and there is this much justification for believing that whatever is there is of a wholly divine, eternal and perfect nature. (i. 9. 279 a 11.)

Within this spherical envelope lie, one within the other, the spheres which carry the planets (including sun and moon). A number of spheres controls the motion of each planet, in the innermost of which the planet itself is set. (Referred to at ii. 12. 293 a 5, but only fully expounded in the *Metaphysics*, Λ ch. 8.) These spheres, being introduced to explain the apparent irregularities in the paths of the planets, do not revolve about the same poles or in the same direction as the sphere of the fixed stars, and Aristotle has an ingenious argument to prove that the existence of this multiplicity of circular motions, as well as of the stationary earth, is a necessary precondition of the primary movement itself. (ii. 3.) The planetary spheres are like the primary sphere composed of the fifth body, which however suffers contamination and declines in purity as we approach the lower strata of the Universe. (*Meteor.* 340 b 6.) The stars and planets remain fixed at a definite point in their spheres, and are carried round by the revolution of the whole sphere. They do not move of themselves. (ii. 8.) Since they are no longer supposed to be made of fire as in earlier cosmogonies, a different explanation has to be sought of the light and (in the case of the sun) heat which they emit. This is due to the friction set up by contact with the air or fire beneath them as they swing round in their spheres. (ii. 7. See note (ii) at beginning of chapter.) They are spherical in shape. (ii. 11.)

Below the heavenly spheres of *aither* come the sublunary regions of the inferior elements. (Books iii. and iv.) These are four, fire and earth (" the extremes "), air and water (" the intermediates "). The essential and definitive property of each is the possession of an inherent source of motion, or natural tendency in a certain direction, and this in turn depends on the possession of a natural place in the Universe, towards which the nature of each is constantly impelling it. Once it has arrived at this place, the same nature which was the cause of its motion is the cause of its quiescence. (iii. 2, iv. 3, 4.) This doctrine affords the true explanation of weight and lightness. Weight is motion towards the centre, lightness motion away from the centre. Thus fire seeks and rests at the circumference,[a] earth the

---

[a] Not of course the circumference of the whole Universe, which is the place of *aither*, but only of " the space in which they perform their motion " (312 a 4). Yet A.'s language often does suggest that in describing the inferior elements he has temporarily forgotten that they are not in his system, as in those of his predecessors, the only bodies in the world.

centre, air the region immediately below fire, and water the region immediately above earth. Fire and earth are therefore absolutely light and heavy respectively, air and water relatively so. The motion (φορά) of an element towards its proper place may be expressed in terms which show it to be only an instance of the wider formula descriptive of every sort of change (κίνησις), as the actualization of a potency, or the final (310 b 32) stage in the progress from matter to form. Only in its proper place is an element fully actual. (iv. 3. For the general law, see *Phys.* iii., 201 a 11, etc.)

None of the elements is eternal as such, but they are generated out of each other and pass into each other again. (iii. 6.) The Universe as a whole is ungenerated and indestructible. (i. 10-12.)

The earth, as the foregoing arguments suggest, is situated at the centre of the Universe and is at rest. It is spherical in shape, and is of no great size relatively to the stars. (ii. 14.)

II. The *De caelo* in relation to Aristotle's Philosophical Development

The development of Aristotle's theology, and of the theory of motion on which it depends, has attracted considerable attention since the publication of Professor Jaeger's book in 1923.[a] For this topic the *De caelo* is of central importance, representing as it clearly

[a] W. Jaeger, *Aristoteles, Grundlegung einer Geschichte seiner Entwicklung*, Berlin, 1923 (trans. R. Robinson, Oxford, 1934); H. von Arnim, *Die Entstehung der Gotteslehre des Arist.*, Vienna, 1931; W. K. C. Guthrie, "The Development of Aristotle's Theology, i." in *Class. Quart.* xxvii. (1933), pp. 162-171; Sir W. D. Ross, *Aristotle's Physics*, Oxford, 1936, pp. 94-102.

does a transitional stage in his views. It should nevertheless be understood at the outset that a single work need not necessarily correspond wholly to a single stage of his thought, and that the presence in the same treatise of elements believed to belong to different periods is no evidence that the whole theory of development is false. The *De caelo* is not a finished product, trimmed and tidied for the press. It was never planned for publication, but is a manuscript intended to serve Aristotle himself and his pupils as a basis for teaching and research. When we take into consideration that, as I have shown elsewhere,[a] the progress of his theory of motion was a simple development and never a contradiction of what had gone before, it is only to be expected that such a manuscript will have been subject to additions by the hand of the master himself or of his pupils. To admit this may be dangerous, since it brings with it the temptation to impose an artificial consistency by the abuse of dissecting methods, but it is a fact which careful reading of the *De caelo* puts beyond doubt.

The discussions have shown that there are two questions which especially attract the attention of a student of the *De caelo*. Though not unconnected, they may conveniently be treated successively. They are (i) the question whether the belief in an unmoved and hence incorporeal first mover was from the beginning a feature of Aristotle's theory of motion, and if not, at what point in his writings it was introduced ; (ii) the question whether the doctrine of natural motions expounded in this treatise has so overlaid his belief in the *aliveness* of the heavenly substance that for a time Aristotle is

[a] *C.Q.* 1933, pp. 167 ff. (Ross is in agreement, *Physics*, p. 98.)

virtually explaining the movement of the spheres on purely mechanistic lines.

(i) Aristotle's final theory of motion is briefly this. Everything that is in motion is moved by something else. Self-motion is impossible because motion correctly defined is the actualization of a potency, and the agent of actualization must itself be in actuality in respect of the particular change or movement in question. That is, the agent must be already in the state towards which the motion of the patient is tending. (Whatever heats is itself hot, etc.) We may not believe in either an uncaused motion or an infinite series of moved movers. Therefore the original cause must be something which can originate motion while itself remaining unmoved. (*Phys.* vii. 1, viii. 4-5.) At the same time everything can be spoken of as having, in so far as it is a natural object, an internal cause or principle of motion. This is that potency, or natural capacity, which has just been spoken of as being realized in the act of motion itself. But an object in motion is not necessarily exercising its natural capacity. Motion may be either natural or unnatural. If I hold a stone aloft and let it go, its own nature is the cause of its movement towards the ground. But I may hurl it up into the air, in which case its motion will be " enforced " or " contrary to its nature." There are thus two possible causes of motion, the thing's own nature or an external force [a] : and it is obvious that the external force ($\beta\acute{\iota}a$) which moves a body contrary to its own nature is to be sharply distinguished from the external mover which is postulated out of respect to the

---

[a] It is even noted once that constraint may *hasten* natural motion instead of counteracting it—*De caelo*, 301 b 17-22.

philosopher's conviction that nothing can move itself, and whose function is to call latent powers into activity, fulfilling, not frustrating, the nature of each thing.

In the last resort, then, the possible causes or sources (ἀρχαί) of motion emerge as three : (i) " nature," defined as " a source of motion in the thing itself " (*De caelo* iii. 2. 301 b 17, *cf. Phys.* ii. 192 b 20) ; (ii) an external mover which energizes the nature of the moved by virtue of having itself reached the goal to which the latter inclines ; (iii) any external force which may overcome the nature of the object and constrain it to move in a way unnatural to it.

Now these three causes can perfectly well exist side by side as parts of a single coherent theory of motion. Failure to see this detracted seriously from the value of von Arnim's arguments about the *De caelo*, in so far as they were based on the assumption that belief in an internal source of motion is inconsistent with belief in an external mover or energizer. In the face of Aristotle's fundamental doctrines of matter and form, potentiality and act, the inconsistency vanishes, since, as has been noted, according to these doctrines the agent whereby a potentiality is actualized must itself be actual.[a] The " nature " of things is constantly referred to as a power or capacity, and sometimes (*De caelo* iv. 1. 307 b 31-33) explicitly contrasted with activity or actuality.

It is clear, therefore, that when Aristotle had ceased to believe in the possibility of self-motion, the necessary modification of his philosophy did not lead him to deny factors which he had previously affirmed.

---

[a] Von Arnim, *Gotteslehre*, pp. 10 ff. The above criticism is more fully stated in *C.Q.* 1933, p. 167.

INTRODUCTION

The internal source of motion is not annihilated by the external mover, but subordinated to it. But this does not show that the external mover was there all the time, and that no modification ever took place. In truth the three sources of motion which we have enumerated are uneasy bedfellows. It is not easy to say in the same breath that a thing is moved by its own indwelling nature and that it is moved by something external, even with the knowledge that if the breath would only hold out long enough for a full explanation of the doctrine of movement as the passage from potency to act, the statement would be found to be perfectly logical. We find therefore that in the *De caelo*, where one of the main topics is the natural or internally-caused motion of bodies, there is almost complete silence about the transcendental and unmoved mover. There are one or two isolated hints that the body's own nature is not the ultimate cause, but in the overwhelming majority of arguments the possibility of anything higher is left entirely out of account.

Now Aristotle learned his philosophy from Plato. In many things he never ceased to be Plato's disciple, and as a young man he accepted the Platonic system in all essentials. It was undoubtedly the starting-point for his own work. But for Plato self-motion in the true sense was no impossibility. He divided motion only into spontaneous and communicated. Spontaneous motion is prior to communicated, and the prime mover of all is a self-mover, which Plato identified with soul, the life-principle.[a] This there-

---

[a] *Laws* x. 894 c ff. Soul is the primary cause of movement and carries round the stars and planets. Three possible methods are suggested by which it might accomplish this. (i) The stars have souls just as we do, *i.e.* are alive. (ii) The

fore was Aristotle's starting-point too. The doctrines of form and matter, potency and act, were his own contribution, and so of course was the postulate of the unmoved prime mover which was the outcome of those doctrines. This makes it *a priori* possible that certain of his writings belong to a stage of thought before the doctrines were carried to their logical conclusion, and at the same time unlikely that, having demonstrated the necessity for this novel feature, he should have kept it so completely in the background as he does in the *De caelo*.

In general, then, the language of the *De caelo* suggests that Aristotle is thinking of the outermost heaven as the primary being, which by its own self-caused revolution is responsible for the motion of everything else in the Universe, although logically it could be reconciled with the notion of a superior and unmoved mover. Yet there are one or two passages which make even the logical reconciliation difficult. I propose to end this section by mentioning first (a) these passages, then (b) those which on the contrary seem to presuppose the transcendent mover, and thirdly (c) those passages in other works of Aristotle which are relevant as external evidence for his development on this point.

---

moving soul takes to itself a body with which to impel the stars. (Probably a reference to the view of Eudoxus, adopted by Aristotle, that the stars are carried round by their spheres —*De caelo* ii. 8.) (iii) It conducts without body by means of " certain other powers excelling in wonder." This third view is described by Sir W. D. Ross as the belief in a transcendent prime mover (so also Jaeger, *Aristotle*, Eng. tran., pp. 141 f.), but we must be on our guard against confusing it with the transcendent mover of Aristotle, from which it differs essentially as what moves itself from what is totally unmoved.

INTRODUCTION

(a) *Passages which exclude the transcendent mover*

At i. 9. 279 a 30 ff. the heavenly system is described as " the foremost and highest divinity," and the reason given is that " there is nothing more powerful so as to move it." [a] Aristotle goes on, " It is too in unceasing motion, as is reasonable . . .", and here as often the attitude of his Greek commentator is illuminating. Simplicius is worried about the passage and would like to read the active (κινεῖ—" sets in motion ") for the passive or middle (κινεῖται—" is in motion "), because the word is clearly descriptive of the highest substance of all, which Simplicius, innocent of development-theories, knows to be the " intelligible and unmoved causes."

The passage ii. 1. 284 a 18 ff. is scarcely compatible with the presence of a transcendent mover in the background. It will be discussed in connexion with the question whether or not it is soul which causes the movement of the heavens (p. xxxi, below).

At iii. 2. 300 b 18, Aristotle is criticizing the pre-cosmic chaos of Plato's *Timaeus*, and says : " The motion must have been either enforced or natural. But if it was natural, careful consideration will show that there must have been a cosmos. For the self-caused motion of the first heaven must be natural. . . ." [b] Von Arnim treated this passage as proof that

---

[a] Note also the language of line 28. When A. wrote of the οὐρανός, ὅθεν καὶ τοῖς ἄλλοις ἐξήρτηται, τοῖς μὲν ἀκριβέστερον τοῖς δ' ἀμαυρῶς, τὸ εἶναί τε καὶ ζῆν, he could hardly have had behind him the sentence applied to the unmoved mover in the *Met.* (1072 b 13): ἐκ τοιαύτης ἄρα ἀρχῆς ἤρτηται ὁ οὐρανὸς καὶ ἡ φύσις.

[b] Or " The prime mover must cause motion in virtue of its own natural movement." So Stocks, who (followed by

Aristotle was still regarding the ultimate cause as a self-mover. One might hesitate to accept this, on the ground that in criticizing the *Timaeus* he was temporarily accepting Plato's own premises for the purposes of the argument. It is nevertheless striking that this is not the explanation offered by either Alexander or Simplicius, although both were anxious to escape the difficulty of attributing to Aristotle a self-moving first cause.

ii. 3. 286 a 9 [a] : " The activity of a god is immortality, that is, eternal life. *Therefore* the god must be characterized by eternal motion." Aristotle goes on to apply this argument to the " first body," the necessity of whose movement is thus seen to follow from its divinity. In the *Metaphysics* (Λ ch. 7), where the necessity for the transcendent mover has been proved and its nature is being described, it too is said to be god and to possess eternal life ; but there these same characteristics are deduced from the fact that it consists of pure intellectual activity and is therefore entirely *unmoved*.

iv. 2. 309 b 17. Criticizing the Atomists, Aristotle says that their theory amounts to making the void the primary cause of motion. " Yet it is illogical that bodies should move upwards on account of the

---

Allan) reads κινεῖν, αὐτὸ for κινεῖν αὐτό. This was suggested by Alexander, though all our mss. have αὐτό. The reasons for the change are not strong, especially when we remember that the purpose of Alex. in making it was (as Simpl. expressly says) to avoid attributing a self-mover to Aristotle. Once again the commentator's attitude is illuminating, but since with either reading the first mover is described as being itself in motion, the action is hardly effective, and makes no difference to the argument above.

[a] These last two passages have not, I think, been previously cited in the discussion.

void if the void does not do so itself." On this assumption, that their theory involves attributing motion to the void itself, Aristotle proceeds to point out the absurdities to which it leads. But it is difficult to see on what grounds he could have made the assumption, unless he still held as a fundamental tenet that the first cause of motion must be that which moves itself. Once admit in principle that a mover can operate without any movement on its own part, and the assumption would surely need separate justification. This passage could not perhaps be relied on in isolation, but may be offered in corroboration of the general attitude of the treatise.

(b) *Passages which imply the transcendent mover*

Books i. and iii. contain no mention of it. It is unambiguously referred to in only two passages, one in book ii. and one in book iv.

The thesis of ii. 6 is that the motion of the outermost sphere is at a constant speed. No less than four proofs are given, of which the first and third are consistent with the view that the *aither* as self-mover is the supreme being. The fourth argument (288 b 22) seems to envisage an external mover when it says that it is unreasonable to suppose that the mover should first show incapacity for an infinite time, and afterwards capacity for another infinity. The second argument starts (288 a 27) with the thesis established in the *Physics* that " everything in motion is moved by some agent," and goes on to say that therefore any irregularity in the movement must proceed either from the mover or from the object moved. But it has been proved that the object moved, the *aither*, is simple and indestructible and altogether free from change of any sort ; *a fortiori* then it is impossible that irregularity should come from the side of the mover, for that which moves another is even less subject to change than that which it moves, because it is more fully actual.

The thesis of iv. 3 is that lightness and weight, upward and downward movement, may be explained on the same general principles as all other forms of change, namely as instances of the passage from potentiality to act. Fire, *e.g.*, has not completed its becoming, not realized its form, until it has moved upwards to its proper place at the circumference. The following reference to Aristotle's mature theory of motion is added at the end of the discussion (311 a 9) : " But movement is also due to the original creative force and to that which removes the hindrance . . . as was explained in the first part of our discussions when we tried to show that none of these things moves itself."

It is permissible to notice that in both these chapters the mentions of the unmoved mover occur as appendages to arguments that have already proved their point without them. Many passages could be quoted to show that it was Aristotle's habit to jot down any supplementary proofs of a thesis as they occurred to him, and there is nothing against supposing that the sentences in question were added afterwards to arguments which proved the point at issue in a different way. The sentence in iv. 3 especially is not an apt conclusion to a series of arguments which explain the nature of things by reference to the principles of potency and act. It is an excellent illustration of what has been said, that the doctrine of the unmoved mover was a development and not a contradiction of the doctrine of the internal source of motion, but that nevertheless the two look ill-assorted when they are baldly juxtaposed.

The above are the only two passages mentioned by von Arnim in this connexion, but notice should also be taken of i. 8. 277 b 9. The thesis of this chapter is that there cannot be more than one world. It is proved by the doctrine of the natural places of the elements, but according to his custom Aristotle ends the chapter by briefly noting two or three other arguments in favour of it. Thus at 277 b 9 he says : " It might also be shown by means of the arguments of first philosophy." There is no more, and the reference may be thought to be left extremely vague, but in fact it can apply to little else but the proof of the uniqueness of the world in *Met.* Λ 8. 1074 a 31 ff. This proof is that, since the existence of a world implies the existence of a transcendent being to move it, a plurality of worlds would entail a plurality of transcendent movers, which is an impossibility. The reference in the *De caelo* partakes of the character of a footnote to an even greater degree than the other passages which have been cited, and the possibility of its being a later insertion is correspondingly strong.

(c) *Relevant passages outside the* De caelo

Aristotle's dialogue *De philosophia* contained his earliest independent views on the question. The work itself is lost, but we can gather something from Cicero's references to it in the *De natura deorum.* According to this (ii. 16. 44), Aristotle laid down three possible causes of motion, mutually exclusive : nature, force and free will. The motion of the stars, he proceeds, cannot be natural, for natural motion is either upward or downward ; nor can it be enforced, for there cannot be any force greater than that of the stars themselves which could move them contrary to nature. Therefore it must be voluntary. This passage, together with one in the preceding chapter of the *De nat. deor.* which ascribes sense-perception, intelligence and divinity to the stars, was taken by von Arnim as proving the absence of a transcendent mover. We must agree with Sir W. D. Ross that it does not necessarily do this, since the idea of voluntary motion is by no means ruled out by the presence of a transcendent mover. Indeed, the transcendent mover operates, in Aristotle's developed theology, by inspiring in the souls of the moved a desire for its own perfection, which they seek to imitate by voluntary action. The only external mover ruled out by the present passage is one which exerts a compulsion contrary to nature. It is nevertheless to be remarked that the passage does offer an explanation of the motion of the stars which is at variance with that of the *De caelo.* In the latter, the contrast between the voluntary motion of the stars and natural motion has disappeared ; the circular movement of *aither* is as natural as the upward or downward movement of the other simple bodies, and is explained on identical lines. There is no hint of the trichotomy of movement into natural, enforced and voluntary. It has been replaced by a dichotomy into natural and enforced, if we exclude the isolated references to a transcendent mover which have been mentioned above, and which have no organic connexion with the general arguments of the treatise. We have then in the *De philosophia* an earlier attempt to explain the motion of the stars, which has been considerably modified in the *De caelo* ; and considering the probability that in the *De caelo* itself the unmoved mover has not yet become a part of the scheme, it is unlikely that it figured in the dialogue.

Another passage in the *De nat. deor.* (i. 13. 33) was held by Jaeger to prove the presence of the transcendent, unmoved mover as early as the *De philosophia*. His arguments have however been adequately refuted already, and it is sufficient here to refer to von Arnim, *Gotteslehre*, pp. 1-7, Guthrie, *Class. Quart.* 1933, pp. 164-165, Ross, *Aristotle's Physics*, pp. 95-96.[a] With this passage disposed of, we find no reference to the unmoved mover in a context which either need be or usually is accounted earlier than the *De caelo*. Ross (*Physics*, p. 99) cites as probably the earliest

---

[a] The view that the unmoved mover had a place in the early, " exoteric " writings of Aristotle has more recently been upheld by E. Bignone on different grounds (*L'Aristotele perduto e la formazione filosofica di Epicuro*, ii. 398 f.). Philodemus (Περὶ Θεῶν III, col. x. Diels, in *Abh. preuss. Akad. Wiss.* 1916, No. 4, p. 30) combats the theory of unmoved gods (ἀκινήτους θεούς), and Bignone maintains that in the time of Philodemus polemic against Aristotle could only have been directed against the " exoteric " works. This is by no means certain, as P. Merlan has rightly pointed out (*Phil. Woch.* 1938, 67), quoting the passage of Cicero (*De fin.* v. 5. 12) which shows at least awareness of the existence of the two classes of Aristotelian writing. Merlan concludes judiciously that the passage from Philodemus is nevertheless remarkable, and suggests the possibility that the unmoved mover may have occurred, if not where Jaeger thought, then elsewhere in Aristotle's early writings. The arguments of the present essay may perhaps give grounds for thinking the possibility remote.

reference *De motu anim.* 2-4. The need for an unmoved being is there argued from a simple analogy with the movements of animals, and it is fairly clear that Aristotle has not yet worked out the full doctrine of motion on which its existence is ultimately based. We have also a clear reference to an unmoved mover in *Phys.* ii. 198 a 35, and the seventh and eighth books of the *Physics* contain the orthodox Aristotelian proofs of its indispensability as summarized above (p. xvii). It forms the subject of the latter half of *Metaphysics* Λ.

I have said that none of the references to an unmoved mover in other treatises need be supposed to be earlier in date than the main argument of the *De caelo.* But it can hardly be proper to say this without mentioning the fact that there are some ten references to the *Physics* in the *De caelo* itself. It may well be true, indeed it is probable, that these have, in Professor Jaeger's convenient phrase, " no chronological significance," but the average reader may be pardoned if on meeting them in the text he feels misgivings about a development theory which ignores their presence. The following are the passages of the *Physics* referred to, and the topics which they are used to illustrate :

i. 7-9 ; part played by opposites in change (*De caelo* 270 a 17).

iii. 4-8, vi. 7, viii. 8, vii. 10 ; infinity (*De caelo* 274 a 21, 272 a 30, 273 a 18, 275 b 23).

vi. 1 and 2 ; indivisible magnitudes (*De caelo* 299 a 10, 303 a 23).

iii. 6 (207 a 8) ; definition of " complete " (*De caelo* 286 b 20).

iv. 8 ; impossibility of " separate " void (*De caelo* 305 a 22).

vii. or viii. ; impossibility of self-motion (*De caelo* 311 a 12, discussed above, p. xxiv).

It is legitimate to argue that, since Aristotle's theory of motion and theology show a development only and not a radical change of view, then considering the nature of the surviving treatises, cross-references may well have been added to manuscripts already in existence. In this connexion we may note especially that the reference to the proofs of the *Physics* that self-motion is impossible is not only unique but seems particularly loosely attached to the argument of its context (p. xxiv, above). How much or how little weight we think it right to give to considerations of this sort must depend on the strength of our conviction that the transcendent unmoved mover has no place in the main discussions of the *De caelo*. My own conviction of this is strong.

(ii) We may grant, then, that in the *De caelo* we are enabled to see a stage of Aristotle's thought at which the sphere of the fixed stars, the highest corporeal entity, is at the same time the highest entity of all. It is this which, swinging round with the ceaseless self-caused motion that is the outcome of its inner nature, brings about the motion of everything else in the Universe and deserves the name of " foremost and highest god, entirely immutable and owning no superior " (i. 9). The question that remains is this. In the explanation of the motion of the heavens as " natural," what has become of the soul or souls of the stars, which in the dialogue *De philosophia*, as in Plato, are said to be the cause of their motion ? We have disentangled three versions of Aristotle's cosmology, each an improvement on the last. In the first (that of the *De phil.*), it is denied that the motions of the stars can be natural, on the ground that none but rectilinear motions can be so. Nor can it be enforced, because there is no force greater than the stars. Therefore it is voluntary, *i.e.* it is accounted for by the fact that they are living, sentient and intelligent beings. The second stage (that of the *De caelo*) agrees with the first in ruling out the notion of an external force or compulsion, not only because there is believed to be no stronger power in existence (though that too is repeated in i. 9), but more especially on the general ground that no enforced, that is unnatural, motion can be eternal. On the other hand it differs from the first stage in arguing that circular motion is no less natural than rectilinear, thus abolishing the contrast between natural and voluntary motion and attributing the motion of the stars, like that of the four sublunary elements, to their nature (*physis*). The third stage (expounded in *Met.* Λ) admits the doctrine, foreign to the second, that self-motion is an impossibility. It therefore explains the motion of the heavens as due not only to their own indwelling nature but also to the influence of an external, unmoved and therefore incorporeal being. This being does not work by compulsion. It calls into activity the powers of motion (*physis*) in the heavens, which otherwise must needs have remained dormant, by arousing in them the desire for its own perfection. Now we see at once that this final explanation of their motion has one important feature in common with the earliest, namely that it relies for its efficacy on the belief that the stars (or rather the spheres in which they are set) are alive and sentient. The influence of the transcendent mover on them is compared to that which is exercised on a lover by the beloved, and no other explanation is offered. The account of the *De caelo* is radically different in that it does not, in so far as it is an account of motion, demand the attribution of life to the heavenly substance as a part of the cause. This is a real distinction and must not be obscured, whether or not we feel bound to conclude finally that Aristotle could not, even temporarily, have renounced his belief in the divinity of the heavenly bodies.

In *De caelo* ii. ch. 1 (284 a 18-23 and 25-27), Aristotle censures those who would attribute the eternal movement of the heavens to " a compelling soul " or " a living constraint," a theory which he compares to the myth of Atlas. This passage has been mentioned already as being difficult to reconcile with the idea of an external mover. At first sight at least it seems equally to dispose of the belief that the heavens owed their movement to the fact that they were themselves alive, that is, to the soul immanent in them. Nevertheless Sir W. D. Ross has recently shown that this conclusion is unnecessary. The following quotation may be taken to summarize his own view (*Physics*, p. 98) : " In the light of this passage (*sc.* ii. 12. 292 a 18-21, b 1-2) and that in ch. 6 we must realize that in ii. 1 what Aristotle is denying is not soul, but soul which constrains the heavenly bodies to motion contrary to their natural motion. . . . Aristotle when he wrote the *De caelo* explained the movements of the heavenly bodies by the action of immanent souls or powers of initiating movement." [a]

[a] Dr. Philipp Merlan, in an admirable but unfortunately very brief discussion, has pointed out how, since interest in the early Aristotle was reawakened by Jaeger's book, the parties in the discussion have taken up positions very

INTRODUCTION

It is of course true that a denial of compulsion or constraint exercised by a soul and acting contrary to the nature of the moved does not rule out altogether the possibility that soul may be the cause of motion. (*Cf.* the three possible causes enumerated above, p. xviii). Yet there remains a difficulty in his view, for it seems to destroy the parallelism which is pressed upon the reader in the first book between the movements of the fifth, heavenly element and those of the other four. It destroys the parallelism between rectilinear and circular motions. Aristotle has tried to explain them all as due to the nature of the material. If the movement of *aither* is due to the action of immanent souls, we can scarcely avoid attributing the upward movement of fire and the downward movement of earth to the same causes. The arguments of i. 2 make it difficult to escape from this conclusion. All natural bodies are capable of locomotion as such ; for by their " nature " we mean a principle of motion. And the motions attributable to this principle are of two main sorts, rectilinear and circular.

Now it need hardly be said that Aristotle did not intend to attribute the movement of the sublunary

---

similar to those of ancient criticism. Ross's resembles that of Simplicius, according to whom A. is here rejecting only a mechanical propulsion (ὠθισμός) of the soul. My own views, and those now propounded by Bignone (*o.c.*, p. xxvii above), are nearer to those of Alexander, who regarded the criticism as directed against the Platonic doctrine of the world-soul (P. Merlan, review of Walzer, *Aristotelis dialogorum fragmenta* in *Phil. Woch.* 1938, 67). As will appear later, however, I consider my earlier assertion of a materialistic stage in Aristotle's thought (*Class. Quart.* 1933, p. 169) to have been too positive in expression.

elements to the fact that they were alive, and we may suspect that the question has been over-simplified. There are in fact two kinds of natural motion, well distinguished by Simplicius thus : " If a thing has a natural motion, then it either moves by nature in the sense of the so-called natural bodies like earth and fire, or in the sense of so-called self-moving creatures which are moved by the soul within them." [a] But if we have to decide to which of these two classes the substance of the stars belongs, the arguments of i. 2 leave us no choice. We must assume that it moves " like earth and fire," even al-though owing to the perfection of circular motion it is of a higher nature than they and is indeed eternal.

Yet Aristotle calls it in the same chapter a bodily substance not only prior to but *more divine than* the other simple bodies (269 a 31), and in the next chapter, appealing to experience for confirmation of his results, he brings forward the belief in gods as testimony for the existence of the fifth body. He does the same again in ii. 1 (284 a 2), when in support of his view of the *aither* as immortal and eternal he refers to " the ancient accounts, belonging especially to our own tradition, that there is something *immortal and divine* in the class of things in motion. . . .' There are also the two passages mentioned by Ross in ii. 6 and ii. 12. That in ii. 6 (288 a 27 ff., discussed above) fairly obviously refers to an external mover and is therefore beside the present point. The sentence in ii. 12 is as follows (292 a 18-21) : " But we are thinking of them (*sc.* the stars) as if they were

---

[a] Simpl. on *De caelo* 242, 4-6 : εἰ κατὰ φύσιν (*sc.* κινεῖται), ἢ φύσει ὡς τὰ φυσικὰ λεγόμενα οἷον γῆ καὶ πῦρ ἢ ὡς τὰ αὐτοκίνητα λεγόμενα τὰ ὑπὸ τῆς ἐν ἑαυτοῖς κινούμενα ψυχῆς.

mere bodies, units arranged in a certain order but entirely lifeless, whereas we ought to regard them as partaking of action and life." This passage seems to Ross to make it impossible for us to believe that in the *De caelo* Aristotle explained the movements of the heavenly bodies otherwise than by the action of immanent souls. But a possible interpretation of these words would be that by " we " Aristotle means himself, and that the sentence betrays an uneasiness about the nature of the arguments by which in this treatise he has been accounting for the motion of the stars, and an attempt to recall himself to what his instincts tell him to be the truth. Possibly, that is, he is taking himself to task for the materialistic trend of his earlier arguments and rousing his Platonic conscience to activity.[a] Whether or not this is so, what has happened seems to be this. The divinity of the stars was an article of the Platonic faith which it could never occur to Aristotle to doubt. This must be emphasized, since otherwise the present discussion may be thought to go too far and make Aristotle, at one stage of his thought, into a materialist. All that is suggested is that he was temporarily in difficulties

---

[a] I mention this tentatively, for the possibility is at least equally strong that the sentence has reference only to the problem of its immediate context, and means " If we find this a stumbling-block, it is only because we are forgetting that the stars are alive." " We " would then mean " mankind in general." If this is the true meaning, I do not think the general position is altered, since what I have assumed on Aristotle's part is not disbelief but a difficulty in reconciling his belief intellectually with the account of the stars' movement which he has just thought out. For this difficulty the evidence must remain the identity between the accounts of the movement of *aither* and of the four sublunary elements.

INTRODUCTION

over the intellectual reconciliation of his belief in the life and divinity of the heavenly bodies and his rational explanation of their movement.[a] He had carried on the search for this explanation on independent lines, and the result as reached in book i. ch. 2 is not in complete accord with his inherited Platonic belief. It never occurred to him to doubt that the *aither* had a soul, and that that soul was the principle of its movement, although his explanation of its movement should in fact have rendered superfluous not only " a soul which constrains the heavenly bodies contrary to their natural motion," but a soul as the principle of their natural motion as well.

The argument of ii. 8 and 9 should be taken into account here. These chapters explain that the stars do not move of themselves, but are embedded in moving spheres which carry them round. " Therefore," he concludes, " their motion is neither the motion of life (ἔμψυχος) nor is it enforced." It is natural without being caused by soul, and possibly this is one of the statements that Aristotle has in mind if we suppose him to be accusing himself, in ii. 12, of speaking of the stars as if they were lifeless. In itself, of course, it might be thought simply to transfer the attribute of life from the individual stars to the spheres which carry them, and so fluid does Aristotle's thought seem to have been at this stage that he may even have intended to give that impression. It is nevertheless a strange way to speak of the stars, either for a Platonist or for the Aristotle of the *Metaphysics* ; and it remains true that accord-

---

[a] That he *wished* to connect them is again not open to doubt. *Cf. e.g.* ii. 2. 285 a 29 : ὁ δ' οὐρανὸς ἔμψυχος καὶ ἔχει κινήσεως ἀρχήν.

ing to the description of the motion of the *aither* in
i. 2, soul is an unnecessary addition.[a]

What is needed, then, and at this stage lacking, is
an explanation of motion which will at the same time
satisfy the reason and make room for the belief in
the divinity of the stars, or of their spheres, which
Aristotle refused to relinquish. The solution lay in
the thesis that self-motion was impossible, and in the
postulate of the transcendent unmoved mover which
was the outcome of that thesis. For the only way
in which the transcendent mover can operate is by
arousing desire in the souls of the moved. Lifeless
matter could not respond to this impulse. Therefore
soul is once more indispensable as the internal condition of movement. If, then, as has appeared
probable, Aristotle when he wrote the *De caelo* had
(a) given up the contrast between the rectilinear
motions of the sublunary elements as " natural " and
the circular motion of the *aither* as " voluntary," and
brought the latter into line with the former by the
assertion that circular motion was natural no less
than rectilinear ; but (b) not yet thought of the
impossibility of self-motion nor arrived at the concept
of the unmoved mover, it is easy to see how the souls
of the heavenly bodies, considered as the source of
their motion, were left temporarily in an ambiguous
and unsatisfactory position.

[a] It might be noted before we leave the argument, that the
soul in sublunary creatures is regarded by A. as a force which
prevents the elements of which a creature is composed from
performing their proper motion. In this sense the soul of a
living creature is a constraining force, and this should be borne
in mind when we are considering A.'s objection to an ἀνάγκη
ἔμψυχος as the cause of celestial motion. *Cf.* 288 b 16
(pp. 172-173) and note *c* on p. 64.

ARISTOTLE
ON THE HEAVENS

ΑΡΙΣΤΟΤΕΛΟΥΣ
ΠΕΡΙ ΟΥΡΑΝΟΥ

A

CHAPTER I

ARGUMENT

The subject of physical science is material substance, or body, and the living creatures which are made out of it. It is also necessary to get first of all a grasp of the general principles on which material substances are constructed (matter, form, etc.), the laws of change and so forth. These have been dealt with in the Physics, *and we now approach the subject of body itself.*

Body is defined as a species of the continuous. This in its turn means " a magnitude which is divisible to infinity," and consists of three species—the line, the surface and the solid body. Since there are only three dimensions, body may be called, on this argument, the complete magnitude. Pythagorean notions of the perfection of the triad, as well as popular custom and language, give further colour to this view, whose proof lies simply in the appeal to experience.

Body, then, is that which has extension in three, i.e. in all, directions, and hence is divisible in all directions. For that reason we speak, on this geometrical argument, of all bodies as " complete magnitudes," but it is of course only in this

2

ARISTOTLE
ON THE HEAVENS

BOOK I

CHAPTER I

ARGUMENT (*continued*)

limited sense that they are complete. We also speak of the whole Universe as complete, and we must not be thought to be confusing that sense of the word with this in which we apply it to any body whatsoever. All bodies are complete in the geometrical sense (i.e. it is impossible to add another dimension to them), but only the Universe as a whole can be said to be complete in all respects, i.e. to be the whole of which the separate bodies are parts, and which itself is not the part of any larger whole.

[The arguments of this and some of the following chapters naturally laid themselves open to the charge of using mathematical language in describing concepts that were intended to be physical. To this Simplicius replies (p. 25 Heiberg) : " If we spoke of lines in a mathematical sense, we should indeed be wide of the mark. But if, taking into consideration that all motion takes place within linear dimensions (simple motion following a simple line and composite motion a complex) we introduce the different dimensions in illustration of the different varieties of motion, how can we be said to be explaining physical matters by mathematical arguments ? The physicist

ARISTOTLE

*and the mathematician must alike make use of lines, as also
of surfaces and solid bodies. Simply to make use of lines*

268 a 'Η περὶ φύσεως ἐπιστήμη σχεδὸν ἡ πλείστη
φαίνεται περί τε σώματα καὶ μεγέθη καὶ τὰ τούτων
οὖσα πάθη καὶ τὰς κινήσεις, ἔτι δὲ περὶ τὰς ἀρχάς,
ὅσαι τῆς τοιαύτης οὐσίας εἰσίν· τῶν γὰρ φύσει
5 συνεστώτων τὰ μέν ἐστι σώματα καὶ μεγέθη, τὰ δ'
ἔχει σῶμα καὶ μέγεθος, τὰ δ' ἀρχαὶ τῶν ἐχόντων
εἰσίν.

Συνεχὲς μὲν οὖν ἐστι τὸ διαιρετὸν εἰς ἀεὶ διαιρετά, σῶμα δὲ τὸ πάντῃ διαιρετόν. μεγέθους
δὲ τὸ μὲν ἐφ' ἓν γραμμή, τὸ δ' ἐπὶ δύο ἐπίπεδον,
τὸ δ' ἐπὶ τρία σῶμα· καὶ παρὰ ταῦτα οὐκ ἔστιν
10 ἄλλο μέγεθος διὰ τὸ τὰ τρία πάντα εἶναι καὶ τὸ
τρὶς πάντῃ. καθάπερ γάρ φασι καὶ οἱ Πυθαγόρειοι,
τὸ πᾶν καὶ τὰ πάντα τοῖς τρισὶν ὥρισται· τελευτὴ
γὰρ καὶ μέσον καὶ ἀρχὴ τὸν ἀριθμὸν ἔχει τὸν τοῦ
παντός, ταῦτα δὲ τὸν τῆς τριάδος. διὸ παρὰ τῆς
φύσεως εἰληφότες ὥσπερ νόμους ἐκείνης, καὶ πρὸς
15 τὰς ἁγιστείας χρώμεθα τῶν θεῶν τῷ ἀριθμῷ τούτῳ.
ἀποδίδομεν δὲ καὶ τὰς προσηγορίας τὸν τρόπον
τοῦτον· τὰ γὰρ δύο ἄμφω μὲν λέγομεν καὶ τοὺς δύο
ἀμφοτέρους, πάντας δ' οὐ λέγομεν, ἀλλὰ κατὰ τῶν

---

[a] πάθος is (a) a property in respect of which a thing is liable
to change (ποιότης καθ' ἣν ἀλλοιοῦσθαι ἐνδέχεται), (b) change
itself (ἀλλοίωσις ἤδη), *Met.* Δ 1022 b 15 foll. Simpl. says
πάθος here is included in κίνησις as species in genus.

[b] *e.g.* the elements (fire, water, etc.) and substances like
stone or wood (Simpl.).

[c] *i.e.* animate nature, plants and animals (Simpl.).

4

therefore is not peculiarly mathematical, but only if they are used in a mathematical way."]

WE may say that the science of nature is for the most part plainly concerned with bodies and magnitudes and with their changing properties [a] and motions, as also with the principles which belong to that class of substance ; for the sum of physically constituted entities consists of (*a*) bodies and magnitudes,[b] (*b*) beings possessed of body and magnitude,[c] (*c*) the principles or causes of these beings.

The continuous may be defined as that which is divisible into parts which are themselves divisible to infinity, body as that which is divisible in all ways.[d] Magnitude divisible in one direction is a line, in two directions a surface, in three directions a body. There is no magnitude not included in these ; for three are all, and " in three ways " is the same as " in all ways." It is just as the Pythagoreans say, the whole world and all things in it are summed up in the number three [e] ; for end, middle and beginning give the number of the whole, and their number is the triad. Hence it is that we have taken this number from nature, as it were one of her laws, and make use of it even for the worship of the gods.[f] Our language too shows the same tendency, for of two things or people we say " both," not " all." This latter term we first

---

[d] That is, the continuous is the genus to which body belongs as a species (Simpl.). On divisibility see Introd. to Loeb *Physics* (vol. i), pp. lxxx ff.

[e] Compare F. M. Cornford in *Class. Quart.* 1923, p. 2.

[f] Examples from Greek practice in the taking of oaths and in sacrifices may be found in P. Stengel, *Griechische Kultusaltertümer* (Munich, 1920), pp. 86, 135.

268 a

τριῶν ταύτην τὴν προσηγορίαν φαμὲν πρῶτον.
ταῦτα δ᾽, ὥσπερ εἴρηται, διὰ τὸ τὴν φύσιν αὐτὴν
20 οὕτως ἐπάγειν ἀκολουθοῦμεν· ὥστ᾽ ἐπεὶ τὰ πάντα
καὶ τὸ πᾶν καὶ τὸ τέλειον οὐ κατὰ τὴν ἰδέαν δια-
φέρουσιν ἀλλήλων, ἀλλ᾽ εἴπερ ἄρα, ἐν τῇ ὕλῃ καὶ
ἐφ᾽ ὧν λέγονται, τὸ σῶμα μόνον ἂν εἴη τῶν μεγεθῶν τέλειον· μόνον γὰρ ὥρισται τοῖς τρισίν,
τοῦτο δ᾽ ἐστὶ πᾶν. τριχῇ δὲ ὂν διαιρετὸν πάντη
25 διαιρετόν ἐστιν· τῶν δ᾽ ἄλλων τὸ μὲν ἐφ᾽ ἕν, τὸ δ᾽
ἐπὶ δύο· ὡς γὰρ τοῦ ἀριθμοῦ τετυχήκασιν, οὕτω
καὶ τῆς διαιρέσεως καὶ τοῦ συνεχοῦς· τὸ μὲν γὰρ
ἐφ᾽ ἓν συνεχές, τὸ δ᾽ ἐπὶ δύο, τὸ δὲ πάντη τοιοῦτον.

Ὅσα μὲν οὖν διαιρετὰ τῶν μεγεθῶν, καὶ συνεχῆ
30 ταῦτα. εἰ δὲ καὶ τὰ συνεχῆ πάντα διαιρετά, οὔπω
δῆλον ἐκ τῶν νῦν· ἀλλ᾽ ἐκεῖνο μὲν δῆλον, ὡς οὐκ
268 b ἔστιν εἰς¹ ἄλλο γένος μετάβασις, ὥσπερ ἐκ μήκους
εἰς ἐπιφάνειαν, εἰς δὲ σῶμα ἐξ ἐπιφανείας· οὐ γὰρ
ἂν ἔτι τὸ τοιοῦτον τέλειον εἴη μέγεθος· ἀνάγκη γὰρ
γίγνεσθαι τὴν ἔκβασιν κατὰ τὴν ἔλλειψιν, οὐχ οἷόν
5 τε δὲ τὸ τέλειον ἐλλείπειν· πάντη γάρ ἐστιν.

Τῶν μὲν οὖν ἐν μορίου εἴδει σωμάτων κατὰ τὸν
λόγον ἕκαστον τοιοῦτόν ἐστιν· πάσας γὰρ ἔχει τὰς
διαστάσεις. ἀλλ᾽ ὥρισται πρὸς τὸ πλησίον ἁφῇ,
διὸ τρόπον τινὰ πολλὰ τῶν σωμάτων ἕκαστόν ἐστιν.

---

¹ εἰς is omitted by Bekker, presumably through a printing
error.

___

ᵃ This vague phrase is no doubt a reminder that A. is speaking with Pythagorean notions in his mind, according to which
the dimensions are represented by numbers, the point = 1,
the line = 2 and so on. Since the point is indivisible, the line
must be the *first* divisible number. In a sense it is also the

6

employ when there are three in question ; and in behaving thus, as I have said, we are accepting nature
herself for our guide. Furthermore, " all," " the
whole " and " the complete " do not differ from one
another in form, but only, if at all, in their matter, and
the subjects of which they are predicated. In this
sense therefore body is the only complete magnitude,
since it is the only one which is defined by extension
in three directions, that is, which is an " all." Being
divisible in three directions, it is divisible in all. Other
magnitudes are divisible in one or two, for according
to the number which can be appropriately applied to
the different magnitudes,[a] in so many directions is
their divisibility and continuity. One is continuous
in one direction, another in two, and the third in all.

We have seen that magnitudes which are divisible
are continuous. Whether all continuous magnitudes
are divisible has not emerged from the present inquiry.[b] This much, however, is clear, that there is
no further change to a fourth species of magnitude
like the changes from length to surface and from surface to body. Otherwise body would not be the complete magnitude that we have shown it to be, for any
advance on it could only be made where it fell short ;
but that which is complete cannot fall short ; it extends in every possible direction.

Bodies which are parts of a whole[c] are each complete in the sense here laid down, i.e. each has all the
dimensions. But each one is limited by contact with
the neighbouring part, so that in a sense each of such

first number, for the monad stands outside the numerical
series, as the ἀρχή of the whole.
   [b] " from the present inquiry," because it has been demonstrated elsewhere, viz. in *Phys.* vi. 1.
   [c] As the elements are of the Universe (Simpl.).

263 b

τὸ δὲ πᾶν οὗ ταῦτα μόρια, τέλειον ἀναγκαῖον εἶναι καὶ καθάπερ τοὔνομα σημαίνει πάντῃ, καὶ μὴ
10 τῇ μὲν τῇ δ' οὔ.

ᵃ It is not easy to say in what sense limitation by contact can make each incomplete body " many." A. may possibly have in mind the doctrine expressed by Plato at *Parmenides* 138 A, that a body thus limited cannot be a unity in the full sense of being without parts and indivisible (like a point).

CHAPTER II

ARGUMENT

(1) To prove that the substance of which the heavens are made, moving as they do with a circular motion beyond the confines of the sublunary world, is a fifth element distinct from the four which make up the world below (268 b 11—269 a 19).

The elements are simple natural bodies, i.e. they contain a principle of movement within themselves, and since they are simple, their natural movement is also simple. The only simple motions are straight (=up and down) and circular. Of these the straight motions belong respectively to the four elements. But every simple motion is the motion of a simple body. (If a composite body is seen to move with a simple motion, that is only because one element in the compound so predominates as to impart its own direction to the whole mass.) Hence there must be a simple body whose nature it is to move in a circle.

Might it not be that this circular motion was of a simple body being carried round against its own nature? No, for (a) supposing it was one of the four known elements, then circular motion (being itself one of the simple motions) would be for that element the motion contrary to its nature, since un- natural is contrary to natural and a thing can have only one

8

bodies is many.[a]   The whole of which these are parts,
on the other hand, is of necessity complete, and, as
its name suggests, wholly so, not complete in one
respect and incomplete in another.

" If (the One) were in something else, it would be encom-
passed all round by that within which it lay, and so would
have numerous contacts with it at various points ; but as the
One is without parts . . ." (Professor Taylor's trans.).

CHAPTER II

ARGUMENT (*continued*)

*contrary.   But the motions of the elements are up or down,
and their contraries can therefore only be down or up.*   (b)
*Supposing it was some other simple body, then, if circular
motion was contrary to its nature, it would have to have a
natural simple motion contrary to the circular.   But that is
impossible.   If its natural motion is up or down, it will be one
of the four known elements, and there are no other simple
motions.*

(2) To prove that the fifth substance is prior in nature
to, and therefore more divine than, the four known elements
(269 a 19-32).

*Of the simple lines, only the circle is perfect or com-
plete.   (A straight line must be either infinite or finite.   If
infinite it can by definition never be complete, if finite it is
always capable of extension and therefore cannot be said to
be complete.)   But the perfect is prior in nature to the imperfect.   Hence circular motion is prior to rectilinear, and
the body whose natural motion it is must therefore be prior
in nature to the bodies which move in straight lines.   Hence,
since these latter are simple bodies, the body whose natural
motion is circular must also be simple, and moreover of a
higher nature than the others.*

(3) *Supplementary proofs* (a) *of the existence of the fifth*

9

ARISTOTLE

body (269 a 32–b 2). *All movement is either natural or unnatural to the moving body. Motion unnatural to one body
is natural to another, as e.g. upward motion being unnatural
to earth is natural to fire. Circular motion is unnatural to
the four elements, therefore there must be another body to
which it is natural.*

(b) *That circular motion is natural to the body so moved*

268 b 11 Περὶ μὲν οὖν τῆς τοῦ παντὸς φύσεως, εἴτ' ἄπειρός
ἐστι κατὰ τὸ μέγεθος εἴτε πεπέρανται τὸν σύνολον
ὄγκον, ὕστερον ἐπισκεπτέον· περὶ δὲ τῶν κατ' εἶδος
αὐτοῦ μορίων νῦν λέγωμεν ἀρχὴν ποιησάμενοι
15 τήνδε. πάντα γὰρ τὰ φυσικὰ σώματα καὶ μεγέθη
καθ' αὑτὰ κινητὰ λέγομεν εἶναι κατὰ τόπον· τὴν
γὰρ φύσιν κινήσεως ἀρχὴν εἶναί φαμεν αὐτοῖς.
πᾶσα δὲ κίνησις ὅση κατὰ τόπον, ἣν καλοῦμεν
φοράν, ἢ εὐθεῖα ἢ κύκλῳ ἢ ἐκ τούτων μικτή· ἁπλαῖ
γὰρ αὗται δύο μόναι. αἴτιον δ' ὅτι καὶ τὰ μεγέθη
ταῦτα ἁπλᾶ μόνον, ἥ τ' εὐθεῖα καὶ ἡ περιφερής.
20 κύκλῳ μὲν οὖν ἐστιν ἡ περὶ τὸ μέσον, εὐθεῖα δ' ἡ
ἄνω καὶ κάτω. λέγω δ' ἄνω μὲν τὴν ἀπὸ τοῦ
μέσου, κάτω δὲ τὴν ἐπὶ τὸ μέσον. ὥστ' ἀνάγκη
πᾶσαν εἶναι τὴν ἁπλῆν φορὰν τὴν μὲν ἀπὸ τοῦ
μέσου, τὴν δ' ἐπὶ τὸ μέσον, τὴν δὲ περὶ τὸ μέσον.
25 καὶ ἔοικεν ἠκολουθηκέναι κατὰ λόγον τοῦτο τοῖς
ἐξ ἀρχῆς· τό τε γὰρ σῶμα ἀπετελέσθη ἐν τρισὶ καὶ
ἡ κίνησις αὐτοῦ.

Ἐπεὶ δὲ τῶν σωμάτων τὰ μέν ἐστιν ἁπλᾶ
τὰ δὲ σύνθετα ἐκ τούτων (λέγω δ' ἁπλᾶ ὅσα κινή-

10

THE question of the nature of this Whole, whether it is of infinite magnitude or its total bulk is limited, must be left until later.[a] We have now to speak of its formally distinct parts,[b] and we may start from this, that all natural bodies and magnitudes are capable of moving of themselves in space; for nature we have defined as the principle of motion in them.[c] Now all motion in space (locomotion) is either straight or circular or a compound of the two, for these are the only simple motions, the reason being that the straight and circular lines are the only simple magnitudes. By " circular motion " I mean motion around the centre, by " straight," motion up and down. " Up " means away from the centre, " down " towards the centre. It follows that all simple locomotion is either away from the centre or towards the centre or around the centre. This appears to follow consistently on what was said at the beginning : body was completed by the number three, and so now is its motion.

Of bodies some are simple, and some are compounds of the simple. By " simple " I mean all bodies which

---

[a] It is taken up in chs. v.-vii.

[b] *i.e.* the elements, which are the " immediate " parts of the whole, the rest being parts of parts (Simpl.). The elements are also the *summa genera* or ultimate distinctions of kind among bodies (Stocks).

[c] *Phys.* ii. 1. 192 b 20.

268 b

σεως ἀρχὴν ἔχει κατὰ φύσιν, οἷον πῦρ καὶ γῆν
καὶ τὰ τούτων εἴδη καὶ τὰ συγγενῆ τούτοις),
30 ἀνάγκη καὶ τὰς κινήσεις εἶναι τὰς μὲν ἁπλᾶς τὰς
269 a δὲ μικτάς πως, καὶ τῶν μὲν ἁπλῶν ἁπλᾶς, μικτὰς
δὲ τῶν συνθέτων, κινεῖσθαι δὲ κατὰ τὸ ἐπικρατοῦν.

Εἴπερ οὖν ἐστιν ἁπλῆ κίνησις, ἁπλῆ δ' ἡ κύκλῳ
κίνησις, καὶ τοῦ τε ἁπλοῦ σώματος ἁπλῆ ἡ κίνησις
καὶ ἡ ἁπλῆ κίνησις ἁπλοῦ σώματος (καὶ γὰρ ἂν
5 συνθέτου ᾖ, κατὰ τὸ ἐπικρατοῦν ἔσται), ἀναγκαῖον
εἶναί τι σῶμα ἁπλοῦν ὃ πέφυκε φέρεσθαι τὴν κύκλῳ
κίνησιν κατὰ τὴν ἑαυτοῦ φύσιν· βίᾳ μὲν γὰρ ἐνδέχεται τὴν ἄλλου καὶ ἑτέρου, κατὰ φύσιν δὲ
ἀδύνατον, εἴπερ μία ἑκάστου κίνησις ἡ κατὰ φύσιν
10 τῶν ἁπλῶν. ἔτι εἰ ἡ παρὰ φύσιν ἐναντία τῇ κατὰ
φύσιν καὶ ἓν ἑνὶ ἐναντίον, ἀνάγκη, ἐπεὶ ἁπλῆ ἡ
κύκλῳ, εἰ μὴ ἔσται κατὰ φύσιν τοῦ φερομένου σώ-

---

[a] This mention of the " kinds " of an element is probably
a reference to the *Timaeus* (58 c foll.), where there are said to
be different varieties of each element, all pure but owing
their differences to the different sizes of their elementary
pyramids. (I owe this suggestion to Professor Cornford.)
There seems no point in Stocks's demand for " a variety of
movement corresponding to variety of kind."

[b] In saying " bodies which contain a principle of natural
motion," A. is not thinking of natural beings in the wide sense
defined in *Phys.* ii., where the term includes plants and
animals, but in the more restricted sense of the elements only.
Strictly speaking (ἀκριβέστερον Simpl.), only these can be
said to have a principle of natural motion (the motion of a
simple natural substance left to itself), since the motions of
plants and animals are determined by the life-principle in
them, which again is dependent on their possessing a certain
complicated structure. Hence Simpl. is probably right in
saying that even the phrase " composite bodies " in this sentence refers to the popular elements, earth, water, etc., as they
appear to the senses. We never see them in a perfectly pure

12

contain a principle of natural motion, like fire and earth and their kinds,[a] and the other bodies of the same order. Hence motions also must be similarly divisible, some simple and others compound in one way or another; simple bodies will have simple motions and composite bodies composite motions, though the movement may be according to the prevailing element in the compound.[b]

If we take these premises, (a) that there is such a thing as simple motion, (b) that circular motion is simple, (c) that simple motion is the motion of a simple body (for if a composite body moves with a simple motion, it is only by virtue of a simple body prevailing and imparting its direction to the whole), then it follows that there exists a simple body naturally so constituted as to move in a circle in virtue of its own nature. By force it can be brought to move with the motion of another, different body, but not naturally, if it is true that each of the simple bodies has one natural motion only. Moreover, granted that (a) unnatural motion is the contrary of natural, (b) a thing can have only one contrary, then circular motion, seeing it is one of the simple motions,[c] must, if it is not the motion natural to the moved body, be contrary to its

form, but they each conform to the natural motions of the pure element, because that prevails sufficiently in the compound to govern the direction of the whole. The argument however does not require that it be limited to these. It could at least include inanimate compounds of the elements (*e.g.* metals), and where the clause occurs again (269 a 28), Simpl. himself illustrates it by the example of a man falling off a roof.

[c] This caution is necessary because, if circular motion were composite, then the axiom " one thing one contrary " could not be applied. A composite motion would be neither natural to a simple body nor directly contrary to its nature, but only, as Simpl. says, " not according to its nature."

ματος, παρὰ φύσιν αὐτοῦ εἶναι. εἰ οὖν πῦρ ἢ ἄλλο
τι τῶν τοιούτων ἐστὶ τὸ κύκλῳ φερόμενον, ἐναντία
ἡ κατὰ φύσιν αὐτοῦ φορὰ ἔσται τῇ κύκλῳ. ἀλλ᾽
15 ἐν ἑνὶ ἐναντίον· ἡ δ᾽ ἄνω καὶ κάτω ἀλλήλαις ἐναντίαι. εἰ δ᾽ ἕτερόν τί ἐστι σῶμα τὸ φερόμενον
κύκλῳ παρὰ φύσιν, ἔσται τις αὐτοῦ ἄλλη κίνησις
κατὰ φύσιν. τοῦτο δ᾽ ἀδύνατον· εἰ μὲν γὰρ ἡ
ἄνω, πῦρ ἔσται ἢ ἀήρ, εἰ δ᾽ ἡ κάτω, ὕδωρ ἢ γῆ.

Ἀλλὰ μὴν καὶ πρώτην γε ἀναγκαῖον εἶναι τὴν
20 τοιαύτην φοράν. τὸ γὰρ τέλειον πρότερον τῇ φύσει
τοῦ ἀτελοῦς, ὁ δὲ κύκλος τῶν τελείων, εὐθεῖα δὲ
γραμμὴ οὐδεμία· οὔτε γὰρ ἡ ἄπειρος (ἔχοι γὰρ ἂν
πέρας καὶ τέλος) οὔτε τῶν πεπερασμένων οὐδεμία
(πασῶν γάρ ἐστί τι ἐκτός· αὐξῆσαι γὰρ ἐνδέχεται
ὁποιανοῦν). ὥστ᾽ εἴπερ ἡ μὲν προτέρα κίνησις προ-
25 τέρου τῇ φύσει σώματος, ἡ δὲ κύκλῳ προτέρα τῆς
εὐθείας, ἡ δ᾽ ἐπ᾽ εὐθείας τῶν ἁπλῶν σωμάτων ἐστί
(τό τε γὰρ πῦρ ἐπ᾽ εὐθείας ἄνω φέρεται καὶ τὰ
γεηρὰ κάτω πρὸς τὸ μέσον), ἀνάγκη καὶ τὴν κύκλῳ
κίνησιν τῶν ἁπλῶν τινὸς εἶναι σωμάτων· τῶν γὰρ
μικτῶν τὴν φορὰν ἔφαμεν εἶναι κατὰ τὸ ἐπικρατοῦν
30 ἐν τῇ μίξει τῶν ἁπλῶν. ἔκ τε δὴ τούτων φανερὸν
ὅτι πέφυκέ τις οὐσία σώματος ἄλλη παρὰ τὰς ἐνταῦθα συστάσεις, θειοτέρα καὶ προτέρα τούτων
ἁπάντων, κἂν εἴ τις ἔτι λάβοι πᾶσαν εἶναι κίνησιν

---

a This is demonstrated also, from similar premises but more
fully, in *Phys.* viii. 9.

nature. Suppose now that the body which is moving in a circle be fire or some other of the four elements, then its natural motion must be contrary to the circular. But a thing can have only one contrary, and the contrary of upward is downward, and *vice versa*. Suppose on the other hand that this body which is moving in a circle contrary to its own nature is something other than the elements, there must be some other motion which is natural to it. But that is impossible : for if the motion were upward, the body would be fire or air, if downward, water or earth.

Furthermore, circular motion must be primary.[a] That which is complete is prior in nature to the incomplete, and the circle is a complete figure, whereas no straight line can be so. An infinite straight line cannot, for to be complete it would have to have an end or completion, nor yet a finite, for all finite lines have something beyond them : any one of them is capable of being extended. Now if (*a*) a motion which is prior to another is the motion of a body prior in nature, (*b*) circular motion is prior to rectilinear, (*c*) rectilinear motion is the motion of the simple bodies (as *e.g.* fire moves in a straight line upwards and earthy bodies move downwards towards the centre), then circular motion also must of necessity be the motion of some simple body. (We have already made the reservation that the motion of composite bodies is determined by whatever simple body predominates in the mixture.) From all these premises therefore it clearly follows that there exists some physical substance besides the four in our sublunary world, and moreover that it is more divine than, and prior to, all these. The same can also be proved on the further assumption that all motion is either

269 a

ἢ κατὰ φύσιν ἢ παρὰ φύσιν, καὶ τὴν ἄλλῳ παρὰ
φύσιν ἑτέρῳ κατὰ φύσιν, οἷον ἡ ἄνω καὶ ἡ κάτω
35 πέπονθεν· ἡ μὲν γὰρ τῷ πυρί, ἡ δὲ τῇ γῇ παρὰ
269 b φύσιν καὶ κατὰ φύσιν· ὥστ᾽ ἀναγκαῖον καὶ τὴν
κύκλῳ κίνησιν, ἐπειδὴ τούτοις παρὰ φύσιν, ἑτέρου
τινὸς εἶναι κατὰ φύσιν. πρὸς δὲ τούτοις εἰ μέν
ἐστιν ἡ κύκλῳ τινὶ φορὰ κατὰ φύσιν, δῆλον ὡς εἴη
ἄν τι σῶμα τῶν ἁπλῶν καὶ πρώτων, ὃ πέφυκεν,
5 ὥσπερ τὸ πῦρ ἄνω καὶ ἡ γῆ κάτω, ἐκεῖνο κύκλῳ
φέρεσθαι κατὰ φύσιν. εἰ δὲ παρὰ φύσιν φέρεται τὰ
φερόμενα κύκλῳ τὴν πέριξ φοράν, θαυμαστὸν καὶ
παντελῶς ἄλογον τὸ μόνην εἶναι συνεχῆ ταύτην
τὴν κίνησιν καὶ ἀΐδιον, οὖσαν παρὰ φύσιν· φαίνεται
10 γὰρ ἔν γε τοῖς ἄλλοις τάχιστα φθειρόμενα τὰ παρὰ
φύσιν. ὥστ᾽ εἴπερ ἐστὶ πῦρ τὸ φερόμενον, καθάπερ
φασί τινες, οὐθὲν ἧττον αὐτῷ παρὰ φύσιν ἡ κίνησίς
ἐστιν αὕτη ἢ ἡ κάτω· πυρὸς γὰρ κίνησιν ὁρῶμεν
τὴν ἀπὸ τοῦ μέσου κατ᾽ εὐθεῖαν.

Διόπερ ἐξ ἁπάντων ἄν τις τούτων συλλογιζό-
μενος πιστεύσειεν ὡς ἔστι τι παρὰ τὰ σώματα
15 τὰ δεῦρο καὶ περὶ ἡμᾶς ἕτερον κεχωρισμένον,
τοσούτῳ τιμιωτέραν ἔχον τὴν φύσιν ὅσῳπερ ἀφέστηκε τῶν ἐνταῦθα πλεῖον.

natural or unnatural, and that motion which is unnatural to one body is natural to another, as the motions up and down are natural or unnatural to fire and earth respectively ; from these it follows that circular motion too, since it is unnatural to these elements, is natural to some other.[a] Moreover, if circular motion is natural to anything, it will clearly be one of the simple and primary bodies of such a nature as to move naturally in a circle, as fire moves upward and earth downward. If on the other hand it be maintained that the revolutionary motion of the body which is carried round in a circle is unnatural, it is strange, in fact quite absurd, that being unnatural it should yet be the only continuous and eternal motion, seeing that in the rest of nature what is unnatural is the quickest to fall into decay. And so, if fire be the body carried round, as some say, this motion will be no less unnatural to it than motion downwards ; for we see the natural motion of fire to be in a straight line away from the centre.

Thus the reasoning from all our premises goes to make us believe that there is some other body separate from those around us here, and of a higher nature in proportion as it is removed from the sublunary world.

[a] In this argument the words παρὰ φύσιν (" unnatural ") cannot have their strongest sense of " contrary to the natural," for this would immediately conflict with the statement of 269 a 9 above, and the doctrine " one thing one contrary." They bear only the weaker sense of " not according to their nature." This is the conclusion reached by Simpl. in his defence of the passage. This being so, we may take it that ἔτι in line 32 (" the further point . . .") is inserted to mark this premise as different from that stated above at line 9.

ARISTOTLE

CHAPTER III

ARGUMENT

Properties of the first body (269 b 18—270 a 35). (i) *It is neither light nor heavy, since lightness implies motion away from the centre, heaviness implies motion to the centre. The first body can have neither of these motions, neither naturally (for its natural motion is circular), nor unnaturally nor by force (for were it to move unnaturally in any of these directions, it would follow that its natural motion was in the other). This applies equally to the body as a whole and to any part of it* (269 b 18—270 a 12).

(ii) *It is ungenerated and indestructible, since it has no opposite (there is no opposite to circular motion, and opposites have opposite motions), and generation and destruction are into and out of opposites, as was shown in the* Physics [a] (270 a 13-23).

269 b 18 Ἐπεὶ δὲ τὰ μὲν ὑπόκειται τὰ δ᾽ ἀποδέδεικται
τῶν εἰρημένων, φανερὸν ὅτι οὔτε κουφότητα οὔτε
20 βάρος ἔχει σῶμα ἅπαν. δεῖ δὲ ὑποθέσθαι τί λέγομεν τὸ βαρὺ καὶ τὸ κοῦφον, νῦν μὲν ἱκανῶς ὡς
πρὸς τὴν παροῦσαν χρείαν, ἀκριβέστερον δὲ πάλιν,
ὅταν ἐπισκοπῶμεν περὶ τῆς οὐσίας αὐτῶν. βαρὺ
μὲν οὖν ἔστω τὸ φέρεσθαι πεφυκὸς ἐπὶ τὸ μέσον,
κοῦφον δὲ τὸ ἀπὸ τοῦ μέσου, βαρύτατον δὲ τὸ
25 πᾶσιν ὑφιστάμενον τοῖς κάτω φερομένοις, κουφότατον δὲ τὸ πᾶσιν ἐπιπολάζον τοῖς ἄνω φερομένοις.
ἀνάγκη δὴ[1] πᾶν τὸ φερόμενον ἢ κάτω ἢ ἄνω ἢ
κουφότητ᾽ ἔχειν ἢ βάρος ἢ ἄμφω, μὴ πρὸς τὸ αὐτὸ

---

[1] δὴ Stocks and Allan with all MSS. but F. δὲ Bekker and Prantl.

---

[a] Book iv. *init.*

18

CHAPTER III

ARGUMENT (*continued*)

(iii) *It cannot grow or diminish, since growth and diminution are only particular instances of generation and destruction* (270 a 23-26).

(iv) *It is unalterable, since changes of property are in physical substances allied with the susceptibility to growth and diminution* (270 a 26-35).

Confirmation of results from experience (270 b 1-26).

(a) *The popular belief in gods and the assignment to them of the highest place in the Universe* (270 b 1-12).

(b) *The evidence of the senses. No alteration has ever been observed in the heavens* (270 b 12-16).

(c) *The existence of a name for this substance*, aither, *derived from* ἀεί *and* θεῖν (270 b 16-25).

There can be no other simple bodies than aither *and the four elements, because there are no other simple motions than circular and straight* (270 b 26-31).

AFTER what has been said, whether laid down as hypothesis or demonstrated in the course of the argument, it becomes clear that not every body has either lightness or weight. However, we must first lay down what we mean by heavy and light, at present only so far as it is necessary for the purpose in hand, but later with more precision,[a] when we come to investigate the real nature of the two. Let " the heavy " then be that whose nature it is to move towards the centre, " the light " that whose nature it is to move away from the centre, " heaviest " that which sinks below all other bodies whose motion is downwards, and " lightest " that which rises to the top of the bodies whose motion is upwards. Thus every body which moves downwards or upwards must have either lightness or weight or both. (A body

19

269 b

δέ· πρὸς ἄλληλα γάρ ἐστι βαρέα καὶ κοῦφα, οἷον
30 ἀὴρ πρὸς ὕδωρ, καὶ πρὸς γῆν ὕδωρ. τὸ δὴ κύκλῳ
σῶμα φερόμενον ἀδύνατον ἔχειν βάρος ἢ κουφότητα·
οὔτε γὰρ κατὰ φύσιν οὔτε παρὰ φύσιν ἐνδέχεται
αὐτῷ κινηθῆναι ἐπὶ τὸ μέσον ἢ ἀπὸ τοῦ μέσου.
κατὰ φύσιν μὲν γὰρ οὐκ ἔστιν αὐτῷ ἡ ἐπ᾽ εὐθείας
φορά· μία γὰρ ἦν ἑκάστου τῶν ἁπλῶν, ὥστ᾽ ἔσται
35 τὸ αὐτὸ τῶν οὕτω τινὶ φερομένων. παρὰ φύσιν δ᾽
270 a ἐνεχθέντος, εἰ μὲν ἡ κάτω παρὰ φύσιν, ἡ ἄνω
ἔσται κατὰ φύσιν, εἰ δ᾽ ἡ ἄνω παρὰ φύσιν, ἡ κάτω
κατὰ φύσιν· ἔθεμεν γὰρ τῶν ἐναντίων ᾧ ἡ ἑτέρα
παρὰ φύσιν, τὴν ἑτέραν εἶναι κατὰ φύσιν. ἐπεὶ
δ᾽ εἰς τὸ αὐτὸ φέρεται τὸ ὅλον καὶ τὸ μόριον κατὰ
5 φύσιν, οἷον πᾶσα γῆ καὶ μικρὰ βῶλος, συμβαίνει
πρῶτον μὲν μήτε κουφότητ᾽ ἔχειν αὐτὸ μηδεμίαν
μήτε βάρος (ἢ γὰρ ἂν πρὸς τὸ μέσον ἢ ἀπὸ τοῦ
μέσου ἠδύνατο φέρεσθαι κατὰ τὴν ἑαυτοῦ φύσιν),
ἔπειθ᾽ ὅτι ἀδύνατον κινηθῆναι τὴν κατὰ τόπον
10 κίνησιν ἢ ἄνω ἢ κάτω κατασπώμενον· οὔτε γὰρ
κατὰ φύσιν ἐνδέχεται κινηθῆναι κίνησιν αὐτῷ ἄλλην οὔτε παρὰ φύσιν, οὔτ᾽ αὐτῷ οὔτε τῶν μορίων
οὐθενί· ὁ γὰρ αὐτὸς λόγος περὶ ὅλου καὶ μέρους.

Ὁμοίως δ᾽ εὔλογον ὑπολαβεῖν περὶ αὐτοῦ καὶ
ὅτι ἀγένητον καὶ ἄφθαρτον καὶ ἀναυξὲς καὶ ἀναλ-
15 λοίωτον, διὰ τὸ γίγνεσθαι μὲν ἅπαν τὸ γιγνόμενον
ἐξ ἐναντίου τε καὶ ὑποκειμένου τινός, καὶ φθείρεσθαι ὡσαύτως ὑποκειμένου τέ τινος καὶ ὑπ᾽ ἐναντίου καὶ εἰς ἐναντίον, καθάπερ ἐν τοῖς πρώτοις

20

cannot of course be both heavy and light in relation
to the same thing, but the elements are so in relation
to each other, *e.g.* air is light in comparison with water,
but water in comparison with earth.)   Now the body
whose motion is circular cannot have either weight or
lightness, for neither naturally nor unnaturally can
it ever move towards or away from the centre.   (*a*)
Naturally it cannot have rectilinear motion, because
it was laid down that each simple body has only one
natural motion, and therefore it would itself be one
of the bodies whose natural motion is rectilinear.
(*b*) But suppose it moves in a straight line contrary to
its nature, then if the motion is downwards, upward
motion will be its natural one, and *vice versa* ; for it
was one of our hypotheses that of two contrary
motions, if one is unnatural the other is natural.
Taking into account then the fact that a whole and
its part move naturally in the same direction (as do
e.g. all earth together and a small clod), we have
established (*a*) that it has neither lightness nor weight,
since otherwise it would have been able to move
naturally either towards the centre or away from the
centre, (*b*) that it cannot move locally by being
violently forced either up or down, for it is impossible
for it to move, either naturally or unnaturally, with
any other motion but its own, either itself as a whole
or any of its parts, seeing that the same argument
applies to whole and part.

   With equal reason we may regard it as ungenerated
and indestructible, and susceptible neither to growth
nor alteration.   (*a*) Everything that is generated
comes into being out of an opposite and a substrate,
and is destroyed only if it has a substrate, and through
the agency of an opposite, and passes into its opposite,

21

270 a

εἴρηται λόγοις· τῶν δ' ἐναντίων καὶ αἱ φοραὶ
ἐναντίαι. εἰ δὴ τούτῳ μηδὲν ἐναντίον ἐνδέχεται
20 εἶναι διὰ τὸ καὶ τῇ φορᾷ τῇ κύκλῳ μὴ εἶναι ἄν τιν'
ἐναντίαν κίνησιν, ὀρθῶς ἔοικεν ἡ φύσις τὸ μέλλον
ἔσεσθαι ἀγένητον καὶ ἄφθαρτον ἐξελέσθαι ἐκ τῶν
ἐναντίων· ἐν τοῖς ἐναντίοις γὰρ ἡ γένεσις καὶ ἡ
φθορά. ἀλλὰ μὴν καὶ τὸ αὐξανόμενον ἅπαν αὐ-
25 ξάνεται [καὶ τὸ φθῖνον φθίνει]¹ ὑπὸ συγγενοῦς
προσιόντος καὶ ἀναλυομένου εἰς τὴν ὕλην· τούτῳ
δ' οὐκ ἔστιν ἐξ οὗ γέγονεν. εἰ δ' ἐστὶ καὶ ἀν-
αύξητον καὶ ἄφθαρτον, τῆς αὐτῆς διανοίας ἐστὶν
ὑπολαβεῖν καὶ ἀναλλοίωτον εἶναι. ἔστι μὲν γὰρ ἡ
ἀλλοίωσις κίνησις κατὰ τὸ ποιόν, τοῦ δὲ ποιοῦ αἱ
μὲν ἕξεις καὶ διαθέσεις οὐκ ἄνευ τῶν κατὰ πάθη
γίγνονται μεταβολῶν, οἷον ὑγίεια καὶ νόσος. κατὰ
30 δὲ πάθος ὅσα μεταβάλλει τῶν φυσικῶν σωμάτων,
ἔχονθ' ὁρῶμεν πάντα καὶ αὔξησιν καὶ φθίσιν, οἷον
τά τε τῶν ζῴων σώματα καὶ τὰ μόρια αὐτῶν καὶ
τὰ τῶν φυτῶν, ὁμοίως δὲ καὶ τὰ τῶν στοιχείων·
ὥστ' εἴπερ τὸ κύκλῳ σῶμα μήτ' αὔξησιν ἔχειν
35 ἐνδέχεται μήτε φθίσιν, εὔλογον καὶ ἀναλλοίωτον
εἶναι.

270 b Διότι μὲν οὖν ἀίδιον καὶ οὔτ' αὔξησιν ἔχον οὔτε
φθίσιν, ἀλλ' ἀγήρατον καὶ ἀναλλοίωτον καὶ ἀπαθές
ἐστι τὸ πρῶτον τῶν σωμάτων, εἴ τις τοῖς ὑποκειμένοις πιστεύει, φανερὸν ἐκ τῶν εἰρημένων
5 ἐστίν. ἔοικε δ' ὅ τε λόγος τοῖς φαινομένοις μαρ-

---

¹ The words καὶ τὸ φθῖνον φθίνει are omitted by Stocks and
Allan. So Simpl., Them., and all mss. but H and M.

ᵃ A.'s reference is to the *Physics* (i. 7-9), but the point is
perhaps put most concisely in *Met.* Λ 1069 b 2-9.

as has been explained in our first discussions.^{a} (b) Opposites have opposite motions. (c) There cannot be an opposite to the body under discussion, because there cannot be an opposite motion to the circular. It looks then as if nature had providently abstracted from the class of opposites that which was to be ungenerated and indestructible, because generation and destruction take place among opposites. Moreover anything which is subject to growth [or diminution] grows [or diminishes] in consequence of substance of the same kind being added to it and dissolving into its matter ^{b}; but this body has no such matter. And if it is subject neither to growth nor to destruction, the same train of thought leads us to suppose that it is not subject to alteration either. Alteration is movement in respect of quality, and the temporary or permanent states of quality, health and disease for example, do not come into being without changes of affection.^{c} But all physical bodies which possess changing affections may be seen to be subject also to growth and diminution. Such are, for example, the bodies of animals and plants and their parts, and also those of the elements. If then the body whose natural motion is circular cannot be subject to growth or diminution, it is a reasonable supposition that it is not subject to alteration either.

From what has been said it is clear why, if our hypotheses are to be trusted, the primary body of all is eternal, suffers neither growth nor diminution, but is ageless, unalterable and impassive. I think too that the argument bears out experience and is borne

^{b} *i.e.* growth and diminution are really only particular examples of generation and destruction (Simpl.).

^{c} For the relation between ποῖον and πάθος (translated " quality " and " affection ") see note on 268 a 2 above.

τυρεῖν καὶ τὰ φαινόμενα τῷ λόγῳ· πάντες γὰρ
ἄνθρωποι περὶ θεῶν ἔχουσιν ὑπόληψιν, καὶ πάντες
τὸν ἀνωτάτω τῷ θείῳ τόπον ἀποδιδόασι, καὶ βάρ-
βαροι καὶ Ἕλληνες, ὅσοι περ εἶναι νομίζουσι θεούς,
δῆλον ὅτι ὡς τῷ ἀθανάτῳ τὸ ἀθάνατον συνηρτη-
10 μένον· ἀδύνατον γὰρ ἄλλως. εἴπερ οὖν ἔστι τι
θεῖον, ὥσπερ ἔστι, καὶ τὰ νῦν εἰρημένα περὶ τῆς
πρώτης οὐσίας τῶν σωμάτων εἴρηται καλῶς.
συμβαίνει δὲ τοῦτο καὶ διὰ τῆς αἰσθήσεως ἱκανῶς,
ὥς γε πρὸς ἀνθρωπίνην εἰπεῖν πίστιν· ἐν ἅπαντι
γὰρ τῷ παρεληλυθότι χρόνῳ κατὰ τὴν παραδεδο-
15 μένην ἀλλήλοις μνήμην οὐθὲν φαίνεται μεταβε-
βληκὸς οὔτε καθ᾽ ὅλον τὸν ἔσχατον οὐρανὸν οὔτε
κατὰ μόριον αὐτοῦ τῶν οἰκείων οὐθέν. ἔοικε δὲ καὶ
τοὔνομα παρὰ τῶν ἀρχαίων διαδεδόσθαι μέχρι καὶ
τοῦ νῦν χρόνου, τοῦτον τὸν τρόπον ὑπολαμβανόντων
ὅνπερ καὶ ἡμεῖς λέγομεν· οὐ γὰρ ἅπαξ οὐδὲ δὶς
20 ἀλλ᾽ ἀπειράκις δεῖ νομίζειν τὰς αὐτὰς ἀφικνεῖσθαι
δόξας εἰς ἡμᾶς. διόπερ ὡς ἑτέρου τινὸς ὄντος τοῦ
πρώτου σώματος παρὰ γῆν καὶ πῦρ καὶ ἀέρα καὶ
ὕδωρ, αἰθέρα προσωνόμασαν τὸν ἀνωτάτω τόπον,
ἀπὸ τοῦ θεῖν ἀεὶ τὸν ἀίδιον χρόνον θέμενοι τὴν
ἐπωνυμίαν αὐτῷ. Ἀναξαγόρας δὲ κατακέχρηται
25 τῷ ὀνόματι τούτῳ οὐ καλῶς· ὀνομάζει γὰρ αἰθέρα
ἀντὶ πυρός.

Φανερὸν δ᾽ ἐκ τῶν εἰρημένων καὶ διότι τὸν
ἀριθμὸν ἀδύνατον εἶναι πλείω τὸν τῶν λεγομένων
σωμάτων ἁπλῶν· τοῦ μὲν γὰρ ἁπλοῦ σώματος
ἀνάγκη τὴν κίνησιν ἁπλῆν εἶναι, μόνας δὲ ταύτας

---

[a] According to Simplicius, it was believed that the astro-

out by it. All men have a conception of gods, and all assign the highest place to the divine, both barbarians and Hellenes, as many as believe in gods, supposing, obviously, that immortal is closely linked with immortal. It could not, they think, be otherwise. If then—and it is true—there is something divine, what we have said about the primary bodily substance is well said. The truth of it is also clear from the evidence of the senses, enough at least to warrant the assent of human faith; for throughout all past time, according to the records handed down from generation to generation,[a] we find no trace of change either in the whole of the outermost heaven or in any one of its proper parts. It seems too that the name of this first body has been passed down to the present time by the ancients, who thought of it in the same way as we do, for we cannot help believing that the same ideas recur to men not once nor twice but over and over again. Thus they, believing that the primary body was something different from earth and fire and air and water, gave the name *aither* to the uppermost region, choosing its title from the fact that it "runs always" (ἀεὶ θεῖν) and eternally. (Anaxagoras badly misapplies the word when he uses *aither* for fire.)[b]

It is also clear from what has been said why the number of the simple bodies, as we call them, cannot be more than we have mentioned. A simple body must have a simple motion, and we hold that these

---

[a] nomical records of the Egyptians went back for 630,000 years, and those of the Babylonians for 1,440,000.

[b] *i.e.* Anaxagoras derived the word from αἴθειν. In a modern work this criticism would probably stand in a footnote. The derivation from ἀεί and θεῖν occurs in Plato's *Cratylus*, 410 B.

270 b

30 εἶναί φαμεν ἁπλᾶς, τήν τε κύκλῳ καὶ τὴν ἐπ'
εὐθείας, καὶ ταύτης δύο μόρια, τὴν μὲν ἀπὸ τοῦ
μέσου, τὴν δ' ἐπὶ τὸ μέσον.

CHAPTER IV

ARGUMENT

There can be no contrary to circular motion.

(a) *Rectilinear motions seem to have first claim to be considered as such, but the simple rectilinear motions are the
contraries of each other, and a simple motion can have only
one contrary (270 b 32—271 a 5).*

(b) *Since rectilinear motions are called contrary in virtue
of moving in opposite directions, it might be thought that,
similarly, motion around the circumference of a circle in one
direction would be the contrary of motion around it in the
opposite direction. Thus one circular motion would be the contrary of another, just as one rectilinear motion is the contrary
of another. But the essence of the contrariety in rectilinear*

32 Ὅτι δ' οὐκ ἔστι τῇ κύκλῳ φορᾷ ἐναντία ἄλλη
φορά, πλεοναχόθεν ἄν τις λάβοι τὴν πίστιν· πρῶτον
μὲν ὅτι τῇ περιφερεῖ τὴν εὐθεῖαν ἀντικεῖσθαι μά-
35 λιστα τίθεμεν· τὸ γὰρ κοῖλον καὶ τὸ κυρτὸν οὐ
271 a μόνον ἀλλήλοις ἀντικεῖσθαι δοκεῖ ἀλλὰ καὶ
τῷ εὐθεῖ, συνδυαζόμενα καὶ λαβόντα σύνθεσιν·
ὥστ' εἴπερ ἐναντία τίς ἐστι, τὴν ἐπὶ τῆς εὐθείας
μάλιστα ἀναγκαῖον ἐναντίαν εἶναι πρὸς τὴν κύκλῳ
κίνησιν. αἱ δ' ἐπὶ τῆς εὐθείας ἀλλήλαις ἀντίκεινται

---

[a] " As the motion which is never deflected to that which is
deflected at every point " (Simpl.).

26

are the only simple motions, circular and rectilinear,
the latter of two sorts, away from the centre and
towards the centre.

CHAPTER IV

ARGUMENT (*continued*)

*motions lay in the places from which they started and to
which they went. These must be opposite for the motions to
be properly described as contrary. Motions around the circumference of a circle, on the other hand, even if in opposite
directions, are nevertheless motions from the same point and
to the same point (271 a 5-22).*

*(c) If there were two contrary circular motions, either they
would be equal, in which case they would neutralize each other,
or one would prevail, in which case the other would be in-
operative. It would follow, since each simple motion is the
motion of a different simple corporeal substance, that there
would exist a body which might as well not exist, since it
would be condemned never to move with its natural motion,
i.e. to exercise its proper function. This is not the way that
nature works (271 a 22-33).*

That there cannot be any motion other than the
circular and contrary to it may be confirmed from many
sides. First of all, we are most accustomed to think
of rectilinear motion as opposed to circular.[a] Concave
and convex are, it would seem, contraries not only of
each other but also of the straight line, when they are
considered together and taken as a unity. If then
there is an opposite to circular motion, it must above
all be rectilinear motion which is that opposite. But
the two rectilinear motions are the contraries of each

2/1 a

5 διὰ τοὺς τόπους· τὸ γὰρ ἄνω καὶ κάτω τόπου τέ
ἐστι διαφορὰ καὶ ἐναντίωσις.

Ἔπειτ᾿ εἴ τις ὑπολαμβάνει τὸν αὐτὸν εἶναι λόγον
ὅνπερ ἐπὶ τῆς εὐθείας, καὶ ἐπὶ τῆς περιφεροῦς
(τὴν γὰρ ἀπὸ τοῦ Α πρὸς τὸ Β φορὰν ἐναντίαν
εἶναι τῇ ἀπὸ τοῦ Β πρὸς τὸ Α), τὴν ἐπὶ τῆς εὐθείας
10 λέγει· αὕτη γὰρ πεπέρανται, περιφερεῖς δ᾿ ἄπειροι
ἂν εἶεν περὶ τὰ αὐτὰ σημεῖα. ὁμοίως δὲ καὶ ἐπὶ
τοῦ ἡμικυκλίου τοῦ ἑνός, οἷον ἀπὸ τοῦ Γ ἐπὶ τὸ Δ
καὶ ἀπὸ τοῦ Δ ἐπὶ τὸ Γ· ἡ γὰρ αὐτὴ τῇ ἐπὶ τῆς
διαμέτρου ἐστίν· ἀεὶ γὰρ ἕκαστον ἀπέχειν τὴν
εὐθεῖαν τίθεμεν. ὁμοίως δὲ κἂν εἴ τις κύκλον
15 ποιήσας τὴν ἐπὶ θατέρου ἡμικυκλίου φορὰν ἐναντίαν θείη τῇ ἐπὶ θατέρου, οἷον ἐν τῷ ὅλῳ κύκλῳ
τὴν ἀπὸ τοῦ Ε πρὸς τὸ Ζ τοῦ Η ἡμικυκλίου τῇ
ἀπὸ τοῦ Ζ πρὸς τὸ Ε ἐν τῷ Θ ἡμικυκλίῳ. εἰ δὲ καὶ
αὗται ἐναντίαι, ἀλλ᾿ οὔτι γε αἱ ἐπὶ τοῦ ὅλου κύκλου

ᵃ The last step of the argument is omitted. It might be:
(a) While the generally admitted case of contrary opposition
in motions (that of up and down) rests on a contrary opposition of places, no such ground can be suggested for the opposition of circular to rectilinear motion (so Stocks); or, perhaps
more likely, simply: (b) This proves that the rectilinear
motions already have contraries, viz. each other; and it has
already been said that each simple motion can have only one
contrary; therefore neither of the rectilinear motions can
have circular motion as its contrary.

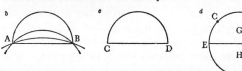

28

other on account of their places, since up and down form a difference, in fact a contrary, in respect of place.[a]

It might be thought that the same thing which has been said of rectilinear motion applies to circular, namely that the motion from a point A in the direction of a point B is the contrary of the motion from B to A. In fact, however, it is rectilinear motion which is meant; for that is definite and limited, whereas there can be an infinite number of circular paths through the same two points.[b] The same holds good even if we take into consideration only the one semicircle, that is, the paths from C to D and from D to C.[c] The result is equivalent to motion along the diameter, for we always measure how far away a thing is by the distance along a straight line. It holds good again even if one were to draw a circle and claim that the motion along one semicircle is contrary to the motion along the other, that is, that in the whole circle the motion from E to F in the semicircle G is contrary to that from F to E in the semicircle H.[d] Even if these are contraries, it does not follow that the motions over the whole circle are contrary to each other.[e] It

---

[e] This becomes clear in conjunction with the following sentence. To consider the motions along the two halves of a circle separately is to impose artificial boundaries; but if they are regarded as parts of the motions round the whole circle, they are seen to be starting from the same point and tending towards the same point. But opposite motions must have opposite ἀρχαί and πέρατα.

φοραὶ ἀλλήλαις διὰ τοῦτο ἐναντίαι. ἀλλὰ μὴν οὐδ'
20 ἡ ἀπὸ τοῦ Α ἐπὶ τὸ Β κύκλῳ φορὰ ἐναντία τῇ
ἀπὸ τοῦ Α ἐπὶ τὸ Γ· ἐκ ταὐτοῦ γὰρ εἰς ταὐτὸ
ἡ κίνησις, ἡ δ' ἐναντία διωρίσθη φορὰ ἐκ τοῦ
ἐναντίου εἰς τὸ ἐναντίον εἶναι.

Εἰ δὲ καὶ ἦν ἡ κύκλῳ τῇ κύκλῳ ἐναντία, μάτην
ἂν ἦν ἡ ἑτέρα· ἐπὶ τὸ αὐτὸ γάρ, ὅτι[1] ἀνάγκη τὸ
25 κύκλῳ φερόμενον ὁποθενοῦν ἀρξάμενον εἰς πάντας
ὁμοίως ἀφικνεῖσθαι τοὺς ἐναντίους τόπους (εἰσὶ δὲ
τόπου ἐναντιότητες τὸ ἄνω καὶ κάτω καὶ τὸ πρόσθεν καὶ ὀπίσθεν καὶ τὸ δεξιὸν καὶ ἀριστερόν), αἱ δὲ
τῆς φορᾶς ἐναντιώσεις κατὰ τὰς τῶν τόπων εἰσὶν
ἐναντιώσεις· εἰ μὲν γὰρ ἴσαι ἦσαν, οὐκ ἂν ἦν
30 κίνησις αὐτῶν, εἰ δ' ἡ ἑτέρα κίνησις ἐκράτει, ἡ
ἑτέρα οὐκ ἂν ἦν· ὥστ' εἰ ἀμφότερα ἦν, μάτην ἂν
θάτερον ἦν σῶμα μὴ κινούμενον τὴν αὑτοῦ κίνησιν·
μάτην γὰρ ὑπόδημα τοῦτο λέγομεν, οὗ μή ἐστιν
ὑπόδεσις. ὁ δὲ θεὸς καὶ ἡ φύσις οὐδὲν μάτην
ποιοῦσιν.

---

[1] ὅτι first hand of E, Simpl. (who discusses both readings),
Alex., Stocks, Allan; ἔτι with all other mss. Bekker; ἐστιν
Prantl *ex coniectura*.

---

[a] γάρ must refer back, as Stocks notes, to the remark "one
of the two would be ineffective." Unless, then, we follow

CHAPTER V

ARGUMENT

There cannot exist an infinite body.
*Every body is either simple or composite, and, since a com-
posite body can be no greater than the sum of its elements, it*

is not even true that motion along the circumference from a point A to a point B is contrary to the motion from A to C : it is motion setting out from the same point to go to the same point, whereas contrary motion was defined as being from an opposite point to its opposite.

Moreover, suppose one circular motion were the contrary of another, the second motion would be purposeless, for it is motion to the same place, since a body revolving in a circle, from whatever point it begins, must touch at all the opposed places alike. ("Opposed places" are top and bottom, front and back, right hand and left.) But contrarieties of motion correspond to contrarieties of place. If then [a] the two motions were of equal strength, no movement would take place, but if one were stronger, the other would disappear. Thus if both existed, the one body [b] would exist to no purpose, not moving with its proper motion, in the same sense as we should call a shoe purposeless which is never worn. But God and nature create nothing that does not fulfil a purpose.

[a] him in repeating that sentence here, the translation "for" cannot be retained. (Prantl wished to alter to ἄρ'.)

[b] It must be remembered, to see the force of this argument, that for Aristotle the existence of a simple motion immediately implies the existence of a body whose natural motion it is. The conception of two contrary circular motions amounts in fact to a conception of two heavenly vaults tending in opposite directions.

CHAPTER V

ARGUMENT (continued)

is sufficient to demonstrate that none of the simple bodies can be infinite (271 b 17-25).

(1) *The primary simple body cannot be infinite, for its*

*natural motion is circular, and no body which revolves in a
circle can be infinite.*

(a) *If an infinite body revolves in a circle, the radii from
the centre of its revolution to the confines of the body must be
infinite. If they are infinite, then the space between any two
of these radii is infinite. Hence to travel over the space between any two of these radii the body will have to traverse an
infinite distance, which is impossible* (271 b 28—272 a 7).

(b) *If a body is spoken of as revolving in a circle, it must be
supposed capable of completing its revolution in a finite time
(as in fact the heaven does, according to our own experience);
and any fraction of a finite time must itself be finite. Now
suppose a line infinite in one direction and revolving about its
other end as a centre. Suppose also another line [in the same
plane] infinite both ways. The first line must be supposed to
cut the second during a finite period of time, since it must do
so during a part of its total revolution. In fact, however, it
cannot. Hence no infinite body (of which this first line is
imagined as a radius drawn from the centre about which it
rotates) can complete a revolution* (272 a 7-20).

271 b   Ἀλλ' ἐπεὶ δῆλον περὶ τούτων, περὶ τῶν λοιπῶν
σκεπτέον, καὶ πρῶτον πότερον ἔστι τι σῶμα ἄπειρον, ὥσπερ οἱ πλεῖστοι τῶν ἀρχαίων φιλοσόφων
ᾠήθησαν, ἢ τοῦτ' ἐστὶν ἕν τι τῶν ἀδυνάτων· τὸ
5 γὰρ οὕτως ἢ ἐκείνως ἔχειν οὔ τι μικρὸν ἀλλ' ὅλον
διαφέρει καὶ πᾶν πρὸς τὴν περὶ τῆς ἀληθείας
θεωρίαν· σχεδὸν γὰρ αὕτη πασῶν ἀρχὴ τῶν ἐναν-
τιώσεων τοῖς ἀποφηναμένοις τι περὶ τῆς ὅλης
φύσεως καὶ γέγονε καὶ γένοιτ' ἄν, εἴπερ καὶ τὸ
μικρὸν παραβῆναι τῆς ἀληθείας ἀφισταμένοις γί-
10 νεται πόρρω μυριοπλάσιον. οἷον εἴ τις ἐλάχιστον
εἶναί τι φαίη μέγεθος· οὗτος γὰρ τοὐλάχιστον
εἰσαγαγὼν τὰ μέγιστ' ἂν κινήσειε τῶν μαθημα-
32

(c) *A moving finite line, whatever its length, would require an infinite time to pass an infinite line : b t the converse must also be true, and an infinite line would require an infinite time to traverse the length of a finite line, however short. Hence an infinite line cannot move at all, from which it can be shown that the heavens, if infinite, could not revolve in a circle* (272 a 21–b 17).

(d) *An infinite circle or sphere is a contradiction in terms : but an infinite body, to revolve, must move in an infinite circle* (272 b 17-24).

(e) *Suppose an infinite moving radius to cut another infinite straight line at a point. Then, however much it rotates, it can never diverge from the other line sufficiently to become parallel to it. Thus it is impossible for the infinite radius ever to complete its circle* (272 b 25-28).

(f) *If an infinite body can complete a revolution, it can traverse an infinite distance in a finite time, since the path of its revolution must be as great as itself. This is impossible* (272 b 28—273 a 6).

THIS, then, is now clear, and we must turn to consider the rest of our problems, of which the first is whether there exists any infinite body, as most of the early philosophers believed, or whether that is an impossibility. This is a point whose settlement one way or the other makes no small difference, in fact all the difference, to our investigation of the truth. It is this, one might say, which has been, and may be expected to be, the origin of all the contradictions between those who make pronouncements in natural science, since a small initial deviation from the truth multiplies itself ten-thousandfold as the argument proceeds. Suppose for instance someone maintained that there is a minimum magnitude ; that man with his minimum would shake the foundations of mathe-

271 b

τικῶν. τούτου δ' αἴτιον ὅτι ἡ ἀρχὴ δυνάμει μείζων
ἢ μεγέθει, διόπερ τὸ ἐν ἀρχῇ μικρὸν ἐν τῇ τελευτῇ
γίνεται παμμέγεθες. τὸ δ' ἄπειρον καὶ ἀρχῆς ἔχει
15 δύναμιν καὶ τοῦ ποσοῦ τὴν μεγίστην, ὥστ' οὐδὲν
ἄτοπον οὐδ' ἄλογον τὸ θαυμαστὴν εἶναι τὴν διαφορὰν ἐκ τοῦ λαβεῖν ὡς ἔστι τι σῶμα ἄπειρον. διὸ
περὶ αὐτοῦ λεκτέον ἐξ ἀρχῆς ἀναλαβοῦσιν.

Ἀνάγκη δὴ πᾶν σῶμα ἢ τῶν ἁπλῶν εἶναι ἢ τῶν
συνθέτων, ὥστε καὶ τὸ ἄπειρον ἢ ἁπλοῦν ἔσται ἢ
20 σύνθετον. ἀλλὰ μὴν καὶ ὅτι γε πεπερασμένων τῶν
ἁπλῶν ἀνάγκη πεπερασμένον εἶναι τὸ σύνθετον,
δῆλον· τὸ γὰρ ἐκ πεπερασμένων καὶ πλήθει καὶ
μεγέθει συγκείμενον πεπέρανται καὶ πλήθει καὶ
μεγέθει· τοσοῦτον γάρ ἐστιν ἐξ ὅσων ἐστὶ συγκείμενον. λοιπὸν τοίνυν ἰδεῖν πότερον ἐνδέχεταί τι
25 τῶν ἁπλῶν ἄπειρον εἶναι τὸ μέγεθος, ἢ τοῦτ'
ἀδύνατον. προχειρισάμενοι δὴ περὶ τοῦ πρώτου
τῶν σωμάτων, οὕτω σκοπῶμεν καὶ περὶ τῶν
λοιπῶν.

Ὅτι μὲν τοίνυν ἀνάγκη τὸ σῶμα τὸ κύκλῳ
φερόμενον πεπεράνθαι πᾶν, ἐκ τῶνδε δῆλον. εἰ γὰρ
ἄπειρον τὸ κύκλῳ φερόμενον σῶμα, ἄπειροι ἔσον-
30 ται αἱ ἀπὸ τοῦ μέσου ἐκβαλλόμεναι. τῶν δ'
ἀπείρων τὸ διάστημα ἄπειρον· διάστημα δὲ λέγω
τῶν γραμμῶν, οὗ μηδέν ἐστιν ἔξω λαβεῖν μέγεθος
ἁπτόμενον τῶν γραμμῶν. τοῦτ' οὖν ἀνάγκη ἄ-
πειρον εἶναι· τῶν γὰρ πεπερασμένων ἀεὶ ἔσται
272 a πεπερασμένον. ἔτι δ' ἀεὶ ἔστι τοῦ δοθέντος μεῖζον
λαβεῖν, ὥστε καθάπερ ἀριθμὸν λέγομεν ἄπειρον,

matics. A starting-point is greater in its potentiality than in its extent, so that an assumption which at the start is small in the end becomes all-important. But as for infinity, that is a conception which not only has the potentiality of a starting-point but in the sphere of quantity the widest of all potentialities, so that it is nothing wonderful or unreasonable that a vast difference results from the assumption of an infinite body. We must therefore take up the question from the beginning.

Every body must be either simple or composite : therefore an infinite body is either simple or composite. But it is clear also that if the simple bodies are finite, any composite body must be finite too ; for that which is composed of elements limited both in number and size is itself limited in number and size, seeing that in quantity it is the sum of its constituents. It remains therefore to see whether it is possible for one of the simple bodies to be infinite in size, or whether this is impossible. Let us start then with the first body, and so pass on to the rest.

The following arguments make it plain that every body which revolves in a circle must be finite. If the revolving body be infinite, the straight lines radiating from the centre [a] will be infinite. But if they are infinite, the intervening space must be infinite. "Intervening space" I am defining as space beyond which there can be no magnitude in contact with the lines. This must be infinite. In the case of finite lines it is always finite, and moreover it is always possible to take more than any given quantity of it, so that this space is infinite in the sense in which we

[a] That is, the centre of the circular path of the supposed revolving body.

ὅτι μέγιστος οὐκ ἔστιν, ὁ αὐτὸς λόγος καὶ περὶ τοῦ
διαστήματος· εἰ οὖν τὸ μὲν ἄπειρον μὴ ἔστι διελθεῖν, ἀπείρου δ' ὄντος ἀνάγκη ἄπειρον τὸ διάστημα
5 εἶναι, οὐκ ἂν ἐνδέχοιτο κινηθῆναι κύκλῳ· τὸν δ'
οὐρανὸν ὁρῶμεν κύκλῳ στρεφόμενον, καὶ τῷ λόγῳ
δὲ διωρίσαμεν ὅτι ἐστί τινος ἡ κύκλῳ κίνησις.

Ἔτι ἀπὸ πεπερασμένου χρόνου ἐὰν ἀφέλῃς πεπερασμένον, ἀνάγκη καὶ τὸν λοιπὸν εἶναι πεπερασμένον
καὶ ἔχειν ἀρχήν. εἰ δ' ὁ χρόνος ὁ τῆς βαδίσεως
10 ἔχει ἀρχήν, ἔστιν ἀρχὴ καὶ τῆς κινήσεως, ὥστε καὶ
τοῦ μεγέθους ὃ βεβάδικεν. ὁμοίως δὲ τοῦτο καὶ
ἐπὶ τῶν ἄλλων. ἔστω δὴ γραμμὴ ἄπειρος, ἐφ' ᾗ
ΑΓΕ, ἐπὶ θάτερα, ᾗ τὸ Ε· ἡ δ' ἐφ' ᾗ τὰ ΒΒ, ἐπ'
ἀμφότερα ἄπειρος. εἰ δὴ γράψει κύκλον ἡ τὸ ΑΓΕ
15 ἀπὸ τοῦ Γ κέντρου, τέμνουσά ποτε οἰσθήσεται κύκλῳ τὴν ΒΒ ἡ τὸ ΑΓΕ πεπερασμένον χρόνον· ὁ
γὰρ πᾶς χρόνος ἐν ὅσῳ κύκλῳ ἠνέχθη ὁ οὐρανός,
πεπερασμένος. καὶ ὁ ἀφῃρημένος ἄρα, ὃν ἡ τέ-
μνουσα ἐφέρετο. ἔσται ἄρα τις ἀρχὴ ᾗ πρῶτον ἡ
τὰ ΑΓΕ τὴν τὰ ΒΒ ἔτεμεν. ἀλλ' ἀδύνατον.
20 οὐκ ἄρα ἔστι κύκλῳ στραφῆναι τὸ ἄπειρον. ὥστ'
οὐδὲ τὸν κόσμον, εἰ ἦν ἄπειρος.

Ἔτι δὲ καὶ ἐκ τῶνδε φανερόν, ὅτι τὸ ἄπειρον
ἀδύνατον κινηθῆναι. ἔστω γὰρ ἡ τὸ Α φερομένη
παρὰ τὴν Β, πεπερασμένη παρὰ πεπερασμένην.

say that number is infinite, because there exists no greatest number. If then it is impossible to traverse an infinite space, and in an infinite body the space between the radii is infinite, the body cannot move in a circle. But we ourselves see the heaven revolving in a circle, and also we established by argument that circular motion is the motion of a real body.

Again, if a finite time be subtracted from a finite time, the remainder must also be finite and have a beginning. But if the time of the journey has a beginning, so also must the movement, and hence the distance which is traversed. This applies equally to everything else. Let ACE be a straight line infinite in the direction of E, and BB another straight line infinite in both directions. If the line ACE describes a circle about C[a] as centre, it will be expected to cut BB in its revolution for a certain finite time (for the whole time taken by the heaven to complete its revolution is finite, therefore the subtracted time, during which the line in its movement cuts the other, is also finite). There will therefore be a point of time at which the line ACE first cuts the line BB. But this is impossible. Therefore it is impossible for an infinite body to revolve in a circle. Neither then could the heaven, if it were infinite.

The following argument also shows that it is impossible for that which is infinite to move. Suppose a line A moving past a line B, both lines being

[a] So Bekker, with all MSS. but F. Allan reads " A," following F and Simpl. This is more satisfactory, for it adds a needless confusion to the problem to suppose that the line ACE revolves not about its starting-point but about some other point farther along it.

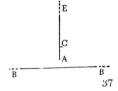

272 a

ἀνάγκη δὴ ἅμα τήν τε Α τῆς Β ἀπολελύσθαι
25 καὶ τὴν Β τῆς Α· ὅσον γὰρ ἡ ἑτέρα ἐπιβάλλει
τῆς ἑτέρας, καὶ ἡ ἑτέρα ἐκείνης τοσοῦτον. εἰ
μὲν οὖν ἄμφω κινοῖντο εἰς τοὐναντίον, θᾶττον ἂν
ἀπολύοιντο, εἰ δὲ παρὰ μένουσαν παραφέροιτο,
βραδύτερον, τῷ αὐτῷ τάχει κινουμένου τοῦ παρα-
φερομένου. ἀλλ' ἐκεῖνό γε φανερόν, ὅτι ἀδύνατον
τὴν ἄπειρον διελθεῖν ἐν πεπερασμένῳ χρόνῳ. ἐν
30 ἀπείρῳ ἄρα· δέδεικται γὰρ τοῦτο πρότερον ἐν τοῖς
περὶ κινήσεως. διαφέρει δέ γε οὐθὲν ἢ τὴν πεπερασμένην φέρεσθαι παρὰ τὴν ἄπειρον ἢ τὴν
272 b ἄπειρον παρ' ἐκείνην· ὅταν γὰρ ἐκείνη παρ' ἐκείνην,
κἀκείνη παραλλάττει[1] ἐκείνην, ὁμοίως κινουμένη
καὶ ἀκίνητος· πλὴν θᾶττον, ἐὰν κινῶνται ἀμφότεραι,
ἀπολυθήσονται. καίτοι ἐνίοτ' οὐθὲν κωλύει τὴν
κινουμένην παρ' ἠρεμοῦσαν θᾶττον παρελθεῖν ἢ τὴν
5 ἀντικινουμένην, ἐάν τις ποιήσῃ τὰς μὲν ἀντικινου-
μένας ἀμφοτέρας φερομένας βραδέως, τὴν δὲ παρὰ
τὴν ἠρεμοῦσαν πολλῷ ἐκείνων θᾶττον φερομένην.
οὐδὲν οὖν πρὸς τὸν λόγον ἐμπόδιον ὅτι παρ' ἠρεμοῦσαν, ἐπείπερ κινουμένην ἐνδέχεται τὴν Α παρὰ
κινουμένην τὴν Β βραδύτερον παρελθεῖν. εἰ οὖν

---

[1] παραλλάττει FHMJ, Stocks, Allan; παρ' E, Bekker;
παραλλάττῃ L.

[a] *Phys.* vi. 7. For the appellation see Stocks's note here,
and Ross, *Physics* (1936), introd. 1 ff.

[b] Bekker's παρ' ἐκείνην is not intolerable on grounds of
meaning, as Stocks maintains. He objects that "it must
stand for φέρεται παρά and thus attributes movement to B,

38

finite. Obviously A must be clear of B at the same time that B is clear of A, since A overlaps B to the same extent that B overlaps A. If both are moving in opposite directions, they will get clear of each other more quickly than if one is stationary and the other moving past it, provided that the latter moves with the same speed in both instances. Now this is clear, that it is impossible to traverse an infinite line in a finite time : the time must be infinite. (This has been demonstrated previously in the work on motion.[a]) Incidentally it would make no difference whether we had a finite line moving past an infinite or an infinite past a finite ; for when the first is moving past the second, the second is virtually [b] moving past the first, whether it be in motion or not. They will simply get clear of each other more quickly if both are moving, though there is nothing against supposing cases where a moving line passes a stationary one more quickly than one which is moving in the opposite direction. One has only to imagine the two moving lines as moving slowly, and the one which moves past the stationary line as moving much quicker than they. It does not therefore affect the argument to suppose a line moving past a stationary line, in view of the possibility that if the second line were moving also, yet the first might be even slower in passing it. If then the

of which it is said in the same sentence that it may be un-moved." But the point Aristotle wishes to make is that it is only relative motion that is in question, so that it makes no difference whether one line is, regarded absolutely, stationary, since it is none the less moving past the other, if the other is moving past it. On the other hand the reading παραλλάττει ἐκείνην, which Stocks and Allan adopt, certainly has better authority. See critical note 1.

272 b

10 ἄπειρος ὁ χρόνος ὂν ἡ πεπερασμένη ἀπολύεται
κινουμένη, καὶ ἐν ᾧ ἡ ἄπειρος τὴν πεπερασμένην
ἐκινήθη ἀνάγκη ἄπειρον εἶναι. ἀδύνατον ἄρα τὸ
ἄπειρον κινεῖσθαι ὅλως· ἐὰν γὰρ καὶ τοὐλάχιστον
κινηθῇ, ἀνάγκη ἄπειρον γίγνεσθαι χρόνον. ἀλλὰ
μὴν ὅ γ᾽ οὐρανὸς περιέρχεται καὶ στρέφεται ὅλος¹
15 κύκλῳ ἐν πεπερασμένῳ χρόνῳ, ὥστε περίεισιν
ἅπασαν τὴν ἐντός, οἷον τὴν ΑΒ πεπερασμένην.
ἀδύνατον ἄρα ἄπειρον εἶναι τὸ κύκλῳ.

Ἔτι ὥσπερ γραμμὴν ἧς² πέρας ἐστὶν ἀδύνατον
εἶναι ἄπειρον, ἀλλ᾽ εἴπερ, ἐπὶ μῆκος, καὶ ἐπίπεδον
ὡσαύτως ᾗ πέρας οὐκ ἐνδέχεται· ὅταν δ᾽ ὁρισθῇ,
20 οὐθαμῇ, οἷον τετράγωνον ἄπειρον ἢ κύκλον ἢ
σφαῖραν, ὥσπερ οὐδὲ ποδιαίαν ἄπειρον. εἰ οὖν
μήτε σφαῖρα μήτε τετράγωνον μήτε κύκλος ἐστὶν

---

¹ ὅλος, so Allan. Bekker, following HM, has ὅλως.
² ἧς. ᾗ coni. Ross.

ᵃ I have retained the text, which seems to make good
sense. The arrangement in the comparison between line
and surface is chiasmic. The correspondence is this : a line
may be described as (a) infinite, in which case we must make
the qualification that we mean infinite only in length [since
by definition a line has no breadth or depth], or (b) finite, in
which case we mean that it is not infinite in any direction at
all. Similarly a surface, if it is described as infinite, must
be understood as extending infinitely in one plane only,
since in depth it is limited by the definition of a surface as
having no depth. (That is the direction ᾗ πέρας ἐστὶν αὐτῷ.
It does not seem necessary to make ἐπίπεδον the subject of
the understood ἐστίν if ᾗ is understood in a local sense rather
than with the meaning " qua limit.") If on the other hand
it is defined in a way which implies limitation in its own
plane, then it cannot be infinite in any direction at all.
(This surface corresponds to the line ἧς πέρας ἐστί.) But

40

time taken by the finite moving line to clear the
infinite must be infinite, so also must the time in
which the infinite line moves the length of the
finite. Hence it is impossible for the infinite line to
move at all, for if it move even the slightest bit, it
must take an infinite time. In fact however the
heaven goes round and revolves in a circle, as a
whole, in a finite time. It therefore passes round
any line within that circle, *e.g.* the finite line AB.
Hence it is impossible for the body which revolves
in a circle to be infinite.

Again, just as a line, if it have a limit, cannot be
infinite, but if it is infinite, can be so only in length;
so also a surface cannot be infinite in that direction
in which it has a limit, and if it be by its definition
determinate cannot be infinite in any direction at
all, *i.e.* an infinite square or circle or sphere is as
much an impossibility as an infinite line-one-foot-
long.[a] If then (*a*) neither a sphere nor a square nor
a circle can be infinite, (*b*) without a circle there

the definitions of square, circle, sphere do imply limitation
in the surface even as a surface. Hence an infinite square
etc. is an impossibility.

Simpl. knew of a reading ἐπὶ θατέρα for ἐπὶ μῆκος, which
would translate: " a finite line cannot be infinite, or if so,
in one direction only." Sir W. D. Ross (see Stocks and Allan)
suggests ᾗ for ἧς in l. 17, *i.e.* " a line cannot be infinite in
the direction in which it is a limit, but only in length " (the
line being the limit of breadth). This is supported by the
translation of Argyropulos (*ex ea parte qua finis est*), and
makes excellent sense. I am however tempted to keep the
text, translating as above, since it gives an argument holding
well together as a whole. γραμμή alone, of course, not
γραμμὴ ἧς πέρας ἐστί, must be the subject of the next clause
(ἀλλ᾽ εἴπερ), but this is quite in Aristotle's manner. ποδιαία
in l. 20 will on this interpretation be intended as an example
of a γραμμὴ ἧς πέρας ἐστίν.

272 b

ἄπειρος, μὴ ὄντος δὲ κύκλου οὐδ' ἂν ἡ κύκλῳ εἴη
φορά, ὁμοίως δὲ μηδ' ἀπείρου ὄντος οὐκ ἂν εἴη
ἄπειρος, εἰ μηδ' ὁ κύκλος ἄπειρός ἐστιν, οὐκ ἂν
κινοῖτο κυκλικῶς ἄπειρον σῶμα.

25 Ἔτι εἰ τὸ Γ κέντρον, ἡ δὲ τὸ ΑΒ ἄπειρος καὶ ἡ
τὸ Ε πρὸς ὀρθὴν ἄπειρος καὶ ἡ τὸ ΓΔ κινουμένη,
οὐδέποτ' ἀπολυθήσεται τῆς Ε, ἀλλ' ἀεὶ ἕξει ὥσπερ
ἡ ΓΕ· τέμνει γὰρ ᾗ τὸ Ζ. οὐκ ἄρα περίεισι
κύκλῳ ἡ ἄπειρος.

Ἔτι εἴπερ ἄπειρος ὁ οὐρανός, κινεῖται δὲ κύκλῳ,
30 ἐν πεπερασμένῳ χρόνῳ ἄπειρον ἔσται διεληλυθώς.
ἔστω γὰρ ὁ μὲν μένων οὐρανὸς ἄπειρος, ὁ δ' ἐν
τούτῳ κινούμενος ἴσος. ὥστ' εἰ περιελήλυθε κύκλῳ
ἄπειρος ὤν, ἄπειρον τὸ ἴσον αὐτῷ διελήλυθεν ἐν
273 a πεπερασμένῳ χρόνῳ. ἀλλὰ τοῦτ' ἦν ἀδύνατον. ἔστι
δὲ καὶ ἀντεστραμμένως εἰπεῖν, ὅτι εἰ πεπερασμένος
ὁ χρόνος ἐν ᾧ περιεστράφη, καὶ τὸ μέγεθος ὃ
διελήλυθεν ἀνάγκη εἶναι πεπερασμένον· ἴσον δ'
αὐτῷ διελήλυθεν· πεπέρανται ἄρα καὶ αὐτός.

5 Ὅτι μὲν οὖν τὸ κύκλῳ κινούμενον οὐκ ἔστιν ἀ-
τελεύτητον οὐδ' ἄπειρον, ἀλλ' ἔχει τέλος, φανερόν.

cannot be circular motion, and similarly (c) if the circle is not infinite the motion cannot be infinite, then, the circle itself not being infinite, an infinite body cannot move in a circle.

Again, let C be a centre, AB an infinite line, E another infinite line at right angles to AB, and CD another infinite line moving about C. The line CD will never free itself from the line E, but will always be in a position analogous to that of CE, *i.e.* it will always cut the line E, say at F.[a] Therefore the infinite line will never describe a complete circle.

Again, if the heaven be infinite, and revolve in a circle, it will have traversed an infinite distance in a finite time. Imagine one stationary heaven which is infinite, and the other moving within it and of equal extent. Should the moving heaven, being infinite, have completed the circle, it will have traversed its equivalent, the infinite, in a finite time. But this we know to be impossible. It is also possible to assert the converse, that if the time of its revolution be finite, the distance which it has traversed must also be finite. But this distance is equal to the heaven itself; therefore it too is finite.

It is now clear that the body which revolves in a circle is not endless or infinite, but has a limit.

[a] In other words, if two infinite lines are convergent, then however much they may subsequently diverge they can never become parallel.

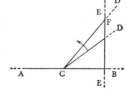

ARISTOTLE

CHAPTER VI

ARGUMENT

There cannot exist an infinite body (*continued*).

(2) *Neither can any of the other elements be infinite.*

(a) *The elements other than the primary one have the contrary motions of up and down, i.e. they have motions to opposite places, and one of these, the centre of the world, is determined, from which it follows that both the upper limit and the space between the two are determined. Hence the bodies which fill this space cannot be infinite* (273 a 7-21).

(b) *An infinite body must have infinite weight, for if its weight were finite it would be possible to cut off from it a portion whose weight was equal to the whole. (Cut off a small portion : the weight of this will bear a definite ratio to the*

273 a 7   Ἀλλὰ μὴν οὐδὲ τὸ ἐπὶ τὸ μέσον οὐδὲ τὸ ἀπὸ τοῦ μέσου φερόμενον ἄπειρον ἔσται· ἐναντίαι γὰρ αἱ φοραὶ ἡ ἄνω καὶ ἡ κάτω, αἱ δ' ἐναντίαι εἰς
10 ἐναντίους τόπους. τῶν δ' ἐναντίων εἰ θάτερον ὥρισται, καὶ θάτερον ὡρισμένον ἔσται. τὸ δὲ μέσον ὥρισται· εἰ γὰρ ὁποθενοῦν φέροιτο κάτω τὸ ὑφιστάμενον, οὐκ ἐνδέχεται πορρωτέρω διελθεῖν τοῦ μέσου. ὡρισμένου οὖν τοῦ μέσου καὶ τὸν ἄνω τόπον ἀνάγκη ὡρίσθαι. εἰ δ' οἱ τόποι ὡρισμένοι
15 καὶ πεπερασμένοι, καὶ τὰ σώματα ἔσται πεπερασμένα. ἔτι εἰ τὸ ἄνω καὶ κάτω ὥρισται, καὶ τὸ μεταξὺ ἀνάγκη ὡρίσθαι. εἰ γὰρ μὴ ὥρισται, ἄπειρος ἂν εἴη κίνησις· τοῦτο δ' ὅτι ἀδύνατον, δέδεικται πρότερον.

Ὥρισται ἄρα τὸ μέσον, ὥστε καὶ τὸ ἐν τούτῳ σῶμα ἢ ὂν ἢ γενέσθαι δυνατόν. ἀλλὰ μὴν τὸ
20 ἄνω καὶ κάτω φερόμενον σῶμα δύναται ἐν τούτῳ

ᵃ *Phys.* viii. 8.

CHAPTER VI

ARGUMENT (*continued*)

finite weight of the whole. Multiply the portion a sufficient
number of times—for any finite quantity may be taken from
an infinite—and you have a portion of the original body whose
weight is equal to the whole.)   But infinite weight is an im-
possibility.   Bodies move at a speed proportionate to their
weights.   A body of infinite weight would therefore have at
the same time both (i) *to move faster than any body of finite*
weight, and (ii) *not to move at all, since the time in which it*
could move must be infinitely short, or in other words no time
at all : which is absurd.   Hence there cannot be an infinite
body (273 a 21—274 a 18).

YET it is equally true that neither the simple body
which moves towards the centre nor that which
moves away from the centre can be infinite.   Upward
and downward motions are contraries, and contrary
motions are motions to opposite places ; and if one
of a pair of opposites is determinate, the other must
also be determinate.   But the centre is determined,
for wherever the downward-moving body may come
from, it cannot pass farther than the centre.   The
centre then being determined, the upper place
must also be determined ; and if their places are
determined and limited, the bodies themselves must
be limited.   Moreover if the upper and lower places
are determined, the space between must also be
determined.   If it were not, there would be infinite
motion, and it has already been shown that this is
impossible.[a]

The intermediate region, as we have said, is
determinate, and so therefore is the body which
either is or has the potentiality of occupying it.
But upward- and downward-moving bodies have the

45

273 a

γενέσθαι· πέφυκε γὰρ τὸ μὲν ἀπὸ τοῦ μέσου
κινεῖσθαι, τὸ δ' ἐπὶ τὸ μέσον.

Ἔκ τε δὴ τούτων φανερὸν ὅτι οὐκ ἐνδέχεται
σῶμα εἶναι ἄπειρον, καὶ πρὸς τούτοις εἰ βάρος μή
ἐστιν ἄπειρον, οὐδ' ἂν τούτων τῶν σωμάτων οὐθὲν εἴη
ἄπειρον· ἀνάγκη γὰρ τοῦ ἀπείρου σώματος ἄπειρον
25 εἶναι καὶ τὸ βάρος. (ὁ δ' αὐτὸς λόγος ἔσται καὶ
ἐπὶ τοῦ κούφου· εἰ γάρ ἐστιν ἄπειρος βαρύτης, ἔστι
καὶ κουφότης, ἂν ἄπειρον ᾖ τὸ ἐπιπολάζον.) δῆλον
δ' ἐκ τῶνδε. ἔστω γὰρ πεπερασμένον, καὶ εἰλήφθω
τὸ μὲν ἄπειρον σῶμα ἐφ' ᾧ τὸ ΑΒ, τὸ δὲ βάρος
αὐτοῦ ἐφ' ᾧ τὸ Γ. ἀφῃρήσθω οὖν ἀπὸ τοῦ ἀπείρου
30 πεπερασμένον μέγεθος ἐφ' ᾧ τὸ ΒΔ· καὶ τὸ βάρος
αὐτοῦ ἔστω ἐφ' ᾧ τὸ Ε. τὸ δὴ Ε τοῦ Γ ἔλαττον
ἔσται· τὸ γὰρ τοῦ ἐλάττονος βάρος ἔλαττον. κατα-
273 b μετρείτω δὴ τὸ ἔλαττον ὁποσακισοῦν, καὶ ὡς τὸ
βάρος τοὔλαττον πρὸς τὸ μεῖζον, τὸ ΒΔ πρὸς τὸ
ΒΖ γεγενήσθω· ἐνδέχεται γὰρ ἀφελεῖν τοῦ ἀπείρου
ὁποσονοῦν. εἰ τοίνυν ἀνάλογον τὰ μεγέθη τοῖς
5 βάρεσι, τὸ δ' ἔλαττον βάρος τοῦ ἐλάττονός ἐστι
μεγέθους, καὶ τὸ μεῖζον ἂν εἴη τοῦ μείζονος. ἴσον
ἄρα ἔσται τὸ τοῦ πεπερασμένου καὶ τὸ τοῦ ἀπείρου
βάρος. ἔτι εἰ τοῦ μείζονος σώματος μεῖζον τὸ
βάρος, τὸ τοῦ ΗΒ μεῖζον ἔσται βάρος ἢ τὸ τοῦ
ΖΒ, ὥστε τὸ τοῦ πεπερασμένου βάρος μεῖζον ἢ τὸ
τοῦ ἀπείρου. καὶ τῶν ἀνίσων δὲ μεγεθῶν ταὐτὸν
10 βάρος ἔσται· ἄνισον γὰρ τῷ πεπερασμένῳ τὸ
ἄπειρον. οὐθὲν δὲ διαφέρει τὰ βάρη σύμμετρα

---

[a] On this interpretation, which is that of Simpl. and is
probably correct, A. uses τὸ μέσον in one sentence to mean
" the intermediate region " (= τὸ μεταξύ), and in the next,
only two lines lower, to mean the centre. If so, it is a

potentiality of being there, for it is their nature to move from and to the centre respectively.[a]

The foregoing arguments make it clear that there cannot exist an infinite body. It may be said in addition that if there is no such thing as infinite weight, that again makes it impossible for any of the simple bodies to be infinite ; for the weight of an infinite body must be infinite. (This applies to lightness too, for if infinite weight is possible, so is infinite lightness, if the rising body is infinite.) The proof of that is as follows. Suppose the weight to be finite, and take an infinite body AB, of weight C. Subtract from the infinite body a finite quantity BD, and let the weight of BD be E. Now E will be less than C, for a smaller quantity has a smaller weight. Suppose now that the smaller weight goes into the greater so many times—as many as you choose—and let the quantity BD bear to another quantity BF the same proportion as the smaller weight bears to the greater. (One can of course subtract as much as one likes from the infinite.) If then quantity is proportionate to weight, and the smaller weight is that of the smaller quantity, the greater will be that of the larger quantity. Therefore the weights of the finite and the infinite quantity will be equal. Again, if the larger body have the greater weight, the weight of the body GB will be greater than that of FB, *i.e.* the weight of a finite body will be greater than that of the infinite. Also, the weight of unequal quantities will be the same, for the infinite and the finite are not equal. It makes no difference whether the weights are com-

striking example of A.'s incorrigible carelessness in the use of terms.

εἶναι ἢ ἀσύμμετρα· καὶ γὰρ ἀσυμμέτρων ὄντων ὁ
αὐτὸς ἔσται λόγος· οἷον εἰ τὸ Ε τρίτον ὑπερβάλλει
μετροῦν τὸ Γ βάρος· τῶν γὰρ ΒΔ μεγεθῶν τριῶν
ὅλων ληφθέντων μεῖζον ἔσται τὸ βάρος ἢ τὸ ἐφ' ᾧ
15 Γ. ὥστε τὸ αὐτὸ ἔσται ἀδύνατον. ἔτι δὲ καὶ
ἐγχωρεῖ σύμμετρα λαβεῖν· οὐθὲν γὰρ διαφέρει ἄρ-
χεσθαι ἀπὸ τοῦ βάρους ἢ ἀπὸ τοῦ μεγέθους· οἷον
ἂν ληφθῇ σύμμετρον βάρος τῷ Γ τὸ ἐφ' ᾧ τὸ Ε,
καὶ ἀπὸ τοῦ ἀπείρου ἀφαιρεθῇ τὸ ἔχον τὸ ἐφ' ᾧ
τὸ Ε βάρος, οἷον τὸ ΒΔ, εἶτα ὡς τὸ βάρος πρὸς τὸ
20 βάρος, τὸ ΒΔ πρὸς ἄλλο γένηται μέγεθος, οἷον
πρὸς τὸ ΒΖ· ἐνδέχεται γὰρ ἀπείρου ὄντος τοῦ
μεγέθους ὁποσονοῦν ἀφαιρεθῆναι· τούτων γὰρ ληφθέντων σύμμετρα ἔσται καὶ τὰ μεγέθη καὶ τὰ
βάρη ἀλλήλοις. οὐδὲ δὴ τὸ μέγεθος ὁμοιοβαρὲς
εἶναι ἢ ἀνομοιοβαρὲς οὐδὲν διοίσει πρὸς τὴν ἀπό-
25 δειξιν· ἀεὶ γὰρ ἔσται λαβεῖν ἰσοβαρῆ σώματα τῷ
ΒΔ ἀπὸ τοῦ ἀπείρου ὁποσαοῦν ἢ ἀφαιροῦντας ἢ
προστιθέντας.

Ὥστε δῆλον ἐκ τῶν εἰρημένων ὅτι οὐκ ἔσται τοῦ
ἀπείρου σώματος πεπερασμένον τὸ βάρος. ἄπειρον
ἄρα. εἰ τοίνυν τοῦτ' ἀδύνατον, καὶ τὸ ἄπειρόν τι
εἶναι σῶμα ἀδύνατον. ἀλλὰ μὴν ὅτι γ' ἄπειρόν τι
30 εἶναι βάρος ἀδύνατον, ἐκ τῶνδε φανερόν. εἰ γὰρ
τὸ τοσονδὶ βάρος τὴν τοσήνδε ἐν τῷδε τῷ χρόνῳ
κινεῖται, τὸ τοσοῦτον καὶ ἔτι ἐν ἐλάττονι, καὶ τὴν
274 a ἀναλογίαν ἣν τὰ βάρη ἔχει, οἱ χρόνοι ἀνάπαλιν ἕξου-
σιν, οἷον εἰ τὸ ἥμισυ βάρος ἐν τῷδε, τὸ διπλάσιον ἐν

mensurate or incommensurate. If they are incommensurate the argument holds good, *e.g.* if the weight E when taken three times into C has a remainder left over. It follows that if the whole quantity BD be taken thrice over, its weight will exceed C; which produces the same impossibility. Or we may take commensurate weights (for it makes no difference whether we start from the weight or from the quantity), as *e.g.* if a weight E be taken which goes exactly into C. Then if from the infinite body there be taken a quantity BD of the weight E, BD will bear the same proportion to another quantity as the weight E to the weight C. Let this quantity be BF, for since the original quantity is infinite we may take away as much as we like. In this case both the quantities and the weights will be commensurate. Nor again does it affect our demonstration for the body to have its weight evenly or unevenly distributed: it will always be possible to take from the infinite mass bodies of equal weight to BD, by subtracting or adding whatever quantities may be necessary.

It is clear from what has been said that the weight of an infinite body cannot be finite. It must then be infinite, so that if that is impossible, the existence of any infinite body is itself impossible; and the impossibility of an infinite weight is clear from the following arguments. (*a*) If a certain weight move a certain distance in a certain time, a greater weight will move the same distance in a shorter time, and the proportion which the weights bear to one another, the times too will bear to one another, *e.g.* if the half weight cover the distance in

274 a

ἡμίσει τούτου. ἔτι τὸ πεπερασμένον βάρος ἅπασαν
πεπερασμένην δίεισιν ἔν τινι χρόνῳ πεπερασμένῳ.
ἀνάγκη ἄρα ἐκ τούτων, εἴ τι ἔστιν ἄπειρον βάρος,
5 κινεῖσθαι μὲν ᾗ τοσόνδε ὅσον τὸ πεπερασμένον καὶ
ἔτι, μὴ κινεῖσθαι δέ, ᾗ ἀνάλογον μὲν δεῖ κατὰ τὰς
ὑπεροχὰς κινεῖσθαι, ἐναντίως δὲ τὸ μεῖζον ἐν τῷ
ἐλάττονι. λόγος δ' οὐθείς ἐστι τοῦ ἀπείρου πρὸς τὸ
πεπερασμένον, τοῦ δ' ἐλάττονος χρόνου πρὸς τὸν
μείζω πεπερασμένον. ἀλλ' ἀεὶ ἐν ἐλάττονι. ἐλάχι-
10 στος δ' οὐκ ἔστιν. οὐδ' εἰ ἦν, ὄφελός τι ἂν ἦν· ἄλλο
γὰρ ἄν τι πεπερασμένον ἐλήφθη ἐν τῷ αὐτῷ λόγῳ,
ἐν ᾧ τὸ ἄπειρον πρὸς ἕτερον μεῖζον, ὥστ' ἐν ἴσῳ
χρόνῳ τὴν ἴσην ἂν ἐκινεῖτο τὸ ἄπειρον τῷ πεπερασμένῳ. ἀλλ' ἀδύνατον. ἀλλὰ μὴν ἀνάγκη γε, εἴπερ
15 ἐν ὁπηλικῳοῦν χρόνῳ πεπερασμένῳ δὲ κινεῖται τὸ
ἄπειρον, καὶ ἄλλο ἐν τῷ αὐτῷ τούτῳ πεπερασμένον βάρος κινεῖσθαί τινα πεπερασμένην. ἀδύνατον
ἄρα ἄπειρον εἶναι βάρος, ὁμοίως δὲ καὶ κουφότητα.
καὶ σώματα ἄρ' ἄπειρον βάρος ἔχοντα καὶ κουφότητα ἀδύνατον.

---

[a] Taking τοσόνδε καὶ ἔτι together, with Stocks and Bonitz
(*Ind. s.v. ἔτι*), as τοσοῦτον καὶ ἔτι at 273 b 31.

[b] The argument would have gained in clarity if A. had
left this step out, for it follows directly from the premise
" In a finite time, however small, a finite weight can move,"
that if we suppose any minimum time, short of none at all,
for the movement of the infinite, it will be a time in which a
finite weight could have moved the same distance.   A. however wishes to make full use of his argument about the
inverse ratios of weights and times.   Consequently he puts
it in this more involved way : if we suppose the infinite to
move at all, we must suppose it to move in a certain minimum
finite time, however small.   This minimum time must bear

x, the whole weight will cover it in $\frac{x}{2}$. (b) Secondly, a finite weight will cover any finite distance in a certain finite time. It follows from these premises that if there is an infinite weight, it must on the one hand move, inasmuch as it is as great as, and greater than,[a] the finite weight, but on the other hand it must not move at all, inasmuch as weights must move in a time related inversely to the excess of greater over smaller, i.e. the greater weight in the shorter time. There is no relation of the infinite to the finite; a shorter time bears a relation to a longer only if both are finite. It may be argued that the weight, as it increases, simply moves in an ever-decreasing time. But there will be no minimum time; nor, if there were, would it be any help, for it would only mean that another finite body had been assumed greater than a given finite body in the same proportion as the infinite is greater.[b] Hence the infinite would have moved the same distance in the same time as the finite, which is impossible. Yet the conclusion is inescapable, that if the infinite move in any time at all, provided the time be finite, then another, finite weight can move a certain finite distance in the same time. It is therefore impossible that there should be infinite weight, or, on similar arguments, infinite lightness, and so it is also impossible that there should be bodies possessing infinite weight or infinite lightness.

a ratio to a longer time in which a certain smaller weight moves the same distance. Hence we must suppose a finite weight bearing the same ratio to that smaller weight which the shorter time bears to the longer, and this finite weight will be that which moves in the shorter of the two times, i.e. in the time taken by the infinite weight.

274 a

Ὅτι μὲν οὖν οὐκ ἔστιν ἄπειρον σῶμα, δῆλον διά
20 τε τῶν κατὰ μέρος θεωροῦσι τοῦτον τὸν τρόπον,
καὶ καθόλου σκοπουμένοις μὴ μόνον κατὰ τοὺς
λόγους τοὺς ἐν τοῖς περὶ τὰς ἀρχὰς εἰρημένους ἡμῖν
(διωρίσθη γὰρ κἀκεῖ καθόλου πρότερον περὶ ἀπείρου πῶς ἔστι καὶ πῶς οὐκ ἔστιν) ἀλλὰ καὶ νῦν
ἄλλον τρόπον. μετὰ δὲ ταῦτ' ἐπισκεπτέον κἂν εἰ
25 μὴ ἄπειρον μὲν τὸ σῶμα τὸ πᾶν, οὐ μὴν ἀλλὰ
τοσοῦτόν γε ὥστ' εἶναι πλείους οὐρανούς· τάχα γὰρ
ἄν τις τοῦτ' ἀπορήσειεν, ὅτι καθάπερ ὁ περὶ ἡμᾶς
κόσμος συνέστηκεν, οὐθὲν κωλύει καὶ ἑτέρους εἶναι
πλείους μὲν ἑνός, μὴ μέντοι γε ἀπείρους. πρῶτον
δ' εἴπωμεν καθόλου περὶ τοῦ ἀπείρου.

---

^a *Phys.* iii. 4-8. For the appellation *cf.* note on 272 a 30
above.

CHAPTER VII

ARGUMENT

There cannot exist an infinite body (*continued*).

(3) *In general, an infinite body is an impossibility.*

(a) *A heterogeneous infinite body is impossible, for it can
neither* (i) *consist of an infinite diversity of elements* (*they
would have to have different natural motions, and there is
only a finite number of motions*), *nor* (ii) *consist of elements
themselves infinite in extent* (274 a 30–b 22).

(b) *A homogeneous infinite body is impossible, whether it
be heavy or light or have a natural circular motion. This is
proved mainly by reference to the arguments of the preceding
two chapters* (274 b 22–32).

(c) *An infinite body cannot act or be acted upon, whether
in relation to a finite or to another infinite body. The general*

That there is no infinite body is clear from the examination of particular cases which we have just made, but it also emerges from general considerations, not only from the arguments brought forward in our work on principles [a] (for there too we began by determining in general under what conditions an infinite exists or cannot exist), but also in another way, as we shall now demonstrate. After that it will be necessary to inquire whether, even if the sum total of matter is not infinite, it may yet be sufficiently great for the existence of several worlds : for it might be raised as a difficulty that there is no reason against other worlds being formed similarly to the one around us, many, though not infinite, in number. First, however, let us make our general observations about the infinite.

CHAPTER VII

ARGUMENT (*continued*)

argument in each case is to show that a finite portion of the infinite could be taken, which must be capable of acting or suffering in a time bearing a definite proportion to the time in which the infinite itself acted or suffered to the same extent. (If the original action took place at all, it must have taken place in a finite time.) The smaller body could thus be shown to bear a definite proportion to the infinite ; but there can be no proportion between the infinite and the finite.

But every perceptible body is capable of acting or suffering, and every body which exists in space is perceptible. Therefore no infinite body exists in space (274 b 33—275 b 11).

(d) A. closes the theme with some general observations, to the effect that there could be no motion proper to an infinite body, which are partly reminders of previous arguments.

ARISTOTLE

ARGUMENT (continued)

(i) *An infinite body cannot have any of the natural motions, either circular or straight.* (ii) *Its motion cannot be either natural or enforced. Natural motion implies the possibility of unnatural, and that would require an infinite force, which means a second infinite body to apply it. It cannot be that it moves itself, i.e. is alive, for an infinite animal would be an absurdity.* (iii) *If one supposes, with the atomists, an in-*

274 a 30 Ἀνάγκη δὴ σῶμα πᾶν ἤτοι ἄπειρον εἶναι ἢ πεπερασμένον, καὶ εἰ ἄπειρον, ἤτοι ἀνομοιομερὲς ἅπαν ἢ ὁμοιομερές, κἂν εἰ ἀνομοιομερές, ἤτοι ἐκ πεπερασμένων εἰδῶν ἢ ἐξ ἀπείρων. ὅτι μὲν τοίνυν οὐχ οἷόν τε ἐξ ἀπείρων, φανερόν, εἴ τις ἡμῖν ἐάσει
274 b μένειν τὰς πρώτας ὑποθέσεις· πεπερασμένων γὰρ τῶν πρώτων κινήσεων οὐσῶν, ἀνάγκη καὶ τὰς ἰδέας τῶν ἁπλῶν σωμάτων εἶναι πεπερασμένας. ἁπλῆ μὲν γὰρ ἡ τοῦ ἁπλοῦ σώματος κίνησις, αἱ δ' ἁπλαῖ πεπερασμέναι κινήσεις εἰσίν· ἀνάγκη δὲ ἀεὶ
5 κίνησιν ἔχειν σῶμα πᾶν φυσικόν. ἀλλὰ μὴν εἴγε ἐκ πεπερασμένων ἔσται τὸ ἄπειρον, ἀνάγκη καὶ τῶν μορίων ἕκαστον εἶναι ἄπειρον, λέγω δ' οἷον τὸ ὕδωρ ἢ τὸ πῦρ. ἀλλ' ἀδύνατον· δέδεικται γὰρ ὅτι οὔτε βάρος οὔτε κουφότης ἐστὶν ἄπειρος. ἔτι ἀναγκαῖον ἀπείρους τῷ μεγέθει εἶναι καὶ τοὺς τόπους
10 αὐτῶν, ὥστε καὶ τὰς κινήσεις ἀπείρους εἶναι πάντων. τοῦτο δ' ἀδύνατον, εἰ θήσομεν ἀληθεῖς εἶναι τὰς πρώτας ὑποθέσεις, καὶ μήτε τὸ κάτω φερόμενον εἰς ἄπειρον ἐνδέχεσθαι φέρεσθαι μήτε τὸ ἄνω κατὰ τὸν αὐτὸν λόγον. ἀδύνατον γὰρ γίνεσθαι

54

ARGUMENT (*continued*)

finite number of discrete particles, they must all have the same motion, since they are described as homogeneous. But what is this motion? There cannot be an up or down in the infinite, nor a centre, therefore there cannot be any motion at all, either rectilinear (of heavy or light bodies) or circular. In any case, experience teaches us that the elements have not all the same natural motion (275 b 12—276 a 17).

EVERY body must be either infinite or finite. Suppose a body to be infinite; then it must be either heterogeneous or homogeneous; suppose it again to be heterogeneous, then it must be composed of elements either finitely or infinitely diverse. Now it clearly cannot be composed of an infinite diversity of elements, if our first assumptions may be allowed to stand, for since the primary movements were finite in number it followed that the different forms of simple bodies were also finite in number. The movement of a simple body is simple, but the simple movements are finite in number, and every natural body must always have a movement. If on the other hand the infinite body must be composed of a finite number of formally different elements, each one of the elements must be infinite, the water, say, or the fire. This is impossible, for it has been demonstrated that there is no infinite weight or lightness. Moreover it would be necessary also for their natural places to be infinite in extent, so that all their movements would be infinite. This is impossible, if we maintain that our first assumptions are true and that neither the downward-moving body can move to infinity nor (by the same argument) the upward-moving. For it is impossible for that to be in the process of happening which can

274 b

ὃ μὴ ἐνδέχεται γενέσθαι, ὁμοίως ἐπὶ τοῦ τοιόνδε
15 καὶ τοσόνδε καὶ τοῦ ποῦ. λέγω δ', εἰ ἀδύνατον
γενέσθαι λευκὸν ἢ πηχυαῖον ἢ ἐν Αἰγύπτῳ, καὶ
γίνεσθαί τι τούτων ἀδύνατον. ἀδύνατον ἄρα καὶ
φέρεσθαι ἐκεῖ οὗ μηθὲν δυνατὸν ἀφικέσθαι φερόμενον. ἔτι εἰ καὶ διεσπασμένον ἐστίν, οὐδὲν ἧττον
ἐνδέχοιτ' ἂν τὸ ἐξ ἁπάντων πῦρ ἄπειρον εἶναι.
20 ἀλλὰ σῶμα ἦν τὸ πάντῃ διάστασιν ἔχον· ὥστε πῶς
οἷόν τε πλείω μὲν ἀνόμοια, ἕκαστον δ' αὐτῶν
ἄπειρον εἶναι; πάντῃ γὰρ ἕκαστον δεῖ ἄπειρον
εἶναι.

Ἀλλὰ μὴν οὐδὲ πᾶν ὁμοιομερὲς ἐνδέχεται τὸ
ἄπειρον εἶναι. πρῶτον μὲν γὰρ οὐκ ἔστιν ἄλλη
παρὰ ταύτας κίνησις. ἕξει οὖν μίαν τούτων. εἰ δὲ
25 τοῦτο, συμβήσεται ἢ βάρος ἄπειρον ἢ κουφότητα
εἶναι ἄπειρον. ἀλλὰ μὴν οὐδ' οἷόν τε τὸ κύκλῳ
σῶμα φερόμενον ἄπειρον. ἀδύνατον γὰρ τὸ ἄπειρον φέρεσθαι κύκλῳ· οὐθὲν γὰρ διαφέρει τοῦτο
λέγειν ἢ τὸ τὸν οὐρανὸν φάναι ἄπειρον εἶναι, τοῦτο
δὲ δέδεικται ὅτι ἀδύνατον. ἀλλὰ μὴν οὐδ' ὅλως
30 γε τὸ ἄπειρον ἐνδέχεται κινεῖσθαι. ἢ γὰρ κατὰ
φύσιν κινηθήσεται ἢ βίᾳ· καὶ εἰ βίᾳ, ἔστιν αὐτῷ
καὶ ἡ κατὰ φύσιν, ὥστε καὶ τόπος ἄλλος ἴσος[1] εἰς
ὃν οἰσθήσεται. τοῦτο δ' ἀδύνατον.

Ὅτι δ' ὅλως ἀδύνατον ἄπειρον ὑπὸ πεπερασμένου

---

[1] ἴσος EL, Simpl., Stocks, Allan; ἴδιος H and second hand
of F, Bekker; om. JM and first hand of F.

---

[a] The infinite body must move either naturally or by
constraint. That it cannot move naturally has just been
shown, and even if it moves by constraint, that presupposes
a natural motion against which the constraint is brought to
bear. The same difficulties therefore arise, or, as he puts it
here, the difficulty that it would have to have a natural place

never actually happen, alike in the categories of quality, quantity and place ; *e.g.* if it is impossible actually to be white, or a cubit long, or in Egypt, it is also impossible to be in the process of becoming any of these. It is impossible therefore even to be moving to a place where nothing can ever in its movement actually arrive. If again the element is dispersed throughout the whole, it might be thought possible for the total sum, say of fire, to be infinite. But body is, as we saw, that which has extension in all directions. How then is it possible for there to be several bodies differing in kind, and each of them infinite, when each of them must be infinite in every direction ?

But on the other hand, it is equally impossible for the infinite body to be all homogeneous. In the first place, there is no other kind of motion besides those that we have noted. The infinite body therefore must have one of these, but if so, the result will be an infinite weight or infinite lightness. Nor can the body whose motion is circular be infinite. It is impossible for that which is infinite to revolve in a circle, for to say that amounts to an assertion that the heaven is infinite, which has been demonstrated to be impossible. But in fact it is impossible for the infinite to move at all. It must move either naturally or by constraint, and if by constraint, it will have also a natural motion, and hence also a separate place as large as itself to which its motion is directed. This is impossible.[a]

That in general an infinite body cannot suffer any change by the agency of a finite, nor itself act upon

different from those of the other elements, which, since it is infinite, is clearly impossible.

274 b

225 a

παθεῖν τι ἢ ποιῆσαι τὸ πεπερασμένον, ἐκ τῶνδε
φανερόν. ἔστω γὰρ ἄπειρον ἐφ᾽ οὗ Α, πεπερασμένον ἐφ᾽ οὗ Β, χρόνος ἐν ᾧ ἐκίνησέ τι ἢ ἐκινήθη
Γ. εἰ δὴ ὑπὸ τοῦ Β τὸ Α ἐθερμάνθη ἢ ὤσθη ἢ
ἄλλο τι ἔπαθεν ἢ καὶ ὁτιοῦν ἐκινήθη ἐν τῷ χρόνῳ
ἐφ᾽ οὗ Γ, ἔστω τὸ Δ τοῦ Β ἔλαττον, καὶ τὸ ἔλαττον
5 ἐν τῷ ἴσῳ χρόνῳ ἔλαττον κινείτω· ἔστω δὲ τὸ ἐφ᾽
ᾧ Ε ὑπὸ τοῦ Δ ἠλλοιωμένον. ὃ δή ἐστι τὸ Δ πρὸς
τὸ Β, τὸ Ε ἔσται πρὸς πεπερασμένον τι. ἔστω δὴ
τὸ μὲν ἴσον ἐν ἴσῳ χρόνῳ ἴσον ἀλλοιοῦν, τὸ δ᾽
ἔλαττον ἐν τῷ ἴσῳ ἔλαττον, τὸ δὲ μεῖζον μεῖζον,
τοσοῦτον δὲ ὅσον ἀνάλογον ἔσται ὅπερ τὸ μεῖζον
10 πρὸς τὸ ἔλαττον. οὐκ ἄρα τὸ ἄπειρον ὑπ᾽ οὐδενὸς
πεπερασμένου κινηθήσεται[1] ἐν οὐθενὶ χρόνῳ· ἔλαττον γὰρ ἄλλο ἐν τῷ ἴσῳ ὑπὸ ἐλάττονος κινηθήσεται, πρὸς ὃ τὸ ἀνάλογον πεπερασμένον ἔσται· τὸ
γὰρ ἄπειρον πρὸς τὸ πεπερασμένον ἐν οὐθενὶ λόγῳ
ἐστίν.

Ἀλλὰ μὴν οὐδὲ τὸ ἄπειρον ἐν οὐθενὶ χρόνῳ
15 κινήσει τὸ πεπερασμένον. ἔστω γὰρ ἐφ᾽ ᾧ τὸ Α
ἄπειρον, τὸ δὲ Β πεπερασμένον, χρόνος ἐν ᾧ τὸ Γ.
οὐκοῦν τὸ Δ ἐν τῷ Γ ἔλαττον τοῦ Β κινήσει· ἔστω
τὸ Ζ. ὃ δή ἐστι τὸ ΒΖ ὅλον πρὸς τὸ Ζ, τὸ Ε ἔχον
τὸν λόγον τοῦτον ἔστω πρὸς τὸ Δ. κινήσει ἄρα τὸ

---

[1] κινήσεται E, Bekker.

---

[a] *Summary of argument that the infinite cannot be acted on
by the finite.*

Axiom : Equal forces will affect equal patients in the
same time to the same degree.

Let P¹ be infinite, A¹ finite, and T the time in which P¹
is heated, moved or otherwise acted on by A¹. (All action
takes place in time.)

the finite, may be proved as follows. Let A be infinite, B finite, C the time in which the one causes a certain movement in the other. That is, suppose that A is heated, or pushed, or moved in any respect whatsoever by B in the time C. Now let D be less than B, and let us assume that the lesser agent in an equal time moves a smaller quantity. Then let E be the quantity altered by D. As D is to B, so will E be to some finite quantity. But we may assume that in the same time equal forces will cause the same amount of alteration, a lesser force less, and a greater more, and more in proportion as the greater force exceeds the less. It follows that the infinite cannot be moved by the finite in any time at all: for a smaller quantity will be moved in the same time by a lesser force, and anything which bears a proportionate relation to this force will be finite, since the infinite stands in no sort of proportion to the finite.[a]

[This proves that the infinite cannot be acted on by the finite.] Nor again can the infinite act upon the finite in any time at all. Let A be infinite, B finite, C the time. In the time C, D will act upon a quantity smaller than B. Let F be this lesser amount. Now suppose that E bears the same relation to D as the whole BF does to F. Then

Let A^2 be a lesser force than A^1. Then in the time T, A^2 will heat etc. less than A^1. Let P^2 be the quantity which is changed by A^2.

Then as A^2 is to A^1 (both finite), so will P^2 be to x, *i.e.* if we take something as many times greater than P^2 as A^1 is greater than A^2, that something will be finite.

> But x should be equal to P^1.
> And P^1 was infinite.
> ∴ P^1 cannot be acted on by A^1.

275 a
Ε τὸ ΒΖ ἐν τῷ Γ. τὸ πεπερασμένον τοίνυν καὶ
20 τὸ ἄπειρον ἐν ἴσῳ χρόνῳ ἀλλοιώσει. ἀλλ' ἀδύ-
νατον· ἐν ἐλάττονι γὰρ τὸ μεῖζον ὑπέκειτο. ἀλλ'
ἀεὶ ὁ ληφθεὶς χρόνος ταὐτὸ ποιήσει, ὥστ' οὐκ ἔσται
χρόνος οὐθεὶς ἐν ᾧ κινήσει. ἀλλὰ μὴν ἐν ἀπείρῳ
γε οὐκ ἔστι κινῆσαι[1] οὐδὲ κινηθῆναι· πέρας γὰρ οὐκ
ἔχει, ἡ δὲ ποίησις καὶ τὸ πάθος ἔχει.

25 Οὐδ' ἄπειρον δὴ ὑπ' ἀπείρου ἐνδέχεται οὐθὲν
παθεῖν. ἔστω γὰρ τὸ Α ἄπειρον καὶ τὸ Β, χρόνος
δ' ἐν ᾧ ἔπαθε τὸ Β ὑπὸ τοῦ Α, ἐφ' ᾧ ΓΔ. τὸ δὴ
ἐφ' ᾧ τὸ Ε τοῦ ἀπείρου μέρος, ἐπεὶ ὅλον πέπονθε
τὸ Β, οὐκ ἐν ἴσῳ χρόνῳ τὸ αὐτό· ὑποκείσθω γὰρ
ἐν ἐλάττονι κινεῖσθαι τὸ ἔλαττον χρόνῳ. ἔστω τὸ
30 Ε κεκινημένον ὑπὸ τοῦ Α ἐν τῷ Δ. ὃ δὴ τὸ Δ
πρὸς τὸ ΓΔ, τὸ Ε ἐστι πρός τι τοῦ Β πεπερασμένον. τοῦτο τοίνυν ἀνάγκη ὑπὸ τοῦ Α κινηθῆναι
ἐν τῷ ΓΔ χρόνῳ· ὑπὸ γὰρ τοῦ αὐτοῦ ὑποκείσθω
275 b ἐν τῷ πλείονι καὶ ἐλάττονι χρόνῳ τὸ μεῖζον καὶ
τὸ ἔλαττον πάσχειν, ὅσα ἀνάλογον τῷ χρόνῳ

---

[1] κινῆσαι. Bekker by a slip prints κινήσει.

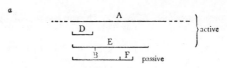

BF in line 17 = B in line 15. " A lack of clarity is introduced
into the argument by calling B (the object moved by the
infinite force) BF as the discussion proceeds, simply because
60

E will act upon BF in the time C. Thus the finite and the infinite will cause the same alteration in an equal time. This is impossible, for it was taken as axiomatic that the greater force will use less time. Whatever time is taken, the result will be the same, so that there can be no time in which the infinite will act upon the finite ; but in infinite time nothing can act or be acted upon, for infinite time has no limit, whereas action and passion have a limit.[a]

Nor, thirdly, can one infinite be acted upon by another. Let A and B both be infinite, and let CD be the time in which B is acted by A. Now if E is a part of the infinite, then since the whole infinite B was acted upon in the given time, E cannot be acted upon in the same time to an equal degree ; for we may take it as an axiom that a smaller quantity is moved [to an equal extent] in a shorter time. Let D therefore be the time in which E is acted upon by A. Now suppose that E bears the same relation to another finite part of B as D bears to CD. It follows that this other part will be moved by A in the time CD ; for given the same force, the greater and smaller quantities will be acted upon in a longer and a shorter time respectively, provided that the bodies acted upon are proportionate to the times. There-

it includes F, the smaller object, in itself'' (Simpl.). A.'s first thought may be expressed by the diagram

As he proceeds, he pictures it like this

διῄρηται. ἐν οὐδενὶ ἄρα χρόνῳ δυνατὸν πεπερασμένῳ ἄπειρον ὑπ' ἀπείρου κινηθῆναι· ἐν ἀπείρῳ
ἄρα. ἀλλ' ὁ μὲν ἄπειρος χρόνος οὐκ ἔχει τέλος,
τὸ δὲ κεκινημένον ἔχει.

5 Εἰ τοίνυν πᾶν σῶμα αἰσθητὸν ἔχει δύναμιν
ποιητικὴν ἢ παθητικὴν ἢ ἄμφω, ἀδύνατον σῶμα
ἄπειρον αἰσθητὸν εἶναι. ἀλλὰ μὴν καὶ ὅσα γε
σώματα ἐν τόπῳ, πάντα αἰσθητά. οὐκ ἔστιν ἄρα
σῶμα ἄπειρον ἔξω τοῦ οὐρανοῦ οὐθέν. ἀλλὰ μὴν
οὐδὲ μέχρι τινός. οὐθὲν ἄρα ὅλως σῶμα ἔξω τοῦ
10 οὐρανοῦ. εἰ μὲν γὰρ νοητόν, ἔσται ἐν τόπῳ· τὸ
γὰρ ἔξω καὶ ἔσω τόπον σημαίνει. ὥστ' ἔσται
αἰσθητόν. αἰσθητὸν δ' οὐθὲν μὴ ἐν τόπῳ.

Λογικώτερον δ' ἔστιν ἐπιχειρεῖν καὶ ὧδε. οὔτε
γὰρ κύκλῳ οἷόν τε κινεῖσθαι τὸ ἄπειρον ὁμοιομερὲς
ὄν· μέσον μὲν γὰρ τοῦ ἀπείρου οὐκ ἔστι, τὸ δὲ
15 κύκλῳ περὶ τὸ μέσον κινεῖται. ἀλλὰ μὴν οὐδ' ἐπ'
εὐθείας οἷόν τε φέρεσθαι τὸ ἄπειρον· δεήσει γὰρ

---

[a] Since the infinite quantity cannot bear any proportion to the finite time, as the immediately preceding clause demanded that it should.

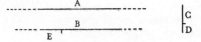

[b] *Cf.* Plato, *Sophist* 247 D, where the "Giants," who will not admit anything to be real except what can be perceived by the senses, are said to accept as a definition of "the real," τὸ καὶ ὁποιανοῦν κεκτημένον δύναμιν εἴτ' εἰς τὸ ποιεῖν ἕτερον ὁτιοῦν πεφυκὸς εἴτ' εἰς τὸ παθεῖν.

[c] This parenthesis is no more than a disconnected jotting. The objection which it meets is scarcely tenable for a moment, since "intelligible body" is so obviously a contradiction in terms. But A. is constantly aware of the transcendent

fore it is not possible for one infinite to be acted upon by another in any finite time whatsoever.[a] The time taken then must be infinite ; but infinite time has no end, whereas the object moved has an end of its movement.

Thus if every perceptible body is capable of either acting or being acted on or both,[b] it is impossible for an infinite body to be perceptible. But, further, all bodies that occupy a place are perceptible. Therefore there is no infinite body outside the heaven. Nor, however, is there a finite. Therefore there is no body at all outside the heaven. (If it be intelligible, it will still be in a place ; for the words " inside " and " outside " themselves imply space. Therefore it will be perceptible. Nothing that does not occupy place is perceptible.)[c]

It is also possible to attempt the proof on more general lines [d] as follows. The infinite and homogeneous body (a) cannot move in a circle. For there is no centre of the infinite, whereas that which moves in a circle moves about a centre. But (b) nor can the infinite move in a straight line. For there will need to be a second equivalent (i.e. infinite)

intelligible entities of Platonism, and constantly in fear of being thought to have overlooked, rather than consciously rejected them. Plato certainly uses spatial terms when describing his Intelligibles, e.g. the ὑπερουράνιος τόπος of the Phaedrus provides A. with just the sort of handle that he is using here.

[d] Arguments which are λογικά are contrasted with those which are φυσικά and οἰκεῖα (De gen. et corr. 316 a 10-14), or (as in Simpl.) πραγματικά. The order here is typical of A.'s philosophical predilections. The (to him) concrete arguments must come first, and only after them may the more general considerations be allowed their place.

275 b

ἕτερον εἶναι τοσοῦτον τόπον ἄπειρον εἰς ὃν οἰσθήσεται κατὰ φύσιν, καὶ ἄλλον τοσοῦτον εἰς ὃν
παρὰ φύσιν. ἔτι εἴτε φύσει ἔχει κίνησιν τοῦ εἰς
εὐθὺ εἴτε βίᾳ κινεῖται, ἀμφοτέρως δεήσει ἄπειρον
20 εἶναι τὴν κινοῦσαν ἰσχύν· ἥ τε γὰρ ἄπειρος ἀπείρου
καὶ τοῦ ἀπείρου ἄπειρος ἡ ἰσχύς· ὥστ᾽ ἔσται καὶ
τὸ κινοῦν ἄπειρον (λόγος δ᾽ ἐν τοῖς περὶ κινήσεως
ὅτι οὐθὲν ἔχει ἄπειρον δύναμιν τῶν πεπερασμένων,
οὐδὲ τῶν ἀπείρων πεπερασμένην). εἰ οὖν τὸ κατὰ
φύσιν καὶ παρὰ φύσιν ἐνδέχεται κινηθῆναι, ἔσται
25 δύο ἄπειρα, τό τε κινοῦν οὕτω καὶ τὸ κινούμενον.
ἔτι τὸ κινοῦν τὸ ἄπειρον τί ἐστιν; εἰ μὲν γὰρ αὐτὸ
ἑαυτό, ἔμψυχον ἔσται. τοῦτο δὲ πῶς δυνατόν,
ἄπειρον εἶναι ζῷον; εἰ δ᾽ ἄλλο τι τὸ κινοῦν, δύο
ἔσται ἄπειρα, τό τε κινοῦν καὶ τὸ κινούμενον,
διαφέροντα τὴν μορφὴν καὶ τὴν δύναμιν.

30 Εἰ δὲ μὴ συνεχὲς τὸ πᾶν, ἀλλ᾽ ὥσπερ λέγει

---

^a Not because natural movement requires a force—it does
not—but only because natural motion implies the possibility
of unnatural (275 b 23 below). Simpl. himself points this
out (εἰκότως εἶπεν ὅτι, κἂν φύσει κἂν βίᾳ τὸ ἄπειρον ἐπ᾽ εὐθὺ
κινῆται, ὑπὸ ἀπείρου κινηθήσεται, οὐχ ὅτι κατὰ φύσιν κινεῖται,
ἀλλ᾽ ὅτι ἐνδέχεται τὸ φύσει κινούμενον ἐπ᾽ εὐθείας καὶ βίᾳ
κινηθῆναι, p. 240, 19 ff.), though it may be doubted whether
in general he interprets the argument correctly.

^b Phys. viii. 10. For the appellation cf. note on 272 a 30
above.

^c The previous sentence surely shows that only " un-
natural " movement is in question. If this is so, A. must
mean (though Simpl. interprets differently) that the peculiar
power of a living creature is to move its body in directions
which are unnatural to it qua body. (Cf. on this point ii. 6,
288 b 16 below.) The body is earthy, therefore its natural
motion is downwards, but the ψυχή is a force which inter-
venes and prevents it from performing that natural motion.
This may also remind us that according at least to the fully

place for it to move into naturally, and yet another into which it may go when moved contrary to its nature. Again, whether its rectilinear movement be natural [a] or enforced, in both instances the moving force will be infinite; for infinite force must be exerted by an infinite body, and conversely the force exerted by an infinite body must be infinite. Therefore the body which moves it will also be infinite. (There is an argument in our work on motion [b] to show that no finite body has infinite potency, nor an infinite body finite potency.) Seeing then that that which moves naturally can also be moved unnaturally, there will be two infinite bodies, the one which causes this unnatural motion, and the other which suffers it. What moreover is it which moves the infinite? If (a) it moves itself, it must be alive.[c] Yet how could this be possible, that there should be an infinite animal? But if (b) the mover is something else, there must be two infinite bodies, the mover and the moved, differing in character and function.

If the whole is not continuous, but its elements are separated by the void (as in the theory of

developed philosophy of A., a self-mover is strictly an impossibility. An animal may appear to move itself, but in fact it is one part (soul) moving the other part (body), and even the soul does not move itself (*Phys.* viii. 2; *cf. ib.* 4 and 5). But it is likely (see introd.) that the *De caelo* was written before the doctrine of the impossibility of self-motion (as in *Phys.* vii. and viii.) had been worked out, and that in speaking here of an animal as moving itself A. is still accepting the Platonic definition of ψυχή as τὸ αὐτὸ ἑαυτὸ κινοῦν. (Stocks's note on this sentence was written before the work of Jaeger and von Arnim on the development of A.'s thought.)

275 b

Δημόκριτος καὶ Λεύκιππος, διωρισμένα τῷ κενῷ, μίαν ἀναγκαῖον εἶναι πάντων τὴν κίνησιν. διώρισται μὲν γὰρ τοῖς σχήμασιν· τὴν δὲ φύσιν εἶναί 276 a φασιν αὐτῶν μίαν, ὥσπερ ἂν εἰ χρυσὸς ἕκαστον εἴη κεχωρισμένον. τούτων δέ, καθάπερ λέγομεν, ἀναγκαῖον εἶναι τὴν αὐτὴν κίνησιν· ὅπου γὰρ μία βῶλος, καὶ ἡ σύμπασα γῆ φέρεται, καὶ τό τε πᾶν πῦρ καὶ σπινθὴρ εἰς τὸν αὐτὸν τόπον. ὥστ' οὔτε κοῦφον ἁπλῶς οὐθὲν ἔσται τῶν σωμάτων, εἰ πάντ' ἔχει βάρος· εἰ δὲ κουφότητα, βαρὺ οὐδέν. ἔτι εἰ βάρος ἔχει ἢ κουφότητα, ἔσται ἢ ἔσχατόν τι τοῦ παντὸς ἢ μέσον. τοῦτο δ' ἀδύνατον ἀπείρου γ' ὄντος. ὅλως τε, οὗ μή ἐστι μέσον μηδ' ἔσχατον, μηδὲ τὸ μὲν ἄνω τὸ δὲ κάτω, τόπος οὐθεὶς ἔσται
10 τοῖς σώμασι τῆς φορᾶς. τούτου δὲ μὴ ὄντος κίνησις οὐκ ἔσται· ἀνάγκη γὰρ κινεῖσθαι ἤτοι κατὰ φύσιν ἢ παρὰ φύσιν, ταῦτα δ' ὥρισται τοῖς τόποις τοῖς τ' οἰκείοις καὶ τοῖς ἀλλοτρίοις. ἔτι εἰ οὗ παρὰ φύσιν τι μένει ἢ φέρεται, ἀνάγκη τινὸς ἄλλου εἶναι τοῦτον τὸν τόπον κατὰ φύσιν (τοῦτο δὲ πιστὸν ἐκ
15 τῆς ἐπαγωγῆς), ἀνάγκη δὴ μὴ πάντα ἢ βάρος ἔχειν ἢ κουφότητα, ἀλλὰ τὰ μὲν τὰ δ' οὔ.

Ὅτι μὲν τοίνυν οὐκ ἔστι τὸ σῶμα τοῦ παντὸς ἄπειρον, ἐκ τούτων φανερόν.

Democritus and Leucippus), then the motion of all will of necessity be one. For the atoms are differentiated by their shapes : the nature of them all is, they say, the same, just as if, *e.g.*, each one separately were a piece of gold. All of these must, as we have just said, have the same motion ; for the whole earth moves in the same direction as a single clod, and similarly the whole sum of fire and a single spark seek the same place. Therefore none of the atoms will be absolutely light,[a] if they all have weight, nor heavy if all have lightness. Again, if they have either weight or lightness, the universe will have either a farthest limit or a centre. But this is impossible when it is infinite. In general, where there is neither centre nor circumference, and one cannot point to one direction as up and another as down, bodies have no place to serve as the goal of their motion. And if this is lacking, there cannot be movement ; for movement must be either natural or unnatural, and these terms are defined in relation to places, *i.e.* the one which is proper and the one which is alien to the body. Again, if when a body rests or moves contrary to its nature, the place of the action must be proper to some other body (a fact which experience leads us to believe), then it is impossible for everything to have weight or everything lightness : some will have one and some the other.

Thus it is clear from these arguments that the body of the world is not infinite.

[a] One of them may be lighter (less heavy) than another, *i.e.* it may move downwards more slowly ; but none of them will actually have an upward motion, like that of fire.

CHAPTER VIII

ARGUMENT

There cannot be more than one world.
1. Argument from the doctrine of natural motions and places.

Every element moves naturally in a certain direction and to a certain fixed goal. If it moves one way only when forced, then it may be taken that its natural motion is in the opposite direction to that. If there are several worlds, they must all be composed of the same elements, therefore the elements of all alike must have the same natural motions. This means that all the earth must move naturally towards the same centre and all the fire towards the same circumference. This is impossible if there are several worlds, each with its own centre and circumference. There can be only one centre and circumference, or in other words only one world (276 a 18–b 21).

Possible objections : (a) The elements of other worlds than this may take on a different nature through being so far removed from their natural places. But a difference of mere distance cannot alter the formal nature of a substance. (b) Their motions are by constraint. But enforced motion implies a natural motion as its contrary, and this must be the same as that of the elements in this world, since all possess the same form. (c) Individuals may be numerically many though the same in form. May not this apply also to the goals of motion of the elements in the different worlds ? But if difference of goal is justified in this way, by the numerical difference between one piece of earth and another, why does

276 a 18   Διότι δ' οὐδὲ πλείους οἷόν τ' οὐρανοὺς εἶναι,
λέγωμεν· τοῦτο γὰρ ἔφαμεν ἐπισκεπτέον, εἴ τις
20 μὴ νομίζει καθόλου δεδεῖχθαι περὶ τῶν σωμάτων
ὅτι ἀδύνατον ἐκτὸς εἶναι τοῦ κόσμου τοῦδε ὁτιοῦν

ᵃ In the wide sense of change of any sort.   There are four

68

CHAPTER VIII

ARGUMENT (*continued*)

not each separate piece of earth in our own world move towards a different goal ? Since the particles in our world and those in another are formally indistinguishable, there is no more reason for all the earth of another world to be separated from all that of our own than for some of the earth of our own to be separated from the rest (276 b 21—277 a 12).

2. Argument from the general nature of motion.[a]

These general considerations are used in support of the doctrine of natural places. All change is between opposite states which are formally different and finite. This must be so with locomotion, and the opposites in this case are top and bottom. The third simple motion, the circular, has also its opposites in a qualified sense (277 a 12-27).

3. *That locomotion must be finite is argued from the increase of speed observable as a body approaches its natural place. Motion to infinity would mean infinite speed, i.e. infinite weight, which has been proved to be impossible (277 a 27-33).*

4. *The atomists' theory of " extrusion " is refuted by the observation that a large mass of any element moves more quickly to its natural place than a small. This could not happen were the motion due to force (277 a 33–b 9).*

5. *A. refers to the evidence of metaphysics on the point (277 b 9-12).*

6. *A further argument is adduced from the doctrine of natural places (277 b 12-24).*

WE must now explain why there cannot even be more than one world. This was a question which we noted for consideration, to meet the objection that no general proof has been given that no body whatsoever can exist beyond this world, since the

sorts of change, affecting respectively substance, quality, quantity or place. (*Phys.* 200 b 32, *Met.* 1069 b 9.)

276 a

αὐτῶν, ἀλλὰ μόνον ἐπὶ τῶν ἀορίστως κειμένων
εἰρῆσθαι τὸν λόγον.

Ἅπαντα γὰρ καὶ μένει καὶ κινεῖται βίᾳ καὶ κατὰ
φύσιν, καὶ κατὰ φύσιν μέν, ἐν ᾧ μένει μὴ βίᾳ, καὶ
25 φέρεται, καὶ εἰς ὃν φέρεται, καὶ μένει· ἐν ᾧ δὲ βίᾳ,
καὶ φέρεται βίᾳ, καὶ εἰς ὃν βίᾳ φέρεται, βίᾳ καὶ
μένει. ἔτι εἰ βίᾳ ἥδε ἡ φορά, ἡ ἐναντία κατὰ
φύσιν. ἐπὶ δὴ[1] τὸ μέσον τὸ ἐνταῦθα εἰ βίᾳ οἰσθήσεται ἡ γῆ ἐκεῖθεν, ἐντεῦθεν οἰσθήσεται ἐκεῖ κατὰ
φύσιν· καὶ εἰ μένει ἐνταῦθα ἡ ἐκεῖθεν μὴ βίᾳ, καὶ
30 οἰσθήσεται κατὰ φύσιν δεῦρο. μία δ' ἡ κατὰ
φύσιν. ἔτι ἀνάγκη πάντας τοὺς κόσμους ἐκ τῶν
αὐτῶν εἶναι σωμάτων, ὁμοίους γ' ὄντας τὴν φύσιν.
ἀλλὰ μὴν καὶ τῶν σωμάτων ἕκαστον ἀναγκαῖον τὴν
276 b αὐτὴν ἔχειν δύναμιν, οἷον λέγω πῦρ καὶ γῆν καὶ
τὰ μεταξὺ τούτων· εἰ γὰρ ὁμώνυμα ταῦτα καὶ μὴ
κατὰ τὴν αὐτὴν ἰδέαν λέγονται τἀκεῖ τοῖς παρ'
ἡμῖν, καὶ τὸ πᾶν ὁμωνύμως ἂν λέγοιτο κόσμος.
δῆλον τοίνυν ὅτι τὸ μὲν ἀπὸ τοῦ μέσου φέρεσθαι
πέφυκε, τὸ δ' ἐπὶ τὸ μέσον αὐτῶν, εἴπερ πᾶν ὁμο-
ειδὲς τὸ πῦρ τῷ πυρὶ καὶ τῶν ἄλλων ἕκαστον,
ὥσπερ καὶ τὰ ἐν τούτῳ μόρια τοῦ πυρός. ὅτι δ'

---

[1] δὴ EHL, Simpl., Prantl, Stocks, Allan; δὲ JFM Bekker.

---

[a] κεῖσθαι, as Professor Cornford pointed out to me, is more
likely to refer to situation than extent, and this sense fits the
context well. In infinite space, bodies (*e.g.* the atoms of
Democritus) can have no proper region and hence no
natural motion (such as A. is discussing in this and the
previous chapters). The view now to be considered is that,

foregoing discussion applied only to those with no definite situation.[a]

All bodies both rest and move naturally and by constraint. A body moves naturally to that place where it rests without constraint, and rests without constraint in that place to which it naturally moves. It moves by constraint to that place in which it rests by constraint, and rests by constraint in that place to which it moves by constraint. Further, if a certain movement is enforced, then its opposite is natural. Thus if it is by constraint that earth moves to the centre here from wherever else it is, its movement thither from here will be natural : and if, having come from there, it remains here without constraint, its movement hither will be natural also. And the natural movement of each is one. Further, all the worlds must be composed of the same bodies, being similar in nature. But at the same time each of these bodies must have the same potentialities, fire, that is to say, and earth, and the bodies intermediate between them ; for if the bodies of another world resemble our own in name only, and not in virtue of having the same form, then it would only be in name that the whole which they compose could be pronounced a world. It clearly follows that one of them will be of a nature to move away from the centre, and another towards the centre, seeing that all fire must have the same form as other fire, just as the different portions of fire in this world have the same form ; and the same may be said about each of the other simple

even though the whole be not infinite, it may yet contain several *cosmoi*, in each of which the elements will have their definite places as in ours.

The reference is to ch. vi. (274 a 24-28).

ἀνάγκη οὕτως ἔχειν, ἐκ τῶν περὶ τὰς κινήσεις
ὑποθέσεων φανερόν· αἵ τε γὰρ κινήσεις πεπερασμέναι, ἕκαστόν τε τῶν στοιχείων λέγεται καθ᾽
10 ἑκάστην τῶν κινήσεων. ὥστ᾽ εἴπερ καὶ αἱ κινήσεις
αἱ αὐταί, καὶ τὰ στοιχεῖα ἀνάγκη εἶναι πανταχοῦ
ταὐτά. πέφυκεν ἄρα φέρεσθαι καὶ ἐπὶ τόδε τὸ
μέσον τὰ ἐν ἄλλῳ κόσμῳ τῆς γῆς μόρια, καὶ πρὸς
τόδε τὸ ἔσχατον τὸ ἐκεῖ πῦρ. ἀλλ᾽ ἀδύνατον· τού-
15 του γὰρ συμβαίνοντος ἀνάγκη φέρεσθαι ἄνω μὲν
τὴν γῆν ἐν τῷ οἰκείῳ κόσμῳ, τὸ δὲ πῦρ ἐπὶ τὸ
μέσον, ὁμοίως δὲ καὶ τὴν ἐντεῦθεν γῆν ἀπὸ τοῦ
μέσου φέρεσθαι κατὰ φύσιν πρὸς τὸ ἐκεῖ φερομένην μέσον, διὰ τὸ τοὺς κόσμους οὕτω κεῖσθαι
πρὸς ἀλλήλους. ἢ γὰρ οὐ θετέον τὴν αὐτὴν εἶναι
φύσιν τῶν ἁπλῶν σωμάτων ἐν τοῖς πλείοσιν οὐρα-
20 νοῖς, ἢ λέγοντας οὕτως τὸ μέσον ἓν ποιεῖν ἀνάγκη
καὶ τὸ ἔσχατον· τούτου δ᾽ ὄντος [ἀτόπου]¹ ἀδύνατον
εἶναι κόσμους πλείους ἑνός.

Τὸ δ᾽ ἀξιοῦν ἄλλην εἶναι φύσιν τῶν ἁπλῶν σωμάτων, ἂν ἀποσχῶσιν ἔλαττον ἢ πλεῖον τῶν
οἰκείων τόπων, ἄλογον· τί γὰρ διαφέρει τοσονδὶ
25 φάναι μῆκος ἀποσχεῖν ἢ τοσονδί; διοίσει γὰρ
κατὰ λόγον, ὅσῳ πλεῖον μᾶλλον, τὸ δ᾽ εἶδος τὸ
αὐτό. ἀλλὰ μὴν ἀνάγκη γ᾽ εἶναί τινα κίνησιν
αὐτῶν· ὅτι μὲν γὰρ κινοῦνται, φανερόν. πότερον
οὖν βίᾳ πάσας ἐροῦμεν κινεῖσθαι καὶ τὰς ἐναντίας;

---

¹ ὄντος ἀτόπου is printed by Bekker with no ms. authority;
EHLM and Simpl. have ὄντος alone (so Stocks and Allan);
ὄντος τοῦ ἀτόπου JF.

ᵃ " A thing that did not move would not be a body at all "
—Stocks. *Cf.* ch. vii. (275 b 4-5) πᾶν σῶμα αἰσθητὸν ἔχει

bodies. The necessity for this emerges clearly from our assumptions about the motions of simple bodies, namely that they are limited in number and that each of the elements has a particular motion assigned to it. Consequently if the motions are the same, the elements also must be the same wherever they are. It must be natural therefore for the particles of earth in another world to move towards the centre of this one also, and for the fire in that world to move towards the circumference of this. This is impossible, for if it were to happen the earth would have to move upwards in its own world and the fire to the centre ; and similarly earth from our own world would have to move naturally away from the centre, as it made its way to the centre of the other, owing to the assumed situation of the worlds relatively to each other. Either, in fact, we must deny that the simple bodies of the several worlds have the same natures, or if we admit it we must, as I have said, make the centre and the circumference one for all ; and this means that there cannot be more worlds than one.

It is wrong to suppose that the elements have a different nature if they are removed less or more from their proper places; for what difference does it make to say that they are removed by this distance or that ? They will differ in proportion, more as the distance increases, but the form will remain the same. Again, there must be a movement assignable to them, for they obviously do move.[a] Shall we then say that they all move by constraint, even when their motions are mutually contrary ?

δύναμιν ποιητικὴν ἢ παθητικήν, and, e.g., the division of substance into αἰσθητή and ἀκινητός in *Met.* Λ ch. i.

276 b

ἀλλ' ὃ μὴ πέφυκεν ὅλως κινεῖσθαι, ἀδύνατον τοῦτο κινεῖσθαι βίᾳ. εἰ τοίνυν ἐστί τις κίνησις αὐτῶν

30 κατὰ φύσιν, ἀνάγκη τῶν ὁμοειδῶν καὶ τῶν καθ' ἕκαστον πρὸς ἕνα ἀριθμῷ τόπον ὑπάρχειν τὴν κίνησιν, οἷον πρὸς τόδε τι μέσον καὶ πρὸς τόδε

277 a τι ἔσχατον. εἰ δὲ πρὸς εἴδει ταὐτά, πλείω δέ, διότι καὶ τὰ καθ' ἕκαστα πλείω μέν, εἴδει δ' ἕκαστον ἀδιάφορον, οὐ τῷ μὲν τῷ δ' οὐ τοιοῦτον ἔσται τῶν μορίων, ἀλλ' ὁμοίως πᾶσιν· ὁμοίως γὰρ ἅπαντα κατ' εἶδος ἀδιάφορα ἀλλήλων, ἀριθμῷ δ' ἕτερον

5 ὁτιοῦν ὁτουοῦν. λέγω δὲ τοῦτο, ὅτι εἰ τὰ ἐνταῦθα μόρια πρὸς ἄλληλα καὶ τὰ ἐν ἑτέρῳ κόσμῳ ὁμοίως ἔχει, καὶ τὸ ληφθὲν ἐντεῦθεν οὐδὲν διαφερόντως πρὸς τῶν ἐν ἄλλῳ τινὶ κόσμῳ μορίων καὶ πρὸς τῶν ἐν τῷ αὐτῷ, ἀλλ' ὡσαύτως· διαφέρουσι γὰρ οὐθὲν εἴδει ἀλλήλων. ὥστ' ἀναγκαῖον ἢ κινεῖν ταύτας

10 τὰς ὑποθέσεις, ἢ τὸ μέσον ἓν εἶναι καὶ τὸ ἔσχατον. τούτου δ' ὄντος ἀνάγκη καὶ τὸν οὐρανὸν ἕνα μόνον εἶναι καὶ μὴ πλείους, τοῖς αὐτοῖς τεκμηρίοις τούτοις καὶ ταῖς αὐταῖς ἀνάγκαις.

Ὅτι δ' ἔστι τι οὗ πέφυκεν ἡ γῆ φέρεσθαι καὶ τὸ πῦρ, δῆλον καὶ ἐκ τῶν ἄλλων. ὅλως γὰρ τὸ κινού-

15 μενον ἔκ τινος εἴς τι μεταβάλλει, καὶ ταῦτα ἐξ οὗ καὶ εἰς ὃ εἴδει διαφέρει. πᾶσα δὲ πεπερασμένη

ᵃ I translate τὸ ληφθὲν ἐντεῦθεν thus, following a suggestion of Professor Cornford's, rather than " the portion which is taken hence " (so Stocks). As regards the rest of this difficult clause, would not Stocks's rendering require οὐδέ instead of καί at 277 a 7 ?

But a thing whose nature it is not to move at all cannot be moved by constraint. If then they have a natural motion, it must be supposed that, since they are individuals possessed of the same form, their motion is towards one and the same place, *i.e.* to one individual centre and one individual circumference. It might be argued that the goals of their motions are numerically many though the same in form, on the ground that the individuals themselves are many but indistinguishable in form. I answer that in that case we cannot pick and choose among the particles to which we assign a different goal; the same rule must apply to all, since all alike exhibit formal identity with each other but numerical individuality. My meaning is this, that if the relation of particles in this world to each other and their relation to those in another world are the same, then any given[a] particle from this world will not behave otherwise towards the particles in another world than towards those in its own, but similarly : for in form they do not differ from one another at all. Either, therefore, the initial assumptions must be rejected, or there must be only one centre and one circumference ; and given this latter fact, it follows from the same evidence and by the same compulsion that the world must be unique. There cannot be several worlds.

A consideration of moving objects in general affords additional proof that there does exist a certain place to which it is natural for earth to move, and another for fire. Motion in general is a change from one state to another, and these two states are formally different. Now every change is

277 a

μεταβολή, οἷον τὸ ὑγιαζόμενον ἐκ νόσου εἰς ὑγίειαν
καὶ τὸ αὐξανόμενον ἐκ μικρότητος εἰς μέγεθος.
καὶ τὸ φερόμενον ἄρα· καὶ γὰρ τοῦτο γίνεταί ποθεν
ποῖ. δεῖ ἄρα εἴδει διαφέρειν ἐξ οὗ καὶ εἰς ὃ πέφυκε
20 φέρεσθαι· ὥσπερ τὸ ὑγιαζόμενον οὐχ οὗ ἔτυχεν,
οὐδ᾽ οὗ βούλεται ὁ κινῶν. καὶ τὸ πῦρ ἄρα καὶ ἡ
γῆ οὐκ εἰς ἄπειρον φέρονται, ἀλλ᾽ εἰς ἀντικείμενα·
ἀντίκειται δὲ κατὰ τόπον τὸ ἄνω τῷ κάτω, ὥστε
ταῦτα ἔσται πέρατα τῆς φορᾶς. (ἐπεὶ καὶ ἡ κύκλῳ
ἔχει πως ἀντικείμενα τὰ κατὰ διάμετρον· τῇ δ᾽ ὅλῃ
25 οὐκ ἔστιν ἐναντίον οὐδέν. ὥστε καὶ τούτοις τρόπον
τινὰ ἡ κίνησις εἰς τὰ ἀντικείμενα καὶ πεπερασμένα.) ἀνάγκη ἄρα εἶναί τι τέλος καὶ μὴ εἰς
ἄπειρον φέρεσθαι.

Τεκμήριον δὲ τοῦ μὴ εἰς ἄπειρον φέρεσθαι καὶ
τὸ τὴν γῆν μέν, ὅσῳ ἂν ἐγγυτέρω ᾖ τοῦ μέσου,
θᾶττον φέρεσθαι, τὸ δὲ πῦρ, ὅσῳ ἂν τοῦ ἄνω. εἰ
30 δ᾽ ἄπειρον ἦν, ἄπειρος ἂν ἦν καὶ ἡ ταχυτής, εἰ
δ᾽ ἡ ταχυτής,[1] καὶ τὸ βάρος καὶ ἡ κουφότης· ὡς
γὰρ τὸ κατωτέρω ταχυτῆτι[2] ἑτέρου τῷ βάρει[3]
ἂν ἦν ταχύ, οὕτως εἰ ἄπειρος ἦν ἡ τούτου ἐπί-

---

[1] εἰ δ᾽ ἡ ταχυτής. These words are accidentally omitted
by Bekker.
[2] ταχυτῆτι secl. Allan.
[3] βάρει : βαρεῖ Bekker.

76

within fixed limits, *e.g.* for a patient who is being cured it is between sickness and health, for anything growing it is between smallness and greatness.[a] This must be true also for that which is being moved locally, for it too in its change has a place whence and a place whither. Therefore the starting-point and the goal of its natural motion must differ formally, just as with the patient the direction of his change is not haphazard nor decided by the wishes of the mover. Similarly therefore fire and earth do not move to infinity, but towards opposite points; and in speaking of place, the opposition is between top and bottom, so that these will be the limits of their movement. (Even circular motion has quasi-opposites in the opposite ends of the diameter, though there is no opposite to the motion as a whole. In this qualified sense it too is the motion of things passing between opposed and finite goals.) There must therefore be an end, and motion cannot go on to infinity.

Further evidence for the finite character of local motion is provided by the fact that earth moves more quickly, the nearer it is to the centre, and fire, the nearer it is to the upper limit. If the movement were to infinity, its speed would be infinite also, and if the speed were infinite, the weight or lightness of the object would be infinite also; for just as a body which, by reason of its speed, occupied a lower position than another, would owe that speed to its weight, so an infinite

---

[a] The repunctuation undertaken here by Stocks and Allan does not improve the sense. With this use of health and sickness as an illustration of change within fixed limits compare *Eth. Nic.* 1173 a 23 ὑγίεια ὡρισμένη οὖσα δέχεται τὸ μᾶλλον καὶ ἧττον.

277 a

δοσις, καὶ ἡ τῆς ταχυτῆτος ἐπίδοσις ἄπειρος
ἂν ἦν.

277 b

Ἀλλὰ μὴν οὐδ' ὑπ' ἄλλου φέρεται αὐτῶν τὸ μὲν
ἄνω τὸ δὲ κάτω· οὐδὲ βίᾳ, ὥσπερ τινές φασι τῇ
ἐκθλίψει. βραδύτερον γὰρ ἂν ἐκινεῖτο τὸ πλεῖον
πῦρ ἄνω καὶ ἡ πλείων γῆ κάτω· νῦν δὲ τοὐναντίον
ἀεὶ τὸ πλεῖον πῦρ θᾶττον φέρεται καὶ ἡ πλείων
5 γῆ εἰς τὸν αὑτῆς τόπον. οὐδὲ θᾶττον ἂν πρὸς τῷ
τέλει ἐφέρετο, εἰ τῇ βίᾳ καὶ τῇ ἐκθλίψει· πάντα γὰρ
τοῦ βιασαμένου πορρωτέρω γιγνόμενα βραδύτερον
φέρεται, καὶ ὅθεν βίᾳ, ἐκεῖ φέρεται οὐ βίᾳ. ὥστ'
ἐκ τούτων θεωροῦσιν ἔστι λαβεῖν τὴν πίστιν περὶ
ὧν λέγομεν ἱκανῶς.

10 Ἔτι δὲ καὶ διὰ τῶν ἐκ τῆς πρώτης φιλοσοφίας
λόγων δειχθείη ἄν, καὶ ἐκ τῆς κύκλῳ κινήσεως,
ἣν ἀναγκαῖον ἀίδιον ὁμοίως ἐνταῦθά τ' εἶναι καὶ
ἐν τοῖς ἄλλοις κόσμοις.

Δῆλον δὲ κἂν ὧδε γένοιτο σκοπουμένοις ὅτι ἀνάγκη
ἕνα εἶναι τὸν οὐρανόν. τριῶν γὰρ ὄντων τῶν σωμα-

---

a The elements move more quickly as they approach their
natural places. If therefore their movements continued to
infinity, they would attain an infinite speed. But that is
equivalent to saying that they acquire infinite weight, a
thing which A. has already in this treatise proved to be an
impossibility. The Greek of the last sentence is difficult,
and there is much to be said for Mr. Allan's proposal to
excise ταχυτῆτι in line 31.

A note of Simpl. at this point deserves mention (266. 35).
Its sense is as follows : " Personally I should like to see an
investigation of what everyone refers to as admitted, namely
that the velocity of objects is greater in proximity to their
natural places. If an addition of weight or lightness occurs,
it will follow that an object which is weighed in the air,
suppose one were to stretch forth from a high tower or tree
or cliff and weigh it, will be found to be heavier when the

increase in the weight would mean an infinite increase in the speed.[a]

It cannot be objected that an external agent is the cause of the elements moving up or down, nor that they are moved by force, the " extrusion " which some allege.[b] If that were so, a larger quantity of fire would move more slowly upwards, and a larger quantity of earth more slowly downwards ; whereas on the contrary the larger quantity of fire or earth always moves more quickly than a smaller to its natural place. Nor would an element move more quickly near the end of its motion, if the movement were due to force and extrusion ; for all things move more slowly as they recede from the source of their enforced motion, and move without the exercise of force towards the place whence force was used to move them. These considerations, then, are sufficient to give us confidence in the truth of what we assert.

The same thing might also be demonstrated from the arguments of first philosophy,[c] and from the nature of circular motion, which would have to be eternal both here and in the other worlds.

From the following standpoint too it might be made clear that the heaven must be unique. There are three corporeal elements, therefore there must

weigher is standing on the earth-level beneath. This appears to be a fiction, unless it is claimed that in such experiments the difference is imperceptible."

[b] *i.e.* the atomists. After A., the opinion was retained by Strato and Epicurus (Simpl.). All elements were naturally heavy, and each was only prevented from sinking to the centre of the universe by the presence of the one next below it, which " squeezed it out " and forced it upwards.

[c] Because a plurality of worlds would mean a plurality of Unmoved Movers, and this is an impossibility. (*Met.* 1074 a 31-38. *Cf.* introd. p. xxv.)

τικῶν στοιχείων, τρεῖς ἔσονται καὶ οἱ τόποι τῶν
15 στοιχείων, εἷς μὲν ὁ τοῦ ὑφισταμένου σώματος ὁ
περὶ τὸ μέσον, ἄλλος δὲ ὁ τοῦ κύκλῳ φερομένου,
ὅσπερ ἐστὶν ἔσχατος, τρίτος δ᾽ ὁ μεταξὺ τούτων ὁ
τοῦ μέσου σώματος. ἀνάγκη γὰρ ἐν τούτῳ εἶναι
τὸ ἐπιπολάζον. εἰ γὰρ μὴ ἐν τούτῳ, ἔξω ἔσται ἀλλ᾽
ἀδύνατον ἔξω. τὸ μὲν γὰρ ἀβαρὲς τὸ δ᾽ ἔχον βάρος
20 κατωτέρω δὲ ὁ τοῦ βάρος ἔχοντος σώματος τόπος,
εἴπερ ὁ πρὸς τῷ μέσῳ τοῦ βαρέος. ἀλλὰ μὴν οὐδὲ
παρὰ φύσιν· ἄλλῳ γὰρ ἔσται κατὰ φύσιν, ἄλλο δ᾽
οὐκ ἦν. ἀνάγκη ἄρα ἐν τῷ μεταξὺ εἶναι. τούτου
δ᾽ αὐτοῦ τίνες εἰσὶ διαφοραί, ὕστερον ἐροῦμεν.

Περὶ μὲν οὖν τῶν σωματικῶν στοιχείων, ποῖά
25 τ᾽ ἐστὶ καὶ πόσα, καὶ τίς ἑκάστου τόπος, ἔτι δ᾽
ὅλως πόσοι τὸ πλῆθος οἱ τόποι, δῆλον ἡμῖν ἐκ τῶν
εἰρημένων.

---

[a] The argument is expressed with more than usual awkwardness. τὸ ἐπιπολάζον would naturally mean τὸ πᾶσιν ἐπιπολάζον, *i.e.* fire (312 a 4 below), but must here refer to the intermediate body, which rises to and stays on the surface of earth. It must stay there, and not pass upward through fire to the outside, for of a weightless body (fire) and a body possessed of a certain weight (the intermediate body), the latter (τὸ βάρος ἔχον) will occupy the lower place. The reason for this is that the place of the absolutely heavy (τὸ βαρύ) is the centre, and therefore the relatively heavy must be nearer the centre than that which has no weight at all. I believe, though it is perhaps doubtful, that A. is leaving

CHAPTER IX

ARGUMENT

There cannot be more than one world (*continued*).
7. Evidence from the doctrine of form and matter.
This seems at first sight unfavourable, since the ever-

be three natural places for them, one around the
centre for the element which sinks, a second (the
outermost) for the revolving element, and a third
between them for the body of intermediate nature.
For that (*i.e.* between centre and circumference) is
where the body must be which stays on the surface.
If it is not there, it will be outside ; but it cannot
be outside, for here are a weightless body and one
with weight, and the lower place belongs to the
body possessing weight, since the region about the
centre is proper to the heavy.[a] Nor again could
it be in a position unnatural to it, for that position
would be natural to something else, and there is,
as we saw, nothing else. It must therefore be in
the space between. What differences there are in
the intermediate itself, we shall discuss later.[b]

We have now said sufficient to clear up the subject of the nature and number of the physical
elements, and what is the natural place of each,
and also in general how many places there are.

his fifth body out of the account, and is supposing a Universe
constructed only out of the four elements recognized by
previous and contemporary thought. (*Cf.* introd. p. xiv,
n. *a*.) For if τὸ κύκλῳ φερόμενον = *aither* and τὸ ἐπιπολάζον
= fire, it would seem that fire must be the " body with weight "
of the next sentence.

[b] The intermediate region, here treated as a unity, contains of course both air and water, whose specific characters
are discussed in the fourth book.

CHAPTER IX

ARGUMENT (*continued*)

present distinction within material objects between absolute
form and form-in-matter seems to show that every form is
realizable more than once in different matter, i.e. *that there*

*either are or can be more than one of every class of material
object.   This suggests at least the possibility of several worlds,
seeing that the world is material.   But the possibility is not
present in an instance where the one object uses up all the
material appropriate to the realization of its particular form.
This condition is fulfilled by the world, for none of the only
three varieties of simple natural body (cf. ch. ii.) can exist
outside it (277 b 27—279 a 11).*

277 b 27   Ὅτι δ' οὐ μόνον εἷς ἐστιν οὐρανός, ἀλλὰ καὶ
ἀδύνατον γενέσθαι πλείους, ἔτι δ' ὡς ἀΐδιος ἄ-
φθαρτος ὢν καὶ ἀγένητος, λέγωμεν, πρῶτον δια-
30 πορήσαντες περὶ αὐτοῦ.   δόξειε γὰρ ἂν ὡδὶ
σκοπουμένοις ἀδύνατον ἕνα καὶ μόνον εἶναι αὐτόν·
ἐν ἅπασι γὰρ καὶ τοῖς φύσει καὶ τοῖς ἀπὸ τέχνης
συνεστῶσι καὶ γεγενημένοις ἕτερόν ἐστιν αὐτὴ καθ'
αὑτὴν ἡ μορφὴ καὶ μεμιγμένη μετὰ τῆς ὕλης· οἷον
278 a τῆς σφαίρας ἕτερον τὸ εἶδος καὶ ἡ χρυσῆ καὶ ἡ
χαλκῆ σφαῖρα, καὶ πάλιν τοῦ κύκλου ἑτέρα ἡ
μορφὴ καὶ ὁ χαλκοῦς καὶ ὁ ξύλινος κύκλος· τὸ γὰρ
τί ἦν εἶναι λέγοντες σφαίρᾳ ἢ κύκλῳ οὐκ ἐροῦμεν
ἐν τῷ λόγῳ χρυσὸν ἢ χαλκόν, ὡς οὐκ ὄντα ταῦτα
5 τῆς οὐσίας· ἐὰν δὲ τὴν χαλκῆν ἢ χρυσῆν, ἐροῦμεν,
καὶ ἐὰν μὴ δυνώμεθα νοῆσαι μηδὲ λαβεῖν ἄλλο τι
παρὰ τὸ καθ' ἕκαστον.   ἐνίοτε γὰρ οὐθὲν κωλύει

---

[a] This means "even though individual examples of spheres
etc. are the only realities that we can apprehend," *i.e.* we
must recognize the distinction between pure form and form-
in-matter even when it is least apparent.   The sentence does
not mean " even though we can apprehend no other example
of a concrete object than the one we are looking at."   The
following sentence might at first sight suggest that it did
(" even if we could only apprehend one circle "), but the
reasoning is this : it is the existence of a plurality of objects

ARGUMENT (*continued*)

Corollary. *This proof of the necessary uniqueness of the world carries with it the corollary that outside the heavens there can be neither place nor void nor time, since all these depend on the actual or potential presence of body. Whatever there may be there must be exempt from the vicissitudes of space and time, and hence must be (as indeed it is commonly held to be) the chief and highest divinity* (279 a 11–b 3).

WE have now to show not only that the world is in fact unique, but that there could not possibly be more than one, and also that it is eternal, being indestructible and ungenerated. But let us first discuss some difficulties, since from one point of view it would seem impossible for it to be unique. In all the formations and products of nature and art alike a distinction can be drawn between the shape in and by itself and the shape as it is combined with the matter. With a sphere, for example, the form is one thing and the golden or bronze ball is another, and similarly with a circle the shape is distinguishable from the ring of bronze or wood. In defining the essence of a sphere or circle we do not include gold or bronze in the definition, because we do not consider them to belong to the substance of what we are defining, but we do include them if it is a bronze or gold ball that we are trying to define ; and we proceed in this way even if we cannot conceive or apprehend any other entity beside the concrete individual thing.[a]

of the same kind that brings home to us the distinction between form and matter, because they exhibit the same form in different matter. If then an object existed which was the sole member of its class, it would tend to obscure for us the existence of anything παρὰ τὸ καθ’ ἕκαστον. It would be difficult, in this instance, to distinguish between form and matter.

τοῦτο συμβαίνειν, οἷον εἰ μόνος εἷς ληφθείη κύκλος·
οὐθὲν γὰρ ἧττον ἄλλο ἔσται τὸ κύκλῳ εἶναι καὶ
τῷδε τῷ κύκλῳ, καὶ τὸ μὲν εἶδος, τὸ δ' εἶδος ἐν
10 τῇ ὕλῃ καὶ τῶν καθ' ἕκαστον. ἐπεὶ οὖν ἐστιν ὁ
οὐρανὸς αἰσθητός, τῶν καθ' ἕκαστον ἂν εἴη· τὸ
γὰρ αἰσθητὸν ἅπαν ἐν τῇ ὕλῃ ὑπῆρχεν. εἰ δὲ τῶν
καθ' ἕκαστον, ἕτερον ἂν εἴη τῷδε τῷ οὐρανῷ εἶναι
καὶ οὐρανῷ ἁπλῶς. ἕτερον ἄρα ὅδε ὁ οὐρανὸς καὶ
οὐρανὸς ἁπλῶς, καὶ τὸ μὲν ὡς εἶδος καὶ μορφή, τὸ
15 δ' ὡς τῇ ὕλῃ μεμιγμένον. ὧν δ' ἐστὶ μορφή τις
καὶ εἶδος, ἤτοι ἔστιν ἢ ἐνδέχεται πλείω γενέσθαι
τὰ καθ' ἕκαστα. εἴτε γὰρ ἔστιν εἴδη, καθάπερ
φασί τινες, ἀνάγκη τοῦτο συμβαίνειν, εἴτε καὶ
χωριστὸν μηθὲν τῶν τοιούτων, οὐθὲν ἧττον· ἐπὶ
πάντων γὰρ οὕτως ὁρῶμεν, ὅσων ἡ οὐσία ἐν ὕλῃ
20 ἐστίν, πλείω καὶ ἄπειρα ὄντα τὰ ὁμοιοειδῆ. ὥστε
ἤτοι εἰσὶ πλείους οὐρανοί¹ ἢ ἐνδέχεται πλείους
εἶναι.

Ἐκ μὲν οὖν τούτων ὑπολάβοι τις ἂν καὶ εἶναι
καὶ ἐνδέχεσθαι πλείους εἶναι οὐρανούς· σκεπτέον
δὲ πάλιν τί τούτων λέγεται καλῶς καὶ τί οὐ καλῶς.
τὸ μὲν οὖν ἕτερον εἶναι τὸν λόγον τὸν ἄνευ τῆς ὕλης
25 καὶ τὸν ἐν τῇ ὕλῃ τῆς μορφῆς καλῶς τε λέγεται,
καὶ ἔστω τοῦτ' ἀληθές. ἀλλ' οὐδὲν ἧττον οὐδεμία

---

¹ πλείους οὐρανοί. So Stocks and Allan, with all mss. but
J; πλείους οἱ οὐρανοί J, Bekker.

There is no reason why this should not happen sometimes. Suppose for instance only one example of a circle were apprehended, the distinction would none the less remain between the essential nature of the circle and the essential nature of this particular circle. The one is simply form, the other is form-in-matter and must be counted among particulars. Now since the world is perceptible, it must be reckoned a particular, for as we have seen, everything that is perceptible is in matter. And if it is a particular, the essential nature of this world of ours must be different from the essential nature of world in general. " This world " and " world in general " are therefore two different things, the latter being distinguishable as form or shape and the former as something compounded with matter. And, finally, it may be said of those particulars which possess a shape or form that there either are or can be more than one of them. This must be so, whether there are forms with an existence of their own as some assert, or, no less, if no entity of that sort is separable from the particulars. It is universal in our experience that, among things whose substance is bound up with matter, there are many—indeed an infinite number—of particulars similar in form, so that there either are or can be many worlds.

From the foregoing arguments one might assume that there either are or may be several worlds ; but we must turn back and test the soundness or unsoundness of each one. The distinction between two definitions of form, without matter and in the matter, is sound, and may be taken to represent a truth. Nevertheless it does not carry with it

278 a

ἀνάγκη διὰ τοῦτο πλείους εἶναι κόσμους, οὐδ'
ἐνδέχεται γενέσθαι πλείους, εἴπερ οὗτος ἐξ ἁπάσης
ἐστὶ τῆς ὕλης, ὥσπερ ἔστιν. ὡδὶ δὲ μᾶλλον ἴσως
τὸ λεγόμενον ἔσται δῆλον. εἰ γάρ ἐστιν ἡ γρυπότης
30 καμπυλότης ἐν ῥινὶ ἢ σαρκί, καὶ ἔστιν ὕλη τῇ
γρυπότητι ἡ σάρξ, εἰ ἐξ ἁπασῶν τῶν σαρκῶν μία
γένοιτο σὰρξ καὶ ὑπάρξειεν ταύτῃ τὸ γρυπόν, οὐθὲν
ἂν ἄλλ' οὔτ' εἴη γρυπὸν οὔτ' ἐνδέχοιτο γενέσθαι.
ὁμοίως δὲ καὶ εἰ τῷ ἀνθρώπῳ ἐστὶν ὕλη σάρκες
καὶ ὀστᾶ, εἰ ἐκ πάσης τῆς σαρκὸς καὶ πάντων τῶν
35 ὀστῶν ἄνθρωπος γένοιτο ἀδυνάτων ὄντων δια-
λυθῆναι, οὐκ ἂν ἐνδέχοιτο εἶναι ἄλλον ἄνθρωπον.
278 b ὡσαύτως δὲ καὶ ἐπὶ τῶν ἄλλων· ὅλως γὰρ ὅσων
ἐστὶν ἡ οὐσία ἐν ὑποκειμένῃ τινὶ ὕλῃ, τούτων οὐδὲν
ἐνδέχεται γενέσθαι μὴ ὑπαρχούσης τινὸς ὕλης. ὁ
δ' οὐρανὸς ἔστι μὲν τῶν καθ' ἔκαστα καὶ τῶν ἐκ
τῆς ὕλης· ἀλλ' εἰ μὴ ἐκ μορίου αὐτῆς συνέστηκεν
5 ἀλλ' ἐξ ἁπάσης, τὸ μὲν εἶναι αὐτῷ οὐρανῷ καὶ τῷδε
τῷ οὐρανῷ ἕτερόν ἐστιν, οὐ μέντοι οὔτ' ἂν εἴη
ἄλλος οὔτ' ἂν ἐνδέχοιτο γενέσθαι πλείους, διὰ τὸ
πᾶσαν τὴν ὕλην περιειληφέναι τοῦτον.

Λείπεται ἄρα τοῦτο δεῖξαι, ὅτι ἐξ ἅπαντος τοῦ
φυσικοῦ καὶ τοῦ αἰσθητοῦ συνέστηκε σώματος.
10 εἴπωμεν δὲ πρῶτον τί λέγομεν εἶναι τὸν οὐρανὸν

---

a This is the word which so far in this chapter has been
translated " world." Elsewhere in the treatise it is rendered
as " world," " heavens " or " sky " according to that one of
the three senses here enumerated which A. is employing at
any particular moment. In this passage a repetition of the
Greek is unavoidable, since no one English word covers all

the necessity for a plurality of worlds, nor even the possibility of their coming into being, provided that (as is the fact) our own world contains all the matter there is. My meaning will perhaps be clearer if I put it in this way. Suppose " aquilinity " to mean a curvature in the nose or in flesh, and flesh to be the matter appropriate to aquilinity. Now if every particle of flesh were made into one mass, and that mass were aquiline, nothing else would be aquiline nor would there be a possibility of anything becoming so. Suppose, again, that the material of a human being is flesh and bones ; then if a man were made out of all the flesh and bones in existence, and if they could not be broken up again, then it would be impossible for there to be another man. This holds good in all instances, and may be put generally thus : of the things which have their substance in an underlying matter, none may come into being unless a certain quantity of matter already exists. Now the world must be counted among particulars and things made from matter ; but if it is composed, not of a portion of matter, but of all matter whatsoever, then we may admit that its essential nature as " world " and as " this world " are distinct, but nevertheless there will not be another world, nor could there be more than one, for the reason that all the matter is contained in this one.

This therefore remains to be demonstrated, that our own world is composed of the whole sum of natural perceptible body. Let us first establish what we mean by *ouranos*,[a] and in how many senses

the three senses which *ouranos* is here stated to possess. *Cf.* introd. pp. xi f.

278 b

καὶ ποσαχῶς, ἵνα μᾶλλον ἡμῖν δῆλον γένηται τὸ
ζητούμενον. ἕνα μὲν οὖν τρόπον οὐρανὸν λέγομεν
τὴν οὐσίαν τὴν τῆς ἐσχάτης τοῦ παντὸς περιφορᾶς,
ἢ σῶμα φυσικὸν τὸ ἐν τῇ ἐσχάτῃ περιφορᾷ τοῦ
παντός· εἰώθαμεν γὰρ τὸ ἔσχατον καὶ τὸ ἄνω
15 μάλιστα καλεῖν οὐρανόν, ἐν ᾧ καὶ τὸ θεῖον πᾶν
ἱδρῦσθαί φαμεν. ἄλλον δ' αὖ τρόπον τὸ συνεχὲς
σῶμα τῇ ἐσχάτῃ περιφορᾷ τοῦ παντός, ἐν ᾧ σελήνη
καὶ ἥλιος καὶ ἔνια τῶν ἄστρων· καὶ γὰρ ταῦτα ἐν
τῷ οὐρανῷ εἶναί φαμεν. ἔτι δ' ἄλλως λέγομεν
20 οὐρανὸν τὸ περιεχόμενον σῶμα ὑπὸ τῆς ἐσχάτης
περιφορᾶς· τὸ γὰρ ὅλον καὶ τὸ πᾶν εἰώθαμεν
λέγειν οὐρανόν.

Τριχῶς δὴ λεγομένου τοῦ οὐρανοῦ, τὸ ὅλον τὸ
ὑπὸ τῆς ἐσχάτης περιεχόμενον περιφορᾶς ἐξ
ἅπαντος ἀνάγκη συνεστάναι τοῦ φυσικοῦ καὶ τοῦ
αἰσθητοῦ σώματος διὰ τὸ μήτ' εἶναι μηδὲν ἔξω
25 σῶμα τοῦ οὐρανοῦ μήτ' ἐνδέχεσθαι γενέσθαι. εἰ
γὰρ ἔστιν ἔξω τῆς ἐσχάτης περιφορᾶς σῶμα
φυσικόν, ἀνάγκη αὐτὸ ἤτοι τῶν ἁπλῶν εἶναι σωμάτων ἢ τῶν συνθέτων, καὶ ἢ κατὰ φύσιν ἢ παρὰ
φύσιν ἔχειν. τῶν μὲν οὖν ἁπλῶν οὐθὲν ἂν εἴη. τὸ
μὲν γὰρ κύκλῳ φερόμενον δέδεικται ὅτι οὐκ ἐνδέχεται μεταλλάξαι τὸν αὑτοῦ τόπον. ἀλλὰ μὴν
30 οὐδὲ τὸ ἀπὸ τοῦ μέσου δυνατόν, οὐδὲ τὸ ὑφιστάμενον. κατὰ φύσιν μὲν γὰρ οὐκ ἂν εἴησαν (ἄλλοι
γὰρ αὐτῶν οἰκεῖοι τόποι), παρὰ φύσιν δ' εἴπερ
εἰσίν, ἄλλῳ τινὶ ἔσται κατὰ φύσιν ὁ ἔξω τόπος·

ᵃ i.e. the planets.   The fixed stars are in *ouranos* no. 1.
ᵇ Chapters ii. and iii. above.

the word is used, in order that we may more clearly
understand the object of our questions. (1) In one
sense we apply the word *ouranos* to the substance
of the outermost circumference of the world, or to
the natural body which is at the outermost circumference of the world ; for it is customary to
give the name of *ouranos* especially to the outermost and uppermost region, in which also we believe
all divinity to have its seat. (2) Secondly we apply
it to that body which occupies the next place to
the outermost circumference of the world, in which
are the moon and the sun and certain of the stars [a] ;
for these, we say, are in the *ouranos*. (3) We apply
the word in yet another sense to the body which
is enclosed by the outermost circumference ; for
it is customary to give the name of *ouranos* to the
world as a whole.

The word, then, is used in these three senses,
and the whole which is enclosed by the outermost
circumference must of necessity be composed of
the whole sum of natural perceptible body, for the
reason that there is not, nor ever could be, any
body outside the heaven. For if there is a natural
body beyond the outermost circumference, it must
be either simple or composite, and its position there
must be either natural or unnatural. It cannot be
one of the simple bodies, for (*a*) with regard to the
body which revolves it has been shown [b] that it
cannot change its place ; (*b*) but no more can it
be either the body which moves away from the
centre or that which settles towards it. They
could not be there naturally (for their proper places
are elsewhere), but if they are there unnaturally,
then this outside region will belong naturally to

278 b

τὸν γὰρ τούτῳ παρὰ φύσιν ἀναγκαῖον ἄλλῳ εἶναι
35 κατὰ φύσιν. ἀλλ' οὐκ ἦν ἄλλο σῶμα παρὰ ταῦτα.
οὐκ ἄρ' ἐστὶ δυνατὸν οὐθὲν τῶν ἁπλῶν ἔξω εἶναι
279 a τοῦ οὐρανοῦ σῶμα. εἰ δὲ μὴ τῶν ἁπλῶν, οὐδὲ τῶν
μικτῶν· ἀνάγκη γὰρ εἶναι καὶ τὰ ἁπλᾶ τοῦ μικτοῦ
ὄντος. ἀλλὰ μὴν οὐδὲ γενέσθαι δυνατόν· ἤτοι γὰρ
κατὰ φύσιν ἔσται ἢ παρὰ φύσιν, καὶ ἢ ἁπλοῦν ἢ
μικτόν, ὥστε πάλιν ὁ αὐτὸς ἥξει λόγος· οὐθὲν γὰρ
διαφέρει σκοπεῖν εἰ ἔστιν ἢ εἰ γενέσθαι δυνατόν.

Φανερὸν τοίνυν ἐκ τῶν εἰρημένων ὅτι οὔτ' ἔστιν
ἔξω οὔτ' ἐγχωρεῖ γενέσθαι σώματος ὄγκον οὐθενός·
ἐξ ἁπάσης γάρ ἐστι τῆς οἰκείας ὕλης ὁ πᾶς κόσμος
(ὕλη γὰρ ἦν αὐτῷ τὸ φυσικὸν σῶμα καὶ αἰσθητόν),
10 ὥστ' οὔτε νῦν εἰσὶ πλείους οὐρανοὶ οὔτ' ἐγένοντο,
οὔτ' ἐνδέχεται γενέσθαι πλείους· ἀλλ' εἷς καὶ μόνος
καὶ τέλειος οὗτος οὐρανός ἐστιν. ἅμα δὲ δῆλον
ὅτι οὐδὲ τόπος οὐδὲ κενὸν οὐδὲ χρόνος ἐστὶν ἔξω
τοῦ οὐρανοῦ. ἐν ἅπαντι γὰρ τόπῳ δυνατὸν ὑπάρξαι
σῶμα· κενὸν δ' εἶναί φασιν ἐν ᾧ μὴ ἐνυπάρχει
15 σῶμα, δυνατὸν δ' ἐστὶ γενέσθαι· χρόνος δὲ ἀριθμὸς
κινήσεως· κίνησις δ' ἄνευ φυσικοῦ σώματος οὐκ
ἔστιν. ἔξω δὲ τοῦ οὐρανοῦ δέδεικται ὅτι οὔτ'
ἔστιν οὔτ' ἐνδέχεται γενέσθαι σῶμα. φανερὸν ἄρα
ὅτι οὔτε τόπος οὔτε κενὸν οὔτε χρόνος ἐστὶν ἔξωθεν·
διόπερ οὔτ' ἐν τόπῳ τἀκεῖ πέφυκεν, οὔτε χρόνος
αὐτὰ ποιεῖ γηράσκειν, οὐδ' ἐστὶν οὐδενὸς οὐδεμία

some other body ; for the place which is unnatural to one must be natural to another. But we have seen that there is no other body besides these three. Therefore it is impossible that any of the simple bodies should lie outside the heaven. And if this is true of the simple bodies, it is true also of composite, for where the composite body is the simple bodies must be also. It is equally impossible that a body should ever come to be there, for its coming to be there will be either natural or unnatural, and it will be either simple or composite, in fact the same argument will recur : it makes no difference whether we ask " Is it there ? " or " Can it come to be there ? "

It is plain, then, from what has been said, that there is not, nor do the facts allow there to be, any bodily mass beyond the heaven. The world in its entirety is made up of the whole sum of available matter (for the matter appropriate to it is, as we saw, natural perceptible body), and we may conclude that there is not now a plurality of worlds, nor has there been, nor could there be. This world is one, solitary and complete. It is clear in addition that there is neither place nor void nor time beyond the heaven ; for (a) in all place there is a possibility of the presence of body, (b) void is defined as that which, although at present not containing body, can contain it, (c) time is the number of motion, and without natural body there cannot be motion. It is obvious then that there is neither place nor void nor time outside the heaven, since it has been demonstrated that there neither is nor can be body there. Wherefore neither are the things there born in place, nor does time cause them to age, nor

279 a
20 μεταβολὴ τῶν ὑπὲρ τὴν ἐξωτάτω τεταγμένων
φοράν, ἀλλ' ἀναλλοίωτα καὶ ἀπαθῆ τὴν ἀρίστην
ἔχοντα ζωὴν καὶ τὴν αὐταρκεστάτην διατελεῖ τὸν
ἅπαντα αἰῶνα. καὶ γὰρ τοῦτο τοὔνομα θείως
ἔφθεγκται παρὰ τῶν ἀρχαίων. τὸ γὰρ τέλος τὸ
περιέχον τὸν τῆς ἑκάστου ζωῆς χρόνον, οὗ μηθὲν
25 ἔξω κατὰ φύσιν, αἰὼν ἑκάστου κέκληται. κατὰ
τὸν αὐτὸν δὲ λόγον καὶ τὸ τοῦ παντὸς οὐρανοῦ
τέλος καὶ τὸ τὸν πάντα χρόνον καὶ τὴν ἀπειρίαν
περιέχον τέλος αἰών ἐστιν, ἀπὸ τοῦ ἀεὶ εἶναι
εἰληφὼς τὴν ἐπωνυμίαν, ἀθάνατος καὶ θεῖος. ὅθεν
καὶ τοῖς ἄλλοις ἐξήρτηται, τοῖς μὲν ἀκριβέστερον
30 τοῖς δ' ἀμαυρῶς, τὸ εἶναί τε καὶ ζῆν. καὶ γὰρ
καθάπερ ἐν τοῖς ἐγκυκλίοις φιλοσοφήμασι περὶ τὰ
θεῖα πολλάκις προφαίνεται τοῖς λόγοις ὅτι τὸ θεῖον
ἀμετάβλητον ἀναγκαῖον εἶναι πᾶν τὸ πρῶτον καὶ
ἀκρότατον· ὃ[1] οὕτως ἔχον μαρτυρεῖ τοῖς εἰρημένοις.
οὔτε γὰρ ἄλλο κρεῖττόν ἐστιν ὅ τι κινήσει (ἐκεῖνο
35 γὰρ ἂν εἴη θειότερον) οὔτ' ἔχει φαῦλον οὐθέν, οὔτ'
279 b ἐνδεὲς τῶν αὑτοῦ καλῶν οὐδενός ἐστιν. καὶ
ἄπαυστον δὴ κίνησιν κινεῖται εὐλόγως· πάντα γὰρ

---

[1] ὃ om. E, Jaeger.

---

[a] Jaeger (*Aristoteles* p. 318, *Eng. tr.* p. 302 with different
punctuation) follows E in omitting ὃ at 279 a 33, thus giving
formal correctness to the sentence. But anacoluthon is not
foreign to A., and the omission of ὃ makes impossible the
rendering given above. (Allan avoids the asyndeton without alteration of the text, by putting the words καθάπερ . . .
τὰ θεῖα between commas.) As J. sees the passage, A. is
claiming that the results of this chapter confirm the arguments of the " popular works "; on the rendering here
offered, he is introducing the arguments of the " popular
works " in support of his present conclusions. Stocks's

does change work in any way upon any of the
beings whose allotted place is beyond the outermost motion : changeless and impassive, they have
uninterrupted enjoyment of the best and most
independent life for the whole aeon of their existence. Indeed, our forefathers were inspired when
they made this word, *aeon*. The total time which
circumscribes the length of life of every creature,
and which cannot in nature be exceeded, they
named the *aeon* of each. By the same analogy
also the sum of existence of the whole heaven,
the sum which includes all time even to infinity,
is *aeon*, taking the name from ἀεὶ εἶναι (" to
be everlastingly "), for it is immortal and divine.
In dependence on it all other things have their
existence and their life, some more directly, others
more obscurely. In the more popular philosophical
works, where divinity is in question, it is often
made abundantly clear by the discussion that the
foremost and highest divinity must be entirely
immutable, a fact which affords testimony to what
we have been saying.[a] For there is nothing superior
that can move it—if there were it would be
more divine—and it has no badness in it nor is
lacking in any of the fairness proper to it. It is
too in unceasing motion, as is reasonable ; for

translation is in agreement with this, and it has the support
of Simpl. 288. 28 ὅτι δὲ ἀΐδιον τὸ θεῖον μαρτυρεῖ, φησί, καὶ τὰ
ἐν τοῖς ἐγκυκλίοις φιλοσοφήμασι πολλαχοῦ προφαινόμενα ἐν τοῖς
λόγοις, ὅτι τὸ θεῖον ἀμετάβλητον ἀναγκαῖον εἶναι πᾶν τὸ πρῶτον
καὶ ἀκρότατον. J.'s punctuation in *Aristoteles* p. 318 also
goes against Simpl. (291. 46.)

The evidence of Simpl. seems conclusive for identifying the
ἐγκύκλια φιλοσοφήματα, like the ἐξωτερικοὶ λόγοι, with A.'s
own published works. He refers to the dialogue Περὶ
φιλοσοφίας by name for the present passage.

παύεται κινούμενα ὅταν ἔλθῃ εἰς τὸν οἰκεῖον τόπον,
τοῦ δὲ κύκλῳ σώματος ὁ αὐτὸς τόπος ὅθεν ἤρξατο
καὶ εἰς ὃν τελευτᾷ.

CHAPTER X

ARGUMENT

The world is ungenerated and indestructible.
1. Review of previous theories. *All agree that it is generated. Of its destructibility there are three views : (a) that
it is indestructible, (b) that it is destructible, (c) that it is
subject to an everlasting alternation between existence and
non-existence.*

(a) *It is impossible for it to be generated but indestructible.*
(i) *That would contradict a universal fact of observation, that
everything which has a beginning may come to an end.* (ii)
*Its generation implies matter pre-existing in a different state.
That matter must be capable of change, since otherwise the
world would never have been generated out of it. It must
therefore be possible for it to change again.*

*Some claim that their statement of the generation of the
world is not literally meant : they only use the narrative
form of exposition in order to lay bare more clearly the present
composition of the world. To explain their meaning here,
they use the analogy of geometrical constructions, but in fact
that analogy, being false, makes nonsense of their claims.
The construction of a geometrical figure may well be in reality
no more than a peculiar form of analysis, since the elements
have no essential priority in time to the finished product.
But a construction out of physical materials must take place
in time or else it is meaningless to speak of it (279 b 4—
280 a 10).*

4 Τούτων δὲ διωρισμένων λέγωμεν μετὰ ταῦτα
5 πότερον ἀγένητος ἢ γενητὸς καὶ ἄφθαρτος ἢ
φθαρτός, διεξελθόντες πρότερον τὰς τῶν ἄλλων

things only cease moving when they arrive at their proper places, and for the body whose motion is circular the place where it ends is also the place where it begins.

CHAPTER X

ARGUMENT (*continued*)

(c) *The view that the world is alternately generated and destroyed means no more, on examination, than that the elements combine now into one formation and now into another. In reality there is nothing involved that can be called generation and destruction, but only change of shape or arrangement* (280 a 11-23).

(b) (i) *If there is only one world, then this view that it may be generated, and again finally destroyed, is quite impossible. It can be refuted by a re-use of the argument* (a) (ii) *above. The generated world must have been generated out of pre-existing material, and its destruction can only mean the return of that material to its former state. But if it is in its former state it is obviously possible for a world to be generated out of it again, just as it was before.* (ii) *If there is an infinity of matter, and an infinite number of worlds, this refutation does not hold. We cannot yet say whether in that case a world may be generated and destroyed* (280 a 23-27).

In general, we must face the whole problem of whether anything that is ungenerated can perish, or (as Plato said in the Timaeus) *anything generated be everlasting. We must leave the narrower field of the nature of the world, and consider generation and destruction as a whole* (280 a 27-34).

HAVING established so much, let us next decide whether the world has been from all time or has had a beginning, and whether it is indestructible or destructible. But first let us run over the theories

ὑπολήψεις· αἱ γὰρ τῶν ἐναντίων ἀποδείξεις ἀπορίαι
περὶ τῶν ἐναντίων εἰσίν. ἅμα δὲ καὶ μᾶλλον ἂν
εἴη πιστὰ τὰ μέλλοντα λεχθήσεσθαι προακηκοόσι
τὰ τῶν ἀμφισβητούντων λόγων δικαιώματα. τὸ
10 γὰρ ἐρήμην καταδικάζεσθαι δοκεῖν ἧττον ἂν ἡμῖν
ὑπάρχοι· καὶ γὰρ δεῖ διαιτητὰς ἀλλ' οὐκ ἀντιδίκους
εἶναι τοὺς μέλλοντας τἀληθὲς κρίνειν ἱκανῶς.

Γενόμενον μὲν οὖν ἅπαντες εἶναί φασιν, ἀλλὰ
γενόμενον οἱ μὲν ἀΐδιον, οἱ δὲ φθαρτὸν ὥσπερ
ὁτιοῦν ἄλλο τῶν φύσει συνισταμένων, οἱ δ' ἐναλλὰξ
15 ὁτὲ μὲν οὕτως ὁτὲ δὲ ἄλλως ἔχειν φθειρόμενον, καὶ
τοῦτο ἀεὶ διατελεῖν οὕτως, ὥσπερ Ἐμπεδοκλῆς ὁ
Ἀκραγαντῖνος καὶ Ἡράκλειτος ὁ Ἐφέσιος.

Τὸ μὲν οὖν γενέσθαι μὲν ἀΐδιον δ' ὅμως εἶναι
φάναι τῶν ἀδυνάτων. μόνα γὰρ ταῦτα θετέον
εὐλόγως ὅσα ἐπὶ πολλῶν ἢ πάντων ὁρῶμεν ὑπ-
20 άρχοντα, περὶ δὲ τούτου συμβαίνει τοὐναντίον·
ἅπαντα γὰρ τὰ γινόμενα καὶ φθειρόμενα φαίνεται.
ἔτι δὲ τὸ μὴ ἔχον ἀρχὴν τοῦ ὡδὶ ἔχειν, ἀλλ' ἀδύνατον ἄλλως ἔχειν πρότερον τὸν ἅπαντα αἰῶνα,
ἀδύνατον καὶ μεταβάλλειν· ἔσται γάρ τι αἴτιον, ὅ
25 εἰ ὑπῆρχε πρότερον, δυνατὸν ἂν ἦν ἄλλως ἔχειν τὸ
ἀδύνατον ἄλλως ἔχειν. εἰ δὲ πρότερον ἐξ ἄλλως

---

[a] Orpheus, Hesiod, Plato (Simpl., following Alex.).

[b] The atomists (Alex. ap. Simpl.).

[c] Regarding φθειρόμενον as an additional note, by A. himself, in the nature of a gloss to make the meaning of ἄλλως
ἔχειν clear. This seems better than to speak, with Burnet
and Stocks, of an " alternation in the destructive process,"
a phrase which Stocks himself describes as " somewhat in-
accurate." See his note ad loc.

[d] This does not refer to the cosmos (as one might suspect
at this point, and so feel a difficulty), but to its elements, as
the following sentences make clear. The argument to which

of others, since to expound one theory is to raise the difficulties involved in its contrary. At the same time also the arguments which are to follow will inspire more confidence if the pleas of those who dispute them have been heard first. It will not look so much as if we are procuring judgement by default. And indeed it is arbiters, not litigants who are wanted for the obtaining of an adequate recognition of the truth.

All thinkers agree that it has had a beginning, but some [a] maintain that having begun it is everlasting, others [b] that it is perishable like any other formation of nature, and others again that it alternates, being at one time as it is now, and at another time changing and perishing, [c] and that this process continues unremittingly. Of this last opinion were Empedocles of Acragas and Heracleitus of Ephesus.

Now the view that it has had a beginning but is everlasting is an impossible one. Reason demands that we should only take for our hypotheses what we see to be generally or universally true, and this one is just the opposite, for observation shows us that everything which has a beginning also comes to an end. Further, if the present state of anything [d] has had no beginning, but hitherto it has for all time been impossible for it to be otherwise than it is, that thing cannot change ; for the change will be due to some cause, and if that cause was present already, then the thing which we said could not be otherwise *could* have been otherwise. If then the world

A. is leading is this : all admit that the world had a beginning. If its elements had been incapable of change, it would never have come into being. Since it *has* come into being, proving that its elements are susceptible to change of state, it is obviously possible for them to change again.

279 b

ἐχόντων συνέστη ὁ κόσμος, εἰ μὲν ἀεὶ οὕτως
ἐχόντων καὶ ἀδυνάτων ἄλλως ἔχειν, οὐκ ἂν ἐγέ-
νετο· εἰ δὲ γέγονεν, ἀνάγκη δηλονότι κἀκεῖνα
δυνατὰ εἶναι ἄλλως ἔχειν καὶ μὴ ἀεὶ οὕτως ἔχειν,
ὥστε καὶ συνεστῶτα διαλυθήσεται καὶ διαλελυμένα
30 συνέστη ἔμπροσθεν, καὶ τοῦτ' ἀπειράκις ἢ οὕτως
εἶχεν ἢ δυνατὸν ἦν. εἰ δὲ τοῦτ', οὐκ ἂν εἴη ἄφθαρτος, οὔτ' εἰ ἄλλως εἶχέ ποτε οὔτ' εἰ δυνατὸν ἄλλως
ἔχειν.

Ἧν δέ τινες βοήθειαν ἐπιχειροῦσι φέρειν ἑαυτοῖς
τῶν λεγόντων ἄφθαρτον μὲν εἶναι γενόμενον δέ,
οὐκ ἔστιν ἀληθής· ὁμοίως γάρ φασι τοῖς τὰ δια-
25 γράμματα γράφουσι καὶ σφᾶς εἰρηκέναι περὶ τῆς
280 a γενέσεως, οὐχ ὡς γενομένου ποτέ, ἀλλὰ διδα-
σκαλίας χάριν ὡς μᾶλλον γνωριζόντων, ὥσπερ
τὸ διάγραμμα γιγνόμενον θεασαμένους. τοῦτο δ'
ἐστίν, ὥσπερ λέγομεν, οὐ τὸ αὐτό· ἐν μὲν γὰρ τῇ
ποιήσει τῶν διαγραμμάτων πάντων τεθέντων εἶναι
5 ἅμα τὸ αὐτὸ συμβαίνει, ἐν δὲ ταῖς τούτων ἀπο-
δείξεσιν οὐ ταὐτόν, ἀλλ' ἀδύνατον· τὰ γὰρ λαμ-
βανόμενα πρότερον καὶ ὕστερον ὑπεναντία ἐστίν.
ἐξ ἀτάκτων γάρ ποτε τεταγμένα γενέσθαι φασίν,
ἅμα δὲ τὸ αὐτὸ ἄτακτον εἶναι καὶ τεταγμένον
ἀδύνατον, ἀλλ' ἀνάγκη γένεσιν εἶναι τὴν χωρί-

---

a The view is that of Plato, the defence (according to Simpl.) that of Xenocrates and other Platonists. It represents incidentally the modern interpretation of the *Timaeus*.
98

has been formed out of elements which once were otherwise than they are now, (*a*) if they had always been in that state and it was impossible for them to change, it could never have come into being at all; but (*b*) since it has come into being they obviously must be capable of change and not fixed in their present state for ever. Thus their present formation will be dissolved, and that formation itself arose out of a previous state of dissolution, and this process either has taken place or might have taken place an infinite number of times. If this is true, and the world either has been or might have been other than it is, it cannot be indestructible.

The self-defence attempted by some of those who hold that it is indestructible but generated,[a] is untrue. They claim that what they say about the generation of the world is analogous to the diagrams drawn by mathematicians : their exposition does not mean that the world ever was generated, but is used for instructional purposes, since it makes things easier to understand just as the diagram does for those who see it in process of construction. But the analogy is, as I say, a false one. In the construction of geometrical figures, when all the constituents have been put together the resulting figure does not differ from them ; but in the expositions of these philosophers the result does differ from the elements. It must, for the earlier and later assumptions are contradictory. They say that order arose from disorder,[b] but a thing cannot be at the same time in order and in disorder. The two must be separated by a process involving time.

See Taylor's *Commentary*, pp. 67 f. and Cornford, *Plato's Cosmology*, p. 31. [b] Plato, *Tim.* 30 A.

280 a
10 ζουσαν καὶ χρόνον· ἐν δὲ τοῖς διαγράμμασιν οὐδὲν
τῷ χρόνῳ κεχώρισται.

Ὅτι μὲν οὖν ἀδύνατον αὐτὸν ἅμ' ἀΐδιον εἶναι καὶ
γενέσθαι, φανερόν. τὸ δ' ἐναλλὰξ συνιστάναι καὶ
διαλύειν οὐθὲν ἀλλοιότερον ποιεῖν ἐστὶν ἢ τὸ κατα-
σκευάζειν αὐτὸν ἀΐδιον μὲν ἀλλὰ μεταβάλλοντα τὴν
μορφήν, ὥσπερ εἴ τις ἐκ παιδὸς ἄνδρα γινόμενον
15 καὶ ἐξ ἀνδρὸς παῖδα ὁτὲ μὲν φθείρεσθαι ὁτὲ δ' εἶναι
οἴοιτο· δῆλον γὰρ ὅτι καὶ εἰς ἄλληλα τῶν στοιχείων
συνιόντων οὐχ ἡ τυχοῦσα τάξις γίγνεται καὶ σύστασις, ἀλλ' ἡ αὐτή, ἄλλως τε καὶ κατὰ τοὺς τοῦτον
τὸν λόγον εἰρηκότας, οἳ τῆς διαθέσεως ἑκατέρας
20 αἰτιῶνται τὸ ἐναντίον. ὥστ' εἰ τὸ ὅλον σῶμα
συνεχὲς ὂν ὁτὲ μὲν οὕτως ὁτὲ δ' ἐκείνως διατίθεται
καὶ διακεκόσμηται, ἡ δὲ τοῦ ὅλου σύστασίς ἐστι
κόσμος καὶ οὐρανός, οὐκ ἂν ὁ κόσμος γίγνοιτο καὶ
φθείροιτο, ἀλλ' αἱ διαθέσεις αὐτοῦ.

Τὸ δ' ὅλως γενόμενον φθαρῆναι καὶ μὴ ἀνακάμπτειν ὄντος μὲν ἑνὸς ἀδύνατόν ἐστιν· πρὶν γὰρ
25 γενέσθαι ἀεὶ ὑπῆρχεν ἡ πρὸ αὐτοῦ σύστασις, ἣν
μὴ γενομένην οὐχ οἷόν τ' εἶναί φαμεν μεταβάλλειν·
ἀπείρων δ' ὄντων ἐνδέχεται μᾶλλον.

---

[a] Three straight lines need not be prior in time to a triangle, nor six squares to a cube. But stones and wood must
be prior in time to a house. You cannot say that in an
account of the building of a house the time element is "only
hypothetical and for purposes of instruction." The building
actually does take time. (The illustration is from Simpl.,
who explains and also criticizes this argument.)

[b] καὶ μὴ ἀνακάμπτειν = without returning on its own track,
i.e. without ever coming into existence again.

[c] The generation of a world demands a pre-cosmic state
of matter in which this change (γένεσις is a species of
μεταβολή) can take place. The destruction of the world

In geometrical figures there is no separation by time.[a]

It is now clear that the world cannot at the same time be everlasting and have had a beginning. As for the view that it is alternately combined and dissolved, that is just the same as making it eternal, only changing its shape. It is as if one were to regard the coming-to-be of a man from a child and a child from a man as involving at one stage destruction and at another existence. For it is clear that, similarly, when the elements come together, the resulting order and combination is not fortuitous, but always the same, especially in the words of the authors of this view, since they attribute each arrangement to one of a pair of opposites. If then the whole sum of body, being a continuum, is disposed and ordered now in this way and now in that, and the formation of this whole is a world, then it will not be the world which comes into being and perishes, but its dispositions only.

For the world as a whole to be at one time generated and at another destroyed irrevocably [b] is certainly impossible if it is the only one (for before it was generated there must always have existed a prior formation, without which, as we have been saying, the change could not take place), though if there are an infinite number of worlds it is more feasible.[c]

can only mean the return of this matter to its original state, out of which, if a world was generated once, it can be generated again, and it will be the same world. The theory of the atomists that there is an infinite amount of matter and an infinite number of different worlds everlastingly coming into being and perishing escapes this argument and therefore remains so far unrefuted, though also unconfirmed.

280 a

Ἀλλὰ μὴν καὶ τοῦτο πότερον ἀδύνατον ἢ δυνατόν,
ἔσται δῆλον ἐκ τῶν ὕστερον· εἰσὶ γάρ τινες οἷς
ἐνδέχεσθαι δοκεῖ καὶ ἀγένητόν τι ὂν φθαρῆναι καὶ
30 γενόμενον ἄφθαρτον διατελεῖν, ὥσπερ ἐν τῷ
Τιμαίῳ· ἐκεῖ γάρ φησι τὸν οὐρανὸν γενέσθαι μέν,
οὐ μὴν ἀλλ' ἔσεσθαί γε τὸν λοιπὸν ἀεὶ[1] χρόνον.
πρὸς οὓς φυσικῶς μὲν περὶ τοῦ οὐρανοῦ μόνον
εἴρηται, καθόλου δὲ περὶ ἅπαντος σκεψαμένοις
ἔσται καὶ περὶ τούτου δῆλον.

CHAPTER XI

ARGUMENT

The world is ungenerated and indestructible (*continued*).
*In preparation for the question whether the world is gener-
ated or ungenerated, destructible or indestructible, A. in this
chapter analyses the meanings of the Greek words conveying
those concepts. Since no English words cover exactly the*

280 b

Πρῶτον δὲ διαιρετέον πῶς ἀγένητα καὶ γενητὰ
φαμὲν καὶ φθαρτὰ καὶ ἄφθαρτα· πολλαχῶς γὰρ
λεγομένων, κἂν μηδὲν διαφέρῃ πρὸς τὸν λόγον,
ἀνάγκη τὴν διάνοιαν ἀορίστως ἔχειν, ἄν τις τῷ
5 διαιρουμένῳ πολλαχῶς ὡς ἀδιαιρέτῳ χρῆται· ἄδη-
λον γὰρ κατὰ ποίαν φύσιν αὐτῷ συμβαίνει τὸ
λεχθέν.

---

[1] λοιπὸν ἀεὶ JHLM, Simpl., Allan ; ἀεὶ E, Bekker ; λοιπὸν F.

[a] By a consideration of the whole problem of generation
and destruction.

However, it will be shown from what is coming whether this is possible or impossible. Meanwhile there are those who think it possible both for something ungenerated to perish and for something generated to remain imperishable, as for example in the *Timaeus*, where he says that the world has been generated but nevertheless will last for all future time. The views of these thinkers about the heaven have been answered so far on purely physical grounds and from the nature of the world only. When we have made our speculations more general and all-embracing,[a] the answer to this last question too will become clear.

CHAPTER XI

ARGUMENT (*continued*)

same senses, the discussion loses most of its value in translation and has little intrinsic interest for English readers. In so far as it is translatable, however, it offers a useful, because characteristic, glimpse into the workings of A.'s mind.

FIRST however we must distinguish the senses in which we use the words " ungenerated " (ἀγένητον) and " generated " (γενητόν), and " destructible " (φθαρτόν) and " indestructible " (ἄφθαρτον) ; for when words are used with different meanings, then even if it makes no difference to the argument in hand, the mind cannot but be confused by treating a concept as indivisible which is really divisible, since it remains doubtful to which of its characteristics the word applies.

280 b

Λέγεται δ' ἀγένητον ἕνα μὲν τρόπον ἐὰν ᾖ τι νῦν
πρότερον μὴ ὂν ἄνευ γενέσεως καὶ μεταβολῆς,
καθάπερ ἔνιοι τὸ ἅπτεσθαι καὶ τὸ κινεῖσθαι λέ-
γουσιν· οὐ γὰρ εἶναι γίνεσθαί φασιν ἁπτόμενον,
10 οὐδὲ κινούμενον. ἕνα δ' εἴ τι ἐνδεχόμενον γίνεσθαι
ἢ γενέσθαι μή ἐστιν· ὁμοίως γὰρ καὶ τοῦτο ἀγένητον, ὅτι ἐνδέχεται γενέσθαι. ἕνα δ' εἴ τι ὅλως
ἀδύνατον γενέσθαι, ὥσθ' ὁτὲ μὲν εἶναι ὁτὲ δὲ μή.
(τὸ δ' ἀδύνατον λέγεται διχῶς. ἢ γὰρ τῷ μὴ
ἀληθὲς εἶναι εἰπεῖν ὅτι γένοιτ' ἄν, ἢ τῷ μὴ ῥᾳδίως
μηδὲ ταχὺ ἢ καλῶς.)
15 Τὸν αὐτὸν δὲ τρόπον καὶ τὸ γενητὸν ἕνα μὲν εἰ
μὴ ὂν πρότερον ὕστερον ἔστιν, εἴτε γενόμενον εἴτ'
ἄνευ τοῦ γίνεσθαι, ὁτὲ μὲν μὴ ὄν, πάλιν δ' ὄν·
ἕνα δ' εἰ δυνατόν, εἴτε τῷ ἀληθεῖ διορισθέντος τοῦ
δυνατοῦ εἴτε τῷ ῥᾳδίως· ἕνα δ' ἐὰν ᾖ[1] γένεσις
αὐτοῦ ἐκ τοῦ μὴ ὄντος εἰς τὸ ὄν, εἴτ' ἤδη ὄντος,
διὰ τοῦ γίνεσθαι δ' ὄντος, εἴτε καὶ μήπω ὄντος, ἀλλ'
20 ἐνδεχομένου.

---

[1] ᾖ Hayduck, Stocks ; ᾖ ἡ H, Allan ; ἡ EJFLM, Bekker.

ᵃ It is most natural to assume that sense (c) means " that
which does not exist now and never could come into existence," and so, presumably, it was taken by Alex. (See next
note.) But if so, we have the curious position that A. in
enumerating the uses of ἀγένητον leaves out the sense in
which he himself believes the world to be ungenerated and
on which the question of its " ungenerated " or " generated "
nature would seem most of all to turn. He does not mention
that it can mean " something which never was generated
because it has always existed " (as in ch. xii. at 282 a 27).
Stocks in his note on ch. xii. 282 a 30 takes it that that is the
sense intended here.
ᵇ Alex. (ap. Simpl.) correlates the meanings of ἀγένητον
and γενητόν thus : ἀγένητον (a) is contrasted with γενητόν

104

The word " ungenerated " ($\dot{a}\gamma\acute{\epsilon}\nu\eta\tau o\nu$) is used (*a*) of anything which once was not and now is, if there has been no process of becoming ($\gamma\acute{\epsilon}\nu\epsilon\sigma\iota s$) or change, as happens according to some theorists with touch and motion ; it is not possible, they say, to *become* touching or moving. (*b*) Again it is used of something which does not exist, although it is capable of coming or of having come into existence. For that too is called " ungenerated," to signify that it may yet be generated. (*c*) Thirdly it is used of something whose coming-to-be is in any circumstances impossible, which cannot pass between existence and non-existence. (" Impossible " has two degrees of force, meaning (*a*) that it is untrue to say that a thing might happen, (*b*) that it could not happen easily, or quickly, or well.)[a]

Similarly the word " generated " ($\gamma\epsilon\nu\eta\tau\acute{o}\nu$) is used (*a*) of something which once was not and later is, either with or without a process of coming-to-be ; the only requisite is that it should at one time not be, at another be. (*b*) It is used of something which is *capable* of generation, the possibility being defined either as of fact or of facility. (*c*) Thirdly it is used of anything which is subject to a process of coming-to-be ($\gamma\acute{\epsilon}\nu\epsilon\sigma\iota s$) out of non-existence into existence, whether it already exists, but its existence has been the result of such a process, or its existence is not yet a fact but only a possibility.[b]

(*c*), as that whose existence is never the result of $\gamma\acute{\epsilon}\nu\epsilon\sigma\iota s$ with that whose existence always and necessarily *is* the result of $\gamma\acute{\epsilon}\nu\epsilon\sigma\iota s$; $\dot{a}\gamma\acute{\epsilon}\nu\eta\tau o\nu$ (*b*) is contrasted with $\gamma\epsilon\nu\eta\tau\acute{o}\nu$ (*a*), as that which so far has not come into existence with that which has ; $\dot{a}\gamma\acute{\epsilon}\nu\eta\tau o\nu$ (*c*) is contrasted with $\gamma\epsilon\nu\eta\tau\acute{o}\nu$ (*b*), as that which cannot with that which can come into being in any way at all.

280 b

Καὶ φθαρτὸν δὲ καὶ ἄφθαρτον ὡσαύτως· εἴτε γὰρ
πρότερόν τι ὂν ὕστερον ἢ μή ἐστιν ἢ ἐνδέχεται μὴ
εἶναι, φθαρτὸν εἶναί φαμεν, εἴτε φθειρόμενόν ποτε
καὶ μεταβάλλον, εἴτε μή. ἔστι δ' ὅτε καὶ τὸ διὰ
τοῦ φθείρεσθαι ἐνδεχόμενον μὴ εἶναι φθαρτὸν εἶναί
25 φαμεν, καὶ ἔτι ἄλλως τὸ ῥᾳδίως φθειρόμενον, ὃ
εἴποι ἄν τις εὔφθαρτον.

Καὶ περὶ τοῦ ἀφθάρτου ὁ αὐτὸς λόγος· ἢ γὰρ τὸ
ἄνευ φθορᾶς ὁτὲ μὲν ὂν ὁτὲ δὲ μὴ ὄν, οἷον τὰς
ἁφάς, ὅτι ἄνευ τοῦ φθείρεσθαι πρότερον οὖσαι
ὕστερον οὐκ εἰσίν· ἢ τὸ ὂν μὲν δυνατὸν δὲ μὴ εἶναι,
ἢ οὐκ ἐσόμενόν ποτε, νῦν δ' ὄν· σὺ γὰρ εἶ, καὶ
30 ἡ ἁφὴ νῦν· ἀλλ' ὅμως φθαρτοί,[1] ὅτι ἔσται ποτὲ
ὅτε οὐκ ἀληθές σε εἰπεῖν ὅτι εἶ, οὐδὲ ταῦτα ἅπτεσθαι. τὸ δὲ μάλιστα κυρίως, τὸ ὂν μέν, ἀδύνατον
δὲ φθαρῆναι οὕτως ὥστε νῦν ὂν ὕστερον μὴ εἶναι
ἢ ἐνδέχεσθαι μὴ εἶναι [ἢ καὶ τὸ μήπω ἐφθαρμένον,
ὂν δέ ἐνδεχόμενον δ' ὕστερον μὴ εἶναι].[2] λέγεται
281 a δ' ἄφθαρτον καὶ τὸ μὴ ῥᾳδίως φθειρόμενον.

Εἰ δὴ ταῦθ' οὕτως ἔχει, σκεπτέον πῶς λέγομεν
τὸ δυνατὸν καὶ ἀδύνατον· τό τε γὰρ κυριώτατα
λεγόμενον ἄφθαρτον τῷ μὴ δύνασθαι φθαρῆναι ἄν,

---

[1] φθαρτοί JFM, Allan; φθαρτόν EHL, Bekker.
[2] ἢ καὶ . . . εἶναι secl. Hayduck, Allan.

---

[a] It of course makes nonsense in English to say that
what is destructible may be indestructible, but what is
φθαρτόν (corruptibile) can nevertheless be ἄφθαρτον (adhuc
incorruptum).
[b] Here follow in the mss. words which mean " or it may
even mean that which is not yet destroyed, but exists, though
capable of ceasing to exist in the future." To follow Allan in
omitting these words with Hayduck seems the only possible
course. Stocks in his note gets a false parallelism with the

The meanings of " destructible " ($\phi\theta\alpha\rho\tau\acute{o}\nu$) and " indestructible " ($\check{\alpha}\phi\theta\alpha\rho\tau\sigma\nu$) are divided in the same way. We say that a thing is " destructible " ($\phi\theta\alpha\rho\tau\acute{o}\nu$) (a) if having once existed it either does not exist or need not exist later, whether or not any process of destruction and change is involved. (b) Sometimes also we give the name " destructible " to that which may through a process of destruction cease to exist. (c) Yet another sense describes that which is easily destroyed, " prone to destruction " ($\epsilon\check{v}\phi\theta\alpha\rho\tau\sigma\nu$) as one might say.

The senses of " indestructible " ($\check{\alpha}\phi\theta\alpha\rho\tau\sigma\nu$) are parallel. (a) It means that which passes from being to not-being without a process of destruction ($\phi\theta\sigma\rho\acute{\alpha}$), e.g. contacts, which now exist and now do not, without going through such a process. (b) It means that which exists but is capable of not existing, or will not exist at some future time, though it exists now. You exist now, and so does the contact; but both are destructible,[a] because there will come a time when it will not be true to say that you exist, nor that these things are in contact. (c) But in the primary and most proper sense it means that which exists and which cannot be destroyed in the sense that, existing now, it will later cease to exist or might cease to exist.[b] Finally, that also may be called indestructible which is not easily destroyed.

If these distinctions stand, we must consider what we mean by possible and impossible; for that which is in the fullest sense indestructible was so called in virtue of its *inability* to be destroyed, or

three senses of " ungenerated," since in fact the words omitted cannot do anything but repeat sense (b) of " indestructible " above.

281 a

μηδ' ὁτὲ μὲν εἶναι ὁτὲ δὲ μή· λέγεται δὲ καὶ τὸ
5 ἀγένητον τὸ ἀδύνατον, καὶ τὸ μὴ δυνάμενον γενέσθαι οὕτως ὥστε πρότερον μὲν μὴ εἶναι ὕστερον
δὲ εἶναι, οἷον τὴν διάμετρον σύμμετρον.

Εἰ δή τι δύναται κινηθῆναι [στάδια ἑκατὸν][1] ἢ
ἆραι βάρος, ἀεὶ πρὸς τὸ πλεῖστον λέγομεν, οἷον
10 τάλαντα ἆραι ἑκατὸν ἢ στάδια βαδίσαι ἑκατὸν
(καίτοι καὶ τὰ μόρια δύναται τὰ ἐντός, εἴπερ καὶ
τὴν ὑπεροχήν), ὡς δέον ὁρίζεσθαι πρὸς τὸ τέλος
καὶ τὴν ὑπεροχὴν τὴν δύναμιν. ἀνάγκη μὲν οὖν
τὸ δυνατὸν καθ' ὑπεροχὴν τοσαδὶ καὶ τὰ ἐντὸς
δύνασθαι, οἷον εἰ τάλαντα ἑκατὸν ἆραι, καὶ δύο,
κἂν εἰ στάδια ἑκατόν, καὶ δύο δύνασθαι βαδίσαι.
15 ἡ δὲ δύναμις τῆς ὑπεροχῆς ἐστίν· κἂν εἴ τι ἀδύνατον τοσονδὶ καθ' ὑπερβολὴν εἰπόντων, καὶ τὰ
πλείω ἀδύνατον, οἷον ὁ χίλια βαδίσαι στάδια μὴ
δυνάμενος δῆλον ὅτι καὶ χίλια καὶ ἕν.

Μηθὲν δ' ἡμᾶς παρενοχλείτω· διωρίσθω γὰρ
κατὰ τῆς ὑπεροχῆς τὸ τέλος λεγόμενον τὸ κυρίως
20 δυνατόν. τάχα γὰρ ἐνσταίη τις ἂν ὡς οὐκ ἀνάγκη
τὸ λεχθέν· ὁ γὰρ ὁρῶν στάδιον οὐ καὶ τὰ ἐντὸς
ὄψεται μεγέθη, ἀλλὰ τοὐναντίον μᾶλλον ὁ δυνάμενος ἰδεῖν στιγμὴν ἢ ἀκοῦσαι μικροῦ ψόφου καὶ

---

[1] στάδια ἑκατὸν secl. Stocks, Allan.

---

[a] I take κατὰ τῆς ὑπεροχῆς τὸ τέλος to mean " with reference to the aim of the maximum," *i.e.* the relevant maximum
is not an absolute one, but refers to the purpose at which the
power is directed. In some cases, *e.g.* sight, it takes a
greater power to act upon a smaller object, and therefore, in
speaking of " maximum," a distinction must be drawn (as
A. draws it in the next sentence but one) between (*a*) maximum size in the object and (*b*) maximum power.

at one time to exist and at another not. The ungenerated too was something which was *unable*, in this case unable to come into being so as to pass from not being to being, as *e.g.* the diagonal is unable to become commensurate with the side.

Now if a thing is able to move, or to lift a certain weight, we always speak with reference to the most that it can do, *e.g.* to lift a hundred talents or to walk a hundred stades. It can of course accomplish the parts within that whole, if it can also accomplish what is greater than them, but we consider it right to define the power with reference to the limit or greatest amount. Thus that which has a power at its utmost for so much, is capable also of what lies within that amount, *e.g.* if it can raise a hundred talents it can also raise two, and if it can walk a hundred stades it can also walk two. But " its power " means its *greatest* power. And if a thing is incapable of a certain amount, speaking with reference to its greatest power, then it is also incapable of anything more than that, *e.g.* the man who cannot walk a thousand stades clearly cannot walk a thousand and one.

This point need not cause us any misgivings : possibility in the strict sense must be defined with reference to the maximum *aimed at.*[a] It might be objected that what we have been saying [b] is not necessarily true, since the man who can see a distance of a stade will not see all the magnitudes within it. On the contrary, it is the man who can see a dot or hear a slight sound who will have perception

[b] Referring to the statement that if a power extends over a whole, it will also extend over all the parts within that whole.

281 a

τῶν μειζόνων ἕξει αἴσθησιν. ἀλλ' οὐθὲν διαφέρει
πρὸς τὸν λόγον· διωρίσθω γὰρ ἤτοι ἐπὶ τῆς δυνά-
25 μεως ἢ ἐπὶ τοῦ πράγματος ἡ ὑπερβολή. τὸ γὰρ
λεγόμενον δῆλον· ἡ μὲν γὰρ ὄψις ἡ τοῦ ἐλάττονος
ὑπερέχει, ἡ δὲ ταχυτὴς ἡ τοῦ πλείονος.

CHAPTER XII

ARGUMENT

The world is ungenerated and indestructible (*concluded*).
[*It is assumed that all views of the world as either generated
or destructible must imply an infinite period of non-existence
or existence for it.*] If anything has the faculties both of being
and of not being, it can only exercise each for a limited time.
A thing may certainly possess two opposite potentialities at
once (e.g. of sitting and standing), but cannot realize both at
once. But if it realizes one for an infinite time, there can be
no later time at which it can realize the other, which therefore
—even as a potentiality—disappears. Thus what exists for
an infinite time cannot have even the potentiality of being
destroyed, but must be essentially indestructible (281 a 28–
b 25). By similar arguments it is easily shown to be ungenerated, for the possibility of its generation would involve
the possibility of its not being at some time in the past. We

28 Διωρισμένων δὲ τούτων λεκτέον τὸ ἐφεξῆς. εἰ
δή ἐστιν ἔνια δυνατὰ καὶ εἶναι καὶ μή, ἀνάγκη
30 χρόνον τινὰ ὡρίσθαι τὸν πλεῖστον καὶ τοῦ εἶναι καὶ
τοῦ μή, λέγω δ' ὃν δυνατὸν τὸ πρᾶγμα εἶναι καὶ
ὃν δυνατὸν μὴ εἶναι καθ' ὁποιανοῦν κατηγορίαν,
οἷον ἄνθρωπον ἢ λευκὸν ἢ τρίπηχυ ἢ ἄλλ' ὁτιοῦν
τῶν τοιούτων. εἰ γὰρ μὴ ἔσται ποσός τις, ἀλλ'
ἀεὶ πλείων τοῦ προτεθέντος καὶ οὐκ ἔστιν οὗ

also of the larger objects. But this does not affect the argument, for the maximum as defined may be *either* in the power *or* in the object. The meaning is clear. In speaking of sight, the greater power is that of seeing the smaller thing ; in speaking of speed, the greater the distance covered the greater the power.

CHAPTER XII

ARGUMENT (*continued*)

can only admit the three types, and they are distinct : (1) that which must always be, (2) that which cannot ever be, (3) intermediate between these, that which can both be and not be, i.e. which at one time is and at another time is not (281 b 25— 282 a 22).

There follow various arguments to demonstrate that the terms " ungenerated " and " indestructible " imply each other. Whatever possesses one of these attributes possesses both, and is eternal (282 a 22—283 b 22).

(The notes to Stocks's translation of this chapter are a valuable aid to the understanding of its tortuous arguments.)

HAVING made these distinctions clear, we must proceed to what follows. If certain things have the power both of being and of not being, an outside limit must be set to the time of their being and their not being, the length of time, I mean, for which the thing can be or not be. (We are speaking of being in all the categories—man, white, three-cubits-long and the rest.) For if the time is not of a certain definite length, but is always more than any given time, and there is none laid down which must exceed it, then the same thing

111

281 b ἐλάττων, ἄπειρον ἔσται χρόνον τὸ αὐτὸ δυνατὸν
εἶναι, καὶ μὴ εἶναι ἄλλον ἄπειρον· ἀλλὰ τοῦτ'
ἀδύνατον.

Ἀρχὴ δ' ἔστω ἐντεῦθεν· τὸ γὰρ ἀδύνατον καὶ τὸ
ψεῦδος οὐ ταὐτὸ σημαίνει. ἔστι δὲ τὸ ἀδύνατον καὶ
τὸ δυνατὸν καὶ τὸ ψεῦδος καὶ τὸ ἀληθὲς τὸ μὲν
5 ἐξ ὑποθέσεως (λέγω δ', οἷον τὸ τρίγωνον ἀδύνατον
δύο ὀρθὰς ἔχειν, εἰ τάδε, καὶ ἡ διάμετρος σύμ-
μετρος, εἰ τάδε), ἔστι δ' ἁπλῶς καὶ δυνατὰ καὶ
ἀδύνατα καὶ ψευδῆ καὶ ἀληθῆ. οὐ δὴ ταὐτόν ἐστι
ψεῦδός τέ τι εἶναι ἁπλῶς καὶ ἀδύνατον ἁπλῶς. τὸ
10 γάρ σε μὴ ἑστῶτα φάναι ἑστάναι ψεῦδος μέν, οὐκ
ἀδύνατον δέ. ὁμοίως δὲ καὶ τὸ τὸν κιθαρίζοντα μὲν
μὴ ᾄδοντα δὲ ᾄδειν φάναι ψεῦδος, ἀλλ' οὐκ ἀδύνατον. τὸ δ' ἅμα ἑστάναι καὶ καθῆσθαι, καὶ τὴν
διάμετρον σύμμετρον εἶναι, οὐ μόνον ψεῦδος ἀλλὰ
καὶ ἀδύνατον. οὐ δὴ ταὐτόν ἐστιν ὑποθέσθαι
15 ψεῦδος καὶ ἀδύνατον· συμβαίνει δ' ἀδύνατον ἐξ
ἀδυνάτου. τοῦ μὲν οὖν καθῆσθαι καὶ ἑστάναι ἅμα
ἔχει τὴν δύναμιν, ὅτι ὅτε ἔχει ἐκείνην, καὶ τὴν
ἑτέραν· ἀλλ' οὐχ ὥστε ἅμα καθῆσθαι καὶ ἑστάναι,
ἀλλ' ἐν ἄλλῳ χρόνῳ. εἰ δέ[1] τι ἄπειρον χρόνον ἔχει
πλειόνων δύναμιν, οὐκ ἔστιν ἐν ἄλλῳ χρόνῳ, ἀλλὰ
20 τοῦθ' ἅμα. ὥστ' εἴ τι ἄπειρον χρόνον ὂν φθαρτόν

___

[1] δέ FHMJ, second hand of E, Stocks, Allan; δή L, first
hand of E, Bekker.

112

will have the power of being for an infinite time and not being for another infinite time ; which is impossible.

Let this be our starting-point : the impossible does not mean the same as the false. The impossible and the possible, the false and the true, may be used (*a*) hypothetically, as when we say it is impossible for a triangle to contain two right angles *if such-and-such conditions are fulfilled*, or, the diagonal is commensurate with the sides *if such-and-such conditions are fulfilled* ; and (*b*) there are some things which are possible or impossible, false or true, absolutely. Now it is not the same for a thing to be absolutely false and absolutely impossible. To say that you are standing when you are not is to assert what is false, but not impossible. Similarly if a man is playing the lyre but not singing, to say that he is singing is to say what is false, but not impossible. On the other hand to say that you are standing and sitting at the same time, or that the diagonal is commensurate with the side, is to assert what is not only false but impossible as well. Thus to make a false premise is not the same as to make an impossible premise ; and an impossible conclusion follows from an impossible premise. A man has at the same time the power of sitting and that of standing, in the sense that when he has the one power he also has the other ; but this does not mean that he is able to sit and stand simultaneously, but only successively. But if a thing has more than one power for an infinite time, there is no " successively " : it must realize the other power simultaneously. Thus if anything which exists for an infinite time is de-

ἐστι, δύναμιν ἔχοι ἂν τοῦ μὴ εἶναι. εἰ δὴ ἄπειρον
χρόνον ἐστίν, ἔστω ὑπάρχον ὃ δύναται, μὴ εἶναι.
ἅμα ἄρ' ἔσται τε καὶ οὐκ ἔσται κατ' ἐνέργειαν.
ψεῦδος μὲν οὖν συμβαίνοι ἄν, ὅτι ψεῦδος ἐτέθη.
ἀλλ' εἰ μὴ ἀδύνατον ἦν, οὐκ ἂν καὶ ἀδύνατον ἦν τὸ
25 συμβαῖνον. ἅπαν ἄρα τὸ ἀεὶ ὂν ἁπλῶς ἄφθαρτον.

Ὁμοίως δὲ καὶ ἀγένητον· εἰ γὰρ γενητόν, ἔσται
δυνατὸν χρόνον τινὰ μὴ εἶναι· φθαρτὸν μὲν γάρ
ἐστι τὸ πρότερον μὲν ὄν, νῦν δὲ μὴ ὂν ἢ ἐνδεχό-
μενόν ποτε ὕστερον μὴ εἶναι· γενητὸν δὲ ὃ ἐνδέχεται πρότερον μὴ εἶναι. ἀλλ' οὐκ ἔστιν ἐν ᾧ
30 χρόνῳ δυνατὸν τὸ ἀεὶ ὂν ὥστε μὴ εἶναι, οὔτ'
ἄπειρον οὔτε πεπερασμένον· καὶ γὰρ τὸν πεπερασμένον χρόνον δύναται εἶναι, εἴπερ καὶ τὸν ἄπειρον.
οὐκ ἄρα ἐνδέχεται τὸ αὐτὸ καὶ ἓν ἀεί τε δύνασθαι
εἶναι καὶ ἀεί[1] μὴ εἶναι.

Ἀλλὰ μὴν οὐδὲ τὴν ἀπόφασιν, οἷον λέγω μὴ ἀεὶ
εἶναι. ἀδύνατον ἄρα καὶ ἀεὶ μέν τι εἶναι, φθαρτὸν
232 a δ' εἶναι. ὁμοίως δ' οὐδὲ γενητόν· δυοῖν γὰρ ὅροιν
εἰ ἀδύνατον τὸ ὕστερον ἄνευ τοῦ προτέρου ὑπάρξαι,
ἐκεῖνο δ' ἀδύνατον ὑπάρξαι, καὶ τὸ ὕστερον. ὥστ'
εἰ τὸ ἀεὶ ὂν μὴ ἐνδέχεταί ποτε μὴ εἶναι, ἀδύνατον
καὶ γενητὸν εἶναι.

5 Ἐπεὶ δ' ἡ ἀπόφασις τοῦ μὲν ἀεὶ δυναμένου εἶναι

[1] ἀεὶ JF, Simpl., Stocks, Allan; om. EHLM, Bekker.

structible, it must have the power of not being. It exists, then, for an infinite time, but we may suppose this power of not being to be realized. Then it will both be and not be, in actuality, at the same time. That is, a false conclusion will result, because the premise laid down was false, though if the premise had not been impossible the conclusion would not have been impossible as well as false. Hence everything which exists for ever is absolutely indestructible.

It is also, and by the same arguments, ungenerated. If it was generated, it will have the power of for some time not being; for just as the destructible is that which formerly was but now is not, or has the possibility of not being at some future time, even so the generated is that which at some time past may not have been. But with that which exists for ever, there is no time during which it may not have been, whether finite or infinite, since of course if it has the power for an infinite time it has it also for a finite. Therefore the same thing which has the power of always being cannot also have the power of always not being.

Nor can it have the contradictory of its own power, *i.e.* that of not always being. Therefore it is impossible for a thing both to exist for ever and to be destructible. Similarly, also, it cannot be generated; for if the second of two terms is impossible without the first, and the first is impossible, the second must be impossible also. Thus if that which exists for ever cannot at any time not be, it is also impossible that it should be generated.

Again, the contradictory of that which is always

τὸ μὴ ἀεὶ δυνάμενον εἶναι, τὸ δ' ἀεὶ δυνάμενον μὴ
εἶναι ἐναντίον, οὗ ἀπόφασις τὸ μὴ ἀεὶ δυνάμενον
μὴ εἶναι, ἀνάγκη τὰς ἀποφάσεις ἀμφοῖν τῷ αὐτῷ
ὑπάρχειν, καὶ εἶναι μέσον τοῦ ἀεὶ ὄντος καὶ τοῦ
ἀεὶ μὴ ὄντος τὸ δυνάμενον εἶναι καὶ μὴ εἶναι· ἡ
10 γὰρ ἑκατέρου ἀπόφασίς ποτε ὑπάρξει, εἰ μὴ εἴη
ἀεί. ὥστε καὶ τὸ μὴ ἀεὶ μὴ ὂν ἔσται ποτὲ καὶ
οὐκ ἔσται, καὶ τὸ μὴ ἀεὶ δυνάμενον εἶναι δηλονότι, ἀλλά ποτε ὄν, ὥστε καὶ μὴ εἶναι. τὸ αὐτὸ
ἄρ' ἔσται δυνατὸν εἶναι καὶ μή, καὶ τοῦτ' ἔστιν
ἀμφοῖν μέσον.

Λόγος δὲ καθόλου ὅδε. ἔστω γὰρ τὸ Α καὶ τὸ
15 Β μηδενὶ τῷ αὐτῷ δυνάμενα ὑπάρχειν, ἅπαντι
δὲ τὸ Α ἢ τὸ Γ καὶ τὸ Β ἢ τὸ Δ. ἀνάγκη δὴ ᾧ
μήτε τὸ Α ὑπάρχει μήτε τὸ Β, παντὶ ὑπάρχειν τὰ
ΓΔ. ἔστω δὴ τὸ Ε τὸ μεταξὺ τῶν ΑΒ· ἐναντίων γὰρ τὸ μηθέτερον μέσον. τούτῳ δὴ ἀνάγκη
ἄμφω ὑπάρχειν τό τε Γ καὶ τὸ Δ. παντὶ γὰρ ἢ
20 τὸ Α ἢ τὸ Γ, ὥστε καὶ τῷ Ε· ἐπεὶ οὖν τὸ Α
ἀδύνατον, τὸ Γ ὑπάρξει. ὁ δ' αὐτὸς λόγος καὶ
ἐπὶ τοῦ Δ.

Οὔτε δὴ τὸ ἀεὶ ὂν γενητὸν οὐδὲ φθαρτόν, οὔτε
τὸ ἀεὶ μὴ ὄν. δῆλον δ' ὅτι καὶ εἰ γενητὸν ἢ
φθαρτόν, οὐκ ἀίδιον. ἅμα γὰρ ἔσται δυνάμενον

capable of being is that which is not always capable
of being. The contrary of it is that which is always
capable of not being, and its contradictory in turn
is that which is not always capable of not being.
Now the contradictories of both these contraries
must apply to the same thing, *i.e.* there must be
something intermediate between that which always
is and that which always is not, namely that which
is capable of both being and not being. The contradictory of each of the two contraries will at
some time be true of it, if it does not always exist.
Thus both that which not always is not will at one
time be and at another not be, and also, clearly,
that which not always can be ; at one time it is,
and at another, therefore, it is not. Thus the
same thing will be capable of both being and not
being, and this is the intermediate between the
contraries.

Put generally, the argument is this. Let A and
B be attributes which can never inhere in the
same thing ; but suppose that everything can be
characterized by either A or C and either B or D.
Then everything which is neither A nor B must be
both C and D. Now suppose E to be something
intermediate between A and B. (Since they are
contraries, that which is neither must lie between
them.) This must be both C and D, for since
everything is either A or C, this applies to E, and
so, since it cannot be A, it will be C. It will also
be D by the same argument.

That which always is, then, is neither generated
nor destructible, and likewise that which always is
not. It is clear also that if anything is generated
or destructible, it is not eternal. That would mean

117

282 a

ἀεὶ εἶναι καὶ δυνάμενον μὴ ἀεὶ εἶναι· τοῦτο δ' ὅτι
25 ἀδύνατον, δέδεικται πρότερον. ἆρ' οὖν εἰ καὶ
ἀγένητον, ὂν δέ, τοῦτ' ἀνάγκη ἀΐδιον εἶναι, ὁμοίως
δὲ καὶ εἰ ἄφθαρτον, ὂν δέ; (λέγω δὲ τὸ ἀγένητον
καὶ ἄφθαρτον τὰ κυρίως λεγόμενα, ἀγένητον μὲν
ὃ ἔστι νῦν, καὶ πρότερον οὐκ ἀληθὲς ἦν εἰπεῖν τὸ
μὴ εἶναι, ἄφθαρτον δὲ ὃ νῦν ὂν ὕστερον μὴ ἀληθὲς
30 ἔσται εἰπεῖν μὴ εἶναι.) ἢ εἰ μὲν ταῦτα ἀλλήλοις
ἀκολουθεῖ καὶ τό τε ἀγένητον ἄφθαρτον καὶ τὸ
ἄφθαρτον ἀγένητον, ἀνάγκη καὶ τὸ ἀΐδιον ἑκατέρῳ
282 b ἀκολουθεῖν, καὶ εἴτε τι ἀγένητον, ἀΐδιον, εἴτε τι
ἄφθαρτον, ἀΐδιον. δῆλον δὲ καὶ ἐκ τοῦ ὁρισμοῦ
αὐτῶν· καὶ γὰρ ἀνάγκη, εἰ φθαρτόν, γενητόν. ἢ
γὰρ ἀγένητον ἢ γενητόν· εἰ δὲ ἀγένητον, ἄφθαρτον
ὑπόκειται. καὶ εἰ γενητὸν δή, φθαρτὸν ἀνάγκη· ἢ
5 γὰρ φθαρτὸν ἢ ἄφθαρτον· ἀλλ' εἰ ἄφθαρτον, ἀγένητον ὑπέκειτο.

Εἰ δὲ μὴ ἀκολουθοῦσιν ἀλλήλοις τὸ ἄφθαρτον καὶ
τὸ ἀγένητον, οὐκ ἀνάγκη οὔτε τὸ ἀγένητον οὔτε
τὸ ἄφθαρτον ἀΐδιον εἶναι. ὅτι δ' ἀνάγκη ἀκολουθεῖν, ἐκ τῶνδε φανερόν. τὸ γὰρ γενητὸν καὶ τὸ
φθαρτὸν ἀκολουθοῦσιν ἀλλήλοις. δῆλον δὲ καὶ
10 τοῦτο ἐκ τῶν πρότερον· τοῦ γὰρ ἀεὶ ὄντος καὶ τοῦ

---

^a 281 b 18 ff.
^b i.e. as the mutual implication of " ungenerated " and
" indestructible " itself emerged from previous arguments.
Cf. ὑπόκειται and ὑπέκειτο at 282 b 3 and 5 (where the
reference was to 281 b 25 ff.). But that backward reference
does not prevent A. from subjecting the point to a new proof.
This is typical of the disjointed character of a great part of
his physical works.

that it has at the same time the power of always being and the power of not always being, which has been shown to be impossible.[a] Must we not say therefore, that if it is ungenerated, but in existence, it will be eternal, and also if it is indestructible but in existence? (I am using the words "ungenerated" and "indestructible" in their primary senses, "ungenerated" to mean something which now is, and which could not at any time in the past have been truly said not to be; and "indestructible" something which now is and which cannot at any time in the future be truly said not to be.) Or rather, if each of these terms implies the other (which means that whatever is ungenerated is indestructible, and whatever is indestructible is ungenerated), "eternal" must be implied by them both, so that whatever is ungenerated is eternal and whatever is indestructible is eternal. This is clear also from the definitions of the terms. Whatever is destructible must be generated, for it must be either ungenerated or generated, but if it is ungenerated we have already said that it must be indestructible; and whatever is generated must be destructible, for it must be either destructible or indestructible, but if it is indestructible we have already said that it must be ungenerated.

If the terms "indestructible" and "ungenerated" do not imply each other, neither that which is ungenerated nor that which is indestructible will necessarily be eternal: but that they do imply each other may be proved in the following way. The terms "generated" and "destructible" imply each other. This too[b] is clear from what has already been said, namely that there is something

119

ἀεὶ μὴ ὄντος ἐστὶ μεταξὺ ᾧ μηθέτερον ἀκολουθεῖ,
τοῦτο δ' ἐστὶ τὸ γενητὸν καὶ φθαρτόν. δυνατὸν
γὰρ καὶ εἶναι καὶ μὴ εἶναι ὡρισμένον χρόνον ἑκάτερον. (λέγω δ' ἑκάτερον καὶ εἶναι ποσόν τινα
χρόνον καὶ μὴ εἶναι.) εἰ τοίνυν ἐστί τι γενητὸν ἢ
15 φθαρτόν, ἀνάγκη τοῦτο μεταξὺ εἶναι. ἔστω γὰρ
τὸ Α τὸ ἀεὶ ὄν, τὸ δὲ Β τὸ ἀεὶ μὴ ὄν, τὸ δὲ Γ
γενητόν, τὸ δὲ Δ φθαρτόν. ἀνάγκη δὴ τὸ Γ
μεταξὺ εἶναι τοῦ Α καὶ τοῦ Β. τῶν μὲν γὰρ οὐκ
ἔστι χρόνος ἐπ' οὐδέτερον τὸ πέρας ἐν ᾧ ἢ τὸ Α
οὐκ ἦν ἢ τὸ Β ἦν· τῷ δὲ γενητῷ ἀνάγκη ἢ ἐνεργείᾳ
20 εἶναι ἢ δυνάμει, τοῖς δὲ ΑΒ οὐδετέρως. ποσὸν
ἄρα τινὰ καὶ ὡρισμένον χρόνον καὶ ἔσται καὶ πάλιν
οὐκ ἔσται τὸ Γ. ὁμοίως δὲ καὶ ἐπὶ τοῦ Δ φθαρτοῦ.
γενητὸν ἄρα καὶ φθαρτὸν ἑκάτερον. ἀκολουθοῦσιν
ἄρα ἀλλήλοις τὸ γενητὸν καὶ τὸ φθαρτόν.

Ἔστω δὴ τὸ ἐφ' ᾧ Ε ἀγένητον, τὸ δ' ἐφ' ᾧ Ζ
25 γενητόν, τὸ δ' ἐφ' ᾧ Η ἄφθαρτον, τὸ δ' ἐφ' ᾧ Θ
φθαρτόν. τὰ δὴ ΖΘ δέδεικται ὅτι ἀκολουθεῖ ἀλλήλοις. ὅταν δ' ᾖ οὕτω κείμενα ὡς ταῦτα, οἷον τὸ
μὲν Ζ καὶ τὸ Θ ἀκολουθοῦντα, τὸ δὲ Ε καὶ τὸ Ζ
μηθενὶ τῷ αὐτῷ, ἅπαντι δὲ θάτερον, ὁμοίως δὲ καὶ
τὰ ΗΘ, ἀνάγκη καὶ τὰ ΕΗ ἀκολουθεῖν ἀλλήλοις.
30 ἔστω γὰρ τῷ Η τὸ Ε μὴ ἀκολουθοῦν. τὸ ἄρα Ζ
ἀκολουθήσει· παντὶ γὰρ τὸ Ε ἢ τὸ Ζ. ἀλλὰ μὴν
ᾧ τὸ Ζ, καὶ τὸ Θ. τῷ ἄρα Η τὸ Θ ἀκολουθήσει.

---

^a I take ἑκάτερον to refer to εἶναι and μὴ εἶναι. Stocks
refers it to τὸ γενητόν and τὸ φθαρτόν, but the omission of
the article before φθαρτόν suggests that τὸ γενητὸν καὶ φθαρτόν
is being thought of as one thing. On the interpretation here
suggested the parenthesis is a reminder of the thesis established at the beginning of the chapter, that the realization of

120

between that which always is and that which always is not, something which is not implied by either of them, and this is the generated-and-destructible; for this is capable of both being and not being, each for a limited time. (When I say " each," I mean that it can for a given time be and for a given time not be.)[a] Whatever, therefore, is generated or destructible must be intermediate. Let A stand for that which always is, and B for that which always is not; let C be generated, and D destructible. Then C must lie between A and B, for there is no time, either past or future, in which A is not or B is. For the generated there must be such a time, either actually or potentially, but not for A and B—neither actually nor potentially. Thus C will be, and again will not be, for a certain limited time. And the case of D (the destructible) is parallel, so that C and D must each be both generated and destructible. Therefore the terms " generated " and " destructible " imply each other.

Now let E be ungenerated, F generated, G indestructible and H destructible. F and H have been proved to imply each other. But when terms are related as these are, i.e. when (i) F and H imply each other, (ii) E and F are never attributes of the same thing but one or other of them is an attribute of everything, and (iii) the same may be said about G and H, then E and G must also imply each other. For supposing E is not implied by G, then F will be implied by it, since everything is either E or F. But that which implies F implies also H. Therefore H will be implied by G. But this is by

opposite potentialities must be successive and not simultaneous.

121

283 a ἀλλ' ὑπέκειτο ἀδύνατον εἶναι. ὁ δ' αὐτὸς λόγος
καὶ ὅτι τὸ Η τῷ Ε. ἀλλὰ μὴν οὕτως ἔχει τὸ
ἀγένητον, ἐφ' ᾧ Ε, πρὸς τὸ γενητόν, ἐφ' ᾧ Ζ, καὶ
τὸ ἄφθαρτον, ἐφ' ᾧ Η, πρὸς τὸ φθαρτόν, ἐφ' ᾧ Θ.

Τὸ δὴ φάναι μηδὲν κωλύειν γινόμενόν τι ἄφθαρ-
5 τον εἶναι καὶ ἀγένητον ὂν φθαρῆναι, ἅπαξ ὑπαρχούσης τῷ μὲν τῆς γενέσεως τῷ δὲ τῆς φθορᾶς,
ἀναιρεῖν ἐστὶ τῶν δεδομένων τι. ἢ γὰρ ἄπειρον ἢ
ποσόν τινα ὡρισμένον χρόνον δύναται ἅπαντα ἢ
ποιεῖν ἢ πάσχειν, ἢ εἶναι ἢ μὴ εἶναι, καὶ τὸν ἄπειρον
διὰ τοῦτο, ὅτι ὥρισταί πως ὁ ἄπειρος χρόνος, οὗ
10 οὐκ ἔστι πλείων. τὸ δὲ πῇ ἄπειρον οὔτ' ἄπειρον
οὔθ' ὡρισμένον.

Ἔτι τί μᾶλλον ἐπὶ τῷδε τῷ σημείῳ ἀεὶ ὂν
πρότερον ἐφθάρη ἢ μὴ ὂν ἄπειρον ἐγένετο; εἰ γὰρ
μηθὲν μᾶλλον, ἄπειρα δὲ τὰ σημεῖα, δῆλον ὅτι
ἄπειρον χρόνον ἦν τι γενητὸν καὶ φθαρτόν. δύνα-
15 ται ἄρα μὴ εἶναι τὸν ἄπειρον χρόνον (ἅμα γὰρ ἕξει
δύναμιν τοῦ μὴ εἶναι καὶ εἶναι), τὸ μὲν πρότερον,
εἰ φθαρτόν, τὸ δ' ὕστερον, εἰ γενητόν. ὥστ' ἐὰν
ὑπάρχειν θῶμεν ἃ δύναται,[1] τὰ ἀντικείμενα ἅμα
ὑπάρξει.[2] ἔτι δὲ καὶ τοῦθ' ὁμοίως ἐν ἅπαντι ση-

---

[1] ἃ δύναται FM and later hand of E, Stocks, Allan; ἃ
δύνανται L, probably first hand of E (so Allan *ad loc.*);
ἀδύνατα HJ, Bekker. Simpl. has ἃ δύνανται in the lemma,
ἃ δύναται in the course of his exegesis.
[2] ὑπάρξει; ὑπάρχει Η (with ξ written above), Bekker.

---

[a] The case against Plato, promised in ch. x. 280 a 28-35.
[b] With this example of A.'s *horror infiniti* compare his
dogma that mathematics does not require the existence of

hypothesis impossible. The same argument proves that G is implied by E. At the same time the relation between the ungenerated (E) and the generated (F) is the same as that between the indestructible (G) and the destructible (H).

Thus to say that there is no reason why something generated should not be indestructible,[a] or something ungenerated come to destruction, as if the birth of the one and the destruction of the other took place once for all, is to destroy one of the premises already granted. The capacity for acting or being acted upon, and for being or not being, is possessed by everything for either an infinite or a limited time ; and for an infinite time only in the sense that the infinite time itself is in a way limited. (It means only that there is no greater time.)[b] As for that which is infinite in one direction, it is neither infinite nor limited.

Moreover, why was it destroyed at this particular point of time rather than any other, when up till now it had always existed, or why generated now, when for an infinite time it had not existed ? If there is no reason at all, and the possible points of time are infinite in number, then clearly there existed for an infinite time something susceptible to generation and destruction. Therefore it is for an infinite time capable of not being (since it will have at the same time the power of being and of not being), before its destruction if it is destructible, and after its generation if it is generated. If then we suppose its powers to be realized, both opposites will be present to it simultaneously. Moreover, its

an actual infinite line, but only of a finite line as long as the worker chooses to suppose it (*Phys.* iii. 207 b 29-31).

283 a

μείῳ ὑπάρξει, ὥστ' ἄπειρον χρόνον τοῦ μὴ εἶναι
καὶ τοῦ εἶναι ἕξει δύναμιν· ἀλλὰ δέδεικται ὅτι
20 ἀδύνατον τοῦτο. ἔτι εἰ πρότερον ἡ δύναμις ὑπάρχει τῆς ἐνεργείας, ἅπανθ' ὑπάρξει τὸν χρόνον, καὶ
ὂν[1] ἀγένητον ἦν καὶ μὴ ὂν [τὸν ἄπειρον χρόνον,][2]
γίγνεσθαι δὲ δυνάμενον. ἅμα δὴ οὐκ ἦν καὶ τοῦ
εἶναι δύναμιν εἶχε, καὶ τοῦ τότε εἶναι[3] καὶ ὕστερον·
ἄπειρον ἄρα χρόνον.

25   Φανερὸν δὲ καὶ ἄλλως ὅτι ἀδύνατον φθαρτὸν ὂν
μὴ φθαρῆναί ποτε. ἀεὶ γὰρ ἔσται ἅμα καὶ φθαρτὸν
καὶ ἄφθαρτον ἐντελεχείᾳ, ὥστε ἅμα ἔσται δυνατὸν
ἀεί τε εἶναι καὶ μὴ ἀεί· φθείρεται ἄρα ποτὲ τὸ
φθαρτόν, καὶ εἰ γενητόν, γέγονεν· δυνατὸν γὰρ
γεγονέναι, καὶ μὴ ἀεὶ ἄρα εἶναι.

30   Ἔστι δὲ καὶ ὧδε θεωρῆσαι ὅτι ἀδύνατον ἢ
γενόμενόν ποτε ἄφθαρτόν τι διατελεῖν, ἢ ἀγένητον
ὂν καὶ ἀεὶ πρότερον ὂν φθαρῆναι. οὐδὲν γὰρ ἀπὸ
τοῦ αὐτομάτου οὔτ' ἄφθαρτον οὔτ' ἀγένητον οἷόν
τ' εἶναι. τὸ μὲν γὰρ αὐτόματόν ἐστι καὶ τὸ ἀπὸ

---

[1] ὄν. So Prantl, Stocks, Allan. ὂν Bekker, with F alone.
[2] τὸν ἄπειρον χρόνον secl. Allan.
[3] εἶναι. So Prantl, Stocks, Allan. μὴ εἶναι Bekker, with
H alone.

---

[a] Two opposite potentialities, A. has said, obviously cannot
be actualized at the same time. But neither can they even
co-exist as potentialities, if the time of their supposed co-
existence is infinite (see 281 b 32). I take τοῦτο to be used
loosely for the double capacity, contrasted by καί with the
actuality on which the previous argument was based, and
which might be realized at any one of an infinite number of
moments. If with Stocks we take it to mean one of the
capacities contrasted with the other, it is not so easy to get
this other out of the Greek and so give force to καί.

capacity ^{a} itself will be equally present at every point of time, *i.e.* the thing will have for an infinite time the powers of both being and not being ; but this has been proved to be impossible. Finally, if the potentiality is present prior to the actuality, it will be present for all time, even when the thing was ungenerated and non-existent, but capable of coming into existence. Thus all the time that it was non-existent it possessed the potentiality of existing, either at once or later, *i.e.* for an infinite time.

It is clear also on other grounds that it is impossible for anything to be destructible and yet never destroyed : for it would always and simultaneously with being destructible be not destructible in actuality, which means that it would be at the same time capable of always being and of not always being. The destructible therefore is at some time destroyed, and if it is capable of generation it has come into being ^{b} ; for it is capable of having come into being, *i.e.* of not always existing.

From the following arguments also it may be observed that it is impossible either for anything which has once been generated to remain indestructible, or for anything which is ungenerated and has existed from all time to be destroyed. Nothing can be either indestructible or ungenerated by the agency of chance or luck, for chance and

---

^{b} Stocks objects that " τὸ φθαρτόν can hardly be the subject of γέγονεν," but since everything which is φθαρτόν is also γενητόν, it would, on the contrary, round off the argument neatly. εἰ might almost be translated " since." That εἰ γενητόν should mean " if there is something else which is generated " is difficult to believe, even in Aristotle.

τύχης παρὰ τὸ ἀεὶ καὶ τὸ ὡς ἐπὶ τὸ πολὺ ἢ ὂν ἢ
γινόμενον· τὸ δ' ἄπειρον χρόνον ἢ ἁπλῶς ἢ ἀπό
τινος χρόνου, ἢ ἀεὶ ἢ ὡς ἐπὶ τὸ πολὺ ὑπάρχει ὄν.
ἀνάγκη τοίνυν φύσει τὰ τοιαῦτα ὁτὲ μὲν εἶναι ὁτὲ
5 δὲ μή. τῶν δὲ τοιούτων ἡ αὐτὴ δύναμις τῆς
ἀντιφάσεως, καὶ ἡ ὕλη αἰτία τοῦ εἶναι καὶ μή.
ὥστ' ἀνάγκη ἅμα ὑπάρχειν ἐνεργείᾳ ἀντικείμενα.

Ἀλλὰ μὴν οὐδέν γ' ἀληθὲς εἰπεῖν νῦν ὅτι ἔστι
πέρυσιν, οὐδὲ πέρυσιν ὅτι νῦν ἔστιν.[1] ἀδύνατον ἄρα
μὴ ὄν ποτε ὕστερον ἀΐδιον εἶναι· ἕξει γὰρ ὕστερον
καὶ τὴν τοῦ μὴ εἶναι δύναμιν, πλὴν οὐ τοῦ τότε
10 μὴ εἶναι ὅτε ἔστιν (ὑπάρχει γὰρ ἐνεργείᾳ ὄν), ἀλλὰ
τοῦ πέρυσιν καὶ ἐν τῷ παρελθόντι χρόνῳ. ἔστω
δὴ οὗ ἔχει τὴν δύναμιν ὑπάρχον ἐνεργείᾳ· ἔσται
ἄρα ἀληθὲς εἰπεῖν νῦν ὅτι οὐκ ἔστι πέρυσιν. ἀλλ'
ἀδύνατον· οὐδεμία γὰρ δύναμις τοῦ γεγονέναι ἐστίν,
ἀλλὰ τοῦ εἶναι ἢ ἔσεσθαι. ὁμοίως δὲ καὶ εἰ πρό-
15 τερον ὂν ἀΐδιον ὕστερον μή ἐστιν· ἕξει γὰρ δύναμιν
οὗ ἐνεργείᾳ οὐκ ἔστιν. ὥστ' ἂν θῶμεν τὸ δυνατόν,
ἀληθὲς ἔσται εἰπεῖν νῦν ὅτι τοῦτ' ἔστι πέρυσιν καὶ
ὅλως ἐν τῷ παρελθόντι χρόνῳ.

Καὶ φυσικῶς δὲ καὶ μὴ καθόλου σκοποῦσιν

---

[1] ἔστι ... ἔστιν. Bekker's (and Prantl's) ἐστὶ ... ἐστίν is
thus corrected by Stocks and Allan.

[a] *Phys.* ii. 196 b 10 ff.

lucky events are the contrary of that which always or normally is or comes to pass,[a] whereas that which exists for an infinite time, whether absolutely or starting from a certain point, exists either always or normally. It must therefore be by nature that such things[b] at one time exist and at another do not. In things like that,[c] however, one and the same potentiality is the potentiality of opposite states, and the matter is the cause of the thing's both being and not being. Hence opposite states would have to be present in actuality at the same time.

Again, it is not true to say of anything now that it is last year, nor to say last year that it is now. It is therefore impossible for anything which once did not exist to be later eternal, for it will retain afterwards the potentiality of not being—not, of course, of not being at the time when it is (for then it is extant in actuality), but of not being last year or at any time in the past. Suppose then that that of which it has the potentiality is present in actuality. In that case it will be true to say now that it is not last year. But this is impossible, for no potentiality is of the past, but only of the present or future. A similar argument applies to that which formerly was from all eternity and later is not. It will have the potentiality of something which is not present in actuality, so that if we suppose the realization of that possibility, it will be true to say now, This thing is last year, or at any time in the past.

The impossibility of anything that was once

[b] *i.e.* things which exist for an infinite time.
[c] *i.e.* things whose existence is by nature (φύσει).

ἀδύνατον ἢ ἀΐδιον ὂν πρότερον φθαρῆναι ὕστερον,
ἢ πρότερον μὴ ὂν ὕστερον ἀΐδιον εἶναι. τὰ γὰρ
20 φθαρτὰ καὶ γενητὰ καὶ ἀλλοιωτὰ πάντα· ἀλλοιοῦται
δὲ τοῖς ἐναντίοις, καὶ ἐξ ὧν συνίσταται τὰ φύσει
ὄντα, καὶ ὑπὸ τῶν αὐτῶν τούτων φθείρεται.

eternal afterwards being destroyed, or anything once non-existent afterwards being eternal, may also be seen from less general and more scientific arguments. Things which are destructible or generated are all subject to change. Change takes place by means of contraries, and physical bodies are destroyed by the agency of the same elements of which they are composed.

B

OF THE HEAVENLY BODIES (*continued*)

CHAPTER I

ARGUMENT

Before passing on to other characteristics of the first body, A. recapitulates the most important of those already demonstrated, namely, its eternal duration, without beginning or end. He points out that those who have denied it this property have by the weakness of their arguments merely strengthened his own position, and reminds us that his view is in accordance with old, and particularly with Hellenic, religious beliefs. The beginning and end of all other motions are contained within the everlasting, all-embracing motion of

283 b 26   Ὅτι μὲν οὖν οὔτε γέγονεν ὁ πᾶς οὐρανὸς οὔτ᾽ ἐνδέχεται φθαρῆναι, καθάπερ τινές φασιν αὐτόν, ἀλλ᾽ ἔστιν εἷς καὶ ἀΐδιος, ἀρχὴν μὲν καὶ τελευτὴν οὐκ ἔχων τοῦ παντὸς αἰῶνος, ἔχων δὲ καὶ περιέχων

30   ἐν αὑτῷ τὸν ἄπειρον χρόνον, ἔκ τε τῶν εἰρημένων ἔξεστι λαβεῖν τὴν πίστιν, καὶ διὰ τῆς δόξης τῆς παρὰ τῶν ἄλλως λεγόντων καὶ γεννώντων αὐτόν· εἰ γὰρ οὕτως μὲν ἔχειν ἐνδέχεται, καθ᾽ ὃν δὲ τρόπον ἐκεῖνοι γενέσθαι λέγουσιν οὐκ ἐνδέχεται,

284 a   μεγάλην ἂν ἔχοι καὶ τοῦτο ῥοπὴν εἰς πίστιν περὶ τῆς ἀθανασίας αὐτοῦ καὶ τῆς ἀϊδιότητος. διόπερ

BOOK II

OF THE HEAVENLY BODIES (*continued*)

CHAPTER I

ARGUMENT (*continued*)

*the outermost heaven. Being thus perfect and eternal, it
cannot involve effort, and this disposes of three earlier views,
(a) the myth of Atlas, (b) the theory of a whirl overcoming the
resistance offered by the weight of the heaven, (c) the theory
of a soul moving the body of the heaven as our souls move our
bodies. All these views depend on the fallacious belief that
the heavenly bodies are made of a materia which has weight
like the four earthly elements.*

TRUSTING, then, to the foregoing arguments, we
may take it that the world as a whole was not
generated and cannot be destroyed, as some allege,
but is unique and eternal, having no beginning
or end of its whole life, containing infinite time
and embracing it in itself. The case may be
strengthened by means of the opinions of those
who think differently and call it generated ; for
if it is possible for it to be as I say, but not possible
for it to have been generated in the manner which
they describe, that must in itself incline us strongly
to a belief in its deathlessness and eternity. · There-

284 a

καλῶς ἔχει συμπείθειν ἑαυτὸν τοὺς ἀρχαίους καὶ
μάλιστα πατρίους ἡμῶν ἀληθεῖς εἶναι λόγους, ὡς
ἔστιν ἀθάνατόν τι καὶ θεῖον τῶν ἐχόντων μὲν
5 κίνησιν, ἐχόντων δὲ τοιαύτην ὥστε μηθὲν εἶναι
πέρας αὐτῆς, ἀλλὰ μᾶλλον ταύτην τῶν ἄλλων
πέρας· τό τε γὰρ πέρας τῶν περιεχόντων ἐστί, καὶ
αὕτη ἡ κυκλοφορία¹ τέλειος οὖσα περιέχει τὰς
ἀτελεῖς καὶ τὰς ἐχούσας πέρας καὶ παῦλαν, αὐτὴ
μὲν οὐδεμίαν οὔτ' ἀρχὴν ἔχουσα οὔτε τελευτήν,
10 ἀλλ' ἄπαυστος οὖσα τὸν ἄπειρον χρόνον, τῶν δ'
ἄλλων τῶν μὲν αἰτία τῆς ἀρχῆς, τῶν δὲ δεχομένη
τὴν παῦλαν. τὸν δ' οὐρανὸν καὶ τὸν ἄνω τόπον οἱ
μὲν ἀρχαῖοι τοῖς θεοῖς ἀπένειμαν ὡς ὄντα μόνον
ἀθάνατον· ὁ δὲ νῦν μαρτυρεῖ λόγος ὡς ἄφθαρτος
καὶ ἀγένητος, ἔτι δ' ἀπαθὴς πάσης θνητῆς δυσχε-
15 ρείας ἐστίν, πρὸς δὲ τούτοις ἄπονος διὰ τὸ μηδεμιᾶς προσδεῖσθαι βιαίας ἀνάγκης, ἣ κατέχει
κωλύουσα φέρεσθαι πεφυκότα αὐτὸν ἄλλως· πᾶν
γὰρ τὸ τοιοῦτον ἐπίπονον, ὅσῳπερ ἂν ἀϊδιώτερον
ᾖ, καὶ διαθέσεως τῆς ἀρίστης ἄμοιρον. διόπερ
οὔτε κατὰ τὸν τῶν παλαιῶν μῦθον ὑποληπτέον
20 ἔχειν, οἵ φασιν Ἄτλαντός τινος αὐτῷ προσδεῖσθαι
τὴν σωτηρίαν· ἐοίκασι γὰρ καὶ τοῦτον οἱ συστή-
σαντες τὸν λόγον τὴν αὐτὴν ἔχειν ὑπόληψιν τοῖς

---

¹ Stocks and Allan, with all mss. but L, omit ἡ κυκλοφορία.

ᵃ So Simpl., who by giving the words this meaning rescues
A. from making an invalid second-figure syllogism (" a limit
is in the class of things which embrace, the heaven is in the
class of things which embrace, therefore the heaven is a
limit "). But it is doubtful whether A. deserves his kindness
here, since τὸ πέρας τῶν περιεχόντων ἐστί is much more
naturally translated as " a limit is one of the things which
embrace."

fore we may well feel assured that those ancient beliefs are true, which belong especially to our own native tradition, and according to which there exists something immortal and divine, in the class of things in motion, but whose motion is such that there is no limit to it. Rather it is itself the limit of other motions, for it is a property of that which embraces to be a limit,[a] and the circular motion in question, being complete, embraces the incomplete and finite motions. Itself without beginning or end, continuing without ceasing for infinite time, it causes the beginning of some motions, and receives the cessation of others. Our forefathers assigned heaven, the upper region, to the gods, in the belief that it alone was imperishable ; and our present discussion confirms that it is indestructible and ungenerated. We have shown, also, that it suffers from none of the ills of a mortal body, and moreover that its motion involves no effort, for the reason that it needs no external force of compulsion, constraining it and preventing it from following a different motion which is natural to it. Any motion of that sort would involve effort, all the more in proportion as it is long-lasting, and could not participate in the best arrangement of all. There is no need, therefore, in the first place to give credence to the ancient mythological explanation according to which it owes its safety to an Atlas [b] ; those who made up that story seem to have had the same notion as later thinkers,

[b] Cf. Plato, Phaedo 99 c, a passage which A. no doubt had in mind. The arguments in both places are identical, namely the substitution of the teleological explanation (cf. τῆς ἀρίστης διαθέσεως above) for the mechanical.

284 a

ὕστερον· ὡς γὰρ περὶ βάρος ἐχόντων καὶ γεηρῶν
ἁπάντων τῶν ἄνω σωμάτων ὑπέστησαν αὐτῷ
μυθικῶς ἀνάγκην ἔμψυχον. οὔτε δὴ τοῦτον τὸν
25 τρόπον ὑποληπτέον, οὔτε διὰ τὴν δίνησιν θάττονος
τυγχάνοντα φορᾶς τῆς οἰκείας ῥοπῆς ἔτι σώζεσθαι
τοσοῦτον χρόνον, καθάπερ Ἐμπεδοκλῆς φησίν.
ἀλλὰ μὴν οὐδ' ὑπὸ ψυχῆς εὔλογον ἀναγκαζούσης
μένειν ἀΐδιον· οὐδὲ γὰρ τῆς ψυχῆς οἷόν τ' εἶναι τὴν
τοιαύτην ζωὴν ἄλυπον καὶ μακαρίαν· ἀνάγκη γὰρ
30 καὶ τὴν κίνησιν μετὰ βίας οὖσαν, εἴπερ κινεῖ φέρεσθαι[1] πεφυκότος τοῦ πρώτου σώματος ἄλλως καὶ
κινεῖ[2] συνεχῶς, ἄσχολον εἶναι καὶ πάσης ἀπηλλαγ-
μένην ῥαστώνης ἔμφρονος, εἴ γε μηδ' ὥσπερ τῇ
ψυχῇ τῇ τῶν θνητῶν ζῴων ἐστὶν ἀνάπαυσις ἡ περὶ
τὸν ὕπνον γινομένη τοῦ σώματος ἄνεσις, ἀλλ' ἀναγ-
35 καῖον Ἰξίονός τινος μοῖραν κατέχειν αὐτὴν ἀΐδιον
284 b καὶ ἄτρυτον. εἰ δή, καθάπερ εἴπομεν, ἐνδέχεται
τὸν εἰρημένον ἔχειν τρόπον περὶ τῆς πρώτης φορᾶς,
οὐ μόνον αὐτοῦ περὶ τῆς ἀϊδιότητος οὕτως ὑπολαβεῖν ἐμμελέστερον, ἀλλὰ καὶ τῇ μαντείᾳ τῇ περὶ
τὸν θεὸν μόνως ἂν ἔχοιμεν οὕτως ὁμολογουμένως

---

[1] κινεῖ φέρεσθαι. So Stocks and Allan, with all authorities
but E. κινεῖσθαι, with E, Bekker.
[2] καὶ κινεῖ. Bekker, with E alone, omits καὶ.

---

[a] This criticism must be aimed at the world-soul of Plato's
Timaeus. See introd. p. xxxi.
[b] Thus A.'s theology as we find it here, though apparently
making the revolving heaven the highest divinity, explicitly
avoids the criticism brought against it by the Epicurean in
Cicero's *De nat. deor.* i. 13 : quomodo semper se movens esse
quietus et beatus potest ? It is fairly certain that the present
passage, and the description of the first body as weightless

that is, they thought that in speaking of the upper
bodies they were treating of bodies which were
earthlike and had weight, when they posited for
the heaven the constraint of a living being. We
must not then think in this way, nor in the second
place must we say with Empedocles that it has
been kept up all this time by the cosmic whirl,
i.e. by having imparted to it a motion swifter than
that to which its own weight inclines it. A third
supposition is equally inadmissible, namely that it
is by the constraint of a soul that it endures for
ever [a] : for such a life as the soul would have to
lead could not possibly be painless or blessed. The
motion must be enforced, if it moves the first body
in one way when its natural motion is in another,
and moves it continuously, and therefore it must
be restless, a stranger to leisure and reason,[b] since
it has not the relief granted to the soul of mortal
creatures by the relaxation of the body in sleep.
The doom of an Ixion would hold it in an eternal
and unyielding grasp. To sum up, if it is possible
for the first motion to take place in the way we
have described, then not only is it more accurate
to conceive of its eternity in this way, but moreover
it is the only way in which we can give a consistent
account and one which fits in with our premonitions [c]

on which it depends, constitute a refinement on the theology
of the dialogue *De philosophia*, from which Cicero got his
knowledge of Aristotle. See W. K. C. Guthrie in *Class.
Quart.* 1933, p. 166.

[c] μαντεία here is explained by Simpl. as τὴν κοινὴν ταύτην
ἔννοιαν ἣν ἔχομεν περὶ τῆς ἀπονίας καὶ μακαριότητος τοῦ θεοῦ.
The passage looks consciously antagonistic to the apolo-
getic way in which Plato introduces his mythical cosmology
in the *Timaeus*. Compare ὁμολογουμένους λόγους there with
ὁμολογουμένως here.

284 b
5 ἀποφαίνεσθαι συμφώνους λόγους. ἀλλὰ τῶν μὲν
τοιούτων λόγων ἅλις ἔστω τὰ νῦν.

CHAPTER II

ARGUMENT

Are there top and bottom, left and right sides to the
heavenly sphere ? *The question sounds slightly less absurd
when we recognize that a number of notions were linked together
in A.'s mind which to us are unconnected, and of which he
reminds us in this chapter. In a sense it may be said that all
solid bodies have a top and bottom, front and back, right and
left, but scientifically speaking these are only found in
animate nature, some in the lower forms of life and others in
the higher. This is because the terms " above" and " below,"
etc., properly imply not only position but also a certain power
of movement (δύναμις) in the thing. Things which can only
move up and down (i.e. plants, which grow but do not move
about) have top and bottom only. Front and back go with
the power of sensation (forward motion implies a goal,
which implies the appetitive, which implies sensation), right
and left with locomotion. (From the commonsense point of
view these combinations are justified by the observation that
inanimate objects have no top and bottom, etc., in themselves
—turn them over and you will call top what was the bottom
before (284 b 6—285 a 27).)*

*In face of this, the question answers itself. The heavenly
sphere has been shown to be living and moving, therefore it
must have top and bottom, right and left. (The question of
front and back is not here raised. Cf. ch. v. below.) The
highest and lowest points are provided by the poles about which
the sphere turns, and of these the pole above us is in reality the
bottom : we live in the lower hemisphere (285 a 27—286 a 2).*

Note.—*A.'s reason for this last, surprising statement lies*

of divinity. But enough of this subject for the present.

CHAPTER II

ARGUMENT (*continued*)

in his belief that all natural motion starts from the right. The Pythagoreans believed that the motion of the outermost sphere (= motion of the fixed stars) from E to W was to the right, doubtless because in their table of opposites right was in the " good " list and left in the " evil."   A. however says that to our eyes this motion is leftwards.   Sir T. Heath (Aristarchus, pp. 231 f.) explains the argument thus : " ' Right ' is the place from which motion in space starts ; and the motion of the heaven starts from the side where the stars rise, i.e. the East ; therefore the East is ' right ' and the West is ' left.' If now you suppose yourself to be lying along the world's axis with your head towards the* north *pole, your feet towards the* south *pole, and your right hand towards the East, then clearly the apparent motion of the stars from East to West is over your* back *from your right side towards your left ; this motion, A. maintains, cannot be called*

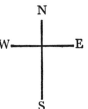

motion ' to the right.' "   A.'s view of the appearances here is in accord with Plato at Laws 760 D τὸ δ' ἐπὶ δεξιὰ γιγνέσθω τὸ πρὸς ἕω *and Epinomis 987 B, though what he says in these two passages does not agree with the* Timaeus (36 c). *This not very important point has by reason of its difficulty called forth much comment.   Of more recent discussions see* Heath, o.c. 160 ff., Rivaud, Timaeus, introd. 55 f., Wicksteed, Aristotle's Physics, Loeb ed., introd. lxii. note (a) (*a particularly interesting note*), Taylor, *Commentary on the* Timaeus, 150 f., *and E. des Places in* Mélanges Cumont

ARISTOTLE

(= Annuaire de l'Institut de Philologie et d'Histoire
Orientales et Slaves de Bruxelles, *tome* iv.), 1936, *fasc* i.
p. 135. *There is doubt about the actual meaning of* ἐπὶ δεξιά.

284 b 6 Ἐπειδὴ δέ τινές εἰσιν οἳ φασιν εἶναί τι δεξιὸν
καὶ ἀριστερὸν τοῦ οὐρανοῦ, καθάπερ οἱ καλούμενοι
Πυθαγόρειοι (ἐκείνων γὰρ οὗτος ὁ λόγος ἐστίν)
σκεπτέον πότερον τοῦτον ἔχει τὸν τρόπον ὡς
10 ἐκεῖνοι λέγουσιν, ἢ μᾶλλον ἑτέρως, εἴπερ δεῖ προσάπτειν τῷ τοῦ παντὸς σώματι ταύτας τὰς ἀρχάς.
εὐθὺς γὰρ πρῶτον, εἰ τὸ δεξιὸν ὑπάρχει καὶ τὸ
ἀριστερόν, ἔτι πρότερον τὰς προτέρας ὑποληπτέον
ὑπάρχειν ἀρχὰς ἐν αὐτῷ. διώρισται μὲν οὖν περὶ
τούτων ἐν τοῖς περὶ τὰς τῶν ζῴων κινήσεις διὰ τὸ
15 τῆς φύσεως οἰκεῖα τῆς ἐκείνων εἶναι· φανερῶς γὰρ
ἔν γε τοῖς ζῴοις ὑπάρχοντα φαίνεται τοῖς μὲν
πάντα τὰ τοιαῦτα μόρια, λέγω δ' οἷον τό τε δεξιὸν
καὶ τὸ ἀριστερόν, τοῖς δ' ἔνια, τοῖς δὲ φυτοῖς τὸ
ἄνω καὶ τὸ κάτω μόνον. εἰ δὲ δεῖ καὶ τῷ οὐρανῷ
προσάπτειν τι τῶν τοιούτων, καὶ τὸ πρῶτον,
20 καθάπερ εἴπομεν, ἐν τοῖς ζῴοις ὑπάρχον εὔλογον
ὑπάρχειν ἐν αὐτῷ· τριῶν γὰρ ὄντων ἕκαστον οἷον
ἀρχή τις ἐστίν. λέγω δὲ τὰ τρία τὸ ἄνω καὶ τὸ
κάτω, καὶ τὸ πρόσθεν καὶ τὸ ἀντικείμενον, καὶ τὸ
δεξιὸν καὶ τὸ ἀριστερόν· ταύτας γὰρ τὰς διαστάσεις
εὔλογον ὑπάρχειν τοῖς σώμασι τοῖς τελείοις πάσας.
25 ἔστι δὲ τὸ μὲν ἄνω τοῦ μήκους ἀρχή, τὸ δὲ δεξιὸν
τοῦ πλάτους, τὸ δὲ πρόσθεν τοῦ βάθους. ἔτι δ'
ἄλλως κατὰ τὰς κινήσεις· ἀρχὰς γὰρ ταύτας λέγω

* *De incessu anim.* chs. iv. and **v.**

ON THE HEAVENS, II. ii.

See Stocks's note on the present passage, and A. F. Braunlich,
" *To the Right in Homer and Attic Greek,*" American
Journal of Philology, *July* 1936.

Now since there are some who say that there is a
right and a left side to the heaven, *e.g.* the school
known as the Pythagoreans (for in fact this contention is theirs), we must consider whether, if
we must attribute these principles to the body
of the whole, it works as they suppose or otherwise. At the very outset, if it has a right and
a left, it must be supposed *a fortiori* to contain the
principles which are prior to those two. This is
something which has been worked out in the
treatises on the movements of animals,[a] being
properly a part of biology, for in living creatures
it is plain and obvious that some have all these
features—right and left and so forth—and others
some, whereas plants have only above and below.
If then we are to attribute anything of this sort to
the heaven, it is natural, as I was saying, that that
which is present in the lowest stage of animal life
is present also in it ; for each of the three pairs in
question is of the nature of a principle. The three I
mean are above and below, the front and its opposite, and right and left. These three dimensional
differences may reasonably be supposed to be possessed by all complete [b] bodies. Above is the principle
of length, right of breadth, and front of depth ;
or alternatively their nature as principles may be
defined with reference to motions, for I mean by
principles the starting-points of the motions of the

[b] *i.e.* three-dimensional, *cf.* bk. i. ch. 1.

285 b
ὅθεν ἄρχονται πρῶτον αἱ κινήσεις τοῖς ἔχουσιν.
ἔστι δὲ ἀπὸ μὲν τοῦ ἄνω ἡ αὔξησις, ἀπὸ δὲ τῶν
δεξιῶν ἡ κατὰ τόπον, ἀπὸ δὲ τῶν ἔμπροσθεν ἡ
30 κατὰ τὴν αἴσθησιν· ἔμπροσθεν γὰρ λέγω ἐφ᾽ ὃ αἱ
αἰσθήσεις.

Διὸ καὶ οὐκ ἐν ἅπαντι σώματι τὸ ἄνω καὶ κάτω
καὶ τὸ δεξιὸν καὶ ἀριστερὸν καὶ τὸ ἔμπροσθεν καὶ
ὄπισθεν ζητητέον, ἀλλ᾽ ὅσα ἔχει κινήσεως ἀρχὴν
ἐν αὑτοῖς ἔμψυχα ὄντα· τῶν γὰρ ἀψύχων ἐν οὐθενὶ
ὁρῶμεν ὅθεν ἡ ἀρχὴ τῆς κινήσεως. τὰ μὲν γὰρ
35 ὅλως οὐ κινεῖται, τὰ δὲ κινεῖται μὲν ἀλλ᾽ οὐ παντα-
285 a χόθεν ὁμοίως, οἷον τὸ πῦρ ἄνω μόνον καὶ ἡ γῆ ἐπὶ
τὸ μέσον. ἀλλ᾽ ἐν μὲν τούτοις λέγομεν τὸ ἄνω καὶ
κάτω καὶ τὸ δεξιὸν καὶ ἀριστερὸν πρὸς ἡμᾶς
ἐπαναφέροντες· ἢ γὰρ κατὰ τὰ ἡμέτερα δεξιά,
ὥσπερ οἱ μάντεις, ἢ καθ᾽ ὁμοιότητα τοῖς ἡμετέροις,
5 οἷον τὰ τοῦ ἀνδριάντος, ἢ τὰ ἐναντίως ἔχοντα τῇ
θέσει, δεξιὸν μὲν τὸ κατὰ τὸ ἡμέτερον ἀριστερόν,
ἀριστερὸν δὲ τὸ κατὰ τὸ ἡμέτερον δεξιόν, [καὶ
ὄπισθεν τὸ κατὰ τὸ ἡμέτερον ἔμπροσθεν].[1] ἐν αὐτοῖς δὲ τούτοις οὐδεμίαν ὁρῶμεν διαφοράν· ἐὰν γὰρ
ἀνάπαλιν στραφῇ, τὰ ἐναντία ἐροῦμεν δεξιὰ καὶ
10 ἀριστερὰ καὶ ἄνω καὶ κάτω καὶ ἔμπροσθεν καὶ
ὄπισθεν.

Διὸ καὶ τῶν Πυθαγορείων ἄν τις θαυμάσειεν ὅτι
δύο μόνας ταύτας ἀρχὰς ἔλεγον, τὸ δεξιὸν καὶ τὸ
ἀριστερόν, τὰς δὲ τέτταρας παρέλιπον οὐθὲν ἧττον
κυρίας οὔσας· οὐθὲν γὰρ ἐλάττω διαφορὰν ἔχει τὰ
ἄνω πρὸς τὰ κάτω καὶ τὰ ἔμπροσθεν πρὸς τὰ
15 ὄπισθεν ἢ τὰ δεξιὰ πρὸς τὰ ἀριστερὰ ἐν ἅπασι τοῖς

---

[1] These last words, which Bekker brackets, are ignored

bodies possessing them. Growth is from above, locomotion from the right, the motion which follows sensation from in front (since the meaning of " front " is that towards which the sensations are directed).

It follows that above and below, right and left, front and back, are not to be looked for in all bodies alike, but only in those which, because living, contain within themselves a principle of motion ; for in no part of an inanimate object can we trace the principle of its motion. Some do not move at all, whereas others, though they move, do not move in every direction alike. Fire, for instance, moves upwards only, earth to the centre. It is in relation to ourselves that we speak of above and below, or right and left, in these objects. We name them either as they correspond with our own right hands (as in augury), or by analogy with our own (as with the right-hand side of a statue), or from the parts which lie on opposite sides to our own, *i.e.* calling *right* in the object that part which is on our left-hand side, and *vice versa* [and *back* that which in relation to ourselves is the front]. But in the objects themselves we detect no difference : if they are turned round, we call the opposite points right and left, above and below, or front and back.

In face of this, one would wonder why it is that the Pythagoreans posited only two of these principles, right and left, to the neglect of the other four, which are no less important ; for above and below, front and back, are as distinctive from each other in all animals as right is from left. Some-

---

by Simpl. and almost certainly spurious, though appearing in all MSS. but E.

285 5 ζῴοις. τὰ μὲν γὰρ τῇ δυνάμει διαφέρει μόνον, τὰ
δὲ καὶ τοῖς σχήμασι, καὶ τὸ μὲν ἄνω καὶ τὸ κάτω
πᾶσι τοῖς ἐμψύχοις ἐστὶν ὁμοίως ζῴοις καὶ φυτοῖς,
τὸ δὲ δεξιὸν καὶ τὸ ἀριστερὸν οὐκ ἐνυπάρχει τοῖς
φυτοῖς. ἔτι δ' ὡς τὸ μῆκος τοῦ πλάτους πρότερον,
20 εἰ τὸ μὲν ἄνω τοῦ μήκους ἀρχή, τό δὲ δ ξιὸν τοῦ
πλάτους, ἡ δὲ τοῦ προτέρου ἀρχὴ προτέρα, πρότερον ἂν εἴη τὸ ἄνω τοῦ δεξιοῦ κατὰ γένεσιν,
ἐπειδὴ πολλαχῶς λέγεται τὸ πρότερον. πρὸς δὲ
τούτοις, εἰ τὸ μὲν ἄνω ἐστὶ τὸ ὅθεν ἡ κίνησις, τὸ
25 δὲ δεξιὸν ἀφ' οὗ, τὸ δ' εἰς τὸ πρόσθεν ἐφ' ὅ, καὶ
οὕτως ἂν ἔχοι τινὰ δύναμιν ἀρχῆς τὸ ἄνω πρὸς τὰς
ἄλλας ἰδέας.

Διά τε δὴ τὸ παραλείπειν τὰς κυριωτέρας ἀρχὰς
δίκαιον αὐτοῖς ἐπιτιμᾶν, καὶ διότι ταύτας ἐν ἅπασιν
ὁμοίως ἐνόμιζον ὑπάρχειν. ἡμῖν δ' ἐπειδὴ ὥρισται
πρότερον ὅτι ἐν τοῖς ἔχουσιν ἀρχὴν κινήσεως αἱ
τοιαῦται δυνάμεις ἐνυπάρχουσιν, ὁ δ' οὐρανὸς
30 ἔμψυχος καὶ ἔχει κινήσεως ἀρχήν, δῆλον ὅτι ἔχει

---

^a i.e. to have breadth a thing must have length, but
(mathematically speaking) it can have length without
breadth.

^b Enumerated as four in Catt. 14 a 26 ff., cf. Met. Δ ch.
xi. (Stocks). Ontologically, the important contrast is between things which are πρότερα γενέσει or χρόνῳ, which
arise at an earlier stage and are less perfect or complete, and
those which are πρότερα εἴδει or οὐσίᾳ, which come at a later
stage of generation, include the πρότερα γενέσει, and are
more nearly perfect.

^c The lowest of all organic substances grow, and growth
is a necessary precondition of the faculties of locomotion
and of sensation involving appetite. Thus the principle of
growth may be said to underlie the principles of these other
faculties, and so to act as principle to them. I have rendered
the sentence so as to bring out the meaning (cf. 284 b 28

times the difference is in function only, sometimes in shape as well. Above and below belong to all living things, plants as well as animals, but right and left are absent from plants. Moreover, length is prior to breadth,[a] so that if above is the principle of length, and right the principle of breadth, and the principle of that which is prior is itself prior, then above must be prior to right (prior, that is, in order of generation; the word "prior" has several senses[b]). Finally, if above is the starting-point of the motion of growth, right the place where locomotion originates, and front the goal of appetitive motion, this too gives above the standing of a first principle in relation to the other forms.[c]

One reason, then, why we may justly censure the Pythagoreans is that they omitted the more important principles, and another is that they supposed the principles which they did recognize to be inherent in all things alike. As for our own position, we have already decided that these functions are found in whatever contains a principle of motion, and that the heaven is alive and contains a principle of motion, so it is clear that the heaven

---

above). Literally translated it is: "Since above is that whence motion comes, right that from which, and front that to which it goes, in this way too above must have a kind of originating function in relation to the other two." It did not seem possible to make "whence" and "from which" indicate a difference of meaning in English: it is doubtful whether ὅθεν and ἀφ' οὗ do so in Greek, save in this instance to A. himself, for whom alone, perhaps, these notes were intended. (Growth "from above." A. believed, like Plato, that the roots of a plant were properly speaking its head. Plato, *Tim.* 90 A, Arist. *De. an.* 416 a 4.)

285 a

καὶ τὸ ἄνω καὶ τὸ κάτω καὶ τὸ δεξιὸν καὶ τὸ
ἀριστερόν. οὐ δεῖ γὰρ ἀπορεῖν διὰ τὸ σφαιροειδὲς
εἶναι τὸ σχῆμα τοῦ παντός, ὅπως ἔσται τούτου τὸ
μὲν δεξιὸν τὸ δὲ ἀριστερὸν ὁμοίων γ' ὄντων τῶν
285 b μορίων ἁπάντων καὶ κινουμένων τὸν ἅπαντα χρόνον, ἀλλὰ νοεῖν ὥσπερ ἂν εἴ τις, ἐν οἷς ἔχει τὸ
δεξιὸν πρὸς τὸ ἀριστερὸν διαφορὰν καὶ τοῖς σχήμασιν, εἶτα περιθείη σφαῖραν· ἕξει μὲν γὰρ τὴν
δύναμιν διαφέρουσαν, δόξει δ' οὐ διὰ τὴν ὁμοιότητα
5 τοῦ σχήματος. τὸν αὐτὸν δὲ τρόπον καὶ περὶ τῆς
ἀρχῆς τοῦ κινεῖσθαι· καὶ γὰρ εἰ μηδέποτ' ἤρξατο,
ὅμως ἔχειν ἀναγκαῖον ἀρχήν, ὅθεν ἂν ἤρξατο, εἰ
ἤρχετο κινούμενον, κἂν εἰ σταίη, κινηθείη ἂν
πάλιν.

Λέγω δὲ μῆκος μὲν αὐτοῦ τὸ κατὰ τοὺς πόλους
διάστημα, καὶ τῶν πόλων τὸν μὲν ἄνω τὸν δὲ
10 κάτω· διαφορὰν γὰρ ἐν τούτοις μόνοις ὁρῶμεν τῶν
ἡμισφαιρίων, τῷ μὴ κινεῖσθαι τοὺς πόλους. ἅμα
δὲ καὶ εἰώθαμεν λέγειν τὰ πλάγια ἐν τῷ κόσμῳ οὐ
τὸ ἄνω καὶ τὸ κάτω, ἀλλὰ τὰ περὶ[1] τοὺς πόλους,
ὡς τούτου μήκους ὄντος· τὸ γὰρ εἰς τὸ πλάγιόν
ἐστι τὸ περὶ[2] τὸ ἄνω καὶ τὸ κάτω.

15 Τῶν δὲ πόλων ὁ μὲν ὑπὲρ ἡμᾶς φαινόμενος τὸ
κάτω μέρος ἐστίν, ὁ δ' ἡμῖν ἄδηλος τὸ ἄνω. δεξιὸν
γὰρ ἑκάστου λέγομεν, ὅθεν ἡ ἀρχὴ τῆς κατὰ τόπον
κινήσεως. τοῦ δ' οὐρανοῦ ἀρχὴν τῆς περιφορᾶς,

___

[1] τὰ περὶ FM, Bekker; τὰ παρὰ Simpl.; τὸ παρὰ EJHL,
Allan.
[2] περὶ F, Bekker; παρὰ ceteri.

___

[a] I have left Bekker's readings unaltered. They make
tolerable sense, but παρά for περί in lines 13 and 14 is probably correct. See critical note. Simpl.'s paraphrase certainly

possesses both upper and lower parts, and right and left. We need not be deterred by the fact that the world is spherical, nor wonder how one side of it can be the right and another the left if all its parts are similar and in eternal motion. We must suppose it to resemble a being of the class whose right differs from their left in shape as well as in function, but which has been enclosed in a sphere : the right will still have a distinctive function, though this will not be apparent owing to the uniformity of shape. The same reasoning applies to the origin of its motion. Even if the motion never had a beginning, nevertheless it must have a principle, from which it would have begun had it had a beginning, and would be started again should it stop.

By the length of the heaven I mean the distance between its poles, and I hold that one pole is the upper and one the lower ; for only two of the possible hemispheres have a distinguishing mark, and that is the immobility of the poles. In ordinary speech too, when we speak of " across " the world we mean, not the line of the poles, but what lies around it, implying that the line of the poles represents above and below ; for " across " means that which lies around the line of above and below.[a]

Of the poles, the one which we see above us is the lowest part, and the one which is invisible to us the uppermost. For we give the name of right-hand to that side of a thing whence its motion through space starts. Now the beginning of the

suggests that παρά stood in his text. Stocks has no note (though Prantl whom he was following read περί), but his translation implies παρά.

285 b

ὅθεν αἱ ἀνατολαὶ τῶν ἄστρων, ὥστε τοῦτ' ἂν εἴη
δεξιόν, οὗ δ' αἱ δύσεις, ἀριστερόν. εἰ οὖν ἄρχεταί
20 τε ἀπὸ τῶν δεξιῶν καὶ ἐπὶ τὰ δεξιὰ περιφέρεται,
ἀνάγκη τὸ ἄνω εἶναι τὸν ἀφανῆ πόλον· εἰ γὰρ
ἔσται ὁ φανερός, ἐπ' ἀριστερὰ ἔσται ἡ κίνησις,
ὅπερ οὔ φαμεν. δῆλον τοίνυν ὅτι ὁ ἀφανὴς πόλος
ἐστὶ τὸ ἄνω, καὶ οἱ μὲν ἐκεῖ οἰκοῦντες ἐν τῷ ἄνω
εἰσὶν ἡμισφαιρίῳ καὶ πρὸς τοῖς δεξιοῖς, ἡμεῖς δ' ἐν
25 τῷ κάτω καὶ πρὸς τοῖς ἀριστεροῖς, ἐναντίως ἢ ὡς
οἱ Πυθαγόρειοι λέγουσιν· ἐκεῖνοι γὰρ ἡμᾶς ἄνω τε
ποιοῦσι καὶ ἐν τῷ δεξιῷ μέρει, τοὺς δ' ἐκεῖ κάτω
καὶ ἐν τῷ ἀριστερῷ. συμβαίνει δὲ τοὐναντίον.
ἀλλὰ τῆς μὲν δευτέρας περιφορᾶς, οἷον τῆς τῶν
πλανήτων, ἡμεῖς μὲν ἐν τοῖς ἄνω καὶ ἐν τοῖς δε-
30 ξιοῖς ἐσμέν, ἐκεῖνοι δὲ ἐν τοῖς κάτω καὶ ἐν τοῖς
ἀριστεροῖς. ἀνάπαλιν γὰρ τούτοις ἡ ἀρχὴ τῆς
κινήσεώς ἐστι διὰ τὸ ἐναντίας εἶναι τὰς φοράς,
ὥστε συμβαίνει ἡμᾶς μὲν εἶναι πρὸς τῇ ἀρχῇ
ἐκείνους δὲ πρὸς τῷ τέλει. περὶ μὲν οὖν τῶν κατὰ
286 a τὰς διαστάσεις μορίων καὶ τῶν κατὰ τόπον ὡρι-
σμένων τοσαῦτα εἰρήσθω.

CHAPTER III

ARGUMENT

Why do the planets, sun and moon have circular motions
which are different from the revolution of the fixed stars?

*The reason for the revolution of the first heaven is obvious.
It is a divine body, the proper activity of the divine is eternal
life, which in a body must be manifested in the form of eternal
motion, and the only motion which can be eternal is revolution*

heaven's revolution is the side from which the stars
rise, so that that must be its right, and where they
set must be its left. If this is true, that it begins
from the right and moves round to the right again,
its upper pole must be the invisible one, since if it
were the visible, the motion would be leftward, which
we deny. Clearly therefore the invisible pole is
the upper, and those who live in the region of it are
in the upper hemisphere and to the right, whereas
we are in the lower and to the left. It is the contrary of the Pythagorean view, for they put us
above and on the right, and the others below and
on the left. The truth is just the reverse. Nevertheless in relation to the secondary revolution,
i.e. that of the planets, we are in the upper and
right-hand part, and they in the lower and left ;
for the place from which these bodies start is on
the opposite side—since they move in the opposite
direction—so that we are at the beginning and
they at the end. So much for the dimensional
parts of the world and those which are defined by
their position.

CHAPTER III

ARGUMENT (*continued*)

*in a circle. It is not so clear why there should exist any
different circular motions, e.g. we cannot say that there
should be a second circular motion to supply a contrary to the
first, as we should in the case of rectilinear motions. (Where
there is an " up " there must be a " down," etc., but there are
no contrary circular motions, bk. i. ch. 4. 271 a 14.)*
    The reasons for the secondary revolutions are as follows :

ARISTOTLE

(a) *If there is a revolving body, there must be something fixed to provide a centre around which it revolves. This cannot be a part of the divine body itself, for it is its essence never to be still. This fixed centre is provided by the earth, which is thus shown to be an essential part of the universe.*

(b) *The existence of the earth involves the existence of its contrary, fire (one member of a pair of natural opposites cannot exist without the other), and these two involve the other elements for similar reasons.*

(c) *The existence of the four elements introduces the necessity for change, coming-to-be and passing-away, for none of*

286 a 3 Ἐπεὶ δ' οὐκ ἔστιν ἐναντία κίνησις ἡ κύκλῳ τῇ κύκλῳ, σκεπτέον διὰ τί πλείους εἰσὶ φοραί, καίπερ
5 πόρρωθεν πειρωμένοις ποιεῖσθαι τὴν ζήτησιν, πόρρω δ' οὐχ οὕτω τῷ τόπῳ, πολὺ δὲ μᾶλλον τῷ τῶν συμβεβηκότων αὐτοῖς περὶ[1] πάμπαν ὀλίγων[2] ἔχειν αἴσθησιν. ὅμως δὲ λέγωμεν. ἡ δ' αἰτία περὶ αὐτῶν ἐνθένδε ληπτέα. ἕκαστόν ἐστιν, ὧν ἐστὶν ἔργον, ἕνεκα τοῦ ἔργου. θεοῦ δ' ἐνέργεια ἀθανασία·
10 τοῦτο δ' ἐστὶ ζωὴ ἀΐδιος. ὥστ' ἀνάγκη τῷ θείῳ κίνησιν ἀΐδιον ὑπάρχειν. ἐπεὶ δ' ὁ οὐρανὸς τοιοῦτος (σῶμα γάρ τι θεῖον), διὰ τοῦτο ἔχει τὸ ἐγκύκλιον σῶμα, ὃ φύσει κινεῖται κύκλῳ ἀεί.

Διὰ τί οὖν οὐχ ὅλον τὸ σῶμα τοῦ οὐρανοῦ τοιοῦτον; ὅτι ἀνάγκη μένειν τι τοῦ σώματος τοῦ

---

[1] περί. So Allan; Bekker with JL πέρι.
[2] ὀλίγων. So Allan; Bekker with HLM ὀλίγην.

---

[a] Simpl. feels bound to remark here that by θεός A. means no more than the θεῖον σῶμα. In fact A. is using the word quite generally to mean the highest divinity. This however

148

*them can be eternal, seeing that they are bodies endowed with
a motion other than circular.*

*(d) And, finally, it is an observed fact that the ultimate
cause of coming-to-be and passing-away is the movements of
certain heavenly bodies in orbits and at speeds which do not
coincide with those of the sphere of the fixed stars, i.e. without
these secondary revolutions there could be no changes of day
and night, summer and winter, etc.*

*Thus the existence of the planetary motions is demonstrated
to be no less than a necessary condition of the motion of the
supremely divine sphere of the fixed stars.*

Now since there exists no circular motion which
is the opposite of another, the question must be
asked why there are several different revolutions,
although we are far removed from the objects of
our attempted inquiry, not in the obvious sense of
distance in space, but rather because very few of
their attributes are perceptible to our senses. Yet
we must say what we can. If we are to grasp their
cause, we must start from this, that everything
which has a function exists for the sake of that
function. The activity of a god [a] is immortality,
that is, eternal life. Necessarily, therefore, the
divine must be in eternal motion. And since the
heaven is of this nature (*i.e.* is a divine body), that
is why it has its circular body, which by nature
moves forever in a circle.

Why, then, is not the whole body of the world
like this? Because when a body revolves in a

for Simpl. could only apply to the incorporeal unmoved
mover, and the coincidence of the term θεός here with
οὐρανός is another indication that the unmoved mover was
not yet a part of **A.**'s theology. See introd. p. xxii.

286 a

φερομένου κύκλῳ τὸ ἐπὶ τοῦ μέσου, τούτου δ'
15 οὐθὲν οἷόν τε μένειν μόριον, οὔθ' ὅλως οὔτ' ἐπὶ
τοῦ μέσου. καὶ γὰρ ἂν ἡ κατὰ φύσιν κίνησις ἦν
αὐτοῦ ἐπὶ τὸ μέσον· φύσει δὲ κύκλῳ κινεῖται· οὐ
γὰρ ἂν ἦν ἀίδιος ἡ κίνησις· οὐθὲν γὰρ παρὰ φύσιν
ἀίδιον. ὕστερον δὲ τὸ παρὰ φύσιν τοῦ κατὰ φύσιν,
20 καὶ ἔκστασίς τίς ἐστιν ἐν τῇ γενέσει τὸ παρὰ φύσιν
τοῦ κατὰ φύσιν. ἀνάγκη τοίνυν γῆν εἶναι· τοῦτο
γὰρ ἠρεμεῖ ἐπὶ τοῦ μέσου. (νῦν μὲν οὖν ὑποκείσθω τοῦτο, ὕστερον δὲ λεχθήσεται περὶ αὐτοῦ.)
ἀλλὰ μὴν εἰ γῆν, ἀνάγκη καὶ πῦρ εἶναι· τῶν γὰρ
ἐναντίων εἰ θάτερον φύσει, ἀνάγκη καὶ θάτερον
εἶναι φύσει, ἐάν περ ᾖ ἐναντίον, καὶ εἶναί τινα
25 αὐτοῦ φύσιν· ἡ γὰρ αὐτὴ ὕλη τῶν ἐναντίων, καὶ
τῆς στερήσεως πρότερον ἡ κατάφασις, λέγω δ'
οἷον τὸ θερμὸν τοῦ ψυχροῦ. ἡ δ' ἠρεμία καὶ τὸ
βαρὺ λέγονται κατὰ στέρησιν κουφότητος καὶ
κινήσεως. ἀλλὰ μὴν εἴπερ ἔστι πῦρ καὶ γῆ,
ἀνάγκη καὶ τὰ μεταξὺ αὐτῶν εἶναι σώματα· ἐναν-
30 τίωσιν γὰρ ἔχει ἕκαστον τῶν στοιχείων πρὸς ἕκαστον. (ὑποκείσθω δὲ καὶ τοῦτο νῦν, ὕστερον δὲ
πειρατέον δεῖξαι.)

Τούτων δ' ὑπαρχόντων φανερὸν ὅτι ἀνάγκη
γένεσιν εἶναι διὰ τὸ μηδὲν οἷόν τ' αὐτῶν εἶναι
ἀίδιον· πάσχει γὰρ καὶ ποιεῖ τἀναντία ὑπ' ἀλλήλων,
καὶ φθαρτικὰ ἀλλήλων ἐστίν. ἔτι δ' οὐκ εὔλογον
35 εἶναί τι κινητὸν ἀίδιον, οὗ μὴ ἐνδέχεται εἶναι κατὰ
φύσιν τὴν κίνησιν ἀίδιον· τούτων δ' ἔστι κίνησις.

---

[a] Ch. 14.   [b] De gen. et corr. ii. 3, 4.
[c] Sc. " and their motion, not being circular, cannot be
eternal." In order to make the text state the whole argument explicitly, Prantl conjectured εἴς τι ἡ for ἔστι.

circle some part of it must remain still, namely that which is at the centre, but of the body which we have described no part can remain still, whether it be at the centre or wherever it be. If it could, then its natural motion would be towards the centre, whereas in fact its natural motion is circular. Otherwise the motion would not be eternal, for nothing contrary to nature is eternal. The unnatural is subsequent to the natural, being an aberration from the natural in the field of becoming. It follows that there must be earth, for it is that which remains at rest in the middle. (Let us accept this last statement for the present : it will be dealt with later.) [a] But if there must be earth, there must also be fire ; for if one of a pair of contraries exists by nature, so also must the other, if it is truly a contrary, and must have a nature of its own. Contraries have indeed the same matter, and the positive element is prior to the negative, as *e.g.* hot is prior to cold. And rest and weight are described as the negation of motion and lightness. Again, if earth and fire exist, so also must the intermediate bodies, seeing that each of the elements is in opposition to the others. (Let this too be assumed for the present : later we must try to demonstrate its truth.) [b]

From the existence of the four elements it clearly follows that there must be coming-to-be, for the reason that none of them is eternal, since contraries act upon each other reciprocally, and are destructive of each other. Moreover it is not reasonable that there should be an eternal movable object whose motion cannot be naturally eternal ; but these bodies have a motion. [c]

286 b "Ὅτι μὲν τοίνυν ἀναγκαῖον εἶναι γένεσιν, ἐκ τούτων δῆλον. εἰ δὲ γένεσιν, ἀναγκαῖον καὶ ἄλλην
εἶναι φοράν, ἢ μίαν ἢ πλείους· κατὰ γὰρ τὴν τοῦ
ὅλου ὡσαύτως ἀναγκαῖον ἔχειν τὰ στοιχεῖα τῶν
5 σωμάτων πρὸς ἄλληλα. λεχθήσεται δὲ καὶ περὶ
τούτου ἐν τοῖς ἑπομένοις σαφέστερον· νῦν δὲ τοσοῦτόν ἐστι δῆλον, διὰ τίνα αἰτίαν πλείω τὰ ἐγκύ-
κλιά ἐστι σώματα, ὅτι ἀνάγκη γένεσιν εἶναι,
γένεσιν δ', εἴπερ καὶ πῦρ, τοῦτο δὲ καὶ τἆλλα,
εἴπερ καὶ γῆν· ταύτην δ' ὅτι ἀνάγκη μένειν τι ἀεί,
εἴπερ κινεῖσθαί τι ἀεί.

CHAPTER IV

ARGUMENT

To demonstrate the sphericity of the heaven.

(a) *The heaven is the primary body, and the sphere the
primary solid, therefore the sphere is the appropriate shape
for the heaven. The primacy of the sphere is made to follow
from its being bounded by a single surface, just as the circle
is primary among plane figures because it is bounded by a
single line. The simple is always prior to the composite, and
the circle and sphere cannot be analysed into any simpler
elements, as e.g. a cube can be analysed into six rectilinear
surfaces. So, too, any system of classifying figures numerically must equate the circle with the unit.*

*Aristotle adds in parenthesis that this sphericity does not
only apply to the outer surface of the universe : the inner
elements are in continuous contact with the outer, so that their
surfaces too are spherical (with the earth as a solid sphere at
the centre) (286 b 10—287 a 11).*

(b) *The universe revolves in a circle, there is no void or
place beyond it (proved in bk. i. ch. 9), therefore the universe*

From these considerations, then, the necessity of coming-to-be is clear. But if there is coming-to-be, there must be another revolution [*sc.* besides that of the fixed stars], or more than one; for the operation of the revolution of the whole could only result in leaving the relations between the four elements unchanged. This too will be discussed more clearly at a later stage,[a] but for the present it is at least evident why there are more revolving bodies than one, namely, because there must be coming-to-be: coming-to-be was inevitable if there was fire, fire and the other elements if there was earth; and the existence of the earth followed from the necessity of having something fixed for ever if there was to be something for ever in motion.

[a] *De gen. et corr.* ii. 10.

CHAPTER IV

ARGUMENT (*continued*)

must be spherical. If it were otherwise, then as it turned it would not occupy the same place all the time, and there would necessarily be place beyond it, ready to receive the projecting parts which from time to time would reach and fill it (287 a 11-22).

(c) The revolution of the heaven is the standard of measurement for all other motions on account of its uniquely constant and eternal character. But " the measure in every class of things is the smallest member," hence the revolution of the heaven must represent the shortest path by which anything can set forth and return again to its starting-point (as the heaven does since its motion is circular). To achieve this the heaven must be spherical (287 a 22-30).

ARGUMENT (*continued*)

(d) *Starting from our own end, we observe the spherical shape of the earth, the sphericity of water on the earth (this is briefly proved), and we may assume that this arrangement is preserved as one goes farther and farther towards the circumference of the universe, since each element is in continuous contact with the one next beyond it.*

This last argument leads naturally to the peroration, ex-

286 b 10 Σχῆμα δ' ἀνάγκη σφαιροειδὲς ἔχειν τὸν οὐρανόν· τοῦτο γὰρ οἰκειότατόν τε τῇ οὐσίᾳ καὶ τῇ φύσει πρῶτον. εἴπωμεν δὲ καθόλου περὶ τῶν σχημάτων, τὸ ποῖόν ἐστι πρῶτον, καὶ ἐν ἐπιπέδοις καὶ ἐν στερεοῖς. ἅπαν δὴ σχῆμα ἐπίπεδον ἢ εὐθύγραμμόν ἐστιν ἢ περιφερόγραμμον. καὶ τὸ μὲν εὐθύγραμ-
15 μον ὑπὸ πλειόνων περιέχεται γραμμῶν, τὸ δὲ περιφερόγραμμον ὑπὸ μιᾶς. ἐπεὶ δὲ πρότερον τῇ φύσει ἐν ἑκάστῳ γένει τὸ ἓν τῶν πολλῶν καὶ τὸ ἁπλοῦν τῶν συνθέτων, πρῶτον ἂν εἴη τῶν ἐπιπέδων σχημάτων ὁ κύκλος.—ἔτι δὲ εἴπερ τέλειόν ἐστιν οὗ μηδὲν ἔξω τῶν αὐτοῦ[1] λαβεῖν δυνατόν, ὥσπερ
20 ὥρισται πρότερον, καὶ τῇ μὲν εὐθείᾳ πρόσθεσίς ἐστιν ἀεί, τῇ δὲ τοῦ κύκλου οὐδέποτε, φανερὸν ὅτι τέλειος ἂν εἴη ἡ περιέχουσα τὸν κύκλον· ὥστ' εἰ τὸ τέλειον πρότερον τοῦ ἀτελοῦς, καὶ διὰ ταῦτα πρότερον ἂν εἴη τῶν σχημάτων ὁ κύκλος. ὡσαύτως δὲ καὶ ἡ σφαῖρα τῶν στερεῶν· μόνη γὰρ περιέχεται
25 μιᾷ ἐπιφανείᾳ, τὰ δ' εὐθύγραμμα πλείοσιν· ὡς γὰρ

---

[1] τῶν αὐτοῦ JHM, Simpl., Stocks, and after λαβεῖν L and second hand of E; *secl.* Allan; αὐτοῦ alone (after λαβεῖν), Bekker with F and first hand of E.

pressed in warmer terms, with which Aristotle is fond of closing a chapter of discussion ; for if we consider the elements from the earth outwards we notice also an increasing fineness of texture. We may conclude that the outermost sphere of aither is smoother and more perfect than any sphere of which we have knowledge here on earth (287 a 30–b 21).

THE shape of the heaven must be spherical. That is most suitable to its substance, and is the primary shape in nature. But let us discuss the question of what is the primary shape, both in plane surfaces and in solids. Every plane figure is bounded either by straight lines or by a circumference ; the rectilinear is bounded by several lines, the circular by one only. Thus since in every genus the one is by nature prior to the many, and the simple to the composite, the circle must be the primary plane figure. Also, if the term " perfect " is applied, according to our previous definition, to that outside which no part of itself can be found,[a] and addition to a straight line is always possible, to a circle never, the circumference of the circle must be a perfect line : granted therefore that the perfect is prior to the imperfect, this argument too demonstrates the priority of the circle to other figures. By the same reasoning the sphere is the primary solid, for it alone is bounded by a single surface, rectilinear solids by several. The place of

---

[a] This is not quite the same as the definition of " perfect " at *Phys.* iii. 207 a 8, to which Stocks refers (οὗ μηδὲν ἔξω, τοῦτο τέλειον. *Cf.* also *Met.* 1055 a 12). In order to bring the two into agreement, Allan would omit the words τῶν αὐτοῦ, but the evidence of Simpl. is strongly in favour of retaining them.

286 b

ἔχει ὁ κύκλος ἐν τοῖς ἐπιπέδοις, οὕτως ἡ σφαῖρα
ἐν τοῖς στερεοῖς. ἔτι δὲ καὶ οἱ διαιροῦντες εἰς
ἐπίπεδα καὶ ἐξ ἐπιπέδων τὰ σώματα γεννῶντες
μεμαρτυρηκέναι φαίνονται τούτοις· μόνην γὰρ τῶν
στερεῶν οὐ διαιροῦσι τὴν σφαῖραν ὡς οὐκ ἔχουσαν
30 πλείους ἐπιφανείας ἢ μίαν· ἡ γὰρ εἰς τὰ ἐπίπεδα
διαίρεσις οὐχ ὡς ἂν τέμνων τις εἰς τὰ μέρη διέλοι
τὸ ὅλον, τοῦτον διαιρεῖται τὸν τρόπον, ἀλλ' ὡς εἰς
ἕτερα τῷ εἴδει.

Ὅτι μὲν οὖν πρῶτόν ἐστιν ἡ σφαῖρα τῶν στερεῶν
σχημάτων, δῆλον. ἔστι δὲ καὶ κατὰ τὸν ἀριθμὸν
35 τὴν τάξιν ἀποδιδοῦσιν οὕτω τιθεμένοις εὐλογώτατον, τὸν μὲν κύκλον κατὰ τὸ ἕν, τὸ δὲ τρίγωνον
287 a κατὰ τὴν δυάδα, ἐπειδὴ δύο ὀρθαί. ἐὰν δὲ τὸ ἓν
κατὰ τὸ τρίγωνον, ὁ κύκλος οὐκέτι ἔσται σχῆμα.
ἐπεὶ δὲ τὸ μὲν πρῶτον σχῆμα τοῦ πρώτου σώματος, πρῶτον δὲ σῶμα τὸ ἐν τῇ ἐσχάτῃ περιφορᾷ,
5 σφαιροειδὲς ἂν εἴη τὸ τὴν κύκλῳ περιφερόμενον
φοράν.

Καὶ τὸ συνεχὲς ἄρα ἐκείνῳ· τὸ γὰρ τῷ σφαιροειδεῖ
συνεχὲς σφαιροειδές. ὡσαύτως δὲ καὶ τὰ πρὸς
τὸ μέσον τούτων· τὰ γὰρ ὑπὸ τοῦ σφαιροειδοῦς
περιεχόμενα καὶ ἁπτόμενα ὅλα σφαιροειδῆ ἀνάγκη
εἶναι· τὰ δὲ κάτω [τῆς τῶν πλανήτων]¹ ἅπτεται

---

¹ τῆς τῶν πλανήτων secl. Allan.

ᵃ The theory of Plato in the *Timaeus*, criticized below,
bk. iii. ch. 1.

ᵇ *i.e.* it is not that a sphere is indivisible, but any division
of it can only be into parts belonging to the same kind
(*sc.* body) as the whole, whereas the " division " which these
thinkers are seeking means theoretical analysis into elements

the sphere among solids is the same as that of the
circle among plane figures. Even those who divide
bodies up into surfaces and generate them out of
surfaces[a] seem to agree with this, for the sphere is
the one solid which they do not divide, holding
that it has only one surface, not a plurality ; for
their division into surfaces does not mean division
in the manner of one cutting a whole into its parts,
but division into elements specifically different.[b]

It is clear, then, that the sphere is the first solid
figure, and it would also be most natural to give
it that place if one ranked figures according to
number, the circle corresponding to one and the
triangle to two, on account of its two right angles—
for if one gives unity to the triangle, the circle
will cease to be a figure. But the primary figure
belongs to the primary body, and the primary
body is that which is at the farthest circumference,
hence it, the body which revolves in a circle, must
be spherical in shape.

The same must be true of the body which is
contiguous[c] to it, for what is contiguous to the
spherical is spherical, and also of those bodies
which lie nearer the centre, for bodies which are
surrounded by the spherical and touch it at all
points must themselves be spherical, and the lower

of a simpler kind—solid bodies into surfaces and surfaces
into lines. Thus a cube can be " divided " into six rect-
angles, a rectangle into four lines, but no similar analysis
can be made of a sphere, if it has only one surface bound-
ing it.

[c] I do not translate συνεχής consistently as = " continuous," because Aristotle does not seem to be consistent in
his use of it. It seems better to keep " continuous " to
represent the strict sense of συνεχής, as described in note
on 287 b 1 below.

287 a
10 τῆς ἐπάνω σφαίρας. ὥστε σφαιροειδὴς ἂν εἴη
πᾶσα· πάντα γὰρ ἅπτεται καὶ συνεχῆ ἐστι ταῖς
σφαίραις.

Ἔτι δὲ ἐπεὶ φαίνεται καὶ ὑπόκειται κύκλῳ
περιφέρεσθαι τὸ πᾶν, δέδεικται δ' ὅτι τῆς ἐσχάτης
περιφορᾶς οὔτε κενόν ἐστιν ἔξωθεν οὔτε τόπος,
ἀνάγκη καὶ διὰ ταῦτα σφαιροειδῆ εἶναι αὐτόν. εἰ
15 γὰρ ἔσται εὐθύγραμμος, συμβήσεται καὶ τόπον
ἔξω εἶναι καὶ σῶμα καὶ κενόν. κύκλῳ γὰρ στρεφόμενον τὸ εὐθύγραμμον οὐδέποτε τὴν αὐτὴν ἐφέξει
χώραν, ἀλλ' ὅπου πρότερον ἦν σῶμα, νῦν οὐκ
ἔσται, καὶ οὗ νῦν οὐκ ἔστι, πάλιν ἔσται, διὰ τὴν
παράλλαξιν τῶν γωνιῶν. ὁμοίως δὲ κἂν εἴ τι ἄλλο
20 σχῆμα γένοιτο μὴ ἴσας ἔχον τὰς ἐκ τοῦ μέσου
γραμμάς, οἷον φακοειδὲς ἢ ὠοειδές· ἐν ἅπασι γὰρ
συμβήσεται καὶ τόπον ἔξω καὶ κενὸν εἶναι τῆς
φορᾶς, διὰ τὸ μὴ τὴν αὐτὴν χώραν κατέχειν τὸ
ὅλον.

Ἔτι δ' εἰ τῶν μὲν κινήσεων τὸ μέτρον ἡ τοῦ
οὐρανοῦ φορὰ διὰ τὸ εἶναι μόνη συνεχὴς καὶ
25 ὁμαλὴς καὶ ἀίδιος, ἐν ἑκάστῳ δὲ μέτρον τὸ ἐλάχιστον, ἐλαχίστη δὲ κίνησις ἡ ταχίστη, δῆλον ὅτι
ταχίστη ἂν εἴη πασῶν τῶν κινήσεων ἡ τοῦ οὐρανοῦ
κίνησις. ἀλλὰ μὴν τῶν ἀφ' αὐτοῦ ἐφ' αὑτὸ[1] ἐλαχίστη ἐστὶν ἡ τοῦ κύκλου γραμμή· κατὰ δὲ τὴν
ἐλαχίστην ταχίστη ἡ κίνησις· ὥστ' εἰ ὁ οὐρανὸς

---

[1] ἀφ' αὑτοῦ ἐφ' αὑτὸ (or ἑαυτοῦ . . . ἑαυτὸ), EJHM, Simpl.
(probably, though his reading is not quite certain), Stocks,
Allan; ἀπὸ τοῦ αὐτοῦ ἐπὶ τὸ αὐτὸ F, Bekker.

158

bodies are in contact with the sphere above. It is, then, spherical through and through, seeing that everything in it is in continuous contact with the spheres.

Again, since it is an observed fact, and assumed in these arguments, that the whole revolves in a circle, and it has been shown that beyond the outermost circumference there is neither void nor place, this provides another reason why the heaven must be spherical. For if it is bounded by straight lines, that will involve the existence of place, body, and void. A rectilinear body revolving in a circle will never occupy the same space, but owing to the change in position *a* of the corners there will at one time be no body where there was body before, and there will be body again where now there is none. It would be the same if it were of some other shape whose radii were unequal, that of a lentil or an egg for example. All will involve the existence of place and void outside the revolution, because the whole does not occupy the same space throughout.

Again, the revolution of the heaven is the measure of all motions, because it alone is continuous and unvarying and eternal, the measure in every class of things is the smallest member, and the shortest motion is the quickest, therefore the motion of the heaven must clearly be the quickest of all motions. But the shortest path of those which return upon their starting-point is represented by the circumference of a circle and the quickest motion is that along the shortest path. If therefore the heaven

---

a For παράλλαξις *cf.* Plato, *Tim.* 22 D and *Politicus* 269 E.

30 κύκλῳ τε φέρεται καὶ τάχιστα κινεῖται, σφαιροειδῆ
αὐτὸν ἀνάγκη εἶναι.

Λάβοι δ᾽ ἄν τις καὶ ἐκ τῶν περὶ τὸ μέσον ἱδρυ-
μένων σωμάτων ταύτην τὴν πίστιν. εἰ γὰρ τὸ μὲν
ὕδωρ ἐστὶ περὶ τὴν γῆν, ὁ δ᾽ ἀὴρ περὶ τὸ ὕδωρ, τὸ
δὲ πῦρ περὶ τὸν ἀέρα, καὶ τὰ ἄνω σώματα κατὰ
τὸν αὐτὸν λόγον· συνεχῆ μὲν γὰρ οὐκ ἔστιν, ἅπτεται
287 b δὲ τούτων. ἡ δὲ τοῦ ὕδατος ἐπιφάνεια σφαιροειδής
ἐστιν, τὸ δὲ τῷ σφαιροειδεῖ συνεχὲς ἢ κείμενον
περὶ τὸ σφαιροειδὲς καὶ αὐτὸ τοιοῦτον ἀναγκαῖον
εἶναι· ὥστε κἂν διὰ τοῦτο φανερὸν εἴη ὅτι σφαιροειδής ἐστιν ὁ οὐρανός.

5 Ἀλλὰ μὴν ὅτι γε ἡ τοῦ ὕδατος ἐπιφάνεια τοιαύτη
φανερόν, ὑπόθεσιν λαβοῦσιν ὅτι πέφυκεν ἀεὶ συρρεῖν
τὸ ὕδωρ εἰς τὸ κοιλότερον· κοιλότερον δέ ἐστι τὸ
τοῦ κέντρου ἐγγύτερον. ἤχθωσαν οὖν ἐκ τοῦ
κέντρου ἡ ΑΒ καὶ ἡ ΑΓ, καὶ ἐπεζεύχθω ἐφ᾽ ἧς ΒΓ.
ἡ οὖν ἀχθεῖσα ἐπὶ τὴν βάσιν, ἐφ᾽ ἧς ΑΔ, ἐλάττων
10 ἐστὶ τῶν ἐκ τοῦ κέντρου· κοιλότερος ἄρα ὁ τόπος.
ὥστε περιρρεύσεται τὸ ὕδωρ, ἕως ἂν ἰσασθῇ. ἴση
δὲ ταῖς ἐκ τοῦ κέντρου ἡ ΑΕ. ὥστ᾽ ἀνάγκη πρὸς
ταῖς ἐκ τοῦ κέντρου εἶναι τὸ ὕδωρ· τότε γὰρ
ἠρεμήσει. ἡ δὲ τῶν ἐκ τοῦ κέντρου ἁπτομένη

---

^a The difference between συνεχές and ἁπτόμενον is ex-

160

(a) revolves in a circle and (b) moves faster than anything else, it must be spherical.

One might also be brought to this belief by consideration of the bodies situated around the centre ; for if water is found around the earth, air around water, and fire around air, the upper bodies will follow the same arrangement, seeing that, although not co-terminous, they are contiguous with the others.ᵃ But the surface of water is spherical, and what is co-terminous with the spherical or lies around it must be of the same shape itself. So by this argument too the spherical shape of the heaven is clear.

As for the sphericity of the surface of water, that is demonstrable from the premise that it always runs together into the hollowest place, and " hollowest " means " nearest to the centre." Let AB and AC be straight lines drawn from the centre, and joined by BC. Then the line AD, drawn as far as the base, is shorter than the original lines from the centre, and the place occupied by D is a hollow. Hence the water will flow round it until it has filled it up. The line AE, on the other hand, is equal to the radii, and thus it is at the extremities of the radii that the water must lie : there it will be at rest. But the line which is at the extremities of the radii is the circumference of a circle. There-

---

plained in *Phys.* v. 3. Things are said to touch (ἅπτεσθαι) when their extremes occupy the same place, but to be co-terminous or continuous (συνεχῆ) when they *share the same extreme limit,* or as A. puts it, when their limits " have become one and the same and are *held together,* as the name implies " (*Phys.* 227 a 13). Hence, as Stocks says, if these bodies were continuous with the heavenly body they would have to move with the same motion as it.

287 b

περιφερής· σφαιροειδὴς ἄρα ἡ τοῦ ὕδατος ἐπιφάνεια, ἐφ' ἧς ΒΕΓ.

15 Ὅτι μὲν οὖν σφαιροειδής ἐστιν ὁ κόσμος, δῆλον ἐκ τούτων, καὶ ὅτι κατ' ἀκρίβειαν ἔντορνος οὕτως ὥστε μηθὲν μήτε χειρόκμητον ἔχειν παραπλησίως μήτ' ἄλλο μηθὲν τῶν παρ' ἡμῖν ἐν ὀφθαλμοῖς φαινομένων. ἐξ ὧν γὰρ τὴν σύστασιν εἴληφεν, οὐδὲν οὕτω δυνατὸν ὁμαλότητα δέξασθαι καὶ ἀκρί-
20 βειαν ὡς ἡ τοῦ πέριξ σώματος φύσις· δῆλον γὰρ ὡς ἀνάλογον ἔχει, καθάπερ ὕδωρ πρὸς γῆν, καὶ τὰ πλεῖον ἀεὶ ἀπέχοντα τῶν στοιχείων.

CHAPTER V

ARGUMENT

Why does the heaven revolve in one direction rather than the other ?

Suppose its movement starts from A, why should it proceed towards B rather than towards C ? The question might be

thought (a) trivial, because in any case there is no opposition between motions round a circle in different directions, or (b) hopelessly difficult. But (a) although there is no opposition involved, yet there must be a reason for the direction taken, since nothing to do with an eternal motion can happen uncaused or by chance ; (b) without boasting that we are capable of determining with strict

fore the surface of water, represented by BEC, is spherical.[a]

Our arguments have clearly shown that the universe is spherical, and so accurately turned that nothing made by man, nor anything visible to us on the earth, can be compared to it. For of the elements of which it is composed, none is capable of taking such a smooth and accurate finish as the nature of the body which encompasses the rest ; for the more distant elements must become ever finer in texture in proportion as water is finer than earth.

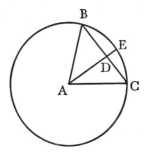

CHAPTER V

ARGUMENT (*continued*)

accuracy the true and inviolable proof, it is yet better to state what is likely to be true than to give up altogether.

The probable reason, then, is that, just as the Universe has been shown to have a top and bottom, right and left, of which one has priority over the other (e.g. the upper regions are the place of divinity), and hence motion to that place (upward) has priority over motion to its opposite (downward), so it also

*has a front and back, and hence a forward and a backward
motion, of which one has priority over the other. Now nature
always follows the best course, therefore the reason for the
direction taken by the heaven is probably that that direction
is forward and therefore prior.*

*[To this there is an obvious objection. A. refers to the dis-
cussions of bk. i, ch. 4, when it was shown that motion one
way round the circumference of a circle was not the contrary
of motion the other way round, because both motions were
from the same point back to the same point, and contrary
motions were motions to opposite termini. How then can one
be forward motion and the other backward? These would
surely be defined as motion to the front and to the back respectively, but as both the motions involved are circular, both
go to the same place. Wicksteed has the following MS. note:
"It has been shown that the South pole is the top, and therefore
the antipodal horizontal hemisphere the superior. Now as*

287 b 22 Ἐπεὶ δ' ἔστι διχῶς ἐπὶ τοῦ κύκλου κινηθῆναι,
οἷον ἀπὸ τοῦ Α τὴν μὲν ἐπὶ τὸ Β τὴν δ' ἐπὶ τὸ Γ,
ὅτι μὲν οὖν οὐκ εἰσὶν ἐναντίαι αὗται, πρότερον
25 εἴρηται. ἀλλ' εἰ μηδὲν ὡς ἔτυχε μηδ' ἀπὸ ταὐτομάτου ἐνδέχεται ἐν τοῖς ἀϊδίοις εἶναι, ὁ δ' οὐρανὸς
ἀΐδιος καὶ ἡ κύκλῳ φορά, διὰ τίνα ποτ' αἰτίαν ἐπὶ
θάτερα φέρεται, ἀλλ' οὐκ ἐπὶ θάτερα; ἀνάγκη
γὰρ καὶ τοῦτο ἢ ἀρχὴν εἶναι ἢ εἶναι αὐτοῦ ἀρχήν.
ἴσως μὲν οὖν τὸ περὶ ἐνίων ἀποφαίνεσθαί τι
30 πειρᾶσθαι καὶ τὸ περὶ πάντων καὶ τὸ παριέναι
μηθὲν τάχ' ἂν δόξειεν εἶναι σημεῖον ἢ πολλῆς
εὐηθείας ἢ πολλῆς προθυμίας. οὐ μὴν δίκαιόν γε
πᾶσιν ὁμοίως ἐπιτιμᾶν, ἀλλ' ὁρᾶν δεῖ τὴν αἰτίαν
τοῦ λέγειν τίς ἐστιν, ἔτι δὲ πῶς ἔχων τῷ πιστεύειν,

*the higher is superior to the lower so is the front to the back.
If the motion of the heaven is perfect, it must be to the front,
and if right and left are as we have said then " front " will
be taken first on counter-clockwise movement of the heavens
regarded from the South regions.   The question we have raised
shows that the heaven has front and back, and which it is is
shown by the actual motion, and caused by the perfect* αἰτία
itself, which makes one region τιμώτερον as evinced by
movement being towards it."   This seems to be Simplicius's
view too (cf. the reference to the North pole at 420. 30), and
although it does not seem to answer the objection that circular
motion in either direction must be to both front and back, the
fact that motion in one direction goes first to front and then
to back may have seemed to Aristotle sufficient justification
for putting forward an argument whose cogency he himself
describes as questionable.*]

CIRCULAR motion has two possible directions ;
beginning from A, it may lead towards B or towards
C. It has already been stated that these two
motions are not mutually contrary,[a] but nevertheless—since nothing which happens by chance and
at random can rank as eternal, and the heaven and
its circular motion are eternal—what is the reason
why it moves in one direction and not the other ?
It must be either itself an ultimate principle or
dependent on an ultimate principle. It may be objected that the attempt to furnish proof of everything
indiscriminately, omitting nothing, seems to betoken
either an excessive simple-mindedness or an excessive zeal. Yet this censure is not always equally
just : one must see what is the reason for speaking,
and what sort of conviction the speaker is aiming at,

---

[a] Bk. i. ch. 4. Both are movements *from* the same
place *to* the same place.

287 b

288 a

πότερον ἀνθρωπίνως ἢ καρτερώτερον.¹ ταῖς μὲν
οὖν ἀκριβεστέραις ἀνάγκαις ὅταν τις ἐπιτύχῃ, τότε
χάριν ἔχειν δεῖ τοῖς εὑρίσκουσι, νῦν δὲ τὸ φαινόμενον ῥητέον.

Εἰ γὰρ ἡ φύσις ἀεὶ ποιεῖ τῶν ἐνδεχομένων τὸ
βέλτιστον, ἔστι δὲ καθάπερ τῶν ἐπὶ τῆς εὐθείας
5 φορῶν ἡ πρὸς τὸν ἄνω τόπον τιμιωτέρα (θειό-
τερος γὰρ ὁ ἄνω τόπος τοῦ κάτω), τὸν αὐτὸν
τρόπον καὶ ἡ εἰς τὸ πρόσθεν τῆς εἰς τοὔπισθεν,
ἔχει δή,² εἴπερ καὶ τὸ δεξιὸν καὶ τὸ ἀριστερόν,
καθάπερ ἐλέχθη πρότερον (καὶ μαρτυρεῖ δ' ἡ
ῥηθεῖσα ἀπορία ὅτι ἔχει), τὸ πρότερον καὶ ὕστερον·
αὕτη γὰρ ἡ αἰτία λύει τὴν ἀπορίαν. εἰ γὰρ ἔχει
10 ὡς ἐνδέχεται βέλτιστα, αὕτη ἂν εἴη αἰτία καὶ τοῦ
εἰρημένου· βέλτιστον γὰρ κινεῖσθαι ἁπλῆν τε κίνησιν
καὶ ἄπαυστον, καὶ ταύτην ἐπὶ τὸ τιμιώτερον.

¹ καρτερώτερον. Bekker follows L in reading καρτερικώ-
τερον, but Stocks refers to Plato, Phaedo 77 A, Theaet. 169 B
for καρτερός in this connexion.
² δὴ Prantl, Stocks, Allan; δὲ EL. Bekker omits, with
FHMJ.

ᵃ In this sentence I have, with Stocks and Allan, followed
Prantl's ἔχει δή, εἴπερ at 288 a 6, and his punctuation of
the whole. The translation also is on the lines of Prantl
and Stocks, but it cannot be said that the subject which it
postulates for ἔχει at 288 a 6 (namely, τὸ πρόσθεν καὶ
τοὔπισθεν) is satisfactory. It seems possible that ὁ οὐρανός
so dominates the chapter as the logical subject of the whole,

CHAPTER VI

ARGUMENT

To demonstrate that the motion of the sphere of the fixed
stars is at a uniform speed.

whether merely human or something more unassailable. Whenever anyone hits upon proofs of a more strictly compelling nature, then we must show due gratitude to the discoverer, but for the present we must state whatever seems plausible.

If nature always produces the best result possible, and if, in the same way as of two rectilinear motions the upward one is superior (because the upper place is more divine than the lower, so forward motion is superior to backward, then this pair of motions too contains a prior and a posterior ; for so indeed do left and right, as has been previously explained and as the difficulty just raised suggests.[a] Here we have an explanation which solves our difficulty, for if the existing state of things is the best, that will be the reason for the fact mentioned ; and the best is to move with a simple and ceaseless motion, and in the superior direction.

that it is in Aristotle's mind as the subject of ἔχει here, although unexpressed. (In the same way it is the real subject of ἔχει at the beginning of the next sentence.) We might then translate : (" If, just as upward motion is superior to downward, so forward motion is superior to backward,) then the universe has, just as it also has a left and a right side . . . a forepart and a hinderpart." (For πρότερος and ὕστερος in a local sense cf. esp. Phys. iv. 219 a 14 τὸ δὴ πρότερον καὶ ὕστερον ἐν τόπῳ πρῶτόν ἐστιν.) Simpl. regards οὐρανός as subject of ἔχει, and seems untroubled about the text. One may suspect that the real explanation is a deeper corruption, with loss of some words before ἔχει.

CHAPTER VI

ARGUMENT (continued)

(a) *The notions of acceleration, retardation, and climax of speed are inextricably connected with different stages of the*

ARISTOTLE

*motion performed—beginning, middle, or end. But in circular
motion no such stages are to be distinguished, therefore its
speed must remain constant* (288 a 13-27).

    (b) *In every movement there are two factors, mover and
moved. Irregularity in the movement must proceed from one
or the other. But in this case the object moved has been
proved to be free from change of any sort : a fortiori it is
impossible that irregularity should come from the side of the
mover, for that which moves another is even less subject to
change than that which it moves (because it exists in fuller
actuality : the principle on which this depends is most clearly
stated in* Phys. viii. 5. 257 b 6-10) (288 a 27–b 7).

    (c) *Motion can be irregular either* (i) *as a whole or* (ii)
because its parts move irregularly. But (ii) *any irregular
motion of parts of the universe separately would have shown
itself by a change in the relative positions of the stars ; no
such change has occurred,* (i) *any retardation of motion could
only be due to a lessening of natural force ; but the heaven
cannot suffer such an unnatural diminution of force. It
suffers no change or decay of any sort, as was demonstrated
in* bk. i. ch. 3. *This rules out all irregularity; acceleration would involve retardation* (288 b 7-22).

    (d) *The argument that diminution of force is unnatural is
applied to the mover, and the case assumed is that the motion
continues to accelerate from an infinite past up to a given
moment, and then slackens. But it would be necessary to*

Περὶ δὲ τῆς κινήσεως αὐτοῦ, ὅτι ὁμαλής ἐστι
καὶ οὐκ ἀνώμαλος, ἐφεξῆς ἂν εἴη τῶν εἰρημένων
15 διελθεῖν. (λέγω δὲ τοῦτο περὶ τοῦ πρώτου οὐρανοῦ
καὶ περὶ τῆς πρώτης φορᾶς· ἐν γὰρ τοῖς ὑποκάτω
πλείους ἤδη αἱ φοραὶ συνεληλύθασιν εἰς ἕν.)

    Εἰ γὰρ ἀνωμάλως κινήσεται, δῆλον ὅτι ἐπίτασις
ἔσται καὶ ἀκμὴ καὶ ἄνεσις τῆς φορᾶς· ἅπασα γὰρ

suppose that the period of slowing down should balance that of acceleration, i.e. the mover must for an infinite time exert no power. That is to say that it exists in an unnatural state for as long as it did in its natural state, but nothing ever in fact does this (22-27).

(e) Acceleration or retardation cannot go on for ever, since no movement is infinite in duration or indeterminate in speed (27-30).

(f) Another reason why the motion cannot go on accelerating continuously for ever. It is necessary to assume a certain minimum finite time in less than which the heaven cannot complete its revolution, since to do that it must traverse a certain finite distance ; and if it were allowed to accelerate, at a uniform or increasing rate, to infinity, it would become possible for it to complete its revolution in an infinitely short time, or no time at all. The same argument can be applied to retardation (288 b 30—289 a 4).

(g) Apart from general arguments against any irregularity in the motion of the heaven, the only particular suppositions so far rebutted are (i) that the motion should have started infinitely far back in the past, accelerated continuously up to a given moment, and then begun a slowing-down which in turn would last to an infinitely remote future, (ii) that the motion should go on either accelerating or slowing-down from infinity to infinity. Aristotle now mentions as being a logically possible alternative the hypothesis that the heaven goes through a series of alternate finite periods of acceleration and retardation, but only to dismiss it at once with contempt (289 a 4-10).

THE next thing which our discussions have to explain is that its motion is regular and not irregular. (I refer to the first heaven and the primary motion ; in the lower regions a number of motions are combined into one.)

If it moves irregularly, there will clearly be an acceleration, climax, and retardation of its motion,

ἡ ἀνώμαλος φορὰ καὶ ἄνεσιν ἔχει καὶ ἐπίτασιν καὶ
20 ἀκμήν. ἀκμὴ δ' ἐστὶν ἢ ὅθεν φέρεται ἢ οἷ ἢ ἀνὰ
μέσον, οἷον ἴσως τοῖς μὲν κατὰ φύσιν οἳ φέρονται,
τοῖς δὲ παρὰ φύσιν ὅθεν, τοῖς δὲ ῥιπτουμένοις ἀνὰ
μέσον. τῆς δὲ κύκλῳ φορᾶς οὐκ ἔστιν οὔτε ὅθεν
οὔτε οἷ οὔτε μέσον· οὔτε γὰρ ἀρχὴ οὔτε πέρας οὔτε
μέσον ἐστὶν αὐτῆς ἁπλῶς· τῷ τε γὰρ χρόνῳ ἀΐδιος
25 καὶ τῷ μήκει συνηγμένη καὶ ἄκλαστος· ὥστ' εἰ μή
ἐστιν ἀκμὴ αὐτοῦ τῆς φορᾶς, οὐδ' ἂν ἀνωμαλία
εἴη· ἡ γὰρ ἀνωμαλία γίγνεται διὰ τὴν ἄνεσιν καὶ
ἐπίτασιν.

Ἔτι ἐπεὶ πᾶν τὸ κινούμενον ὑπό τινος κινεῖται,
ἀνάγκη τὴν ἀνωμαλίαν γίγνεσθαι τῆς κινήσεως ἢ
30 διὰ τὸ κινοῦν ἢ διὰ τὸ κινούμενον ἢ δι' ἄμφω· εἴτε
γὰρ τὸ κινοῦν μὴ τῇ αὐτῇ δυνάμει κινοῖ, εἴτε τὸ
κινούμενον ἀλλοιοῖτο καὶ μὴ διαμένοι τὸ αὐτό, εἴτε
ἄμφω μεταβάλλοι, οὐθὲν κωλύει ἀνωμάλως κινεῖ-

The least unsatisfactory explanation of these words
seems to be that of Alexander, quoted by Simpl., that the
whole of the "missile" movement is to be regarded as
taking place horizontally and therefore "in the middle"
between natural and unnatural motion, since every body
moves naturally either upwards or downwards. But even
this is a very unsatisfactory explanation of Aristotle's argument, according to which all three cases should be parallel,
and ἀνὰ μέσον should mean nothing else but the middle point
of the motion of anything thrown. He first describes a
motion which would be that of a stone upwards. Obviously
the maximum velocity is at the source. Then of a stone
dropped from a height. The maximum velocity is reached
at the end. Then of "something thrown," and we are told
that this object reaches its maximum velocity "in the
middle." Surely one would naturally suppose this to mean
the middle point of the trajectory. The middle is contrasted

since all irregular motion has retardation, acceleration, and climax. The climax may be either at
the source or at the goal or in the middle of the
motion ; thus we might say that for things moving
naturally it is at the goal, for things moving contrary to nature it is at the source, and for things
whose motion is that of a missile it is in the middle.[a]
But circular motion has in itself neither source nor
goal nor middle. There is no absolute beginning
or end or mid-point of it, for in time it is eternal
and in length it returns upon itself and is un-
broken. If then there is no climax to its motion,
there will be no irregularity, for irregularity is the
result of retardation and acceleration.

Secondly, everything moved is moved by something, hence the irregularity of the movement must
proceed either from the mover or from the object
moved or from both. If the mover does not act
with constant force, or if the object changes instead
of remaining constant, or if both alter, then there

with the beginning and end of the motion, not with the
extreme natural and unnatural places of the body. Then
comes the obvious difficulty that this is contrary to fact. At
the middle point of its trajectory a stone from a sling is
moving at its slowest. I do not see how this difficulty is to
be avoided if the text is what A. wrote. But if it were permissible to alter texts simply to suit the sense which the
passage seems to require, there would be a great temptation
to read ἀμφότερα for ἀνὰ μέσον at 288 a 20 and 22. Things
thrown have two maxima, since their motion is a combination
of, first, unnatural, and second, natural motions. The triplet
ὅθεν, οἷ, μέσον at l. 23 might give some slight support to
this, by accounting for an early change. It does not make
ἀνὰ μέσον indispensable in the previous sentence, but it gives
a verbal correspondence which might appeal to a copyist or
corrector.

288 a

σθαι τὸ κινούμενον. οὐθὲν δὲ τούτων δυνατὸν περὶ
τὸν οὐρανὸν γενέσθαι· τὸ μὲν γὰρ κινούμενον
288 b δέδεικται ὅτι πρῶτον καὶ ἁπλοῦν καὶ ἀγένητον
καὶ ἄφθαρτον καὶ ὅλως ἀμετάβλητον, τὸ δὲ κινοῦν
πολὺ μᾶλλον εὔλογον εἶναι τοιοῦτον· τὸ γὰρ πρῶτον
τοῦ πρώτου καὶ τὸ ἁπλοῦν τοῦ ἁπλοῦ καὶ τὸ
ἄφθαρτον καὶ ἀγένητον τοῦ ἀφθάρτου καὶ ἀγενήτου
5 κινητικόν. ἐπεὶ οὖν τὸ κινούμενον οὐ μεταβάλλει
σῶμα ὄν, οὐδ᾽ ἂν τὸ κινοῦν μεταβάλλοι ἀσώματον
ὄν. ὥστε καὶ τὴν φορὰν ἀδύνατον ἀνώμαλον
εἶναι.

Καὶ γὰρ εἰ γίνεται ἀνώμαλος, ἤτοι ὅλη μεταβάλλει καὶ ὁτὲ μὲν γίνεται θάττων ὁτὲ δὲ βρα-
δυτέρα πάλιν, ἢ τὰ μέρη αὐτῆς. τὰ μὲν οὖν μέρη
10 ὅτι οὐκ ἔστιν ἀνώμαλα, φανερόν· ἤδη γὰρ ἂν
ἐγεγόνει[1] διάστασις τῶν ἄστρων ἐν τῷ ἀπείρῳ
χρόνῳ, τοῦ μὲν θᾶττον κινουμένου τοῦ δὲ βραδύτερον. οὐ φαίνεται δ᾽ οὐθὲν ἄλλως ἔχον τοῖς
διαστήμασιν. ἀλλὰ μὴν οὐδὲ τὴν ὅλην ἐγχωρεῖ
μεταβάλλειν· ἡ γὰρ ἄνεσις ἑκάστου γίνεται δι᾽
15 ἀδυναμίαν, ἡ δ᾽ ἀδυναμία παρὰ φύσιν· (καὶ γὰρ
αἱ ἐν τοῖς ζῴοις ἀδυναμίαι πᾶσαι παρὰ φύσιν εἰσίν,
οἷον γῆρας καὶ φθίσις. ὅλη γὰρ ἴσως ἡ σύστασις
τῶν ζῴων ἐκ τοιούτων συνέστηκεν ἃ διαφέρει τοῖς
οἰκείοις τόποις· οὐθὲν γὰρ τῶν μερῶν ἔχει τὴν
αὑτοῦ χώραν.) εἰ οὖν ἐν τοῖς πρώτοις μή ἐστι τὸ
20 παρὰ φύσιν—ἁπλᾶ γὰρ καὶ ἄμικτα καὶ ἐν τῇ οἰκείᾳ
χώρᾳ, καὶ οὐθὲν αὐτοῖς ἐναντίον—οὐδ᾽ ἂν ἀδυναμία

---

[1] ἐγεγόνει FHLMJ, Stocks, Allan. γεγόνει Bekker.

---

[a] Cf. p. 64 note c above.

is nothing to prevent the movement of the object from being irregular. But none of these hypotheses can be applied to the heaven; for the object of the movement has been demonstrated to be primary, simple, ungenerated, indestructible, and altogether changeless, and we may take it that the mover has far better reason to be so : only what is primary can move the primary, what is simple the simple, what is indestructible and ungenerated the indestructible and ungenerated. Since, then, the object moved, which is body, does not change, neither will the mover which is incorporeal change. It is impossible therefore that the motion should be irregular.

Thirdly, if it becomes irregular, either it changes as a whole, becoming now faster and now slower again, or its parts change separately. Clearly, however, the motion of the parts is not irregular ; otherwise the stars would have drawn apart in the infinite course of time, as one moved faster and another more slowly ; whereas no variation in their intervals is in fact observed. On the other hand there is no possibility of a change in the whole. Retardation of the movement of anything takes places owing to loss of power, and loss of power is contrary to nature. (Instances of loss of power in animals are all contrary to nature, *e.g.* old age and decay, and the reason for them is probably that the whole structure of an animal is composed of elements whose proper places are different ; none of its parts is occupying its own place.)[a] But that which is contrary to nature is not to be found in the primary substances, since they are simple and unmixed and in their proper place, and have no contrary.

288 b εἴη, ὥστ᾽ οὐδ᾽ ἄνεσις οὐδ᾽ ἐπίτασις· εἰ γὰρ ἐπίτασις, καὶ ἄνεσις.

Ἔτι δὲ καὶ ἄλογον ἄπειρον χρόνον ἀδύνατον εἶναι
τὸ κινοῦν, καὶ πάλιν ἄλλον ἄπειρον δυνατόν· οὐθὲν
γὰρ φαίνεται ὂν ἄπειρον χρόνον παρὰ φύσιν (ἡ δ᾽
25 ἀδυναμία παρὰ φύσιν), οὐδὲ τὸν ἴσον χρόνον παρὰ
φύσιν καὶ κατὰ φύσιν, οὐδ᾽ ὅλως δυνατὸν καὶ
ἀδύνατον· ἀνάγκη δ᾽, εἰ ἀνίησιν ἡ κίνησις, ἄπειρον
ἀνιέναι χρόνον. ἀλλὰ μὴν¹ οὐδ᾽ ἐπιτείνειν ἀεὶ ἢ
πάλιν ἀνιέναι δυνατόν· ἄπειρος γὰρ ἂν εἴη καὶ
ἀόριστος ἡ κίνησις, ἅπασαν δέ φαμεν ἔκ τινος εἰς
30 τι εἶναι καὶ ὡρισμένην.

Ἔτι δ᾽ εἴ τις λάβοι εἶναί τινα χρόνον ἐλάχιστον,
οὗ οὐκ ἐνδέχεται ἐν ἐλάττονι κινηθῆναι τὸν οὐρα-
νόν· ὥσπερ γὰρ οὐδὲ βαδίσαι οὐδὲ κιθαρίσαι ἐν
ὁτῳοῦν χρόνῳ δυνατόν, ἀλλ᾽ ἑκάστης ἔστι πράξεως
ὡρισμένος ὁ ἐλάχιστος χρόνος κατὰ τὸ μὴ ὑπερ-
289 a βάλλειν, οὕτως οὐδὲ κινηθῆναι τὸν οὐρανὸν ἐν
ὁτῳοῦν χρόνῳ δυνατόν. εἰ οὖν τοῦτ᾽ ἀληθές, οὐκ
ἂν εἴη ἀεὶ ἐπίτασις τῆς φορᾶς (εἰ δὲ μὴ ἐπίτασις,
οὐδ᾽ ἄνεσις· ὁμοίως γὰρ ἄμφω καὶ θάτερον), εἴπερ
τῷ αὐτῷ τε ἐπιτείνεται τάχει ἢ μείζονι καὶ ἄπειρον χρόνον.

5 Λείπεται δὴ λέγειν ἐναλλὰξ εἶναι τῇ κινήσει τὸ
θᾶττον καὶ τὸ βραδύτερον· τοῦτο δὲ παντελῶς

---

¹ μὴν. Bekker misprints as μὲν.

Neither then is there loss of power, nor, in consequence, retardation nor yet acceleration (for that would imply retardation).

Fourthly, it is contrary to reason that the mover should for an infinite time exert no power, and then for another infinite time exert power, for it is observable that nothing exists in an unnatural state for an infinite time (and lack of power is contrary to nature), nor exists as long in an unnatural as in its natural state, nor indeed as long without power as with it. But if the movement slows down, it must be for an infinite time.[a] Nor yet, fifthly, can it either accelerate or slow down for ever, for if so the movement would be infinite and undetermined, whereas we believe that every movement is from one fixed point to another and is determinate.

Sixthly, one may suppose that there is a certain minimum time, in less than which the heaven cannot complete its motion; even the actions of walking or playing the lyre are not possible in any time one chooses, but for each action there is a definite minimum time which cannot be passed, and so too the heaven cannot complete its motion in any and every time. If then this is true, there cannot be an everlasting acceleration of the motion (and if not acceleration, then not retardation either; for the argument applies with equal force to both or one), if the acceleration is uniform or increasing, and lasts for an infinite time.

It is left us to maintain that the movement becomes alternately swifter and slower; but this is

[a] That is, if the preceding acceleration has lasted for an infinite time. There must be equality between the two.

ἄλογον καὶ πλάσματι ὅμοιον. ἔτι δὲ καὶ τὸ μὴ
λανθάνειν ἐπὶ τούτων εὐλογώτερον· εὐαισθητότερα
γὰρ τὰ παρ' ἄλληλα τιθέμενα.

Ὅτι μὲν οὖν εἷς τε μόνος ἐστὶν οὐρανός, καὶ οὗτος
10 ἀγένητος καὶ ἀΐδιος, ἔτι δὲ κινούμενος ὁμαλῶς,
ἐπὶ τοσοῦτον ἡμῖν εἰρήσθω.

CHAPTER VII

ARGUMENT

Composition of the stars.—*The stars are made of the fifth
element in which they move, not of fire. How is it then that
they emit light and, at least in the case of the sun, heat?
These are produced by ignition of the air beneath them, due
to the friction caused by their movement.*

*The chapter raises two main difficulties, both of which were
recognized by Alexander and Simplicius.*

(i) *How is it that the stars produce an effect so different
from the other parts of the spheres in which they are carried,
if they are made of the same simple body?* (πῶς ἁπλῆς οὔσης
τῆς πέμπτης λεγομένης οὐσίας τοῦ κυκλοφορητικοῦ σώματος
τοσαύτη φαίνεται διαφόρα τοῦ τῶν ἄστρων σώματος πρὸς τὸ
οὐράνιον; *Alex.* ap. *Simpl.* p. 436. 4.) *It might be suggested that they differ from the rest in density, consisting of
a high concentration of the fifth element at one point. To
one thinking along the lines of Greek thought, this raises the
difficulty that to speak of density and rarity is to introduce
opposites into the fifth body, and the presence of opposites
would seem to indicate the possibility of change, generation,
and decay, which are " into and out of opposites," whereas
the fifth body is eternal and indestructible owing to its sim-
plicity. But, argues Simpl., the only requirement for its in-
destructibility is that there should be no opposite to its essence*

an altogether unreasonable and obviously artificial
theory. Besides, it would have been more likely
to be observed, since things that occur alternately
are more easily distinguishable by the senses.

Here we may end our account of the uniqueness
of the world, its ungenerated and eternal nature,
and the regularity of its motion.

CHAPTER VII

ARGUMENT (*continued*)

*or form. That it has accidental qualities which admit of
contrariety need not worry us. Snow is destroyed because
there exists an opposite to coldness which is its essence. But
the fact that its accidental attribute whiteness also has an
opposite is irrelevant to the question of its destructibility or
otherwise. Snow is destroyed by heat but not by blackness.
In short, says Simpl., the proposition " where there are no
opposites there is no generation or decay " need not be regarded as convertible.*

*The general question remains, whether we are right in
positing differences between the stars and the spheres in
which they are carried round, at the same time as we affirm
them to be made of the same simple body. Yes, says Simpl.,
because to say that all alike are made of the body which moves
naturally in a circle (as A. does, 289 a 14-16) is only to mention
a very wide genus which they have in common : within that
genus there is room for plenty of specific differences, such as
we in fact find between the four sublunary elements which
share a parallel generic quality, that of rectilinear motion.*

*(ii) The element in contact with the spheres which carry the
stars is not air, but fire. Why, then, does A. say that it is
air which is ignited by the motion of the stars ? He in fact
seems to have believed that it is the fire which is ignited by the*

177

*motion of the stars themselves, and the air beneath by it.
Pure elemental fire is not flame, but inflammable material
(ὑπέκκαυμα), a dry vapour easily ignited by the smallest
motion (Meteor. i. 4. 341 b 18). The idea is therefore
possible, and the order is clearly stated in Meteor. i. 3. 341 a 2:
" Fire is continuous with the upper element, and air with
fire." There remains however the objection that, strictly
speaking, only the innermost of the spheres carrying the stars*

289 a 11 Περὶ δὲ τῶν καλουμένων ἄστρων ἑπόμενον ἂν
εἴη λέγειν, ἐκ τίνων τε συνεστᾶσι καὶ ἐν ποίοις
σχήμασι καὶ τίνες αἱ κινήσεις αὐτῶν. εὐλογώτατον
δὴ καὶ τοῖς εἰρημένοις ἑπόμενον ἡμῖν τὸ ἕκαστον
15 τῶν ἄστρων ποιεῖν ἐκ τούτου τοῦ σώματος ἐν ᾧ
τυγχάνει τὴν φορὰν ἔχον, ἐπειδὴ ἔφαμέν τι εἶναι
ὃ κύκλῳ φέρεσθαι πέφυκεν· ὥσπερ γὰρ οἱ πύρινα
φάσκοντες εἶναι διὰ τοῦτο λέγουσιν, ὅτι τὸ ἄνω
σῶμα πῦρ εἶναί φασιν, ὡς εὔλογον ὂν ἕκαστον
συνεστάναι ἐκ τούτων ἐν οἷς ἕκαστόν ἐστιν,
ὁμοίως καὶ ἡμεῖς λέγομεν.

20 Ἡ δὲ θερμότης ἀπ᾽ αὐτῶν καὶ τὸ φῶς γίνεται
παρεκτριβομένου τοῦ ἀέρος ὑπὸ τῆς ἐκείνων φορᾶς.
πέφυκε γὰρ ἡ κίνησις ἐκπυροῦν καὶ ξύλα καὶ λίθους
καὶ σίδηρον· εὐλογώτερον οὖν τὸ ἐγγύτερον τοῦ
πυρός, ἐγγύτερον δὲ ὁ ἀήρ· οἷον καὶ ἐπὶ τῶν
φερομένων βελῶν· ταῦτα γὰρ αὐτὰ ἐκπυροῦται
25 οὕτως ὥστε τήκεσθαι τὰς μολυβδίδας, καὶ ἐπείπερ
αὐτὰ ἐκπυροῦται, ἀνάγκη καὶ τὸν κύκλῳ αὐτῶν
ἀέρα τὸ αὐτὸ τοῦτο πάσχειν. ταῦτα μὲν οὖν αὐτὰ
ἐκθερμαίνεται διὰ τὸ ἐν ἀέρι φέρεσθαι, ὃς διὰ τὴν

is in contact with the fiery element below. Perhaps A. saw a way of escape in the thesis that the fifth element exists in purity only at the outer extreme of the universe, and gets more and more contaminated at its lower levels (Meteor. i. 3. 340 b 6 τὸ μὲν γὰρ ἄνω καὶ μέχρι σελήνης ἕτερον εἶναι σῶμά φαμεν πυρός τε καὶ ἀερός, οὐ μὴν ἀλλ' ἐν αὐτῷ γε τὸ μὲν καθαρώτερον εἶναι τὸ δὲ ἧττον εἰλικρινές, καὶ διαφορὰς ἔχειν, καὶ μάλιστα ᾗ καταλήγει πρὸς τὸν ἀέρα); *but we have no evidence that he ever elucidated in detail the suggestion here thrown out. Compare Stocks's note on* 289 a 32, *and* Heath, Aristarchus, *p.* 242.

IT falls to us next to speak of the bodies called stars, of what elements they are composed, and what are their shapes and movements. The most logical and consistent hypothesis is to make each star consist of the body in which it moves, since we have maintained that there is a body whose nature it is to move in a circle. Thus we adopt the same line of argument as those who say that the stars are of fire, for their reason is that they call the uppermost body fire, and think it logical that each individual thing should consist of those elements in which it has its being.

The heat and light which they emit are engendered as the air is chafed by their movement. It is the nature of movement to ignite even wood and stone and iron, *a fortiori* then that which is nearer to fire, as air is. Compare the case of flying missiles. These are themselves set on fire so that leaden balls are melted, and if the missiles themselves catch fire, the air which surrounds them must be affected likewise. These then become heated themselves by reason of their flight through

289 a

πληγὴν τῇ κινήσει γίγνεται πῦρ· τῶν δὲ ἄνω
ἕκαστον ἐν τῇ σφαίρᾳ φέρεται, ὥστ' αὐτὰ μὲν μὴ
30 ἐκπυροῦσθαι, τοῦ δ' ἀέρος ὑπὸ τὴν τοῦ κυκλικοῦ
σώματος σφαῖραν ὄντος ἀνάγκη φερομένης ἐκείνης
ἐκθερμαίνεσθαι, καὶ ταύτῃ μάλιστα ᾗ ὁ ἥλιος
τετύχηκεν ἐνδεδεμένος· διὸ δὴ πλησιάζοντός τε
αὐτοῦ καὶ ἀνίσχοντος καὶ ὑπὲρ ἡμᾶς ὄντος γίγνεται
ἡ θερμότης. ὅτι μὲν οὖν οὔτε πύρινά ἐστιν οὔτ'
35 ἐν πυρὶ φέρεται, ταῦθ' ἡμῖν εἰρήσθω περὶ αὐτῶν.

ᵃ This extraordinary notion seems to have been widely
held in antiquity. See *e.g.* Lucr. vi. 178 : plumbea vero
glans etiam longo cursu volvenda liquescit. (*Cf.* also *ib.*
306 f.) Munro, *ad loc.*, refers to Seneca, *Nat. Qu.* 2. 57. 2 :
sic liquescit excussa glans funda et adtritu aeris velut igne
distillat; Ovid, *Met.* xiv. 825 : sic lata plumbea funda missa
solet medio glans intabescere; caelo Lucan, vii. 513 : ut calido
liquefactae pondere glandes[512-513: inde faces et saxa volant,
spatioque solutae aeris et calido liquefactae pondere glandes,
Housman]; Virg. *Aen.* ix. 588 : liquefacto tempora plumbo
diffidit. Add Ovid, *Met.* ii. 727 : non secus exarsit, quam
cum Balearica plumbum funda iacit: volat illud et incan-
descit eundo, et, quos non habuit, sub nubibus invenit ignes.
I can find no other Greek examples, and cannot account for
the origin of a belief so patently at variance with the facts.

CHAPTER VIII

ARGUMENT

That the motion of the stars is not self-caused, but the
result of their being set at fixed points in the revolving
heavens.

*A start is made from the fact that both the stars and the
heaven as a whole can be observed to change their position
relatively to us. Four explanations may be considered*
(289 b 1—290 a 7).

the air,[a] which owing to the impact upon it is made fire by the movement. But the upper bodies are carried each one in its sphere ; hence they do not catch fire themselves,[b] but the air which lies beneath the sphere of the revolving element is necessarily heated by its revolution, and especially in that part where the sun is fixed.[c] That is the reason for the heat experienced as it gets nearer or rises higher or stands above our head. Let this suffice for the point that the stars are neither made of fire nor move in fire.

Bergk's explanation, even if true, seems inadequate (*Römische Schleudergeschosse*, Teubner 1876, p. 97) : "Indem der Schleuderer, ehe er das Geschoss absendet, die Schleuder wiederholt schwingt, erwärmt sich das Metall; diese Hitze wird, namentlich wenn es eine weite Bahn zurückzulegen hat, noch gesteigert, so dass es in dem Getroffenen die Empfindung eines brennenden Schmerzes hervorruft."

[b] Because the revolving element of which they and the spheres are made cannot be transmuted into any of the other elements, since it is not the contrary of any of them.

[c] This is explained in *Meteor.* i. 3, 341 a 19. Perceptible heat is engendered by the sun's motion because it is both rapid and near. The motion of the stars is rapid but distant, that of the moon near but slow.

CHAPTER VIII

ARGUMENT (*continued*)

(1) *Both are in fact at rest. Dismissed because inconsistent with the hypothesis of a stationary earth.*

(2) *Both move independently. Dismissed on account of the improbability that stars moving in circles of different magnitudes (according to their distance from the poles of the sphere) should have their speeds so nicely adjusted that they*

ARGUMENT (*continued*)

*should all complete a revolution in exactly the same time, and
that identical with the time taken by their circles.*

*(3) The sphere is at rest and the stars move by themselves.
Open to the same objection as (2).* [*N.B.—A. refers throughout not to " the sphere " but to " the circles," because he
wishes to differentiate between the paths of stars in different
parts of the sphere, but these " circles " are continuous and
are in fact only reached by a process of mental division of the
one sphere. Cf. esp. 290 a 5-7.*]

*(4) Only the sphere has a motion of its own, and it carries
the stars round because they are fixed in it. This is the only
hypothesis which fits the facts.*

Supplementary arguments. (1) *The stars are spherical,
and only two forms of motion are proper to spherical bodies,
rotation about an axis and rolling. The stars move in*

289 b ᾽Επεὶ δὲ φαίνεται καὶ τὰ ἄστρα μεθιστάμενα καὶ
ὅλος ὁ οὐρανός, ἀναγκαῖον ἤτοι ἠρεμούντων ἀμφοτέρων γίγνεσθαι τὴν μεταβολήν, ἢ κινουμένων, ἢ
τοῦ μὲν ἠρεμοῦντος τοῦ δὲ κινουμένου.

5 ᾽Αμφότερα μὲν τοίνυν ἠρεμεῖν ἀδύνατον ἠρεμούσης
γε τῆς γῆς· οὐ γὰρ ἂν ἐγίγνετο τὰ φαινόμενα. τὴν δὲ
γῆν ὑποκείσθω ἠρεμεῖν. λείπεται δὴ ἢ ἀμφότερα
κινεῖσθαι, ἢ τὸ μὲν κινεῖσθαι τὸ δ' ἠρεμεῖν.

Εἰ μὲν οὖν ἀμφότερα κινήσεται, ἄλογον τὸ ταὐτὰ
τάχη τῶν ἄστρων εἶναι καὶ τῶν κύκλων· ἕκαστον
10 γὰρ ὁμοταχὲς ἔσται τῷ κύκλῳ καθ' ὃν φέρεται.
φαίνεται γὰρ ἅμα τοῖς κύκλοις καθιστάμενα πάλιν

---

a *i.e.* the fixed stars and the outermost heaven according
to Simpl. ; τῆς οὖν ἀμφοῖν μεταβάσεως φαινομένης τοῦ τε
ἀπλανοῦς οὐρανοῦ καὶ τῶν ἀπλανῶν ἄστρων· περὶ γὰρ τούτων νῦν
ὁ λόγος (Simpl. p. 444. 27. *Cf.* 449. 1). Yet ἄστρα included the planets in the previous chapter (*cf.* the reference
to the sun), and seems to do so again at 290 a 14, as it does

*neither of these two ways, therefore they are not moving with
their own proper motion, therefore their motion cannot be
self-caused* (290 a 7-29).

(2) *The stars have no organs of motion like animals which
move through space of their own accord. In fact sphericity,
with its smoothness and absence of projections, is as unlike
as possible to the shape of self-moving* (in the sense of progressing) *bodies, and is the least suitable for locomotion. If,
then, nature has conferred this shape on all the stars, it cannot
be accidental, but must mean that they were never intended
to move through space of their own accord. In just the same
way the heaven as a whole was given spherical shape because
it was destined for rotation in the same place* (290 a 29–b 11).

CHANGE is apparent in the position both of the
stars and of the whole heaven,[a] and this change
must be reconciled with one of three possibilities.
Either (1) both are at rest, or (2) both are in motion,
or (3) one is at rest and the other in motion.

(1) For both to be at rest is impossible, if the
earth is at rest, for that would not produce the
phenomena ; and the immobility of the earth shall
be our hypothesis. There remain the alternatives
that both move or that one moves and the other is
at rest.

(2) If both move, we have the improbable result
that the speeds of the stars and the circles are the
same, for each star would then have the same speed as
the circle in which it moves, seeing that they may be

also in the subsequent chapters. The argument here
certainly does not require a reference to anything beyond
the fixed stars and their " circles," and indeed would gain
in neatness if confined to them, but Simpl.'s statement can
scarcely stand against the evidence of the context. (Prantl
takes the view that the planets are included here.)

289 b

εἰς τὸ αὐτό. συμβαίνει οὖν ἅμα τό τε ἄστρον
διεληλυθέναι τὸν κύκλον καὶ τὸν κύκλον ἐνηνέχθαι
τὴν αὑτοῦ φοράν, διεληλυθότα τὴν αὑτοῦ περι-
φέρειαν. οὐκ ἔστι δ' εὔλογον τὸ τὸν αὐτὸν λόγον
ἔχειν τὰ τάχη τῶν ἄστρων καὶ τὰ μεγέθη τῶν
15 κύκλων. τοὺς μὲν γὰρ κύκλους οὐθὲν ἄτοπον ἀλλ'
ἀναγκαῖον ἀνάλογον ἔχειν τὰ τάχη τοῖς μεγέθεσι,
τῶν δ' ἄστρων ἕκαστον τῶν ἐν τούτοις οὐδαμῶς
εὔλογον· εἴτε γὰρ ἐξ ἀνάγκης τὸ τὸν μείζω κύκλον
φερόμενον θᾶττον ἔσται, δῆλον ὅτι κἂν μετατεθῇ
τὰ ἄστρα εἰς τοὺς ἀλλήλων κύκλους, τὸ μὲν ἔσται
20 θᾶττον τὸ δὲ βραδύτερον· οὕτω δ' οὐκ ἂν ἔχοιεν
οἰκείαν κίνησιν, ἀλλὰ φέροιντ' ἂν ὑπὸ τῶν κύκλων.
εἴτε ἀπὸ ταὐτομάτου συνέπεσεν, οὐδ' οὕτως εὔλογον ὥστ' ἐν ἅπασιν ἅμα τόν τε κύκλον εἶναι μείζω
καὶ τὴν φορὰν θάττω τοῦ ἐν αὐτῷ ἄστρου· τὸ μὲν
γὰρ ἐν ᾗ δύο τοῦτον τὸν τρόπον ἔχειν οὐθὲν
25 ἄτοπον, τὸ δὲ πάνθ' ὁμοίως πλάσματι ἔοικεν.
ἅμα δὲ καὶ οὐκ ἔστιν ἐν τοῖς φύσει τὸ ὡς ἔτυχεν,
οὐδὲ τὸ πανταχοῦ καὶ πᾶσιν ὑπάρχον τὸ ἀπὸ
τύχης.

Ἀλλὰ μὴν πάλιν εἰ οἱ μὲν κύκλοι μένουσιν, αὐτὰ
δὲ τὰ ἄστρα κινεῖται, τὰ αὐτὰ[1] καὶ ὁμοίως ἔσται
ἄλογα· συμβήσεται γὰρ θᾶττον κινεῖσθαι τὰ ἔξω,
καὶ τὰ τάχη εἶναι κατὰ τὰ μεγέθη τῶν κύκλων.

30 Ἐπεὶ τοίνυν οὔτ' ἀμφότερα κινεῖσθαι εὔλογον
οὔτε τὸ ἄστρον μόνον, λείπεται τοὺς μὲν κύκλους

---

[1] τὰ αὐτά. So Stocks and Allan with all mss. and Simpl.
ταῦτα Bekker.

observed to return to the same spot simultaneously with the circles. This means that at the same moment the star has traversed the circle and the circle has completed its own revolution, having traversed its own circumference. But it is not reasonable to suppose that the speeds of the stars are related to one another as the size of their circles. That the circles should have their speeds proportional to their magnitudes is no absurdity, indeed it is a necessity, but that each of the stars in them should show the same proportion is not reasonable. If it is by necessity that the one which moves in the path of the larger circle is the swifter, then it is clear that even if the stars were transposed into each others' circles, still the one in the larger circle would be swifter, and the other slower; but in that case they would possess no motion of their own, but be carried by the circles. If on the other hand it has happened by chance, yet it is equally unlikely that chance should act so that in every case the larger circle is accompanied by a swifter movement of the star in it. That one or two should show this correspondence is conceivable, but that it should be universal seems fantastic. In any case, chance is excluded from natural events, and whatever applies everywhere and to all cases is not to be ascribed to chance.

(3a) But again, if the circles are at rest and the stars move by themselves, the same absurdity arises and in the same way : for the effect will be that the stars which lie far out will move faster, and the speeds will correspond to the size of the circles.

(3b) Since then neither the motion of both nor the motion of the star alone can be defended, we

289 b
κινεῖσθαι, τὰ δὲ ἄστρα ἠρεμεῖν καὶ ἐνδεδεμένα τοῖς
κύκλοις φέρεσθαι· μόνως γὰρ οὕτως οὐθὲν ἄλογον
συμβαίνει· τό τε γὰρ θᾶττον εἶναι τοῦ μείζονος
35 κύκλου τὸ τάχος εὔλογον περὶ τὸ αὐτὸ κέντρον
290 a ἐνδεδεμένων (ὥσπερ γὰρ ἐν τοῖς ἄλλοις τὸ μεῖζον
σῶμα θᾶττον φέρεται τὴν οἰκείαν φοράν, οὕτως καὶ
ἐν τοῖς ἐγκυκλίοις· μεῖζον γὰρ τῶν ἀφαιρουμένων
ὑπὸ τῶν ἐκ τοῦ κέντρου τὸ τοῦ μείζονος κύκλου
5 τμῆμα, ὥστ' εὐλόγως ἐν τῷ ἴσῳ χρόνῳ ὁ μείζων
περιοισθήσεται κύκλος), τό τε μὴ διασπᾶσθαι τὸν
οὐρανὸν διά τε τοῦτο συμβήσεται καὶ ὅτι δέδεικται
συνεχὲς ὂν τὸ ὅλον.

Ἔτι δ' ἐπεὶ σφαιροειδῆ τὰ ἄστρα, καθάπερ
οἵ τ' ἄλλοι φασὶ καὶ ἡμῖν ὁμολογούμενον εἰπεῖν,
ἐξ ἐκείνου γε τοῦ σώματος γεννῶσιν, τοῦ δὲ
10 σφαιροειδοῦς δύο κινήσεις εἰσὶ καθ' αὑτό, κύλισις
καὶ δίνησις, εἴπερ οὖν κινοῖτο τὰ ἄστρα δι' αὑτῶν,
τὴν ἑτέραν ἂν κινοῖτο τούτων· ἀλλ' οὐδετέραν
φαίνεται. δινούμενα μὲν γὰρ ἔμενεν ἂν ἐν ταὐτῷ
καὶ οὐ μετέβαλλε τὸν τόπον, ὅπερ φαίνεταί τε καὶ
πάντες φασίν. ἔτι δὲ πάντα μὲν εὔλογον τὴν αὐτὴν
15 κίνησιν κινεῖσθαι, μόνος δὲ δοκεῖ τῶν ἄστρων ὁ
ἥλιος τοῦτο δρᾶν, ἀνατέλλων ἢ δύνων, καὶ οὗτος
οὐ δι' αὑτὸν ἀλλὰ διὰ τὴν ἀπόστασιν τῆς ἡμετέρας
ὄψεως· ἡ γὰρ ὄψις ἀποτεινομένη μακρὰν ἑλίσσεται
διὰ τὴν ἀσθένειαν. ὅπερ αἴτιον ἴσως καὶ τοῦ

186

are left with the conclusion that the circles move and that the stars stay still and are carried along because fixed in the circles. This is the only hypothesis that does not lead to an absurdity. That the larger circle should have the higher speed is reasonable, seeing that the stars are dotted around one and the same centre. Among the other elements, the larger a body the more swiftly it performed its proper motion, and the same is true of the bodies whose motion is circular. If arcs are cut off by lines radiating from the centre, that of the larger circle will be larger, and it is natural therefore that the larger circle should take the same time as the others to revolve. This too is one reason why the heaven does not spring apart, and another is that the whole has been demonstrated to be continuous.

Again, since the stars are spherical (as others assert, and the statement is consistent with our own opinions, seeing that we construct them out of the spherical body), and there are two motions proper to the spherical as such, namely rolling and rotation about an axis, the stars, if they moved of themselves, would move in one of these two ways. But to all appearances they move in neither. (i) If their motion were rotation, they would remain in the same place and not change their position, which would be contrary to observation and the universal consensus of men. Besides, we may take it that all have the same motion, and none of the stars appears to rotate except the sun at its rising or setting, and that not of itself but only because we view it at such a great distance : that is, our sight, when used at long range, becomes weak and unsteady. This is possibly the reason

στίλβειν φαίνεσθαι τοὺς ἀστέρας τοὺς ἐνδεδε-
20 μένους, τοὺς δὲ πλάνητας μὴ στίλβειν· οἱ μὲν γὰρ
πλάνητες ἐγγύς εἰσιν, ὥστ' ἐγκρατὴς οὖσα πρὸς
αὐτοὺς ἀφικνεῖται ἡ ὄψις· πρὸς δὲ τοὺς μένοντας
κραδαίνεται διὰ τὸ μῆκος, ἀποτεινομένη πόρρω
λίαν. ὁ δὲ τρόμος αὐτῆς ποιεῖ τοῦ ἄστρου δοκεῖν
εἶναι τὴν κίνησιν· οὐθὲν γὰρ διαφέρει κινεῖν τὴν
ὄψιν ἢ τὸ ὁρώμενον.
25 Ἀλλὰ μὴν ὅτι οὐδὲ κυλίεται τὰ ἄστρα, φανερόν·
τὸ μὲν γὰρ κυλιόμενον στρέφεσθαι ἀνάγκη, τῆς δὲ
σελήνης ἀεὶ δῆλόν ἐστι τὸ καλούμενον πρόσωπον.
Ὥστ' ἐπεὶ κινούμενα μὲν δι' αὐτῶν τὰς οἰκείας
κινεῖσθαι κινήσεις εὔλογον, ταύτας δ' οὐ φαίνεται
κινούμενα, δῆλον ὅτι οὐκ ἂν κινοῖτο δι' αὐτῶν.
30 Πρὸς δὲ τούτοις ἄλογον τὸ μηθὲν ὄργανον αὐτοῖς
ἀποδοῦναι τὴν φύσιν πρὸς τὴν κίνησιν—οὐθὲν γὰρ
ὡς ἔτυχε ποιεῖ ἡ φύσις—οὐδὲ τῶν μὲν ζῴων φρον-
τίσαι, τῶν δ' οὕτω τιμίων ὑπεριδεῖν, ἀλλ' ἔοικεν
ὥσπερ ἐπίτηδες ἀφελεῖν πάντα δι' ὧν ἐνεδέχετο
προϊέναι καθ' αὑτά, καὶ ὅτι πλεῖστον ἀποστῆσαι
35 τῶν ἐχόντων ὄργανα πρὸς κίνησιν. διὸ καὶ
290 b εὐλόγως ἂν δόξειεν ὅ τε ὅλος οὐρανὸς σφαιροειδὴς

---

^a Prantl points out as a flaw that the sun is supposed by
A. to be the second nearest of the planets. But A. does not
say that the sun twinkles, nor deny that the planets give
the illusion of rotation, or would do so did they appear large
enough.
^b In this passage A. commits himself to the view, current
until his time, that sight is effected by rays issuing from
the eye, though in his own work on the senses he gave it
up. *Cf.* Plato, *Meno* 76 c-d, Arist. *Top.* 105 b 6, and see
Stocks's note on this passage. The argument of this para-

also why the fixed stars appear to twinkle but the planets do not. The planets are near, so that our vision reaches them with its powers unimpaired [a]; but in reaching to the fixed stars it is extended too far, and the distance causes it to waver. Thus its trembling makes it seem as if the motion were the stars'—the effect is the same whether it is our sight or its object that moves.[b]

(ii) On the other hand it is equally clear that the stars do not roll. Whatever rolls must turn about, but the moon always shows us its face (as men call it).[c]

Thus: if the stars moved of themselves they would naturally perform their own proper motions; but we see that they do not perform these motions; therefore they cannot move of themselves.

Another argument is that it would be absurd for nature to have given them no organs of motion. Nature makes nothing in haphazard fashion, and she would not look after the animals and neglect such superior beings as these.[d] Rather she seems to have purposely deprived them of every means of progressing by themselves, and made them as different as possible from creatures which have organs of motion. The assumption is therefore justified that both the heaven as a whole and the

graph, that the stars do not rotate, contradicts Plato (*Tim.* 40 A).

[c] And therefore does not *roll*, as A. is using the word here, though of course it rotates once about its axis for every revolution it makes around the earth. Heath justifies this sentence in *Aristarchus*, p. 235. *Cf.* also Burnet, *Thales to Plato*, p. 226.

[d] The construction is a little irregular. Presumably οὐδὲ picks up the negative contained in ἄλογον, as if οὐκ εὔλογον had been written.

290 b

εἶναι καὶ ἕκαστον τῶν ἄστρων. πρὸς μὲν γὰρ τὴν
ἐν τῷ αὐτῷ κίνησιν ἡ σφαῖρα τῶν σχημάτων
χρησιμώτατον (οὕτω γὰρ ἂν καὶ τάχιστα κινοῖτο
καὶ μάλιστα κατέχοι τὸν αὐτὸν τόπον), πρὸς δὲ
5 τὴν εἰς τὸ πρόσθεν ἀχρηστότατον· ἥκιστα γὰρ
ὅμοιον τοῖς δι᾽ αὐτῶν κινητικοῖς· οὐδὲν γὰρ ἀπηρ-
τημένον ἔχει οὐδὲ προέχον, ὥσπερ τὸ εὐθύγραμμον,
ἀλλὰ πλεῖστον ἀφέστηκε τῷ σχήματι τῶν πορευ-
τικῶν σωμάτων. ἐπεὶ οὖν δεῖ τὸν μὲν οὐρανὸν
κινεῖσθαι τὴν ἐν αὐτῷ κίνησιν, τὰ ἄλλα δ᾽ ἄστρα
10 μὴ προϊέναι δι᾽ αὐτῶν, εὐλόγως ἂν ἑκάτερον εἴη
σφαιροειδές· οὕτω γὰρ μάλιστα τὸ μὲν κινήσεται
τὸ δ᾽ ἠρεμήσει.

CHAPTER IX

ARGUMENT

Explanation and refutation of the Pythagorean theory
of the harmony of the spheres.

(i) *Explanation (290 b 12-29). The theory is founded on
the two assumptions (a) that movement is necessarily accompanied by sound, and that the sound emitted by the moving
stars must be in relation to their size and speed, i.e. very loud
indeed, (b) that the intervals between the planets and the
sphere of the fixed stars correspond mathematically to the
intervals between the notes of the octave. Thus the sound
produced is musical. To the objection that we do not hear
this music it is answered that we cannot expect to be aware of
a sound which was going on when we were born and has continued without intermission ever since. It is only by contrast with intervals of silence that a sound becomes perceptible.*

190

separate stars are spherical, for the sphere is at once the most useful shape for motion in the same place—since what is spherical can move most swiftly and can most easily maintain its position unchanged—and the least suited to progression,[a] the latter because it least resembles bodies which are self-moving. It has no separate or projecting parts as a rectilinear figure has, and is of a totally different shape from forward-moving bodies. Since, then, the heaven must move within its own boundaries, and the stars must not move forward of themselves, we may conclude that both are spherical. This will best ensure to the one its movement and to the others their immobility.

    [a] Again a contrast to Plato (*Tim.* 55 D, E)

CHAPTER IX

ARGUMENT (*continued*)

(ii) *Refutation* (290 b 30—291 a 26). (a) *There is a more serious objection than the fact that we are not aware of it. Sound has a destructive effect (e.g. stones may be split by thunder), and a noise of the unimaginable loudness which we must attribute to bodies of the size of the sun, moon and stars would long ago have crushed and shattered everything on earth.* (b) *The only reason for the theory was the difficulty felt in supposing that such enormous bodies could move noiselessly. This difficulty disappears as soon as it is recognized that (as demonstrated in the previous chapter) the stars are not moving by themselves through a stationary medium. It is friction which creates noise. The stars are carried passively in their revolving spheres, and their motion is comparable to that of a ship drifting downstream.*

191

ARISTOTLE

290 b 12　Φανερὸν δ' ἐκ τούτων ὅτι καὶ τὸ φάναι γίνεσθαι
φερομένων ἁρμονίαν, ὡς συμφώνων γινομένων τῶν
ψόφων, κομψῶς μὲν εἴρηται καὶ περιττῶς ὑπὸ τῶν
15 εἰπόντων, οὐ μὴν οὕτως ἔχει τἀληθές. δοκεῖ γάρ
τισιν ἀναγκαῖον εἶναι τηλικούτων φερομένων σωμάτων γίγνεσθαι ψόφον, ἐπεὶ καὶ τῶν παρ' ἡμῖν
οὔτε τοὺς ὄγκους ἐχόντων ἴσους οὔτε τοιούτῳ
τάχει φερομένων· ἡλίου δὲ καὶ σελήνης, ἔτι τε
τοσούτων τὸ πλῆθος ἄστρων καὶ τὸ μέγεθος
20 φερομένων τῷ τάχει τοιαύτην φορὰν ἀδύνατον μὴ
γίγνεσθαι ψόφον ἀμήχανόν τινα τὸ μέγεθος. ὑπο-
θέμενοι δὲ ταῦτα καὶ τὰς ταχυτῆτας ἐκ τῶν ἀπο-
στάσεων ἔχειν τοὺς τῶν συμφωνιῶν λόγους,
ἐναρμόνιόν φασι γίνεσθαι τὴν φωνὴν φερομένων
κύκλῳ τῶν ἄστρων. ἐπεὶ δ' ἄλογον ἐδόκει τὸ μὴ
25 συνακούειν ἡμᾶς τῆς φωνῆς ταύτης, αἴτιον τούτου
φασὶν εἶναι τὸ γιγνομένοις εὐθὺς ὑπάρχειν τὸν
ψόφον, ὥστε μὴ διάδηλον εἶναι πρὸς τὴν ἐναντίαν
σιγήν· πρὸς ἄλληλα γὰρ φωνῆς καὶ σιγῆς εἶναι τὴν
διάγνωσιν· ὥστε καθάπερ τοῖς χαλκοτύποις διὰ

ᵃ For the Pythagorean theory of the harmony of the
spheres see Heath, *Aristarchus*, pp. 105-115 (where the
passage 290 b 12-29 is translated).

ᵇ How the upholders of the theory, at least before Plato's
time, estimated the relative distances of the planets and fixed
stars we do not know. (See Heath, *o.c.* p. 111.)　Plato himself, in the myth of Er, implies that the breadths of the
whorls on the spindle of Necessity represent the distances
between successive planets, and he states which is the widest,

192

THESE results clear up another point, namely that the theory that music is produced by their movements, because the sounds they make are harmonious, although ingeniously and brilliantly formulated by its authors, does not contain the truth.[a] It seems to some thinkers that bodies so great must inevitably produce a sound by their movement : even bodies on the earth do so, although they are neither so great in bulk nor moving at so high a speed, and as for the sun and the moon, and the stars, so many in number and enormous in size, all moving at a tremendous speed, it is incredible that they should fail to produce a noise of surpassing loudness. Taking this as their hypothesis, and also that the speeds of the stars, judged by their distances,[b] are in the ratios of the musical consonances, they affirm that the sound of the stars as they revolve is concordant.[c] To meet the difficulty that none of us is aware of this sound, they account for it by saying that the sound is with us right from birth and has thus no contrasting silence to show it up ; for voice and silence are perceived by contrast with each other, and so all mankind is

which the second widest and so on, but without giving any estimate of their relative widths (*Rep.* x. 616 E). One may however compare *Tim.* 36 D (Heath, pp. 163-164, Cornford, *Plato's Cosmology*, p. 79).

[c] It is difficult for us to understand a view according to which all the notes of an octave sounding simultaneously are supposed to produce a harmony, but Heath is no doubt right in saying (p. 115) that the Pythagoreans would not have been alive to this objection. The beauty of their discoveries about the relation between mathematical proportion and music exercised too strong a fascination over them. Heath refers to some later attempts to make the music harmonious in the accepted sense.

290 b
συνήθειαν οὐθὲν δοκεῖ διαφέρειν, καὶ τοῖς ἀνθρώ-
ποις ταὐτὸ συμβαίνειν.

30 Ταῦτα δή, καθάπερ εἴρηται πρότερον, ἐμμελῶς
μὲν λέγεται καὶ μουσικῶς, ἀδύνατον δὲ τοῦτον
ἔχειν τὸν τρόπον. οὐ γὰρ μόνον τὸ μηθὲν ἀκούειν
ἄτοπον, περὶ οὗ λύειν ἐγχειροῦσι τὴν αἰτίαν, ἀλλὰ
καὶ τὸ μηδὲν πάσχειν χωρὶς αἰσθήσεως. οἱ γὰρ
ὑπερβάλλοντες ψόφοι διακαίουσι καὶ τῶν ἀψύχων
35 σωμάτων τοὺς ὄγκους, οἷον ὁ τῆς βροντῆς διΐστησι
291 a λίθους καὶ τὰ καρτερώτατα τῶν σωμάτων. τοσούτων δὲ φερομένων, καὶ τοῦ ψόφου διϊόντος πρὸς
τὸ φερόμενον μέγεθος, πολλαπλάσιον μέγεθος
ἀναγκαῖον ἀφικνεῖσθαί τε δεῦρο καὶ τὴν ἰσχὺν
ἀμήχανον εἶναι τῆς βίας. ἀλλ᾽ εὐλόγως οὔτ᾽
5 ἀκούομεν οὔτε πάσχοντα φαίνεται τὰ σώματα
βίαιον οὐδὲν πάθος, διὰ τὸ μὴ ψοφεῖν· ἅμα δ᾽ ἐστὶ
τό τ᾽ αἴτιον τούτων δῆλον, καὶ μαρτύριον τῶν
εἰρημένων ἡμῖν λόγων, ὡς εἰσὶν ἀληθεῖς· τὸ γὰρ
ἀπορηθὲν καὶ ποιῆσαν τοὺς Πυθαγορείους φάναι
γίγνεσθαι συμφωνίαν τῶν φερομένων ἡμῖν ἐστι
10 τεκμήριον. ὅσα μὲν γὰρ αὐτὰ φέρεται, ποιεῖ
ψόφον καὶ πληγήν· ὅσα δ᾽ ἐν φερομένῳ ἐνδέδεται
ἢ ἐνυπάρχει, καθάπερ ἐν τῷ πλοίῳ τὰ μόρια, οὐχ
οἷόν τε ψοφεῖν, οὐδ᾽ αὖ τὸ πλοῖον, εἰ φέροιτο ἐν
ποταμῷ. καίτοι τοὺς αὐτοὺς λόγους ἂν ἐξείη
λέγειν, ὡς ἄτοπον εἰ μὴ φερόμενος ὁ ἱστὸς καὶ ἡ
15 πρύμνα ποιεῖ ψόφον πολὺν τηλικαύτης νεώς, ἢ
πάλιν αὐτὸ τὸ πλοῖον κινούμενον. τὸ δ᾽ ἐν μὴ
φερομένῳ φερόμενον ποιεῖ ψόφον· ἐν φερομένῳ δὲ

194

undergoing an experience like that of a copper-smith, who becomes by long habit indifferent to the din around him.

Now this theory, I repeat, shows great feeling for fitness and beauty, but nevertheless it cannot be true. The difficulty of our hearing nothing, which they attempt to solve, is not the only one ; there is also the absence of other effects unconnected with sensation. Excessively loud sounds are also able to shatter inanimate masses, *e.g.* the noise of thunder splits stones and other materials of the most enduring kinds. And when so many bodies are in motion, if the noise which travels here is in proportion to the size of the moving body, it must be many times greater than thunder when it reaches us, and of insupportable force and violence. No, there is a good reason why we neither hear any-thing ourselves nor see violence done to inanimate objects, namely that the movement is noiseless. The explanation is obvious, and at the same time bears out the truth of our arguments ; that is, what puzzled the Pythagoreans and made them postulate a harmony for the moving bodies, affords proofs of our own thesis. Things which are them-selves in motion create noise and impact, but whatever is fixed or otherwise contained in some-thing moving, as the different parts are in a ship, cannot create noise ; nor can the ship itself, if it is moving down a river. Yet one might produce the same arguments, that it is absurd for the mast and the poop of so great a ship to move without making considerable noise, or again for the ship as a whole to do so. But what makes a noise is that which is moving in a stationary medium. If

291 a

συνεχὲς καὶ μὴ ποιοῦντι πληγὴν ἀδύνατον ψοφεῖν.
ὥστ᾽ ἐνταῦθα λεκτέον ὡς εἴπερ ἐφέρετο τὰ σώματα
τούτων εἴτ᾽ ἐν ἀέρος πλήθει κεχυμένῳ κατὰ τὸ
20 πᾶν εἴτε πυρός, ὥσπερ πάντες φασίν, ἀναγκαῖον
ποιεῖν ὑπερφυᾶ τῷ μεγέθει τὸν ψόφον, τούτου δὲ
γινομένου καὶ δεῦρ᾽ ἀφικνεῖσθαι καὶ διακναίειν.
ὥστ᾽ ἐπείπερ οὐ φαίνεται τοῦτο συμβαῖνον, οὔτ᾽ ἂν
ἔμψυχον οὔτε βίαιον φέροιτο φορὰν οὐθὲν αὐτῶν,
25 ὥσπερ τὸ μέλλον ἔσεσθαι προνοούσης τῆς φύσεως,
ὅτι μὴ τοῦτον τὸν τρόπον ἐχούσης τῆς κινήσεως
οὐθὲν ἂν ἦν τῶν περὶ τὸν δεῦρο τόπον ὁμοίως ἔχον.

Ὅτι μὲν οὖν σφαιροειδῆ τὰ ἄστρα καὶ ὅτι οὐ
κινεῖται δι᾽ αὐτῶν, εἴρηται.

CHAPTER X

ARGUMENT

*The positions of the stars, relative to the outermost sphere
and to each other, have been adequately dealt with by astro-
nomers. We may note here that the speed at which each moves
in its own circle is proportionate to its distance from the*

29 Περὶ δὲ τῆς τάξεως αὐτῶν, ὃν μὲν τρόπον
30 ἕκαστον κεῖται¹ τῷ τὰ μὲν εἶναι πρότερα τὰ δ᾽
ὕστερα, καὶ πῶς ἔχει πρὸς ἄλληλα τοῖς ἀποστή-

---

¹ κεῖται. So Bekker with F alone. κινεῖται Allan with all
other mss.

---

a The inconsistency with ch. vii., in which friction with the
air is adduced to account for the brightness of the stars,
seems glaring and indefensible. There is no apparent reason

the medium is in motion continuous with that of the object, and produces no impact, there cannot be noise. Let it be said at once then, that if the bodies of the stars moved in a quantity either of air or of fire diffused throughout the whole, as everyone assumes them to do, the noise which they created would inevitably be tremendous, and this being so, it would reach and shatter things here on earth.[a] Since, then, this obviously does not happen, their motions cannot in any instance be due either to soul or to external violence. It is as if nature foresaw the consequences, how if the motion were otherwise than it is, nothing in our own terrestrial region could be the same.

This completes our proof that the stars are spherical and that they do not initiate their own movement.

CHAPTER X

ARGUMENT (continued)

outermost sphere ; for the motion of the latter exerts a counteracting influence, and those whose spheres are farthest removed from it suffer least from this. Here too we may refer to the mathematicians for details.

THE questions of their order, their relative positions [b] before or behind [c] each other, and their distances from one another, may best be studied in astro-

---

why it should not create as much noise as the situation imagined here.
[b] Or " movements," since Allan's κινεῖται for κεῖται has the better authority, and his reference to the κινήσεις of line 33 is pertinent.
[c] " Before " =nearer the sphere of the fixed stars (Simpl.).

291 a

μασιν, ἐκ τῶν περὶ ἀστρολογίαν θεωρείσθω·
λέγεται γὰρ ἱκανῶς. συμβαίνει δὲ κατὰ λόγον
γίγνεσθαι τὰς ἑκάστου κινήσεις τοῖς ἀποστήμασι
τῷ τὰς μὲν εἶναι θάττους τὰς δὲ βραδυτέρας· ἐπεὶ
35 γὰρ ὑπόκειται τὴν μὲν ἐσχάτην τοῦ οὐρανοῦ περι-
291 b φορὰν ἁπλῆν τ᾽ εἶναι καὶ ταχίστην, τὰς δὲ τῶν
ἄλλων βραδυτέρας τε καὶ πλείους (ἕκαστον γὰρ
ἀντιφέρεται τῷ οὐρανῷ κατὰ τὸν αὑτοῦ κύκλον),
εὔλογον ἤδη τὸ μὲν ἐγγυτάτω τῆς ἁπλῆς καὶ πρώτης περιφορᾶς ἐν πλείστῳ χρόνῳ διιέναι τὸν αὑτοῦ
5 κύκλον, τὸ δὲ πορρωτάτω ἐν ἐλαχίστῳ, τῶν δ᾽
ἄλλων ἀεὶ τὸ ἐγγύτερον ἐν πλείονι, τὸ δὲ πορρώτερον ἐν ἐλάττονι. τὸ μὲν γὰρ ἐγγυτάτω μάλιστα
κρατεῖται, τὸ δὲ πορρωτάτω πάντων ἥκιστα διὰ
τὴν ἀπόστασιν· τὰ δὲ μεταξὺ κατὰ λόγον ἤδη τῆς
10 ἀποστάσεως, ὥσπερ καὶ δεικνύουσιν οἱ μαθη-
ματικοί.

CHAPTER XI

ARGUMENT

That the stars are spherical. (a) *It has been shown*
(ch. viii.) *that the stars do not cause their own motion, and
therefore teleology demands that Nature should have given
them the shape which is least suited to motion. This is
the sphere.* (b) *Both direct observation and astronomical de-
duction make plain the sphericity of the moon, and all the
heavenly bodies will have the same shape.*

11 Τὸ δὲ σχῆμα τῶν ἄστρων ἑκάστου σφαιροειδὲς
μάλιστ᾽ ἄν τις εὐλόγως ὑπολάβοι. ἐπεὶ γὰρ
198

nomical writings, where they are adequately discussed. One characteristic is that their movements are faster or slower according to their distances. That is, once it has been admitted that the outermost revolution of the heaven is simple and is the swiftest of all, whereas that of the inner spheres is slower and composite (for each in performing its own revolution is going against the motion of the heaven), then it becomes natural for the star nearest to the simple and primary revolution to complete its own circle in the longest time, and the one farthest away in the shortest, and so with the others—the nearer in a longer time, the farther in a shorter. This is because the nearest one is most strongly counteracted by the primary motion, and the farthest least, owing to its distance. The others are influenced in proportion to their distances, and how this works out is demonstrated by the mathematicians.

CHAPTER XI

ARGUMENT (*continued*)

Simpl. accuses Aristotle's argument of circularity, on the ground that in ch. viii. the spherical shape of the stars was used to prove that they do not move themselves. But Stocks justly points out that the stars' lack of self-motion is first proved on other grounds (by elimination of other possibilities). Only after that is their spherical shape adduced, as something which " others assert," to lend the thesis additional support.

THE shape of each star is spherical, at least according to the most reasonable supposition. For it has been

ARISTOTLE

δέδεικται ὅτι οὐ πεφύκασι κινεῖσθαι δι' αὑτῶν, ἡ
δὲ φύσις οὐδὲν ἀλόγως οὐδὲ μάτην ποιεῖ, δῆλον
15 ὅτι καὶ σχῆμα τοιοῦτον ἀπέδωκε τοῖς ἀκινήτοις
ὃ ἥκιστά ἐστι κινητικόν. ἥκιστα δὲ κινητικὸν ἡ
σφαῖρα διὰ τὸ μηδὲν ἔχειν ὄργανον πρὸς τὴν
κίνησιν. ὥστε δῆλον ὅτι σφαιροειδῆ ἂν εἴη τὸν
ὄγκον.

Ἔτι δ' ὁμοίως μὲν ἅπαντα καὶ ἕν, ἡ δὲ σελήνη
20 δείκνυται διὰ τῶν περὶ τὴν ὄψιν ὅτι σφαιροειδής· οὐ
γὰρ ἂν ἐγίνετο αὐξανομένη καὶ φθίνουσα τὰ μὲν
πλεῖστα μηνοειδὴς ἢ ἀμφίκυρτος, ἅπαξ δὲ διχό-
τομος. καὶ πάλιν διὰ τῶν ἀστρολογικῶν, ὅτι οὐκ
ἂν ἦσαν αἱ τοῦ ἡλίου ἐκλείψεις μηνοειδεῖς. ὥστ'
εἴπερ ἓν τοιοῦτον, δῆλον ὅτι καὶ τἆλλα ἂν εἴη
σφαιροειδῆ.

CHAPTER XII

ARGUMENT

*Two difficulties remain before we leave the subject of the
stars : (1) the first heaven, or outermost sphere, which carries
the fixed stars, has one motion only (i.e. the simple motion
of one revolving sphere accounts for the appearances). But
there seems to be no correlation between the order of the
planets and the complexity of their motions. It is not true
that the planet nearest to the outermost sphere moves, say,
with two motions, the next with three and so on (i.e. there
is no proportionate increase of irregularity. According to
the beliefs of the time, which explained the irregularities of
planetary motion as due to the combined effect of more or
fewer concentric revolving spheres, this is expressed in terms
of " number of motions "). The moon and sun have fewer
motions than the planets which lie between them and the outer-*

demonstrated that they do not naturally move themselves; but Nature makes nothing which is purposeless or doomed to frustration; she must therefore have provided immobile objects with the sort of shape which is least adapted to motion. Now the least adapted to motion is the sphere, for it possesses no instrument to serve for that purpose. Clearly therefore the stars will consist of masses spherical in shape.

Again, one and all are alike, and the moon can be shown by the evidence of sight to be spherical. Were it any other shape, it would not appear crescent-shaped or gibbous during the greater part of its waxing and waning, and only at one moment semicircular. Or the proof can be taken from astronomy, which demonstrates that the sun in eclipse would not be crescent-shaped. If, then, one of the heavenly bodies is spherical, the others will clearly be spherical also.

CHAPTER XII

ARGUMENT (continued)

most sphere, and the earth does not move at all. Can this be explained? (2) Why does the single primary motion carry a whole host of stars, whereas each of the other stars has a separate motion of its own? (291 b 24—292 a 14).

In attempting a solution, we must bear in mind what we have hitherto left out of account, that the stars are no mere dead and passive lumps, but alive and active (292 a 18-22).

(1) Consider that (a) the nearer a thing is to its goal, the fewer steps it will need to reach it, (b) the larger the number of intermediate steps, the greater the chance of failing in one and so not reaching the end at all. Hence there are three

ARISTOTLE

classes : (i) *of things which are nearly perfect and therefore
reach perfection by one action only, (ii) of things which are
farther off and hence need to perform a number of actions
before they reach it, (iii) of things which are so far from perfection that they cannot hope to reach it, but either lie inert or
at most can perform only the first one or two of the actions
which the members of class (ii) successively performed in their
progress towards the ultimate goal. For this class, then,
these lower stages appear not as means but as the highest end
which they can hope to attain. Clearly the actions of class (i)
will be simple, of class (ii) complex, and of class (iii) again
simpler than those of class (ii). The first heaven is in class
(i), the outer planets are in class (ii), the sun, moon and earth
are in class (iii) (292 a 22–b 25).*

291 b 24　Δυοῖν δ' ἀπορίαιν οὔσαιν, περὶ ὧν εἰκότως ἂν
　25 ὁστισοῦν ἀπορήσειε, πειρατέον λέγειν τὸ φαινόμενον, αἰδοῦς ἀξίαν εἶναι νομίζοντας τὴν προθυμίαν
μᾶλλον ἢ θράσους, εἴ τις διὰ τὸ φιλοσοφίας διψῆν
καὶ μικρὰς εὐπορίας ἀγαπᾷ περὶ ὧν τὰς μεγίστας
ἔχομεν ἀπορίας. ἔστι δὲ πολλῶν ὄντων τοιούτων
　30 οὐχ ἥκιστα θαυμαστόν, διὰ τίνα ποτ' αἰτίαν οὐκ
ἀεὶ τὰ πλεῖον ἀπέχοντα τῆς πρώτης φορᾶς κινεῖται
πλείους κινήσεις, ἀλλὰ τὰ μεταξὺ πλείστας. εὔλογον γὰρ ἂν δόξειεν εἶναι τοῦ πρώτου σώματος
μίαν κινουμένου φορὰν τὸ πλησιαίτατον ἐλαχίστας
κινεῖσθαι κινήσεις, οἷον δύο, τὸ δ' ἐχόμενον τρεῖς ἢ
　35 τινα ἄλλην τοιαύτην τάξιν. νῦν δὲ συμβαίνει τοὐ-
ναντίον· ἐλάττους γὰρ ἥλιος καὶ σελήνη κινοῦνται
292 a κινήσεις ἢ τῶν πλανωμένων ἄστρων ἔνια· καίτοι
πορρώτερον τοῦ μέσου καὶ πλησιαίτερον τοῦ πρώ-

ARGUMENT (*continued*)

(2) *Two reasons are given.* (a) *The outermost sphere is far superior in life and energy to the others.* (b) *Each of the other spheres has more work to do than is apparent at first sight. The only acceptable explanation of a planet's motion is that it is carried on the innermost of a nest of concentric spheres revolving in different directions, each sphere imparting its own motion to the one beneath it. It follows that (since the spheres are material) every sphere except the one in which the planet is fixed has to find energy to move one or more other spheres besides itself, including the sphere which carries the actual planet. To accomplish this would be beyond their powers if a number of stars were added in the innermost sphere which all the others help to carry* (292 b 25—293 a 11).

THERE are two difficulties which might naturally be felt, and we must do our best to give the most plausible solution, looking upon a readiness to do so as evidence of modesty rather than of rashness, if the seeker, out of thirst for philosophy, rests content with but a little enlightenment in matters where we are surrounded by such unfathomable obscurities. These obscurities are many, and one of the most incomprehensible is this : how can we explain the fact that it is not the bodies farthest removed from the primary movement that have the most complex motions, but those which lie in between ? Considering that the primary body has only one motion, it would seem natural for the nearest one to it to have a very small number, say two, and the next one three, or some similar proportionate arrangement. But the opposite is true, for the sun and moon perform simpler motions than some of the planets, although the planets are farther from the centre and nearer the primary

του σώματός εἰσιν αὐτῶν. δῆλον δὲ τοῦτο περὶ
ἐνίων καὶ τῇ ὄψει γέγονεν· τὴν γὰρ σελήνην ἑω-
5 ράκαμεν διχότομον μὲν οὖσαν, ὑπελθοῦσαν δὲ τὸν
ἀστέρα τὸν Ἄρεος, καὶ ἀποκρυφθέντα μὲν κατὰ τὸ
μέλαν αὐτῆς, ἐξελθόντα δὲ κατὰ τὸ φανὸν καὶ
λαμπρόν. ὁμοίως δὲ καὶ περὶ τοὺς ἄλλους ἀστέρας
λέγουσιν οἱ πάλαι τετηρηκότες ἐκ πλείστων ἐτῶν
Αἰγύπτιοι καὶ Βαβυλώνιοι, παρ' ὧν πολλὰς πίστεις
ἔχομεν περὶ ἑκάστου τῶν ἄστρων.

10 Τοῦτό τε δὴ δικαίως ἀπορήσειεν ἄν τις, καὶ διὰ
τίνα ποτ' αἰτίαν ἐν μὲν τῇ πρώτῃ φορᾷ τοσοῦτόν
ἐστιν ἄστρων πλῆθος ὥστε τῶν ἀναριθμήτων εἶναι
δοκεῖν τὴν πᾶσαν τάξιν, τῶν δ' ἄλλων ἓν χωρὶς
ἕκαστον, δύο δ' ἢ πλείω οὐ φαίνεται ἐν τῇ αὐτῇ
ἐνδεδεμένα φορᾷ.

15 Περὶ δὴ τούτων ζητεῖν μὲν καλῶς ἔχει καὶ τὴν
ἐπὶ πλεῖον σύνεσιν, καίπερ μικρὰς ἔχοντας ἀφορμὰς
καὶ τοσαύτην ἀπόστασιν ἀπέχοντας τῶν περὶ αὐτὰ
συμβαινόντων· ὅμως δ' ἐκ τῶν τοιούτων θεωροῦσιν
οὐδὲν ἄλογον ἂν δόξειεν εἶναι τὸ νῦν ἀπορούμενον.

ᵃ Cf. The Times for Monday 19 July 1937 : " London
had a perfect view of the eclipsing of Mars by the moon on
Saturday night. Mars showed very brightly as it approached
the unilluminated edge of the moon, and began to fade at
10.13 exactly. Within 30 seconds it had disappeared. The
whole phenomenon was clearly visible to the naked eye.
Mars did not appear to fade out until it was inside the unilluminated edge of the moon. The spectacle was all the
more vivid because, at the moment of the disappearance,
only a very few other stars and planets had become visible."
204

body, as has in certain cases actually been seen; for instance, the moon has been observed, when half-full, to approach the planet Mars, which has then been blotted out behind the dark half of the moon, and come out again on the bright side.[a] Similar observations about the other planets are recorded by the Egyptians and the Babylonians, who have watched the stars from the remotest past, and to whom we owe many incontrovertible facts about each of them.

That is one question which it is proper to raise. Another is this : what can be the reason why the primary motion should include such a multitude of stars that their whole array seems to be beyond counting, whereas each of the other motions involves one only, and we never see two or more caught in the same revolution ?

These are questions on which it is worth while seeking boldly to extend our understanding. It is true that we have very little to start from, and that we are situated at a great distance from the phenomena that we are trying to investigate. Nevertheless if we base our inquiry on what we know, the present difficulty will not appear as

---

Stocks quotes a passage from Kepler (*Astronomia Nova*, 1609, p. 323), in which he estimates that the date of the occultation referred to by Aristotle was 4 April 357 B.C. A modern astronomer (K. Schoch, *Planetentafeln für Jedermann*, Berlin 1927, col. xx.) determines the true time as 4 May 357 B.C. about 9 P.M. Athens time. (I owe this reference to the kindness of Mr. D. H. Sadler, Superintendent of H.M. Nautical Almanac Office, who also informs me that the frequency of occultations of Mars observable under good conditions from any one place is, approximately, 50 in a period of 1000 years. The actual number of occultations is very much larger.)

292 a

ἀλλ' ἡμεῖς ὡς περὶ σωμάτων αὐτῶν μόνον καὶ
20 μονάδων τάξιν μὲν ἐχόντων, ἀψύχων δὲ πάμπαν,
διανοούμεθα· δεῖ δ' ὡς μετεχόντων ὑπολαμβάνειν
πράξεως καὶ ζωῆς· οὕτω γὰρ οὐθὲν δόξει παρά-
λογον εἶναι τὸ συμβαῖνον. ἔοικε γὰρ τῷ μὲν
ἄριστα ἔχοντι ὑπάρχειν τὸ εὖ ἄνευ πράξεως, τῷ δ'
ἐγγύτατα διὰ ὀλίγης καὶ μιᾶς, τοῖς δὲ πορρωτάτω
25 διὰ πλειόνων, ὥσπερ ἐπὶ σώματος τὸ μὲν οὐδὲ
γυμναζόμενον εὖ ἔχει, τὸ δὲ μικρὰ περιπατῆσαν,
τῷ δὲ καὶ δρόμου δεῖ καὶ πάλης καὶ κονίσεως,[1]
πάλιν δ' ἑτέρῳ οὐδ' ὁποσαοῦν πονοῦντι τοῦτό γ'
ἂν ἔτι ὑπάρξαι τἀγαθόν, ἀλλ' ἕτερόν τι. ἔστι δὲ
τὸ κατορθοῦν χαλεπὸν ἢ τὸ πολλὰ ἢ τὸ πολλάκις,
30 οἷον μυρίους ἀστραγάλους Χίους βαλεῖν ἀμήχανον,
ἀλλ' ἕνα ἢ δύο ῥᾷον. καὶ πάλιν ὅταν τοδὶ μὲν δέῃ
τοῦδ' ἕνεκα ποιῆσαι, τοῦτο δ' ἄλλου καὶ τοῦτο
ἑτέρου, ἐν μὲν ἑνὶ ἢ δυσὶ ῥᾷον ἐπιτυχεῖν, ὅσῳ δ'
292 b ἂν διὰ πλειόνων, χαλεπώτερον. διὸ δεῖ νομίζειν
καὶ τὴν τῶν ἄστρων πρᾶξιν εἶναι τοιαύτην οἵα περ

---

[1] κινήσεως FM : κἀκοντίσεως coni. Bywater.

---

[a] κόνισις if genuine is probably unique. (*Cf.* D. W.
Thompson on *Hist. anim.* 623 b 32 (Oxford translation).)
On the other hand, Bywater's reason for changing it, namely
that the third term in the phrase should be a distinct form of
exercise from running or wrestling (*J. Phil.* xxviii. p. 241),

206

anything inexplicable. The fact is that we are inclined to think of the stars as mere bodies or units, occurring in a certain order but completely lifeless; whereas we ought to think of them as partaking of life and initiative. Once we do this, the events will no longer seem surprising. It is reasonable for that which is in the best state to possess the good without taking action, for that which is nearest to the best to obtain it by means of little, or a single, action, and for those things which are farther from it to need more; in the same way as one body may be healthy without any exercise at all, another by means of a little walking, a third may need running and wrestling and violent exertion,[a] and again a fourth despite tremendous efforts cannot preserve this particular good, but only something else. To succeed in many things, or many times, is difficult; for instance, to repeat the same throw ten thousand times[b] with the dice would be impossible, whereas to make it once or twice is comparatively easy. We must consider too that whenever A must be done as a means to B, B as a means to C, and C as a means to some further end, then if the intermediate steps are one or two, it is easier to attain the end, but the more they are the more difficult it becomes. With these considerations in mind, we must suppose the action of the planets to be analogous to that of animals

is not a strong one. The second καί can quite well introduce a general term covering both the previous two, and this either κίνησις or κόνισις (=training in the dust of the palaestra) might be. Simpl.'s explanation suggests that it refers more specifically to πάλη.

[b] The reading here does not affect the argument. See Stocks's and Allan's notes for variants.

292 b

ἡ τῶν ζῴων καὶ φυτῶν. καὶ γὰρ ἐνταῦθα αἱ τοῦ
ἀνθρώπου πλεῖσται πράξεις· πολλῶν γὰρ τῶν εὖ
δύναται τυχεῖν, ὥστε πολλὰ πράττει, καὶ ἄλλων
5 ἕνεκα. τῷ δ᾽ ὡς ἄριστα ἔχοντι οὐθὲν δεῖ πράξεως·
ἔστι γὰρ αὐτὸ τὸ οὗ ἕνεκα, ἡ δὲ πρᾶξις ἀεί ἐστιν
ἐν δυσίν, ὅταν καὶ οὗ ἕνεκα ᾖ καὶ τὸ τούτου ἕνεκα.
τῶν δ᾽ ἄλλων ζῴων ἐλάττους, τῶν δὲ φυτῶν μικρά
τις καὶ μία ἴσως· ἢ γὰρ ἕν τί ἐστιν οὗ τύχοι ἄν,
ὥσπερ καὶ ἄνθρωπος, ἢ καὶ τὰ πολλὰ πάντα πρὸ
10 ὁδοῦ ἐστι πρὸς τὸ ἄριστον. τὸ μὲν οὖν ἔχει καὶ
μετέχει τοῦ ἀρίστου, τὸ δ᾽ ἀφικνεῖται εὐθὺς[1] δι᾽

---

[1] εὐθὺς is a conjecture of Stocks, adopted by Allan. ˙ (Stocks's
reference to line 20 for comparison must be a mistake for
23.) The mss. and Bekker have ἐγγύς.

---

[a] The argument and analogy may perhaps be made clearer
by a diagram.

Outside the comparison
- First Mover (no movement because it = the good).
- First Heaven (simple movement because it is nearest to the good).

Man = Planets with many motions (complex movement because they reach the good by diverse routes and at several removes).

Animals and plants = Sun, moon and earth (simple movement or none at all, because they have no hope of reaching the highest good, but must be content with goods lying near at hand).

208

and plants.[a] For here on earth it is the actions
of mankind that are the most varied, and the reason
is that man has a variety of goods within his reach,
wherefore his actions are many, and directed to
ends outside themselves. That which is in the
best possible state, on the other hand, has no need
of action. It is its own end, whereas action is
always concerned with two factors, occurring when
there is on the one hand an end proposed, and
on the other the means towards that end. Yet
the animals lower than man have less variety of
action than he, and plants might be said to have
one limited mode of action only ; for either there
is only one end for them to attain (as in truth there
is for man also),[b] or if there are many, yet they
all conduce directly to the best. To sum up, there
is one thing which possesses, or shares in, the best,

[b] This seems at first sight to contradict lines 2-4 above,
where the variety of man's actions is accounted for by saying
that he aims at a variety of " goods." The explanation is
that it is possible for something to be both a good in itself
and at the same time a step towards a higher good. *Cf.*
Eth. Nic. 1096 b 16 : καθ᾽ αὑτὰ δὲ (*sc.* ἀγαθὰ) ποῖα θείη τις
ἄν; ἢ ὅσα καὶ μονούμενα διώκεται, οἷον τὸ φρονεῖν καὶ ὁρᾶν
καὶ ἡδοναί τινες καὶ τιμαί; ταῦτα γὰρ εἰ καὶ δι᾽ ἄλλο τι
διώκομεν, ὅμως τῶν καθ᾽ αὑτὰ ἀγαθῶν θείη τις ἄν. The
parenthesis here is thus a refinement on the earlier sentence,
and points out that although man has within his reach a
variety of ends which it is right to call good in themselves,
they are nevertheless not the highest good attainable by him,
which is unique. (It is of course, as the *Ethics* tells us,
theoria.) It is this variety of subordinate goods which
marks him off from the lower creatures.

292 b

ὀλίγων, τὸ δὲ διὰ πολλῶν, τὸ δ' οὐδ' ἐγχειρεῖ, ἀλλ'
ἱκανὸν εἰς τὸ ἐγγὺς τοῦ ἐσχάτου ἐλθεῖν· οἷον εἰ
ὑγίεια τέλος, τὸ μὲν δὴ ἀεὶ ὑγιαίνει, τὸ δ' ἰσχναν-
θέν, τὸ δὲ δραμὸν καὶ ἰσχναθέν, τὸ δὲ καὶ ἄλλο
15 τι πρᾶξαν τοῦ δραμεῖν ἕνεκα, ὥστε πλείους αἱ
κινήσεις· ἕτερον δ' ἀδυνατεῖ πρὸς τὸ ὑγιᾶναι ἐλθεῖν,
ἀλλὰ πρὸς τὸ δραμεῖν μόνον ἢ ἰσχναθῆναι, καὶ
τούτων θάτερον τέλος αὐτοῖς. μάλιστα μὲν γὰρ
ἐκείνου τυχεῖν ἄριστον πᾶσι τοῦ τέλους· εἰ δὲ μή,
ἀεὶ ἄμεινόν ἐστιν ὅσῳ ἂν ἐγγύτερον ᾖ τοῦ ἀρίστου.
20 καὶ διὰ τοῦτο ἡ μὲν γῆ ὅλως οὐ κινεῖται, τὰ δ'
ἐγγὺς ὀλίγας κινήσεις· οὐ γὰρ ἀφικνεῖται πρὸς τὸ
ἔσχατον, ἀλλὰ μέχρι ὅτου δύναται τυχεῖν τῆς
θειοτάτης ἀρχῆς. ὁ δὲ πρῶτος οὐρανὸς εὐθὺς
τυγχάνει διὰ μιᾶς κινήσεως. τὰ δ' ἐν μέσῳ τοῦ
πρώτου καὶ τῶν ἐσχάτων ἀφικνεῖται μέν, διὰ
πλειόνων δ' ἀφικνεῖται κινήσεων.

Περὶ δὲ τῆς ἀπορίας ὅτι κατὰ μὲν τὴν πρώτην
μίαν οὖσαν φορὰν πολὺ πλῆθος συνέστηκεν ἄστρων,
τῶν δ' ἄλλων χωρὶς ἕκαστον εἴληφεν ἰδίας κινήσεις, δι' ἓν μὲν ἄν τις πρῶτον εὐλόγως οἰηθείη
τοῦθ' ὑπάρχειν· νοῆσαι γὰρ δεῖ τῆς ζωῆς καὶ τῆς

ᵃ This sentence is difficult, and I do not see that it helps to
suggest, as Stocks does, that ἀλλά here is used for ἀλλ' ἤ.
That should mean that a thing "does not attain to the
ultimate except with a qualification." The meaning given
by Stocks, that it does not attain to the ultimate at all, but
only comes near to it, would surely be easier to obtain if
ἀλλά kept its normal sense. A.'s meaning must be explained
by his previous sentence that "where it is impossible to
attain the end, a thing gets better and better the nearer it
approaches to the best." We may substitute θειότερον for
ἄμεινον in that sentence. All nature shares to *some* extent in
the divine principle, and divinity is a quality that admits of

a second which reaches it immediately by few
stages, a third which reaches it through many
stages, and yet another which does not even attempt
to reach it, but is content merely to approach near
to the highest. For example, if health is the end,
then one creature is always healthy, another by
reducing, a third by running in order to reduce, a
fourth by doing something else to prepare itself
for running, and so going through a larger number
of motions : another creature cannot attain to
health, but only to running or reducing. To such
creatures one of these latter is the end. To attain
the ultimate end would be in the truest sense best
for all ; but if that is impossible, a thing gets better
and better the nearer it is to the best. This then
is the reason why the earth does not move at all,
and the bodies near it have only few motions.
They do not arrive at the highest, but reach only
as far as it is within their power to obtain a share
in the divine principle.[a] But the first heaven
reaches it immediately by one movement, and the
stars that are between the first heaven and the
bodies farthest from it reach it indeed, but reach it
through a number of movements.

Concerning the difficulty that in the primary
movement, in spite of its uniqueness, a whole host
of stars is involved, whereas each of the other stars
has separate motions of its own, there is one thing
which may be thought of first of all as supplying a
satisfactory cause for this. In considering each of

comparatives. But the earth and the bodies near it do not
arrive at the ultimate, and cannot ever be described by the
superlative. (Simpl.'s explanation is vitiated by Neo-
platonic preoccupations.)

30 ἀρχῆς ἑκάστης πολλὴν ὑπεροχὴν εἶναι τῆς πρώτης
πρὸς τὰς ἄλλας, εἴη δ᾽ ἂν ἥδε συμβαίνουσα κατὰ
λόγον· ἡ μὲν γὰρ πρώτη μία οὖσα πολλὰ κινεῖ τῶν
σωμάτων τῶν θείων, αἱ δὲ πολλαὶ οὖσαι ἓν μόνον
293 a ἑκάστη· τῶν γὰρ πλανωμένων ἓν ὁτιοῦν πλείους
φέρεται φοράς. ταύτῃ τε οὖν ἀνισάζει ἡ φύσις καὶ
ποιεῖ τινὰ τάξιν, τῇ μὲν μιᾷ φορᾷ πολλὰ ἀποδοῦσα
σώματα τῷ δ᾽ ἑνὶ σώματι πολλὰς φοράς.

5 Καὶ ἔτι διὰ τόδε ἓν ἔχουσι σῶμα αἱ ἄλλαι φοραί,
ὅτι πολλὰ σώματα κινοῦσιν αἱ πρὸ τῆς τελευταίας
καὶ τῆς ἓν ἄστρον ἐχούσης· ἐν πολλαῖς γὰρ σφαίραις
ἡ τελευταία σφαῖρα ἐνδεδεμένη φέρεται, ἑκάστη
δὲ σφαῖρα σῶμα τυγχάνει ὄν. ἐκείνης ἂν οὖν
κοινὸν εἴη τὸ ἔργον· αὐτῇ[1] μὲν γὰρ ἑκάστῃ ἡ ἴδιος
10 φύσει φορά, αὕτη δὲ οἷον πρόσκειται. παντὸς δὲ
πεπερασμένου σώματος πρὸς πεπερασμένον ἡ
δύναμίς ἐστιν.

Ἀλλὰ περὶ μὲν τῶν τὴν ἐγκύκλιον φερομένων
κίνησιν ἄστρων εἴρηται ποῖ᾽ ἄττα κατά τε τὴν
οὐσίαν ἐστὶ καὶ κατὰ τὸ σχῆμα, καὶ περὶ τῆς φορᾶς
καὶ τῆς τάξεως αὐτῶν.

---

[1] The reading αὐτῇ is due to Prantl, and adopted by Allan.
M has αὐτὴ, Bekker αὕτη, with all other mss.

---

[a] *i.e.* the motion of the innermost of the set of concentric

CHAPTER XIII

ARGUMENT

*The earth, its situation and shape, and the question
whether and why it is at rest or in motion. Review of extant
theories.*

these living principles, we must bear in mind that the primary one has an immense superiority over the rest, and this falls in with our argument. The primary principle, we say, though one, moves many of the divine bodies, but the others, which are many, move only one each, for any one of the planets moves with several motions. This then is Nature's way of equalizing things and introducing order, by assigning many bodies to the one motion, and to the one body many motions.

Here is a second reason why the other motions carry one body: the motions before the last one, which carries the one star,[a] move many bodies, for the last sphere moves round embedded in a number of spheres, and each sphere is corporeal. The work of the last one, therefore, will be shared by the others. Each one has its own proper and natural motion, and this one is, as it were, added. But every limited body has limited powers.

Here we finish the subject of the revolving stars, their substance and their shape, their motion and their order.

spheres whose combined motions are supposed to account for the irregular path of the planet itself. Stocks's reference to the motion which carries the star as the outermost is a curious aberration.

CHAPTER XIII

ARGUMENT (continued)

The Pythagoreans hold that the earth revolves like a planet round the centre, which is occupied by fire, and believe in the existence of a " counter-earth " revolving opposite to it.

213

(*Some even suppose the possibility of more than one such body, and would account thus for the frequency of lunar eclipses. 293 b 21-25.*) *To the argument that the earth's removal from the centre would disturb the phenomena, they reply that the surface of the earth, from which we observe, is in any case not at the centre. With them may be mentioned some (unnamed) who assign the central place to fire on the grounds that fire is a more honourable element than earth, and the centre, like the boundary, is the place of honour. The Pythagoreans add that the centre being the most important spot needs to be guarded, and call the fire which they assume there the "guard-house of Zeus," ignoring the possibility that geometrical centre and centre of importance may not coincide (293 a 15–b 30).*

Others, e.g. Plato in the Timaeus, *say that it is at the centre but yet in motion (293 b 30-32).*

Some suppose it spherical in shape, others flat and drum-like. The latter adduce as part of their evidence the straight line which it shows against the rising or setting sun, but this fails to take into account the immense size and distance of the bodies concerned (293 b 32—294 a 10).

To account for its immobility, (a) some, like Xenophanes, suppose it to extend downwards to infinity. (b) Others (Thales) say that it rests on water. But (i) what does the water rest on? (ii) Water is lighter than earth, and earth sinks in water. (c) Anaximenes, Anaxagoras and Demo-critus adduce its flatness: it compresses the air beneath it, and air so compressed can bear great weights. But to achieve this compression, it need only be of sufficient size: its shape is irrelevant (294 a 10–b 30).

The question of the rest or motion of the earth should be approached on more general grounds, i.e. by asking whether in general the elements have natural motions. This has already been settled (bk. i. chs. ii.-iv). This approach leads to consideration of the "vortex" theory, according to which the elements underwent an original sorting-out owing to the whirling motion of the Universe, by which the heaviest were forced to the centre. On this theory the earth moved to the centre by constraint, consequently it remains there now by constraint. What is this constraint? Here some adherents of the vortex adduce flatness and size (previously discussed), others (e.g. Empedocles) the swiftness of the motion of the heavens around it. These latter compare the way in which a cup of water can be whirled round on a string without the water spilling. Criticisms: *(i) It is legitimate to ask the question: if the sort of constraint posited (whether air compressed beneath or swiftness of the heavens) were removed, where would the earth go? If it is by constraint that it remains at the centre, it must have a natural motion. In which direction is this? They can give no satisfactory answer. (ii) In the cosmology of Empedocles, there is nothing to account for the earth's immobility at the time when the elements had all been separated by Strife. (iii) Can the vortex account for the fact that at the present time heavy objects move towards the earth? (iv) The vortex will not explain the upward motion of fire. But if this is natural, the earth may have a natural motion too. (v) The theory presupposes weight and lightness, since the vortex could not have separated things if they did not already differ in weight. But how were heavy and light distinguished if not by the doctrine of natural places? (sc. and this doctrine does away with the need for a vortex)* (294 b 30—295 b 9).

A few have argued that the earth is at rest because, being at the centre and in exactly the same relationship to every part of the Universe around it, it has no reason to move in one direction rather than in another. Criticisms: *(i) This makes the earth's immobility depend solely on its position. Are we then to say that fire, if placed at the centre, would remain there no less than earth? (ii) Earth not only rests at the centre but moves towards it. This indicates that the doctrine of natural places, and not the argument from indifferent position, affords the true explanation. (iii) Their answer is too partial. They ask why earth remains at the centre, but not why fire remains at the circumference. The doctrine of natural places accounts for both at once. (iv) The elements exhibit motion as well as rest, but their explanation ignores this. (v) Why should not the earth fly off in all directions at once ? Fire does this, and it is quite compatible with the indifference theory. It is only motion as a whole in one direction which could not be reconciled with it. The difference between the behaviour of earth and fire must be*

293 a 15 Λοιπὸν δὲ περὶ τῆς γῆς εἰπεῖν, οὗ τε τυγχάνει κειμένη, καὶ πότερον τῶν ἠρεμούντων ἐστὶν ἢ τῶν κινουμένων, καὶ περὶ τοῦ σχήματος αὐτῆς.

Περὶ μὲν οὖν τῆς θέσεως οὐ τὴν αὐτὴν ἅπαντες ἔχουσι δόξαν, ἀλλὰ τῶν πλείστων ἐπὶ τοῦ μέσου κεῖσθαι λεγόντων, ὅσοι τὸν ὅλον οὐρανὸν πεπερα-
20 σμένον εἶναί φασιν, ἐναντίως οἱ περὶ τὴν Ἰταλίαν, καλούμενοι δὲ Πυθαγόρειοι λέγουσιν· ἐπὶ μὲν γὰρ τοῦ μέσου πῦρ εἶναί φασι, τὴν δὲ γῆν, ἓν τῶν ἄστρων οὖσαν, κύκλῳ φερομένην περὶ τὸ μέσον νύκτα τε καὶ ἡμέραν ποιεῖν. ἔτι δ᾽ ἐναντίαν ἄλλην ταύτῃ κατασκευάζουσι γῆν, ἣν ἀντίχθονα ὄνομα
25 καλοῦσιν, οὐ πρὸς τὰ φαινόμενα τοὺς λόγους καὶ τὰς αἰτίας ζητοῦντες, ἀλλὰ πρός τινας λόγους καὶ δόξας αὑτῶν τὰ φαινόμενα προσέλκοντες καὶ πειρώμενοι συγκοσμεῖν. πολλοῖς δ᾽ ἂν καὶ ἑτέροις συνδόξειε μὴ δεῖν τῇ γῇ τὴν τοῦ μέσου χώραν ἀποδιδόναι, τὸ πιστὸν οὐκ ἐκ τῶν φαινομένων
30 ἀθροῦσιν ἀλλὰ μᾶλλον ἐκ τῶν λόγων. τῷ γὰρ τιμιωτάτῳ οἴονται προσήκειν τὴν τιμιωτάτην ὑπάρχειν χώραν, εἶναι δὲ πῦρ μὲν γῆς τιμιώτερον, τὸ δὲ πέρας τῶν μεταξύ, τὸ δ᾽ ἔσχατον καὶ τὸ μέσον πέρας· ὥστ᾽ ἐκ τούτων ἀναλογιζόμενοι οὐκ

accounted for otherwise, i.e. by their own natural tendencies. (vi) The indifference theory could not rule out motion in the form of expansion or contraction. All things considered, we must conclude that the assumption of "indifference" is by itself insufficient to account for immobility (295 b 10— 296 a 23).

It remains to speak of the earth, where it is, whether it should be classed among things at rest or things in motion, and of its shape.

Concerning its position there is some divergence of opinion. Most of those who hold that the whole Universe is finite say that it lies at the centre, but this is contradicted by the Italian school called Pythagoreans. These affirm that the centre is occupied by fire, and that the earth is one of the stars, and creates night and day as it travels in a circle about the centre. In addition they invent another earth, lying opposite our own, which they call by the name of " counter-earth," not seeking accounts and explanations in conformity with the appearances, but trying by violence to bring the appearances into line with accounts and opinions of their own. There are many others too who might agree that it is wrong to assign the central position to the earth, men who see proof not in the appearances but rather in abstract theory. These reason that the most honourable body ought to occupy the most honourable place, that fire is more honourable than earth, that a limit is a more honourable place than what lies between limits, and that the centre and outer boundary are the limits. Arguing from these premises, they say it must be

217

οἴονται ἐπὶ τοῦ μέσου κεῖσθαι τῆς σφαίρας αὐτήν, ἀλλὰ μᾶλλον τὸ πῦρ.

Ἔτι δ' οἵ γε Πυθαγόρειοι καὶ διὰ τὸ μάλιστα προσήκειν φυλάττεσθαι τὸ κυριώτατον τοῦ παντὸς —τὸ δὲ μέσον εἶναι τοιοῦτον—[ὃ]¹ Διὸς φυλακὴν ὀνομάζουσι τὸ ταύτην ἔχον τὴν χώραν πῦρ, ὥσπερ 5 τὸ μέσον ἁπλῶς λεγόμενον, καὶ τὸ τοῦ μεγέθους μέσον καὶ τοῦ πράγματος ὂν μέσον καὶ τῆς φύσεως. καίτοι καθάπερ ἐν τοῖς ζῴοις οὐ ταὐτὸν τοῦ ζῴου καὶ τοῦ σώματος μέσον, οὕτως ὑποληπτέον μᾶλλον καὶ περὶ τὸν ὅλον οὐρανόν. διὰ μὲν οὖν ταύτην τὴν αἰτίαν οὐθὲν αὐτοὺς δεῖ θορυβεῖσθαι περὶ τὸ πᾶν, 10 οὐδ' εἰσάγειν φυλακὴν ἐπὶ τὸ κέντρον, ἀλλ' ἐκεῖνο ζητεῖν τὸ μέσον, ποῖόν τι² καὶ ποῦ πέφυκεν. ἐκεῖνο μὲν γὰρ ἀρχὴ τὸ μέσον καὶ τίμιον, τὸ δὲ τοῦ τόπου μέσον ἔοικε τελευτῇ μᾶλλον ἢ ἀρχῇ· τὸ μὲν γὰρ ὁριζόμενον τὸ μέσον, τὸ δ' ὁρίζον τὸ πέρας. τι- μιώτερον δὲ τὸ περιέχον καὶ τὸ πέρας ἢ τὸ περαινό- 15 μενον· τὸ μὲν γὰρ ὕλη τὸ δ' οὐσία τῆς συστάσεως ἐστίν.

Περὶ μὲν οὖν τοῦ τόπου τῆς γῆς ταύτην ἔχουσί τινες τὴν δόξαν, ὁμοίως δὲ καὶ περὶ μονῆς καὶ κινήσεως· οὐ γὰρ τὸν αὐτὸν τρόπον ἅπαντες ὑπο-

---

¹ ὃ secl. Allan.
² τι. So Prantl and Allan. Bekker's τε has the sole sup- port of L.

ᵃ Professor Cornford (*Plato's Cosmology* 126 ff.) discusses the possibility that these " many others " were distinguished from the ordinary Pythagoreans by holding, not the planetary theory of the earth, but the view that, though centrally situated, it had fire at its heart. *Cf.* Simpl. 512. 9-12. These according to Simpl. are a " more genuine " variety

not the earth, but rather fire, that is situated at the centre of the sphere.[a]

The Pythagoreans make a further point. Because the most important part of the Universe—which is the centre—ought more than any to be guarded, they call the fire which occupies this place the Watch-tower of Zeus, as if it were the centre in an unambiguous sense, being at the same time the geometrical centre and the natural centre of the thing itself. But we should rather suppose the same to be true of the whole world as is true of animals, namely that the centre of the animal and the centre of its body are not the same thing.[b] For this reason there is no need for them to be alarmed about the Universe, nor to call in a guard for its mathematical centre ; they ought rather to consider what sort of thing the true centre is, and what is its natural place. For it is that centre which should be held in honour as a starting-point ; the local centre would seem to be rather an end than a starting-point, for that which is defined is the local centre, that which defines it is the boundary : but that which encompasses and sets bounds is of more worth than that which is bounded, for the one is matter, the other the substance of the structure.

This then is the opinion of some about the position of the earth, and on the question of its rest or motion there are conformable views. Here

of Pythagoreans. (His authority is Aristotle himself in his *Pythagorica*.) On the two doctrines see also Hilda Richardson in *Class. Quart.* xx. (1926) pp. 118 ff.

[b] The logical, or real, centre of an animal is the heart. For its position in the body, *cf. De part. anim.* 665 b 21, 666 b 3.

λαμβάνουσιν, ἀλλ' ὅσοι μὲν μηδ' ἐπὶ τοῦ μέσου
κεῖσθαί φασιν αὐτήν, κινεῖσθαι κύκλῳ περὶ τὸ
20 μέσον, οὐ μόνον δὲ ταύτην, ἀλλὰ καὶ τὴν ἀντίχθονα,
καθάπερ εἴπομεν πρότερον. ἐνίοις δὲ δοκεῖ καὶ
πλείω σώματα τοιαῦτα ἐνδέχεσθαι φέρεσθαι περὶ
τὸ μέσον, ἡμῖν δὲ ἄδηλα διὰ τὴν ἐπιπρόσθησιν τῆς
γῆς. διὸ καὶ τὰς τῆς σελήνης ἐκλείψεις πλείους ἢ
τὰς τοῦ ἡλίου γίγνεσθαί φασιν· τῶν γὰρ φερομένων
25 ἕκαστον ἀντιφράττειν αὐτήν, ἀλλ' οὐ μόνον τὴν γῆν.
ἐπεὶ γὰρ οὐκ ἔστιν ἡ γῆ κέντρον, ἀλλ' ἀπέχει τὸ
ἡμισφαίριον αὐτῆς ὅλον, οὐθὲν κωλύειν οἴονται τὰ
φαινόμενα συμβαίνειν ὁμοίως μὴ κατοικοῦσιν ἡμῖν
ἐπὶ τοῦ κέντρου, ὥσπερ κἂν εἰ ἐπὶ τοῦ μέσου ἦν
ἡ γῆ· οὐθὲν γὰρ οὐδὲ νῦν ποιεῖν ἐπίδηλον τὴν
30 ἡμίσειαν ἀπέχοντας ἡμᾶς διάμετρον. ἔνιοι δὲ καὶ
κειμένην ἐπὶ τοῦ κέντρου φασὶν αὐτὴν ἴλλεσθαι καὶ
κινεῖσθαι¹ περὶ τὸν διὰ παντὸς τεταμένον πόλον,
ὥσπερ ἐν τῷ Τιμαίῳ γέγραπται.

---

¹ ἴλλεσθαι καὶ κινεῖσθαι. Bekker with HL omits καὶ κινεῖσθαι,
but cf. 296 a 26 below. For ἴλλεσθαι (M, probably first hand
of E, Simpl. and Alex.), JFHL have εἰλεῖσθαι.

ᵃ *Timaeus* 40 B. This is not the place for discussion of
the famous controversy in which this statement is involved.
It is sufficient to refer to the two most recent contributions,
those of A. E. Taylor in his *Commentary on Plato's Timaeus*
(Oxford 1928) 226 ff. and F. M. Cornford in *Plato's Cosmology* (Kegan Paul 1937) 120 ff., where the other necessary
references can be found. It may be permitted to mention
briefly Professor Cornford's view, because it is the only one
which is consistent with the unambiguous part of Aristotle's
statement here and at the same time provides a satisfactory
explanation of the earth's behaviour in the *Timaeus*. In
Aristotle's words, the earth, according to the account of the

again all do not think alike. Those who deny that it lies at the centre suppose that it moves in a circle about the centre, and not the earth alone, but also the counter-earth, as we have already explained. Some even think it possible that there are a number of such bodies carried round the centre, invisible to us owing to the interposition of the earth. This serves them too as a reason why eclipses of the moon are more frequent than those of the sun, namely that it is blocked by each of these moving bodies, not only by the earth. Since the earth's surface is not in any case the centre, but distant the whole hemisphere from the centre, they do not feel any difficulty in supposing that the phenomena are the same although we do not occupy the centre as they would be if the earth were in the middle. For even on the current view there is nothing to show that we are distant from the centre by half the earth's diameter. Some again say that although the earth lies at the centre, it " winds," *i.e.* is in motion, " round the axis which stretches right through," as is written in the *Timaeus*.ᵃ

Timaeus and some others, " lies at the centre " (κεῖσθαι ἐπὶ τοῦ μέσου). Therefore in Aristotle's opinion at least, it did not slide continually up and down the axis of the Universe, passing and re-passing the centre but never for a moment resting at it, and we need not, in discussing the present passage, linger over the theory of Burnet and Taylor which posits such a motion. It remains to consider whether the " winding " (ἴλλεσθαι) of the earth about the axis means revolution in the same place. To that the chief objection had been that any rotation of the earth would upset the balance of day and night, since the first heaven already revolves once in twenty-four hours : but (if I may put Professor Cornford's argument in a different way) to ensure this balance, the earth must be stationary *relatively to the motion*

Παραπλησίως δὲ καὶ περὶ τοῦ σχήματος ἀμ-
φισβητεῖται· τοῖς μὲν γὰρ δοκεῖ εἶναι σφαιροειδής,
294 a τοῖς δὲ πλατεῖα καὶ τὸ σχῆμα τυμπανοειδής·
ποιοῦνται δὲ τεκμήριον ὅτι δύνων καὶ ἀνατέλλων ὁ
ἥλιος εὐθεῖαν καὶ οὐ περιφερῆ τὴν ἀπόκρυψιν φαίνεται ποιούμενος ὑπὸ τῆς γῆς, ὡς δέον, εἴπερ ἦν
σφαιροειδής, περιφερῆ γίνεσθαι τὴν ἀποτομήν, οὐ
5 προσλογιζόμενοι τό τε ἀπόστημα τοῦ ἡλίου πρὸς
τὴν γῆν καὶ τὸ τῆς περιφερείας μέγεθος, ὡς ἐν τοῖς
φαινομένοις μικροῖς κύκλοις εὐθεῖα φαίνεται πόρρωθεν. διὰ μὲν οὖν ταύτην τὴν φαντασίαν οὐδὲν
αὐτοὺς ἀπιστεῖν δεῖ μὴ κυκλοτερῆ τὸν ὄγκον εἶναι
τῆς γῆς· ἀλλ' ἔτι προστιθέασι, καὶ φασὶ διὰ τὴν
10 ἠρεμίαν ἀναγκαῖον τὸ σχῆμα τοῦτ' ἔχειν αὐτήν.

Καὶ γὰρ δὴ οἱ περὶ τῆς κινήσεως καὶ τῆς μονῆς
εἰρημένοι τρόποι πολλοὶ τυγχάνουσιν. τὸ μὲν οὖν
ἀπορῆσαι πᾶσιν ἀναγκαῖον ἐπελθεῖν· τάχα γὰρ
ἀλυποτέρας διανοίας τὸ μὴ θαυμάζειν πῶς ποτε

---

of the first heaven. But " the revolution of the Same is a
movement of the World-Soul, which, ' everywhere inwoven
from the centre to the extremity of heaven and enveloping the
heaven all round on the outside, revolving upon itself, made
a divine beginning of ceaseless and intelligent life for all
time ' (36 E). Physically, this is that rational movement
whereby the entire spherical body of the world rotates upon
its axis (34 A). This movement must not only carry the
planets with it, . . . but extend from the circumference to
the centre and therefore include the Earth " (Cornford p.
130). If then the earth had no axial rotation of its own, it
would simply be carried round in the same motion as the
fixed stars, and there would be no day and night. (*Cf.* note
on ch. xiv. 296 b 6 below.) For minor difficulties in this view
(*e.g.* Plato's choice of the word ἰλλομένην), the reader must be
referred to Professor Cornford's own discussion.

For a thorough treatment of the purely linguistic side of

There is just as much disagreement about the shape of the earth. Some think it spherical, others flat and shaped like a drum. These latter adduce as evidence the fact that the sun at its setting and rising shows a straight instead of a curved line where it is cut off from view by the horizon, whereas were the earth spherical, the line of section would necessarily be curved. They fail to take into consideration either the distance of the sun from the earth, or the size of the earth's circumference, and the appearance of straightness which it naturally presents when seen on the surface of an apparently small circle a great distance away. This phenomenon therefore gives them no cogent ground for disbelieving in the spherical shape of the earth's mass. But they add to their argument by saying that its immobility necessarily involves the other shape.[a]

It is certainly true that the theories which have been held about the motion or rest of the earth are manifold. Indeed, everyone must be impressed by the difficulty of the question. His must surely be a careless mind who does not wonder how it is

the question (meaning of ἱλλεσθαι and related forms), see K. Burdach in *Neue Jahrbücher für das Klass. Alt.*, 1922, pp. 268 ff. He finally supports the view which goes back to Boeckh (*Untersuchungen über das Kosmische System des Platon*, 1852) that the word in Plato does not involve any motion at all. (So also Sir T. Heath, *Aristarchus*, p. 175.) Of the work of Elizabeth G. Caskey (*The Problem of the Earth in Plato's Timaeus*) I have only been able to see a summary (in *Trans. and Proc. of the American Philological Society*, 1936, p. xxxii). It is written mainly in criticism of Professor Taylor and before the appearance of Professor Cornford's book.

[a] This is discussed below at 294 b 13 ff.

294 a

μικρὸν μὲν μόριον τῆς γῆς, ἂν μετεωρισθὲν ἀφεθῇ,
15 φέρεται καὶ μένειν οὐκ ἐθέλει, καὶ τὸ πλεῖον ἀεὶ
θᾶττον, πᾶσαν δὲ τὴν γῆν εἴ τις ἀφείη μετεωρίσας,
οὐκ ἂν φέροιτο. νῦν δ᾽ ἠρεμεῖ τοσοῦτον βάρος.
ἀλλὰ μὴν καὶ εἴ τις τῶν φερομένων μορίων αὐτῆς,
πρὶν πεσεῖν, ὑφαιροίη τὴν γῆν, οἰσθήσεται κάτω
μηθενὸς ἀντερείσαντος.

Ὥστε τὸ μὲν ἀπορεῖν εἰκότως ἐγένετο φιλο-
20 σόφημα πᾶσιν· τὸ δὲ τὰς περὶ τούτου λύσεις μὴ
μᾶλλον ἀτόπους εἶναι δοκεῖν τῆς ἀπορίας, θαυμάσειεν ἄν τις. οἱ μὲν γὰρ διὰ ταῦτα ἄπειρον τὸ
κάτω τῆς γῆς εἶναί φασιν, ἐπ᾽ ἄπειρον αὐτὴν ἐρ-
ριζῶσθαι λέγοντες, ὥσπερ Ξενοφάνης ὁ Κολοφώ-
νιος, ἵνα μὴ πράγματ᾽ ἔχωσι ζητοῦντες τὴν αἰτίαν·
25 διὸ καὶ Ἐμπεδοκλῆς οὕτως ἐπέπληξεν, εἰπὼν ὡς

εἴ περ ἀπείρονα γῆς τε βάθη καὶ δαψιλὸς αἰθήρ,
ὡς διὰ πολλῶν δὴ γλώσσης ῥηθέντα ματαίως
ἐκκέχυται στομάτων, ὀλίγον τοῦ παντὸς ἰδόντων.

Οἱ δ᾽ ἐφ᾽ ὕδατος κεῖσθαι. τοῦτον γὰρ ἀρχαιό-
τατον παρειλήφαμεν τὸν λόγον, ὅν φασιν εἰπεῖν
30 Θαλῆν τὸν Μιλήσιον, ὡς διὰ τὸ πλωτὴν εἶναι
μένουσαν ὥσπερ ξύλον ἤ τι τοιοῦτον ἕτερον (καὶ
γὰρ τούτων ἐπ᾽ ἀέρος μὲν οὐθὲν πέφυκε μένειν,
ἀλλ᾽ ἐφ᾽ ὕδατος), ὥσπερ οὐ τὸν αὐτὸν λόγον ὄντα
περὶ τῆς γῆς καὶ τοῦ ὕδατος τοῦ ὀχοῦντος τὴν γῆν·

---

a Diels, *Vors.* 21 [11]. A. 47 and B. 28 = Diels-Kranz [5] i.,
pp. 125 and 135. *Cf.* Burnet, *Early Gk. Phil.*[3], p. 125.
b Diels, *Vors.* 31 [21]. B. 39 = Diels-Kranz [5] i., p. 329. In
line 2, Kranz reads γλώσσας ἐλθόντα, following Wilamowitz
(*Hermes* 65 (1930) 249).

that a small particle of the earth, if raised to a height and then set free, should refuse to remain where it was but begin to travel, and travel the quicker the bigger it is, whereas if one held the whole earth in the air and let it go, it would not move. But in fact, for all its weight, it is at rest. Consider too that if one removed the earth from the path of one of its particles before it had fallen, it would travel downwards so long as there was nothing to oppose it.

This question, then, has become, as one might expect, a subject of general inquiry. But one may well wonder that the answers suggested are not recognized as being more incomprehensible than the question which they set out to solve. It has led some to assert that the earth extends downwards indefinitely, saying with Xenophanes of Colophon that it is " infinite in its roots," [a] to save themselves the trouble of looking for a reason. This called forth the censure of Empedocles, in the words :

If verily the depths of the earth were infinite and the ample ether, a saying which has run foolishly off the tongues of many and dropped from their mouths, men who have perceived but little of the whole.[b]

Others say that it rests on water. This is the most ancient explanation which has come down to us, and is attributed to Thales of Miletus. It supposes that the earth is at rest because it can float like wood and similar substances, whose nature it is to rest upon water, though none of them could rest on air. But (i) this is to forget that the same thing may be said of the water supporting the earth as was said of the earth itself. It is not the

294 a

οὐδὲ γὰρ τὸ ὕδωρ πέφυκε μένειν μετέωρον, ἀλλ'

294 b ἐπί τινός ἐστιν. ἔτι δ' ὥσπερ ἀὴρ ὕδατος κουφότερον, καὶ γῆς ὕδωρ· ὥστε πῶς οἷόν τε τὸ κουφότερον κατωτέρω κεῖσθαι τοῦ βαρυτέρου τὴν φύσιν;
ἔτι δ' εἴπερ ὅλη πέφυκε μένειν ἐφ' ὕδατος, δῆλον
ὅτι καὶ τῶν μορίων ἕκαστον· νῦν δ' οὐ φαίνεται
5 τοῦτο γιγνόμενον, ἀλλὰ τὸ τυχὸν μόριον φέρεται
εἰς βυθόν, καὶ θᾶττον τὸ μεῖζον. ἀλλ' ἐοίκασι μέχρι
τινὸς ζητεῖν, ἀλλ' οὐ μέχρι περ οὗ δυνατὸν τῆς
ἀπορίας. πᾶσι γὰρ ἡμῖν τοῦτο σύνηθες, μὴ πρὸς
τὸ πρᾶγμα ποιεῖσθαι τὴν ζήτησιν ἀλλὰ πρὸς τὸν
τἀναντία λέγοντα· καὶ γὰρ αὐτὸς ἐν αὑτῷ ζητεῖ
10 μέχρι περ ἂν οὗ μηκέτι ἔχῃ ἀντιλέγειν αὐτὸς αὑτῷ.
διὸ δεῖ τὸν μέλλοντα καλῶς ζητήσειν ἐνστατικὸν
εἶναι διὰ τῶν οἰκείων ἐνστάσεων τῷ γένει, τοῦτο
δ' ἐστὶν ἐκ τοῦ πάσας τεθεωρηκέναι τὰς διαφοράς.
Ἀναξιμένης δὲ καὶ Ἀναξαγόρας καὶ Δημόκριτος
15 τὸ πλάτος αἴτιον εἶναί φασι τοῦ μένειν αὐτήν. οὐ
γὰρ τέμνειν ἀλλ' ἐπιπωματίζειν τὸν ἀέρα τὸν
κάτωθεν, ὅπερ φαίνεται τὰ πλάτος ἔχοντα τῶν
σωμάτων ποιεῖν· ταῦτα γὰρ καὶ πρὸς τοὺς ἀνέμους
ἔχει δυσκινήτως διὰ τὴν ἀντέρεισιν. ταὐτὸ δὴ
τοῦτο ποιεῖν τῷ πλάτει φασὶ τὴν γῆν πρὸς τὸν
ὑποκείμενον ἀέρα, τὸν δ' οὐκ ἔχοντα μεταστῆναι
20 τόπον ἱκανὸν ἀθρόον τῷ κάτωθεν ἠρεμεῖν, ὥσπερ
τὸ ἐν ταῖς κλεψύδραις ὕδωρ. ὅτι δὲ δύναται πολὺ

---

[a] The principle of the *klepsydra* is shown in fig. i, p. 228,
which is a diagram based on Simplicius's description (" a
narrow-necked vessel having a broader base pierced with
small holes "). Figs. ii and iii show an ancient (6th cent.
B.C.) vessel actually in existence in which the principle is
employed. The handle is hollow and has a thumb-hole at
the top. In this form it was used *e.g.* for lifting wine from

nature of water, any more than of earth, to remain suspended : it rests upon something. (ii) Just as air is lighter than water, so water is lighter than earth. How then can the lighter substance lie underneath that which is naturally heavier ? (iii) If it is the nature of the earth as a whole to float on water, the same should be true of every piece of it : but this is plainly contrary to fact, for a piece taken at random sinks to the bottom, and the larger it is the quicker it sinks. Thus we may say of these theorists that they pursued the difficulty up to a point, but not as far as they might have. This is a habit which we all share, of relating an inquiry not to the subject-matter itself, but to our opponent in argument. A man will even pursue a question in his own mind no farther than the point at which he finds nothing to say against his own arguments. Therefore to be a good investigator a man must be alive to the objections inherent in the genus of his subject, an awareness which is the result of having studied all its differentiae.

Anaximenes, Anaxagoras and Democritus name the flatness of the earth as the cause of its remaining at rest. It does not cleave the air beneath it, but settles on it like a lid, as flat bodies to all appearances do : owing to their resistance, they are not easily moved even by the wind. The earth, they say, owing to its flatness behaves in the same way in relation to the air immediately underneath it, which, not having sufficient room to change its place, is compressed and stays still owing to the air beneath, like the water in *klepsydrae*.[a] For this power

the mixing-bowl, having the advantage that when the wine was low in the bowl it could more readily be extracted than

βάρος φέρειν ἀπολαμβανόμενος καὶ μένων ὁ ἀήρ,
τεκμήρια πολλὰ λέγουσιν. πρῶτον μὲν οὖν εἰ μὴ
πλατὺ τὸ σχῆμα τῆς γῆς ἐστί, διὰ τοῦτο μὲν οὐκ
25 ἂν ἠρεμοῖ. καίτοι τῆς μονῆς οὐ τὸ πλάτος αἴτιον
ἐξ ὧν λέγουσιν, ἀλλὰ τὸ μέγεθος μᾶλλον· διὰ γὰρ
τὴν στενοχωρίαν οὐκ ἔχων τὴν πάροδον ὁ ἀὴρ μένει
διὰ τὸ πλῆθος· πολὺς δ' ἐστὶ διὰ τὸ ὑπὸ μεγέθους
πολλοῦ ἐναπολαμβάνεσθαι τοῦ τῆς γῆς. ὥστε
τοῦτο μὲν ὑπάρξει, κἂν σφαιροειδὴς μὲν ἡ γῆ ᾖ,
30 τηλικαύτη δὲ τὸ μέγεθος· μενεῖ γὰρ κατὰ τὸν
ἐκείνων λόγον.

---

with the ordinary ladle. (Description and sketch by B. Zahn
in *Athenische Mitteilungen*, 1899, p. 339.) The water-clock
used for timing speeches in the law-courts was a large vessel
bearing a superficial resemblance to the *klepsydra* (whose
name it borrowed) in that it had an opening at the top,
through which it was filled, and a hole in the bottom
through which the water could drip out. (See H. Last in
Class. Quart. xviii. 169-173.)

With these vessels two distinct experiments were performed. (i) The vessel was lowered, empty, into water, as for

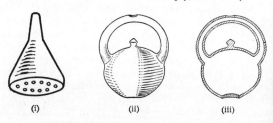

(i)   (ii)   (iii)

its use in wine-serving, but with the thumb of the experi-
menter closing the opening at the top, and it was observed
that until the thumb was removed no water entered through
the holes in the bottom. (ii) The vessel was allowed to

of the air to bear a great weight when it is shut up and its motion stopped, they bring forward plenty of evidence. Now in the first place, if the earth is not flat, it cannot be owing to its flat shape that it is at rest. But in fact their arguments do not make its flatness the cause of its immobility, but rather its size. It is for lack of room that the air stays as it does, because it has no way out and on account of its mass ; and the quantity of it is due to the greatness of the earth confining a large amount. These conditions will be provided, even though the earth is spherical, if it is of the requisite size : it will still be at rest according to their argument.

fill with water, and the thumb placed over the opening. No water escaped through the holes in the bottom. When the thumb was removed, the water dripped out. τὸ ἐν ταῖς κλεψύδραις ὕδωρ means " the water in *klepsydrae*," therefore the reference must be to experiment (ii). This fits the argument if τῷ κάτωθεν in line 20 = τῷ κάτωθεν ἀέρι, and the air immediately beneath the earth is distinguished from the lower air by which it is buoyed up. So Simpl. (who seems to read ἀθρόῳ for ἄθροον), and the rendering is strongly supported by the simile. Stocks translates: "the air, not having room enough to change its place because it is underneath the earth, stays there in a mass, like the water in the case of the water-clock." This would refer the comparison to experiment (i), but the translation of ἐν ταῖς κλεψύδραις is scarcely possible. Allan retains the reference to experiment (i) without forcing the translation by putting the words τὸν δ' οὐκ ἔχοντα . . . ἠρεμεῖν in parenthesis, so that the following words refer to the earth.

Other passages referring to *klepsydrae* are *Probl.* xvi. 914 b 9 ff., *Phys.* iv. 213 a 27, Empedocles fr. 100 Diels. For further information see Ross's note to the passage in the *Physics.* If his translation of ἐναπολαμβάνοντες there is right, then it is being used in a different sense from ἐναπολαμβάνεσθαι here at 294 b 27.

294 b

Ὅλως δὲ πρός γε τοὺς οὕτω λέγοντας περὶ τῆς κινήσεως οὐ περὶ μερῶν ἐστιν ἡ ἀμφισβήτησις, ἀλλὰ περὶ ὅλου τινὸς καὶ παντός. ἐξ ἀρχῆς γὰρ διοριστέον πότερόν ἐστί τις τοῖς σώμασι φύσει κίνησις ἢ οὐδεμία, καὶ πότερον φύσει μὲν οὐκ ἔστι,

295 a βίᾳ δ' ἔστιν. ἐπεὶ δὲ περὶ τούτων διώρισται πρότερον ὅσα κατὰ τὴν παροῦσαν δύναμιν εἴχομεν, χρηστέον ὡς ὑπάρχουσιν. εἰ γὰρ μηδεμία φύσει κίνησίς ἐστιν αὐτῶν, οὐδὲ βίαιος ἔσται· εἰ δὲ μή ἐστι μήτε φύσει μήτε βίᾳ, ὅλως οὐδὲν κινηθήσεται·

5 περὶ γὰρ τούτων ὅτι ἀναγκαῖον συμβαίνειν, διώρισται πρότερον, καὶ πρὸς τούτοις ὅτι οὐδ' ἠρεμεῖν ἐνδέχεται· ὥσπερ γὰρ κίνησις ὑπάρχει ἢ βίᾳ ἢ φύσει, οὕτω καὶ ἠρεμία. ἀλλὰ μὴν εἴ γε ἔστι κίνησίς τις κατὰ φύσιν, οὐκ ἂν ἡ βίαιος εἴη φορὰ μόνον οὐδ' ἠρέμησις· ὥστ' εἰ βίᾳ νῦν ἡ γῆ μένει,

10 καὶ συνῆλθεν ἐπὶ τὸ μέσον φερομένη διὰ τὴν δίνησιν. (ταύτην γὰρ τὴν αἰτίαν πάντες λέγουσιν ἐκ τῶν ἐν τοῖς ὑγροῖς καὶ περὶ τὸν ἀέρα συμβαινόντων· ἐν τούτοις γὰρ ἀεὶ φέρεται τὰ μείζω καὶ τὰ βαρύτερα πρὸς τὸ μέσον τῆς δίνης.) διὸ δὴ[1] τὴν γῆν πάντες ὅσοι τὸν οὐρανὸν γεννῶσιν, ἐπὶ τὸ μέσον

15 συνελθεῖν φασιν· ὅτι δὲ μένει, ζητοῦσι τὴν αἰτίαν, καὶ λέγουσιν οἱ μὲν τοῦτον τὸν τρόπον, ὅτι τὸ πλάτος καὶ τὸ μέγεθος αὐτῆς αἴτιον, οἱ δ' ὥσπερ Ἐμπεδοκλῆς, τὴν τοῦ οὐρανοῦ φορὰν κύκλῳ περι-

---

[1] δὴ E, Allan; καὶ FHMJ; δὴ καὶ L, Bekker.

---

[a] *i.e.* the behaviour of a particular element, earth, must not be considered in isolation, but only as a part of the cosmos with its universal laws.

[b] In book i. chs. ii.-iv.

[c] The close connexion between motion and rest, natural

But we need not argue over details. Our quarrel with the men who talk like that about motion does not concern particular parts, but an undivided whole.[a] I mean that we must decide from the very beginning whether bodies have a natural motion or not, or whether, not having a natural motion, they have an enforced one. And since our decisions on these points have already been made,[b] so far as our available means allowed, we must use them as data. If, we said, they have no natural motion, they will have no enforced motion either ; and if there is neither natural nor enforced motion, nothing will ever move at all. We have already determined what would necessarily happen in these circumstances ; in addition to the foregoing, things could not even be at rest, for rest is either natural or enforced in the same way as motion.[c] But if they have any motion at all by nature, then they cannot have either enforced motion only or enforced rest only ; so that if the earth's rest is due to constraint, it must have been under the action of the vortex that it travelled into the middle. (This is the name which all agree in giving to the cause, reasoning from what happens in liquids and in the air, where larger and heavier things always move towards the middle of a vortex.) Therefore all who hold that the world had a beginning, say that the earth travelled to the middle. They then seek the reason of its remaining there, and some claim, as we have said, that its flatness and size are the cause ; others agree with Empedocles that it is the excessive swiftness of the motion of

or enforced, is due to the definition of both in relation to the doctrine of natural places (bk. i. ch. viii. 276 a 22-26).

θέουσαν καὶ θᾶττον φερομένην τὴν τῆς γῆς φορὰν
κωλύειν, καθάπερ τὸ ἐν τοῖς κυάθοις ὕδωρ· καὶ γὰρ
20 τοῦτο κύκλῳ τοῦ κυάθου φερομένου πολλάκις κάτω
τοῦ χαλκοῦ γινόμενον ὅμως οὐ φέρεται, κάτω
πεφυκὸς φέρεσθαι, διὰ τὴν αὐτὴν αἰτίαν. καίτοι
μήτε τῆς δίνης κωλυούσης μήτε τοῦ πλάτους,
ἀλλ᾽ ὑπελθόντος[1] τοῦ ἀέρος, ποῖ ποτ᾽ οἰσθήσεται;
πρὸς μὲν γὰρ τὸ μέσον βίᾳ, καὶ μένει βίᾳ· κατὰ
25 φύσιν δέ γε ἀναγκαῖον εἶναί τινα αὐτῆς φοράν.
αὕτη οὖν πότερον ἄνω ἢ κάτω, ἢ ποῦ ἐστιν; εἶναι
μὲν γάρ τινα ἀναγκαῖον· εἰ δὲ μηδὲν μᾶλλον κάτω
ἢ ἄνω, ὁ δ᾽ ἄνω ἀὴρ μὴ κωλύει τὴν ἄνω φοράν,
οὐδ᾽ ἂν ὁ ὑπὸ τῇ γῇ κωλύοι τὴν κάτω· τὰ γὰρ
αὐτὰ τῶν αὐτῶν ἀναγκαῖον εἶναι αἴτια τοῖς αὐτοῖς.
30 Ἔτι δὲ πρὸς Ἐμπεδοκλέα κἂν ἐκεῖνό τις εἴπειεν.
ὅτε γὰρ τὰ στοιχεῖα διειστήκει χωρὶς ὑπὸ τοῦ
νείκους, τίς ἡ αἰτία τῇ γῇ τῆς μονῆς ἦν; οὐ γὰρ
δὴ καὶ τότε αἰτιάσεται τὴν δίνην.

Ἄτοπον δὲ καὶ τὸ μὴ συννοεῖν ὅτι πρότερον μὲν
διὰ τὴν δίνησιν ἐφέρετο τὰ μόρια τῆς γῆς πρὸς τὸ
35 μέσον· νῦν δὲ διὰ τίν᾽ αἰτίαν[2] πάντα τὰ βάρος
ἔχοντα φέρεται πρὸς αὐτήν; οὐ γὰρ ἥ γε δίνη
295 b πλησιάζει πρὸς ἡμᾶς. ἔτι δὲ καὶ τὸ πῦρ ἄνω
φέρεται διὰ τίν᾽ αἰτίαν; οὐ γὰρ διά γε τὴν δίνην.
εἰ δὲ τοῦτο φέρεσθαί που πέφυκεν, δῆλον ὅτι καὶ
τὴν γῆν οἰητέον. ἀλλὰ μὴν οὐδὲ τῇ δίνῃ γε τὸ
βαρὺ καὶ τὸ κοῦφον ὥρισται, ἀλλὰ τῶν πρότερον
5 ὑπαρχόντων βαρέων καὶ κούφων τὰ μὲν εἰς τὸ

---

[1] ὑπελθόντος. Stocks suggested ὑπεξελθόντος, on the ground
that there is no parallel to the use of ὑπελθεῖν in the required
sense.

[2] αἰτίαν. Bekker misprints as αἰτία.

the heaven as it swings around in a circle which prevents motion on the part of the earth. They compare it to the water in a cup, which in fact, when the cup is swung round in a circle, is prevented from falling by the same cause, although it often finds itself underneath the bronze and it is its nature to move downwards. Yet if neither the vortex nor its own flatness hindered its falling, but the air had been withdrawn from below, where would it go? It moved to the centre by constraint, and it rests there by constraint; but it must have some natural motion. Is this then upwards or downwards or where? There must be a motion, and if it is as likely to be upwards as downwards, and the air above it does not prevent it from moving upwards, no more would the air beneath it prevent it from moving downwards: for the same causes must produce the same effects on the same objects.

Against Empedocles there is another objection that might be made. When the elements had been separated off by Strife, what was the cause of the earth's immobility? He cannot assert that even at that time the vortex was the cause.

It was irrational too not to take into account the question: if formerly the parts of the earth were brought together by the vortex, what is the reason why at the present time everything that has weight moves towards the earth? Surely the vortex does not come close to us. Again, why does fire move upwards? Not I imagine on account of the vortex. But if it has a natural motion somewhere, we must presume that earth has too. Nor, again, are heavy and light defined by the vortex: rather, heavy and light things existed first, and then the motion

295 b

μέσον ἔρχεται, τὰ δ' ἐπιπολάζει διὰ τὴν κίνησιν.
ἦν ἄρα καὶ πρὶν γενέσθαι τὴν δίνην βαρύ τε καὶ
κοῦφον, ἃ τίνι διώριστο καὶ πῶς ἐπεφύκει φέρεσθαι
ἢ ποῦ; ἀπείρου γὰρ ὄντος ἀδύνατον εἶναι ἄνω ἢ
κάτω, διώρισται δὲ τούτοις τὸ βαρὺ καὶ κοῦφον.

10 Οἱ μὲν οὖν πλεῖστοι περὶ τὰς αἰτίας ταύτας δια-
τρίβουσιν· εἰσὶ δέ τινες οἳ διὰ τὴν ὁμοιότητά φασιν
αὐτὴν μένειν, ὥσπερ τῶν ἀρχαίων Ἀναξίμανδρος·
μᾶλλον μὲν γὰρ οὐθὲν ἄνω ἢ κάτω ἢ εἰς τὰ πλάγια
φέρεσθαι προσήκει τὸ ἐπὶ τοῦ μέσου ἱδρυμένον καὶ
15 ὁμοίως πρὸς τὰ ἔσχατα ἔχον· ἅμα δ' ἀδύνατον εἰς
τἀναντία ποιεῖσθαι τὴν κίνησιν· ὥστ' ἐξ ἀνάγκης
μένειν. τοῦτο δὲ λέγεται κομψῶς μέν, οὐκ ἀληθῶς
δέ· κατὰ γὰρ τοῦτον τὸν λόγον ἀναγκαῖον ἅπαν, ὅ
τι ἂν τεθῇ ἐπὶ τοῦ μέσου, μένειν, ὥστε καὶ τὸ πῦρ
ἠρεμήσει· τὸ γὰρ εἰρημένον οὐκ ἴδιόν ἐστι τῆς γῆς.
20 ἀλλὰ μὴν οὐδ' ἀναγκαῖον· οὐ γὰρ μόνον φαίνεται
μένουσα ἐπὶ τοῦ μέσου, ἀλλὰ καὶ φερομένη πρὸς τὸ
μέσον (ὅπου γὰρ ὁτιοῦν φέρεται μέρος αὐτῆς,

---

^a The meaning of ὁμοιότητα becomes clear from the con-
text. I have adopted the rendering " indifference " from
Burnet and Stocks. See Stocks's note *ad loc.* Compare
Plato, *Phaedo* 108 E foll. πέπεισμαι τοίνυν . . . ὡς . . . εἰ
ἔστιν (sc. ἡ γῆ) ἐν μέσῳ τῷ οὐρανῷ περιφερὴς οὖσα, μηδὲν
αὐτῇ δεῖν μήτε ἀέρος πρὸς τὸ μὴ πεσεῖν μήτε ἄλλης ἀνάγκης
μηδεμιᾶς τοιαύτης, ἀλλὰ ἱκανὴν εἶναι αὐτὴν ἴσχειν τὴν ὁμοιότητα
τοῦ οὐρανοῦ αὐτοῦ ἑαυτῷ πάντῃ καὶ τῆς γῆς αὐτῆς τὴν ἰσορ-
ροπίαν· ἰσόρροπον γὰρ πρᾶγμα ὁμοίου τινὸς ἐν μέσῳ τεθὲν οὐχ
ἕξει μᾶλλον οὐδ' ἧττον οὐδαμόσε κλιθῆναι, ὁμοίως δ' ἔχον
ἀκλινὲς μένει.

caused them to go either to the centre or the surface. Light and heavy, then, were there before the vortex arose, but by what were they distinguished, and how or where was it their nature to move ? In an infinite space there can be no *up* or *down*, yet it is these that distinguish heavy and light.

These are the causes which engage the attention of the majority of thinkers. But there are some who name its " indifference " [a] as the cause of its remaining at rest, *e.g.* among the early philosophers Anaximander. These urge that that which is situated at the centre and is equally related to the extremes has no impulse to move in one direction— either upwards or downwards or sideways—rather than in another; and since it is impossible for it to accomplish movement in opposite directions at once, it necessarily remains at rest. This argument is ingenious, but not true : for according to it, whatever is placed at the centre must remain there, even fire ; the property is not peculiar to earth. But besides that, it is superfluous [b] : for the earth may be seen not only to rest at the centre, but also to travel towards the centre. (For where any part of

---

[b] Stocks and Prantl take ἀναγκαῖον as referring to logical necessity. (" But this does not follow " St. ; " fehlt jener Begründung ja auch die Notwendigkeit " P.) But it seems strange to say that an argument is not true *nor even* (ἀλλὰ μὴν οὐδέ) necessary in this sense, and on general grounds a more natural meaning for the passage is : " Their argument is false, but in any case it is unnecessary because the earth's immobility is sufficiently accounted for by the fact of natural motion implying a natural resting-place." (So Simpl., 534. 7 : δείξας . . . ὅτι πρὸς τὴν τῆς γῆς μονὴν οὐκ ἔστιν ἀναγκαῖος ὁ ἀπὸ τῆς ὁμοιότητος λόγος, ἄλλης οὔσης προχειροτέρας τῆς τοῦ κατὰ φύσιν. . . .)

295 b

ἀναγκαῖον ἐνταῦθα φέρεσθαι καὶ τὴν ὅλην). οὗ δὲ
φέρεται κατὰ φύσιν, καὶ μένει ἐνταυθοῖ κατὰ φύσιν.
οὐκ ἄρα διὰ τὸ ὁμοίως ἔχειν πρὸς τὰ ἔσχατα·
25 τοῦτο μὲν γὰρ πᾶσι κοινόν, τὸ δὲ φέρεσθαι πρὸς τὸ
μέσον ἴδιον τῆς γῆς.

Ἄτοπον δὲ καὶ τοῦτο μὲν ζητεῖν, διὰ τί ποτε
μένει ἡ γῆ ἐπὶ τοῦ μέσου, τὸ δὲ πῦρ μὴ ζητεῖν διὰ
τί ἐπὶ τοῦ ἐσχάτου. εἰ μὲν γὰρ κἀκείνῳ φύσει
τόπος ὁ ἔσχατος, δῆλον ὅτι ἀναγκαῖον εἶναί τινα
καὶ τῇ γῇ φύσει τόπον· εἰ δὲ μὴ ταύτῃ οὗτος ὁ
30 τόπος, ἀλλὰ διὰ τὴν ἀνάγκην μένει τὴν τῆς ὁμοιότητος (ὥσπερ ὁ περὶ τῆς τριχὸς λόγος τῆς ἰσχυρῶς
μὲν ὁμοίως δὲ πάντῃ τεινομένης, ὅτι οὐ διαρραγή-
σεται, καὶ τοῦ πεινῶντος καὶ διψῶντος σφόδρα μέν,
ὁμοίως δέ, καὶ τῶν ἐδωδίμων καὶ ποτῶν ἴσον
ἀπέχοντος· καὶ γὰρ τοῦτον ἠρεμεῖν ἀναγκαῖον),
35 ζητητέον αὐτοῖς περὶ τῆς τοῦ πυρὸς μονῆς ἐπὶ τῶν
ἐσχάτων.

296 a   Θαυμαστὸν δὲ καὶ τὸ περὶ μὲν τῆς μονῆς ζητεῖν,
περὶ δὲ τῆς φορᾶς αὐτῶν μὴ ζητεῖν, διὰ τίν' αἰτίαν
τὸ μὲν ἄνω φέρεται τὸ δ' ἐπὶ τὸ μέσον μηδενὸς
ἐμποδίζοντος.

Ἀλλὰ μὴν οὐδ' ἀληθές ἐστι τὸ λεγόμενον. κατὰ
5 συμβεβηκὸς μέντοι τοῦτ' ἀληθές, ὡς ἀναγκαῖον
μένειν ἐπὶ τοῦ μέσου πᾶν ᾧ μηθὲν μᾶλλον δεῦρο ἢ
δεῦρο κινεῖσθαι προσήκει. ἀλλὰ διά γε τοῦτον τὸν
λόγον οὐ μενεῖ ἀλλὰ κινηθήσεται, οὐ μέντοι ὅλον
ἀλλὰ διεσπασμένον. ὁ γὰρ αὐτὸς ἁρμόσει λόγος
καὶ ἐπὶ τοῦ πυρός· ἀνάγκη γὰρ τεθὲν μένειν ὁμοίως
10 ὥσπερ τὴν γῆν· ὁμοίως γὰρ ἕξει πρὸς τῶν σημείων

236

it moves, we must assume the whole moves too.)
And whither it is natural for it to go, there it is
natural for it to remain. Therefore the reason is
not its impartial relation to the extremes : that
could be shared by any other element, but motion
towards the centre is peculiar to earth.

It was irrational too to ask the question why the
earth remains at the centre, but not why fire remains
at the extremity. If the extremity is the natural
place for fire, there must plainly be some natural
place for earth also. If on the other hand the place
where the earth rests is not its natural place, but
the cause of its remaining there is the constraint
of its " indifference " (on the analogy of the hair
which, stretched strongly but evenly at every point,
will not break, or the man who is violently, but
equally, hungry and thirsty, and stands at an equal
distance from food and drink, and who therefore
must remain where he is), then they ought to have
inquired into the presence of fire at the extremes.

It was also strange to inquire about the resting
of these elements but not their motion, that is,
the reason why, if nothing interferes, the one moves
upward and the other downward.

Finally, what they say is not even true. Thus
much happens accidentally to be true, that everything must remain at the centre which has no
reason to move in one or another particular direction ; but so far as their argument goes, a body need
not remain there but can move—not, however, as a
whole, but scattering in different directions. For the
same reasoning may be applied to fire. Fire when
placed at the centre is under as much necessity to
remain there as earth, for it will be related in the

296 a

τῶν ἐσχάτων ὁτιοῦν· ἀλλ' ὅμως οἰσθήσεται ἀπὸ
τοῦ μέσου, ὥσπερ καὶ φαίνεται φερόμενον, ἂν μή
τι κωλύῃ, πρὸς τὸ ἔσχατον· πλὴν οὐχ ὅλον προς ἕν
σημεῖον (τοῦτο γὰρ ἀναγκαῖον μόνον συμβαίνειν ἐκ
τοῦ λόγου τοῦ περὶ τῆς ὁμοιότητος) ἀλλὰ τὸ
15 ἀνάλογον μόριον πρὸς τὸ ἀνάλογον τοῦ ἐσχάτου,
λέγω δ' οἷον τὸ τέταρτον μέρος πρὸς τὸ τέταρτον
μέρος τοῦ περιέχοντος· οὐθὲν γὰρ στιγμὴ τῶν
σωμάτων ἐστίν. ὥσπερ δὲ κἂν ἐκ μεγάλου συνέλ-
θοι πυκνούμενον εἰς ἐλάττω τόπον, οὕτω κἂν ἐξ
ἐλάττονος εἰς μείζω μανότερον γιγνόμενον· ὥστε
20 κἂν ἡ γῆ τοῦτον τὸν τρόπον ἐκινεῖτο ἀπὸ τοῦ
μέσου διά γε τὸν τῆς ὁμοιότητος λόγον, εἰ μὴ
φύσει τῆς γῆς οὗτος τόπος ἦν.

Ὅσα μὲν οὖν τυγχάνει περί τε τοῦ σχήματος
αὐτῆς ὑπολαμβανόμενα καὶ περὶ τόπου καὶ μονῆς
καὶ κινήσεως, σχεδὸν ταῦτ' ἐστίν.

---

[a] 296 a 3-21. The argument is obscured because only
partially expressed. I take it to be something like this :—
The real (καθ' αὐτό) reason why the earth remains at the
centre is that that is its natural place. It is an incidental
(κατὰ συμβεβηκός) outcome of that essential reason that the
earth, once at the centre, has no incentive to move one way
rather than another, and it is true that this fact prevents its
moving. To prove that he is right in his choice of which is
essential and which incidental, A. shows that the doctrine of
ὁμοιότης, unsupported by the doctrine of natural places, is
insufficient to account for immobility. (a) ὁμοιότης should
apply to fire as well as to earth, and experience shows that
in the case of fire it does not bring about immobility at the
centre. Placed at the centre, fire scatters, each particle
seeking the nearest point on the circumference. Earth then

238

same way to any one of the points on the extremity; but in fact it will leave the centre, and move as we observe it to do, if nothing prevents it, towards the extremity ; only, it will not move as a whole in the direction of a single point (this is the only consequence necessitated by the argument from indifference), but each part towards the corresponding part of the extremity. I mean, for example, a quarter of it will seek a quarter of the outer boundary, since no body is an indivisible point. And just as in the process of condensation a body can contract from a larger place into a smaller, so by rarefaction it can exchange a smaller place for a larger : this then is a form of motion from the centre which the earth too could perform, so far as the argument from indifference goes, were it not that the centre is its natural place.[a]

We may assume that this completes the tale of theories about the shape, the place, and the rest or motion of the earth.

should do the same, were ὁμοιότης alone at work. The mistake made by the holders of the " indifference " doctrine was that they did not envisage any other kind of motion away from the centre save a moving off by the earth as a whole in one direction. This would indeed be incompatible with ὁμοιότης, but not so the scattering of a body from centre to circumference in all directions at once. If, then, earth stays at the centre, this must be because, unlike fire, it has no natural impulse away from it, but on the contrary a natural impulse towards it. (b) There is another sort of motion (possibly suggested to A. at this point by a loose train of thought from the notion of heat), which is compatible with the ὁμοιότης doctrine and therefore helps to show that the doctrine, even if true, does not necessitate complete immobility. This is the motion of *expansion* in all directions equally, which accompanies rarefaction.

CHAPTER XIV

ARGUMENT

The earth (continued). Positive conclusions.
(1) It is at rest in the centre of the Universe (296 a 24—297 a 8).

(a) *The motions which have been ascribed to it could not be natural to it, for the behaviour of its parts shows that its natural motion is in a straight line towards the centre. The order of the world is eternal, therefore it cannot include any unnatural or enforced motions* (296 a 24-34).

(b) *If the earth were in motion, it would travel round the axis of the ecliptic. This would lead to apparent irregularities in the motions of the stars which are not in fact observed* (296 a 34–b 6).

(c) *The natural motion of earth towards the centre, as seen in the behaviour of small pieces, is sufficient evidence that the earth as a whole is at the centre and immobile. (Thus centre of earth and centre of Universe coincide, but it is* qua *centre of Universe that this point attracts earthy bodies.)* (296 b 6—297 a 2.)

(d) *Astronomical observations do not conflict with this hypothesis* (297 a 2-6).

(2) It is spherical in shape. (a) *This also follows from the*

296 a 24 Ἡμεῖς δὲ λέγωμεν πρῶτον πότερον ἔχει κίνησιν
25 ἢ μένει· καθάπερ γὰρ εἴπομεν, οἱ μὲν αὐτὴν ἓν τῶν
ἄστρων ποιοῦσιν, οἱ δ' ἐπὶ τοῦ μέσου θέντες ἴλλεσθαι καὶ κινεῖσθαί φασι περὶ τὸν πόλον μέσον.
ὅτι δ' ἐστὶν ἀδύνατον, δῆλον λαβοῦσιν ἀρχὴν ὡς
εἴπερ φέρεται εἴτ' ἐκτὸς οὖσα τοῦ μέσου εἴτ' ἐπὶ
τοῦ μέσου, ἀναγκαῖον αὐτὴν βίᾳ κινεῖσθαι ταύτην
30 τὴν κίνησιν· οὐ γὰρ αὐτῆς γε τῆς γῆς ἐστιν· καὶ
γὰρ ἂν τῶν μορίων ἕκαστον ταύτην εἶχε τὴν φοράν·
νῦν δ' ἐπ' εὐθείας πάντα φέρεται πρὸς τὸ μέσον.

CHAPTER XIV

ARGUMENT (*continued*)

*fact that every earthy particle moves naturally towards the
centre. An imaginary description of the earth as in process
of generation elucidates this. Whether or not the particles
which made it were evenly distributed around the outer parts
of the Universe, the final result must inevitably be a sphere*
(297 a 8–b 17).

(b) *Heavy bodies do not fall in parallel lines, but so as to
make similar angles with the earth. This, too, indicates that
the earth, towards which their fall is directed, is spherical*
(297 b 17-23).

(c) *The conclusion is borne out by the evidence of the senses.*

(i) *Eclipses of the moon always show a convex outline*
(297 b 24-30).

(ii) *Quite small changes in the position of the observer
lead to perceptible changes in the apparent positions of the stars. This demonstrates a further
point, namely that the earth's sphere is of no very
great size* (297 b 30—298 a 17).

*Conclusion. The earth is spherical, and small in compari-
son with the other stars* (298 a 18-20).

FOR ourselves, let us first state whether it is in
motion or at rest. Some, as we have said, make
it one of the stars, whereas others put it at the
centre but describe it as winding and moving about
the pole as its axis. But the impossibility of these
explanations is clear if we start from this, that if
the earth moves, whether at the centre or at a
distance from it, its movement must be enforced :
it is not the motion of the earth itself, for otherwise
each of its parts would have the same motion, but
as it is their motion is invariably in a straight line

241

διόπερ οὐχ οἷόν τ' ἀΐδιον εἶναι, βίαιόν γ' οὖσαν καὶ
παρὰ φύσιν· ἡ δέ γε τοῦ κόσμου τάξις ἀΐδιός ἐστιν.

35 Ἔτι πάντα τὰ φερόμενα τὴν φορὰν τὴν ἐγκύκλιον
296 b ὑπολειπόμενα φαίνεται καὶ κινούμενα πλείους μιᾶς
φορᾶς[1] ἔξω τῆς πρώτης σφαίρας, ὥστε καὶ τὴν
γῆν ἀναγκαῖον, εἴτε περὶ τὸ μέσον εἴτ' ἐπὶ τοῦ
μέσου κειμένη φέρεται, δύο κινεῖσθαι φοράς. τούτου δὲ συμβαίνοντος ἀναγκαῖον γίγνεσθαι παρόδους
5 καὶ τροπὰς τῶν ἐνδεδεμένων ἄστρων. τοῦτο δ' οὐ
φαίνεται γιγνόμενον, ἀλλ' ἀεὶ ταὐτὰ κατὰ τοὺς
αὐτοὺς ἀνατέλλει τε καὶ δύεται τόπους αὐτῆς.

Ἔτι δ' ἡ φορὰ τῶν μορίων καὶ ὅλης αὐτῆς ἡ
κατὰ φύσιν ἐπὶ τὸ μέσον τοῦ παντός ἐστιν· διὰ
τοῦτο γὰρ καὶ τυγχάνει κειμένη νῦν ἐπὶ τοῦ κέν-
τρου· διαπορήσειε δ' ἄν τις, ἐπεὶ ταὐτὸν ἀμφοτέρων
10 ἐστὶ τὸ μέσον, πρὸς πότερον φέρεται τὰ βάρος
ἔχοντα καὶ τὰ μόρια τῆς γῆς κατὰ φύσιν· πότερον
ὅτι τοῦ παντός ἐστι μέσον, ἢ διότι τῆς γῆς. ἀνάγκη
δὴ πρὸς τὸ τοῦ παντός· καὶ γὰρ τὰ κοῦφα καὶ τὸ
πῦρ εἰς τοὐναντίον φερόμενα τοῖς βάρεσι πρὸς τὸ

---

[1] φορὰς Allan.   φορᾶς codd., Bekker.

---

[a] The criticism depends on the analogy with the planets,
following which A. assumes that if the earth moved with a
motion of its own, as well as being carried round in the
motion of the first heaven, its proper motion would be in the
plane of the ecliptic and not of the equator. Were this so,
the fixed stars would exhibit to our eyes the irregularities
which he describes by the words παρόδους καὶ τροπάς : the

towards the centre. The motion therefore, being enforced and unnatural, could not be eternal ; but the order of the world is eternal.

Secondly, all the bodies which move with the circular movement are observed to lag behind and to move with more than one motion, with the exception of the primary sphere : the earth therefore must have a similar double motion, whether it move around the centre or as situated at it. But if this were so, there would have to be passings and turnings of the fixed stars. Yet these are not observed to take place : the same stars always rise and set at the same places on the earth.[a]

Thirdly, the natural motion of the earth as a whole, like that of its parts, is towards the centre of the Universe : that is the reason why it is now lying at the centre. It might be asked, since the centre of both is the same point, in which capacity the natural motion of heavy bodies, or parts of the earth, is directed towards it ; whether as centre of the Universe or of the earth. But it must be towards the centre of the Universe that they move, seeing that light bodies like fire, whose motion is contrary to that of the heavy, move to the extremity

pole-star would appear to describe a circle in the sky, and the stars would not rise and set as they do. (For the senses of τροπαί, see Heath, *Aristarchus*, p. 33, n. 3. He discusses the present passage *o.c.* p. 241.) The objection is lodged against both the planetary theory and Plato's theory of motion at the centre. If we may accept Prof. Cornford's suggestion (*Plato's Cosmology*, pp. 132 ff.), Plato would reply that he had expressly limited the motion in the ecliptic (= motion of the Different) to the seven planetary circles, and that the motion of the earth, caused by its soul, was independent and around the same axis as the motion of the Same, only in the reverse direction to cancel it.

15 ἔσχατον φέρεται τοῦ περιέχοντος τόπου τὸ μέσον.
συμβέβηκε δὲ ταὐτὸ μέσον εἶναι τῆς γῆς καὶ τοῦ
παντός· φέρεται γὰρ καὶ ἐπὶ τὸ τῆς γῆς μέσον,
ἀλλὰ κατὰ συμβεβηκός, ᾗ τὸ μέσον ἔχει ἐν τῷ τοῦ
παντὸς μέσῳ. ὅτι δὲ φέρεται καὶ πρὸς τὸ τῆς γῆς
20 μέσον, σημεῖον ὅτι τὰ φερόμενα βάρη ἐπὶ ταύτην
οὐ παρ' ἄλληλα φέρεται ἀλλὰ πρὸς ὁμοίας γωνίας,
ὥστε πρὸς ἓν τὸ μέσον φέρεται, καὶ τὸ τῆς γῆς.
φανερὸν τοίνυν ὅτι ἀνάγκη ἐπὶ τοῦ μέσου εἶναι τὴν
γῆν καὶ ἀκίνητον, διά τε τὰς εἰρημένας αἰτίας, καὶ
διότι τὰ βίᾳ ῥιπτούμενα ἄνω βάρη κατὰ στάθμην
25 πάλιν φέρεται εἰς ταὐτό, κἂν εἰς ἄπειρον ἡ δύναμις
ἐκριπτῇ.

Ὅτι μὲν οὖν οὔτε κινεῖται οὔτ' ἐκτὸς κεῖται τοῦ
μέσου, φανερὸν ἐκ τούτων· πρὸς δὲ τούτοις δῆλον
ἐκ τῶν εἰρημένων τὸ αἴτιον τῆς μονῆς. εἰ γὰρ
φύσει πέφυκε φέρεσθαι πάντοθεν πρὸς τὸ μέσον,

---

[a] *Sc.* the upward motion of fire is upward in relation to the
Universe (*i.e.* towards its extremity), not in relation to itself.
Simpl. thinks that " the region which surrounds the centre " is
the region occupied by the air, *i.e.* immediately surrounding
the earth. Fire moves to the outer extremity of this region.
It is true that if Aristotle simply means the circumference of
the Universe, the phrase is unusually elaborate.

[b] *i.e.* at right angles to a tangent. Stocks explains the
Greek as meaning that the angles at each side of the line of
fall of any one body are equal. But does it not more naturally mean that the angles made by one falling body with the
earth are similar to those made by another? *Cf.* the second
occurrence of the phrase at 297 b 19 below. See Fig. on
opposite page.

of the region which surrounds the centre.[a]   It so happens that the earth and the Universe have the same centre, for the heavy bodies do move also towards the centre of the earth, yet only incidentally, because it has its centre at the centre of the Universe.   As evidence that they move also towards the centre of the earth, we see that weights moving towards the earth do not move in parallel lines but always at the same angles to it [b] : therefore they are moving towards the same centre, namely that of the earth.   It is now clear that the earth must be at the centre and immobile.   To our previous reasons we may add that heavy objects, if thrown forcibly upwards in a straight line, come back to their starting-place, even if the force hurls them to an unlimited distance.

From these considerations it is clear that the earth does not move, neither does it lie anywhere but at the centre.   In addition the reason for its immobility is clear from our discussions.   If it is inherent in the nature of earth to move from all

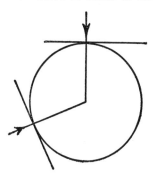

ὥσπερ φαίνεται, καὶ τὸ πῦρ ἀπὸ τοῦ μέσου πάλιν
30 πρὸς τὸ ἔσχατον, ἀδύνατον ἐνεχθῆναι ὁτιοῦν μόριον
αὐτῆς ἀπὸ τοῦ μέσου μὴ βιασθέν· μία γὰρ φορὰ
τοῦ ἑνὸς καὶ ἁπλῆ τοῦ ἁπλοῦ, ἀλλ' οὐχ αἱ ἐναντίαι·
ἡ δ' ἀπὸ τοῦ μέσου τῇ ἐπὶ τὸ μέσον ἐναντία. εἰ
τοίνυν ὁτιοῦν μόριον ἀδύνατον ἐνεχθῆναι ἀπὸ τοῦ
μέσου, φανερὸν ὅτι καὶ τὴν ὅλην ἔτι ἀδυνατώτερον·
35 εἰς ὃ γὰρ τὸ μόριον πέφυκε φέρεσθαι, καὶ τὸ ὅλον
297 a ἐνταῦθα πέφυκεν· ὥστ' εἴπερ ἀδύνατον κινηθῆναι
μὴ ὑπὸ κρείττονος ἰσχύος, ἀναγκαῖον ἂν εἴη μένειν
αὐτὴν ἐπὶ τοῦ μέσου. μαρτυρεῖ δὲ τούτοις καὶ τὰ
παρὰ τῶν μαθηματικῶν λεγόμενα περὶ τὴν ἀστρο-
λογίαν· τὰ γὰρ φαινόμενα συμβαίνει μεταβαλ-
5 λόντων τῶν σχημάτων οἷς ὥρισται τῶν ἄστρων ἡ
τάξις, ὡς ἐπὶ τοῦ μέσου κειμένης τῆς γῆς. περὶ
μὲν οὖν τοῦ τόπου καὶ μονῆς καὶ κινήσεως, ὃν
τρόπον ἔχει, τοσαῦτα εἰρήσθω περὶ αὐτῆς.

Σχῆμα δ' ἔχειν σφαιροειδὲς ἀναγκαῖον αὐτήν·
ἕκαστον γὰρ τῶν μορίων βάρος ἔχει μέχρι πρὸς τὸ
10 μέσον, καὶ τὸ ἔλαττον ὑπὸ τοῦ μείζονος ὠθούμενον
οὐχ οἷόν τε κυμαίνειν, ἀλλὰ συμπιέζεσθαι μᾶλλον
καὶ συγχωρεῖν ἕτερον ἑτέρῳ, ἕως ἂν ἔλθῃ ἐπὶ τὸ
μέσον. δεῖ δὲ νοῆσαι τὸ λεγόμενον ὥσπερ ἂν εἰ
γιγνομένης τὸν[1] τρόπον ὃν καὶ τῶν φυσιολόγων
λέγουσί τινες γενέσθαι. πλὴν ἐκεῖνοι μὲν βίαν

---

[1] τὸν is omitted by Bekker with L alone.

---

[a] The verb (cf. Phys. iv. 216 b 25) signifies the motion of

246

sides to the centre (as observation shows), and of fire to move away from the centre towards the extremity, it is impossible for any portion of earth to move from the centre except under constraint; for one body has one motion and a simple body a simple motion, not two opposite motions, and motion from the centre is the opposite of motion towards it. If then any particular portion is incapable of moving from the centre, it is clear that the earth itself as a whole is still more incapable, since it is natural for the whole to be in the place towards which the part has a natural motion. If then it cannot move except by the agency of a stronger force, it must remain at the centre. This belief finds further support in the assertions of mathematicians about astronomy: that is, the observed phenomena—the shifting of the figures by which the arrangement of the stars is defined—are consistent with the hypothesis that the earth lies at the centre. This may conclude our account of the situation and the rest or motion of the earth.

Its shape must be spherical. For every one of its parts has weight until it reaches the centre, and thus when a smaller part is pressed on by a larger, it cannot surge round it,[a] but each is packed close to, and combines with, the other until they reach the centre. To grasp what is meant we must imagine the earth as in the process of generation in the manner which some of the natural philosophers describe (except that they make external compulsion responsible for the downward

---

a wave, and Simpl. notes that the behaviour of the less heavy particles when in contact with the heavier is being contrasted with the behaviour of liquids under similar pressure.

αἰτιῶνται τῆς κάτω φορᾶς· βέλτιον δὲ τιθέναι
τἀληθές, καὶ φάναι τοῦτο συμβαίνειν διὰ τὸ φύσιν
ἔχειν φέρεσθαι τὸ βάρος ἔχον πρὸς τὸ μέσον. ἐν
δυνάμει οὖν ὄντος τοῦ μίγματος τὰ διακρινόμενα
ἐφέρετο ὁμοίως πάντοθεν πρὸς τὸ μέσον. εἴτ᾽ οὖν
20 ὁμοίως ἀπὸ τῶν ἐσχάτων διῃρημένα τὰ μόρια
συνήχθη πρὸς τὸ μέσον, εἴτ᾽ ἄλλως ἔχοντα, ποιήσει
ταὐτόν. ὅτι μὲν οὖν ὁμοίως γε πανταχόθεν ἀπὸ
τῶν ἐσχάτων φερομένων πρὸς ἓν τὸ μέσον ἀναγκαῖον ὅμοιον γίγνεσθαι πάντῃ τὸν ὄγκον, φανερόν·
25 ἴσου γὰρ πάντῃ προστιθεμένου ἴσον ἀνάγκη ἀπέχειν τοῦ μέσου τὸ ἔσχατον· τοῦτο δὲ τὸ σχῆμα
σφαίρας ἐστίν. οὐδὲν δὲ διοίσει πρὸς τὸν λόγον,
οὐδ᾽ εἰ μὴ πανταχόθεν ὁμοίως συνέθει πρὸς τὸ
μέσον τὰ μόρια αὐτῆς. τὸ γὰρ πλεῖον ἀεὶ τὸ πρὸ
αὑτοῦ ἔλαττον προωθεῖν ἀναγκαῖον μέχρι τοῦ μέσου
τὴν ῥοπὴν ἐχόντων ἀμφοῖν, καὶ τοῦ βαρυτέρου
30 προωθοῦντος μέχρι τούτου τὸ ἔλαττον βάρος.

Ὃ γὰρ ἄν τις ἀπορήσειε, τὴν αὐτὴν ἔχει τούτοις
λύσιν· εἰ γὰρ οὔσης ἐπὶ τοῦ μέσου καὶ σφαιροειδοῦς
τῆς γῆς πολλαπλάσιον βάρος ἐπιγένοιτο πρὸς θάτερον ἡμισφαίριον, οὐκ ἔσται τὸ αὐτὸ μέσον τοῦ ὅλου
καὶ τὸ τῆς γῆς· ὥστε ἢ οὐ μενεῖ ἐπὶ τοῦ μέσου,
297 b ἢ εἴπερ, ἠρεμήσει γε καὶ νῦν[1] καὶ μὴ τὸ μέσον
ἔχουσα, ᾗ πέφυκε κινεῖσθαι. τὸ μὲν οὖν ἀπορούμενον τοῦτ᾽ ἐστίν· ἰδεῖν δ᾽ οὐ χαλεπὸν μικρὸν

---

[1] καὶ νῦν occurs after κινεῖσθαι in the mss. and Bekker. It
is placed as above by Simpl., whom Allan follows.

movement : let us rather substitute the true statement that this takes place because it is the nature of whatever has weight to move towards the centre). In these systems, when the mixture existed in a state of potentiality,[a] the particles in process of separation were moving from every side alike towards the centre. Whether or not the portions were evenly distributed at the extremities, from which they converged towards the centre, the same result will be produced. It is plain, first, that if particles are moving from all sides alike towards one point, the centre, the resulting mass must be similar on all sides ; for if an equal quantity is added all round, the extremity must be at a constant distance from the centre. Such a shape is a sphere. But it will make no difference to the argument even if the portions of the earth did not travel uniformly from all sides towards the centre. A greater mass must always drive on a smaller mass in front of it, if the inclination of both is to go as far as the centre, and the impulsion of the less heavy by the heavier persists to that point.

A difficulty which might be raised finds its solution in the same considerations. If, the earth being at the centre and spherical in shape, a weight many times its own were added to one hemisphere, the centre of the Universe would no longer coincide with that of the earth. Either, therefore, it would not remain at the centre, or, if it did, it might even as it is be at rest although not occupying the centre, *i.e.* though in a situation where it is natural for it to be in motion. That then is the difficulty. But

---

[a] Compare the language used of earlier cosmologies in *Met.* Λ, 1069 b 20-23.

297 b

ἐπιτείναντας, καὶ διελόντας πῶς ἀξιοῦμεν ὁποσονοῦν μέγεθος φέρεσθαι πρὸς τὸ μέσον, βάρος ἔχον.
5 δῆλον γὰρ ὡς οὐχὶ μέχρι τοῦ ἅψασθαι τοῦ κέντρου
τὸ ἔσχατον, ἀλλὰ δεῖ κρατεῖν τὸ πλέον ἕως ἂν λάβῃ
τῷ αὑτοῦ μέσῳ τὸ μέσον· μέχρι τούτου γὰρ ἔχει
τὴν ῥοπήν. οὐδὲν τοίνυν τοῦτο διαφέρει λέγειν ἐπὶ
βώλου καὶ μορίου τοῦ τυχόντος ἢ ἐπὶ ὅλης τῆς γῆς·
οὐ γὰρ διὰ μικρότητα ἢ μέγεθος εἴρηται τὸ συμ-
10 βαῖνον, ἀλλὰ κατὰ παντὸς τοῦ ῥοπὴν ἔχοντος ἐπὶ
τὸ μέσον· ὥστε εἴτε ὅλη ποθὲν ἐφέρετο εἴτε κατὰ
μέρος, ἀναγκαῖον μέχρι τούτου φέρεσθαι ἕως ἂν
πανταχόθεν ὁμοίως λάβῃ τὸ μέσον, ἀνισαζομένων
τῶν ἐλαττόνων ὑπὸ τῶν μειζόνων τῇ προώσει
τῆς ῥοπῆς.

Εἴτ᾽ οὖν ἐγένετο, τοῦτον ἀναγκαῖον γενέσθαι τὸν
15 τρόπον, ὥστε φανερὸν ὅτι σφαιροειδὴς ἡ γένεσις
αὐτῆς, εἴτ᾽ ἀγένητος ἀεὶ διατελεῖ[1] μένουσα, τὸν
αὐτὸν τρόπον ἔχειν ὅνπερ κἂν εἰ γιγνομένη τὸ
πρῶτον ἐγένετο. κατὰ τοῦτόν τε δὴ τὸν λόγον
ἀναγκαῖον εἶναι τὸ σχῆμα σφαιροειδὲς αὐτῆς, καὶ
ὅτι πάντα φέρεται τὰ βαρέα πρὸς ὁμοίας γωνίας,
20 ἀλλ᾽ οὐ παρ᾽ ἄλληλα· τοῦτο δὲ πέφυκε πρὸς
τὸ φύσει σφαιροειδές. ἢ οὖν ἐστι σφαιροειδής, ἢ
φύσει γε σφαιροειδής. δεῖ δ᾽ ἕκαστον λέγειν τοιοῦτον εἶναι ὃ φύσει βούλεται εἶναι καὶ ὃ ὑπάρχει,
ἀλλὰ μὴ ὃ βίᾳ καὶ παρὰ φύσιν.

---

[1] διατελεῖ is in FHMJ and Simpl., and printed by Allan.
Bekker omits with EL.

it is not hard to understand, if we make a little further effort and define the manner in which we suppose any magnitude, possessed of weight, to travel towards the centre. Not, clearly, to the extent of only touching the centre with its edge : the larger portion must prevail until it possesses the centre with its own centre, for its impulse extends to that point. It makes no difference whether we posit this of any chance portion or clod, or of the earth as a whole, for the fact as explained does not depend on smallness or greatness, but applies to everything which has an impulse towards the centre. Therefore whether the earth moved as a whole or in parts, it must have continued in motion until it occupied the centre evenly all round, the smaller portions being equalized by the greater under the forward pressure of their common impulse.

If then the earth has come into being, this must have been the manner of its generation, and it must have grown in the form of a sphere : if on the other hand it is ungenerated and everlasting, it must be the same as it would have been had it developed as the result of a process. Besides this argument for the spherical shape of the earth, there is also the point that all heavy bodies fall at similar angles, not parallel to each other [a] ; this naturally means that their fall is towards a body whose nature is spherical. Either then it *is* spherical, or at least it is natural for it to be so, and we must describe each thing by that which is its natural goal or its permanent state, not by any enforced or unnatural characteristics.

[a] 296 b 19 above.

297 b

Ἔτι δὲ καὶ διὰ τῶν φαινομένων κατὰ τὴν αἴσθη-
25 σιν· οὔτε γὰρ ἂν αἱ τῆς σελήνης ἐκλείψεις τοιαύτας
ἂν εἶχον τὰς ἀποτομάς· νῦν γὰρ ἐν μὲν τοῖς κατὰ
μῆνα σχηματισμοῖς πάσας λαμβάνει τὰς διαιρέσεις
(καὶ γὰρ εὐθεῖα γίνεται καὶ ἀμφίκυρτος καὶ κοίλη),
περὶ δὲ τὰς ἐκλείψεις ἀεὶ κυρτὴν ἔχει τὴν ὁρίζουσαν
γραμμήν, ὥστ' ἐπείπερ ἐκλείπει διὰ τὴν τῆς γῆς
30 ἐπιπρόσθησιν, ἡ τῆς γῆς ἂν εἴη περιφέρεια τοῦ
σχήματος αἰτία σφαιροειδὴς οὖσα. ἔτι δὲ διὰ
τῆς τῶν ἄστρων φαντασίας οὐ μόνον φανερὸν ὅτι
περιφερής, ἀλλὰ καὶ τὸ μέγεθος οὐκ οὖσα μεγάλη·
μικρᾶς γὰρ γιγνομένης μεταστάσεως ἡμῖν πρὸς
μεσημβρίαν καὶ ἄρκτον ἐπιδήλως ἕτερος γίγνεται
298 a ὁ ὁρίζων κύκλος, ὥστε τὰ ὑπὲρ κεφαλῆς ἄστρα
μεγάλην ἔχειν τὴν μεταβολήν, καὶ μὴ ταὐτὰ φαίνεσθαι πρὸς ἄρκτον τε καὶ μεσημβρίαν μεταβαίνου-
σιν· ἔνιοι γὰρ ἐν Αἰγύπτῳ μὲν ἀστέρες ὁρῶνται καὶ
περὶ Κύπρον, ἐν τοῖς πρὸς ἄρκτον δὲ χωρίοις οὐχ
5 ὁρῶνται, καὶ τὰ διὰ παντὸς ἐν τοῖς πρὸς ἄρκτον
φαινόμενα τῶν ἄστρων ἐν ἐκείνοις τοῖς τόποις
ποιεῖται δύσιν. ὥστ' οὐ μόνον ἐκ τούτων δῆλον
περιφερὲς ὂν τὸ σχῆμα τῆς γῆς, ἀλλὰ καὶ σφαίρας
οὐ μεγάλης· οὐ γὰρ ἂν οὕτω ταχὺ ἐπίδηλον ἐποίει
μεθισταμένοις οὕτω βραχύ. διὸ τοὺς ὑπολαμ-
10 βάνοντας συνάπτειν τὸν περὶ τὰς Ἡρακλείους
στήλας τόπον τῷ περὶ τὴν Ἰνδικήν, καὶ τοῦτον τὸν
τρόπον εἶναι τὴν θάλατταν μίαν, μὴ λίαν ὑπολαμβάνειν ἄπιστα δοκεῖν· λέγουσι δὲ τεκμαιρόμενοι καὶ
τοῖς ἐλέφασιν, ὅτι περὶ ἀμφοτέρους τοὺς τόπους
τοὺς ἐσχατεύοντας τὸ γένος αὐτῶν ἐστιν, ὡς τῶν
15 ἐσχάτων διὰ τὸ συνάπτειν ἀλλήλοις τοῦτο πε-

Further proof is obtained from the evidence of the senses. (i) If the earth were not spherical, eclipses of the moon would not exhibit segments of the shape which they do. As it is, in its monthly phases the moon takes on all varieties of shape—straight-edged, gibbous and concave—but in eclipses the boundary is always convex. Thus if the eclipses are due to the interposition of the earth, the shape must be caused by its circumference, and the earth must be spherical. (ii) Observation of the stars also shows not only that the earth is spherical but that it is of no great size, since a small change of position on our part southward or northward visibly alters the circle of the horizon, so that the stars above our heads change their position considerably, and we do not see the same stars as we move to the North or South. Certain stars are seen in Egypt and the neighbourhood of Cyprus, which are invisible in more northerly lands, and stars which are continuously visible in the northern countries are observed to set in the others. This proves both that the earth is spherical and that its periphery is not large, for otherwise such a small change of position could not have had such an immediate effect. For this reason those who imagine that the region around the Pillars of Heracles joins on to the regions of India, and that in this way the ocean is one, are not, it would seem, suggesting anything utterly incredible. They produce also in support of their contention the fact that elephants are a species found at the extremities of both lands, arguing that this phenomenon at the extremes is due to communication between the two.

πονθότων. καὶ τῶν μαθηματικῶν ὅσοι τὸ μέγεθος
ἀναλογίζεσθαι πειρῶνται τῆς περιφερείας, εἰς τετ-
ταράκοντα λέγουσιν εἶναι μυριάδας σταδίων.

Ἐξ ὧν τεκμαιρομένοις οὐ μόνον σφαιροειδῆ τὸν
ὄγκον ἀναγκαῖον εἶναι τῆς γῆς, ἀλλὰ καὶ μὴ μέγαν
20 πρὸς τὸ τῶν ἄλλων ἄστρων μέγεθος.

---

^a *i.e.* 9987 geographical miles.   Prantl (p. 319) remarks
that this is the oldest recorded calculation of the earth's
circumference.   He quotes the following estimates for comparison : Archimedes 7495 geogr. miles ; Eratosthenes and

Mathematicians who try to calculate the circumference put it at 400,000 stades.[a]

From these arguments we must conclude not only that the earth's mass is spherical but also that it is not large in comparison with the size of the other stars.

Hipparchus 6292 ; Posidonius 5992 or 4494 ; present day 5400. (The present-day figure in English miles is 24902.)

This passage of Aristotle is said to have provided a stimulus to the voyage of Columbus. (Ross, *Aristotle*, p. 96, n. 3.)

Γ

OF THE FOUR SUBLUNARY BODIES

CHAPTER I

ARGUMENT

*To treat of the sublunary elements involves a theory of
generation. Previous views on generation : (1) It is all
illusion, since what is is unchangeable and imperishable.
(2) Everything which we see is in a flux of generation,
change, and decay, but there is one persistent underlying substance out of which the world and its phenomena are evolved.
(3) All natural bodies are generated, their ultimate elements
being plane surfaces (298 a 24—299 a 1).*

*The last theory (that of Plato) is criticized in detail, ex-
pressly from the point of view of the natural scientist and not
of the mathematician (299 a 1—300 a 19).*

*(a) Natural bodies have weight, therefore their parts, how-
ever small, must have weight, therefore surfaces must have
weight, and if surfaces then lines and points (since on the
view criticized the elements of body are surfaces, of surfaces
lines, and of lines points). But a point cannot have weight,
because it is by definition indivisible, and everything which
has weight can be shown to be divisible (299 a 25-b 23).*

289 a 24 Περὶ μὲν οὖν τοῦ πρώτου οὐρανοῦ καὶ τῶν
25 μερῶν, ἔτι δὲ περὶ τῶν ἐν αὐτῷ φαινομένων[1] ἄστρων,

---

[1] φαινομένων Bekker with JHM. But other edd. follow
the remaining authorities in printing φερομένων.

BOOK III

OF THE FOUR SUBLUNARY BODIES

CHAPTER I

ARGUMENT (*continued*)

(b) *The* Timaeus *would have us believe that surfaces only combine edge to edge, since they have to form the pyramids, cubes, etc., which on Plato's theory are the constituents of the four primary bodies. But we cannot believe this. It would be just as easy for them to lie one upon another, but if they do, what sort of body would result?* (299 b 23-31.)

(c) *It is said in the* Timaeus *that the primary bodies differ in weight according to the number of equal triangular surfaces comprising each of their " seeds." But if so we are back at the difficulty of supposing that surfaces (and hence points) have weight. Even if we simply affirm earth to be heavy and fire light, this must result from a property of the surfaces which compose their " seeds "* (299 b 31—300 a 7).

The result of the theory then is to dissolve all body and magnitude into thin air. Applied to time, it has the same effect. And the criticisms to which it is open apply with equal force to the Pythagorean theory which generates the world from numbers: weightless monads can never be the sole ultimate components of bodies possessed of weight (300 a 7-19).

WE have treated earlier of the first heaven and its parts, and also of the stars which are visible

298 a

ἐκ τίνων τε συνεστᾶσι καὶ ποῖ' ἄττα τὴν φύσιν
ἐστί, πρὸς δὲ τούτοις ὅτι ἀγένητα καὶ ἄφθαρτα,
διεληλύθαμεν πρότερον. ἐπεὶ δὲ τῶν φύσει λεγομένων τὰ μέν ἐστιν οὐσίαι τὰ δ' ἔργα καὶ πάθη
τούτων (λέγω δ' οὐσίας μὲν τά τε ἁπλᾶ σώματα,
30 οἷον πῦρ καὶ γῆν καὶ τὰ σύστοιχα τούτοις, καὶ ὅσα
ἐκ τούτων, οἷον τόν τε σύνολον οὐρανὸν καὶ τὰ
μόρια αὐτοῦ, καὶ πάλιν τά τε ζῷα καὶ τὰ φυτὰ καὶ
τὰ μόρια τούτων, πάθη δὲ καὶ ἔργα τάς τε κινήσεις
τὰς τούτων ἑκάστου καὶ τῶν ἄλλων, ὅσων ἐστὶν
αἴτια ταῦτα κατὰ τὴν δύναμιν τὴν ἑαυτῶν, ἔτι δὲ
298 b τὰς ἀλλοιώσεις καὶ τὰς εἰς ἄλληλα μεταβάσεις),
φανερὸν ὅτι τὴν πλείστην συμβαίνει τῆς περὶ
φύσεως ἱστορίας περὶ σωμάτων εἶναι· πᾶσαι γὰρ
αἱ φυσικαὶ οὐσίαι ἢ σώματα ἢ μετὰ σωμάτων
γίγνονται καὶ μεγεθῶν. τοῦτο δὲ δῆλον ἔκ τε τοῦ
5 διωρίσθαι τὰ ποῖά ἐστι φύσει, καὶ ἐκ τῆς καθ'
ἕκαστα θεωρίας.

Περὶ μὲν οὖν τοῦ πρώτου τῶν στοιχείων εἴρηται,
καὶ ποῖόν τι τὴν φύσιν, καὶ ὅτι ἄφθαρτον καὶ
ἀγένητον· λοιπὸν δὲ περὶ τοῖν δυοῖν εἰπεῖν. ἅμα δὲ
συμβήσεται περὶ τούτων λέγουσι καὶ περὶ γενέσεως
10 καὶ φθορᾶς διασκέψασθαι· γένεσις γὰρ ἤτοι τὸ
παράπαν οὐκ ἔστιν, ἢ μόνον ἐν τούτοις τοῖς στοι-
χείοις καὶ τοῖς ἐκ τούτων ἐστίν. αὐτὸ δὲ τοῦτο
πρῶτον ἴσως θεωρητέον, πότερον ἔστιν ἢ οὐκ ἔστιν.
οἱ μὲν οὖν πρότερον φιλοσοφήσαντες περὶ τῆς
ἀληθείας καὶ πρὸς οὓς νῦν λέγομεν ἡμεῖς λόγους

ᵃ Not four. *Cf.* the prooemium of Simpl. (p. 1): " By
two he means the two pairs, the light pair (fire and air) and
258

in it, their composition and natural characteristics, and the fact that they are ungenerated and indestructible. Now the word " natural " is applied on the one hand to substances, and on the other to functions and attributes of substances. By substances I refer to the simple bodies, fire and earth and the others of the same order, and things composed of them, *e.g.* the heaven as a whole and its parts, as well as animals and plants and their parts ; attributes and functions include the movements of each of these substances and all movements of the others for which each is responsible by virtue of its proper power, and also their alterations and mutual transmutations. It is obvious therefore that the study of nature is concerned for the most part with bodies, seeing that all natural substances either are bodies or are dependent on bodies and magnitudes. This is plain both from a logical definition of the type of things that are natural, and from a study of each separate species.

Since, then, we have dealt with the first element, its natural characteristics and the fact that it is ungenerated and indestructible, it remains to speak of the other two.[a] But to treat of them involves us at the same time in an investigation of generation and destruction, for generation, if it is not a pure fiction, occurs in these elements and their compounds. Possibly however we ought first to ask this very question, whether generation is a fact or not. Earlier seekers after truth have differed both from

the heavy pair (water and earth)," and also his discussion on bk. i. ch. 2 (Simpl. 20. 10), which concludes διὸ δύο τὰ κυρίως ἁπλᾶ στοιχεῖα, πῦρ καὶ γῆ. As Stocks says, generically the elements are two, since the only generic differences are weight and lightness.

298 b
καὶ πρὸς ἀλλήλους διηνέχθησαν. οἱ μὲν γὰρ αὐτῶν
1 ὅλως ἀνεῖλον γένεσιν καὶ φθοράν· οὐθὲν γὰρ οὔτε
γίγνεσθαί φασιν οὔτε φθείρεσθαι τῶν ὄντων, ἀλλὰ
μόνον δοκεῖν ἡμῖν, οἷον οἱ περὶ Μέλισσόν τε καὶ
Παρμενίδην, οὕς, εἰ καὶ τἆλλα λέγουσι καλῶς, ἀλλ'
οὐ φυσικῶς γε δεῖ νομίσαι λέγειν· τὸ γὰρ εἶναι
20 ἄττα τῶν ὄντων ἀγένητα καὶ ὅλως ἀκίνητα μᾶλλόν
ἐστιν ἑτέρας καὶ προτέρας ἢ τῆς φυσικῆς σκέψεως.
ἐκεῖνοι δὲ διὰ τὸ μηθὲν μὲν ἄλλο παρὰ τὴν τῶν
αἰσθητῶν οὐσίαν ὑπολαμβάνειν εἶναι, τοιαύτας δέ
τινας νοῆσαι πρῶτοι φύσεις, εἴπερ ἔσται τις γνῶσις
ἢ φρόνησις, οὕτω μετήνεγκαν ἐπὶ ταῦτα τοὺς ἐκεῖ-
25 θεν λόγους. ἕτεροι δέ τινες ὥσπερ ἐπίτηδες τὴν
ἐναντίαν τούτοις ἔσχον δόξαν. εἰσὶ γάρ τινες οἳ
φασιν οὐθὲν ἀγένητον εἶναι τῶν πραγμάτων, ἀλλὰ
πάντα γίγνεσθαι, γενόμενα δὲ τὰ μὲν ἄφθαρτα
διαμένειν τὰ δὲ πάλιν φθείρεσθαι, μάλιστα μὲν οἱ
περὶ Ἡσίοδον, εἶτα καὶ τῶν ἄλλων οἱ πρῶτοι
30 φυσιολογήσαντες. οἱ δὲ τὰ μὲν ἄλλα πάντα γίνεσθαί τέ φασι καὶ ῥεῖν, εἶναι δὲ παγίως οὐθέν, ἓν
δέ τι μόνον ὑπομένειν, ἐξ οὗ ταῦτα πάντα μετα-
σχηματίζεσθαι πέφυκεν· ὅπερ ἐοίκασι βούλεσθαι
λέγειν ἄλλοι τε πολλοὶ καὶ Ἡράκλειτος ὁ Ἐφέσιος.
εἰσὶ δέ τινες οἳ καὶ πᾶν σῶμα γενητὸν ποιοῦσι,
299 a συντιθέντες καὶ διαλύοντες εἰς ἐπίπεδα καὶ ἐξ
ἐπιπέδων.

Περὶ μὲν οὖν τῶν ἄλλων ἕτερος ἔστω λόγος· τοῖς

our present statements and from one another. Some of them flatly denied generation and destruction, maintaining that nothing which is either comes into being or perishes; it only seems to us as if they do. Such were the followers of Melissus and Parmenides. Of them we must hold, that though some of what they say may be right, yet they do not speak as students of nature, since the existence of certain substances subject neither to generation nor to any other kind of motion is not a matter for natural science but rather for another and higher study. They, however, being unaware of the existence of anything beyond the substance of sensible objects, and perceiving for the first time that unchangeable entities were demanded if knowledge and wisdom were to be possible, naturally transferred to sensible objects the description of the higher. Others again, as if intentionally, maintained the opposite view. That is to say, it has been suggested that nothing is ungenerated, but everything comes to be: once in being, some things last for ever, others perish again. Of this view are Hesiod and his school, and the earliest natural philosophers. The theory of the latter was that in general everything is in a state of becoming and flux, and nothing is stable, but that there is one substance which persists, and out of which the phenomena of the world, with their various transmutations, are naturally evolved. This seems to have been the meaning of Heracleitus of Ephesus and many others besides. Finally there are those according to whom all bodies are generated, being constructed out of planes and resolved into planes again.

Most of these theories we may leave for another

299 a

δὲ τοῦτον τὸν τρόπον λέγουσι καὶ πάντα τὰ σώματα
συνιστᾶσιν ἐξ ἐπιπέδων ὅσα μὲν ἄλλα συμβαίνει
λέγειν ὑπεναντία τοῖς μαθήμασιν, ἐπιπολῆς ἔστιν
5 ἰδεῖν· καίτοι δίκαιον ἦν ἢ μὴ κινεῖν ἢ πιστοτέροις
αὐτὰ λόγοις κινεῖν τῶν ὑποθέσεων. ἔπειτα δῆλον
ὅτι τοῦ αὐτοῦ λόγου ἐστὶ στερεὰ μὲν ἐξ ἐπιπέδων
συγκεῖσθαι, ἐπίπεδα δ' ἐκ γραμμῶν, ταύτας δ' ἐκ
στιγμῶν· οὕτω δ' ἐχόντων οὐκ ἀνάγκη τὸ τῆς
10 γραμμῆς μέρος γραμμὴν εἶναι· περὶ δὲ τούτων
ἐπέσκεπται πρότερον ἐν τοῖς περὶ κινήσεως λόγοις,
ὅτι οὐκ ἔστιν ἀδιαίρετα μήκη. ὅσα δὲ περὶ τῶν
φυσικῶν σωμάτων ἀδύνατα συμβαίνει λέγειν τοῖς
ποιοῦσι τὰς ἀτόμους γραμμάς, ἐπὶ μικρὸν θεωρή-
σωμεν καὶ νῦν· τὰ μὲν γὰρ ἐπ' ἐκείνων ἀδύνατα
15 συμβαίνοντα καὶ τοῖς φυσικοῖς ἀκολουθήσει, τὰ δὲ
τούτοις ἐπ' ἐκείνων οὐχ ἅπαντα διὰ τὸ τὰ μὲν ἐξ
ἀφαιρέσεως λέγεσθαι, τὰ μαθηματικά, τὰ δὲ φυσικὰ
ἐκ προσθέσεως. πολλὰ δ' ἐστὶν ἃ τοῖς ἀδιαιρέτοις
οὐχ οἷόν τε ὑπάρχειν, τοῖς δὲ φυσικοῖς ἀναγκαῖον.
[οἷον εἴ τί ἐστιν ἀδιαίρετον·][1] ἐν ἀδιαιρέτῳ γὰρ
20 διαιρετὸν ἀδύνατον ὑπάρχειν, τὰ δὲ πάθη διαιρετὰ
πάντα διχῶς· ἢ γὰρ κατ' εἶδος ἢ κατὰ συμβεβηκός, κατ' εἶδος μὲν οἷον χρώματος τὸ λευκὸν καὶ
τὸ μέλαν, κατὰ συμβεβηκὸς δέ, ἂν ᾧ ὑπάρχει ᾗ
διαιρετόν, ὥστε ὅσα ἁπλᾶ τῶν παθημάτων, πάντ'

---

[1] I have followed Allan in omitting οἷον . . . ἀδιαίρετον.
(So, in all probability, Simpl.)

occasion. But as for this last theory, which constructs all bodies out of planes, a glance will reveal
many points in which it is in contradiction to the
findings of mathematics (and unless one can re-
place the hypotheses of a science with something
more convincing, it is best to leave them undis-
turbed). In addition, the composition of solids from
planes clearly involves, by the same reasoning, the
composition of planes from lines and lines from
points (a view according to which a part of a line
need not be a line); and this is something which
we have already considered in the work on motion,[a]
where we concluded that there are no indivisible
lines. Nevertheless, so far as they concern natural
bodies, the impossibilities resulting from an assumption of indivisible lines are worth a little attention
here. The mathematical impossibilities will be
physical impossibilities too, but this proposition
cannot be simply converted, since the method of
mathematics is to abstract, but of natural science
to add together all determining characteristics.[b]
Thus there are many attributes which cannot belong
to indivisibles, but must belong to natural objects,
e.g. in the indivisible there can be nothing divisible, but all attributes of bodies are divisible in one
of two ways. They are divisible either by kinds, as
white and black are kinds of colour, or accidentally,
if the subject to which they belong is divisible. All

---

[a] *Phys.* vi. 1. For the appellation περὶ κινήσεως, cf. Ross,
Physics (1936), introd. 1 ff.

[b] For ἐξ ἀφαιρέσεως, ἐκ προσθέσεως, cf. esp. *Met.* 1061 a 28,
An. post. 87 a 35. Mathematics concerns only certain
properties (viz. those connected with quantity) in isolation
from the rest, natural science tries to define the object as a
whole, by discovering all its differentiae.

299 a

ἐστὶ διαιρετὰ τοῦτον τὸν τρόπον. διὸ τὸ ἀδύνατον
25 ἐν τοῖς τοιούτοις ἐπισκεπτέον.

Εἰ δὴ τῶν ἀδυνάτων ἐστὶν ἑκατέρου μέρους μηδὲν
ἔχοντος βάρος τὰ ἄμφω ἔχειν βάρος, τὰ δ᾽ αἰσθητὰ
σώματα ἢ πάντα ἢ ἔνια βάρος ἔχει, οἷον ἡ γῆ καὶ
τὸ ὕδωρ, ὡς κἂν αὐτοὶ φαῖεν, εἰ ἡ στιγμὴ μηδὲν
ἔχει βάρος, δῆλον ὅτι οὐδ᾽ αἱ γραμμαί, εἰ δὲ μὴ
30 αὗται, οὐδὲ τὰ ἐπίπεδα· ὥστ᾽ οὐδὲ τῶν σωμάτων
οὐθέν.

Ἀλλὰ μὴν ὅτι τὴν στιγμὴν οὐχ οἷόν τε βάρος
ἔχειν, φανερόν. τὸ μὲν γὰρ βαρὺ ἅπαν καὶ βαρύ-
299 b τερον καὶ τὸ κοῦφον καὶ κουφότερον ἐνδέχεταί
τινος εἶναι. τὸ δὲ βαρύτερον ἢ κουφότερον ἴσως
οὐκ ἀνάγκη βαρὺ ἢ κοῦφον εἶναι, ὥσπερ καὶ τὸ μὲν
μέγα μεῖζον, τὸ δὲ μεῖζον οὐ πάντως μέγα· πολλὰ
γάρ ἐστιν ἃ μικρὰ ὄντα ἁπλῶς ὅμως μείζω τινῶν
5 ἑτέρων ἐστίν. εἰ δὴ ὃ ἂν βαρὺ ὂν βαρύτερον ᾖ,
ἀνάγκη βάρει μεῖζον εἶναι, καὶ τὸ βαρὺ ἅπαν διαιρετὸν ἂν εἴη. ἡ δὲ στιγμὴ ἀδιαίρετον ὑπόκειται.
ἔτι εἰ τὸ μὲν βαρὺ πυκνόν τι, τὸ δὲ κοῦφον μανόν,
ἔστι δὲ πυκνὸν μανοῦ διαφέρον τῷ ἐν ἴσῳ ὄγκῳ
πλεῖον ἐνυπάρχειν· εἰ οὖν ἐστὶ στιγμὴ βαρεῖα καὶ
10 κούφη, ἔσται καὶ πυκνὴ καὶ μανή. ἀλλὰ τὸ μὲν
πυκνὸν διαιρετόν, ἡ δὲ στιγμὴ ἀδιαίρετος. εἰ δὲ
πᾶν τὸ βαρὺ ἢ μαλακὸν ἢ σκληρὸν ἀνάγκη εἶναι,
ῥᾴδιον ἐκ τούτων ἀδύνατόν τι συναγαγεῖν. μαλακὸν
μὲν γὰρ τὸ εἰς ἑαυτὸ ὑπεῖκον, σκληρὸν δὲ τὸ μὴ
ὑπεῖκον· τὸ δὲ ὑπεῖκον διαιρετόν.

15 Ἀλλὰ μὴν οὐδ᾽ ἐκ μὴ ἐχόντων βάρος ἔσται
βάρος. τό τε γὰρ ἐπὶ πόσων συμβήσεται τοῦτο

simple attributes, thus regarded, are divisible. Let us then consider the impossibilities in the theories in question.

If each of two parts is weightless, the two together cannot have weight ; but sensible bodies, if not all, at least some, such as earth and water, have weight —so our opponents themselves would admit. Yet if the point is without weight, so also are lines, and if lines, then surfaces as well, and hence bodies.

That the point cannot have weight is clear. (i) It is possible for everything which is heavy to be heavier, and everything which is light lighter, than something else, though that which is heavier or lighter need not, perhaps, be heavy or light. (Similarly the " great " is " greater," but the " greater " is not in all circumstances " great " : there are many things which are intrinsically small though they are greater than others.) Now if to say that a heavy thing is " heavier " necessarily means that it is " greater in weight," then everything heavy must be divisible. But the point is *ex hypothesi* indivisible. (ii) If (*a*) heavy = dense and light = rare (dense differing from rare in that the former contains a greater quantity in an equal bulk), and (*b*) a point is heavy or light, then points must be dense or rare. But that which is dense is divisible, the point is indivisible. If also everything which is heavy must be either soft or hard, an impossible conclusion can be drawn without difficulty ; for the soft is that which can be pressed in upon itself, and the hard is that which cannot ; and anything which can be pressed in is divisible.

Now a weight cannot be composed of parts which are weightless. The question with how many

καὶ ἐπὶ ποίων, πῶς διοριοῦσι μὴ βουλόμενοι πλάτ-
τειν; καὶ εἰ πᾶν μεῖζον βάρος βάρους βάρει,
συμβήσεται καὶ ἕκαστον τῶν ἀμερῶν βάρος ἔχειν·
εἰ γὰρ αἱ τέτταρες στιγμαὶ βάρος ἔχουσι, τὸ δ' ἐκ
20 πλειόνων ἢ τοδὶ βαρέος ὄντος βαρύτερον, ᾧ[1] δὲ
βαρέος βαρύτερον ἀνάγκη βαρὺ εἶναι, ὥσπερ καὶ
ᾧ[1] λευκοῦ λευκότερον λευκόν, ὥστε τὸ μεῖζον μιᾷ
στιγμῇ βαρύτερον ἔσται ἀφαιρεθέντος τοῦ ἴσου.
ὥστε καὶ ἡ μία στιγμὴ βάρος ἕξει.

Ἔτι εἰ μὲν τὰ ἐπίπεδα μόνον κατὰ γραμμὴν
25 ἐνδέχεται συντίθεσθαι, ἄτοπον· ὥσπερ γὰρ καὶ
γραμμὴ πρὸς γραμμὴν ἀμφοτέρως συντίθεται, καὶ
κατὰ μῆκος καὶ κατὰ πλάτος, δεῖ καὶ ἐπίπεδον
ἐπιπέδῳ τὸν αὐτὸν τρόπον. γραμμὴ δὲ δύναται
γραμμῇ συντίθεσθαι κατὰ γραμμὴν ἐπιτιθεμένη,[2]
οὐ μὴν προστιθεμένη.[2] ἀλλὰ μὴν εἴ γε καὶ κατὰ
30 πλάτος ἐνδέχεται συντίθεσθαι, ἔσται τι σῶμα ὃ
οὔτε στοιχεῖον οὔτε ἐκ στοιχείων, συντιθέμενον ἐκ
τῶν οὕτω συντιθεμένων ἐπιπέδων.

Ἔτι εἰ μὲν πλήθει βαρύτερα τὰ σώματα τῶν[3]

---

[1] It seems necessary to adopt, as Allan does, the conjecture of Bonitz, ᾧ for the mss. τὸ in both these lines. (In line 20, L has ὅ.)

[2] Bekker has ἐπιτιθεμένην and προτιθεμένην, with JHL and first hand of E.

[3] τῶν. So Stocks and Allan. τὰ τῶν Bekker, with E alone.

---

[a] It is assumed but not stated by A. that the heavier body contains one more point than the other. Prantl conjectured that the words μίᾳ στιγμῇ should be duplicated to make this explicit.

[b] Plato in the *Timaeus* had described the popular ele-

parts, or with what sort of parts, such a result could be attained, does not admit of an answer other than fictitious. If indeed it is weight that makes one weight greater than another, it follows that every indivisible part has weight : for supposing four points have weight, and a body composed of more than four points is heavier than this heavy body, and that which makes one weight heavier than another must itself be heavy (as that which makes a white thing whiter than another must be white), then subtract the four-point weight from both alike, and the greater weight will be found to be by one point heavier.[a] This one point therefore must have weight.

Further, we cannot be asked to believe that surfaces can only be put together edgewise. Lines can be combined in both ways, end to end and side by side, and it must be the same for surfaces. Lines can be combined as edge to edge by putting one on top of the other, instead of adding it at the end. But if similarly we allow surfaces contact over all their area as well as only at the edges, we shall have a body which is neither an element nor composed of elements, the body, namely, which is made of surfaces combined in this way.[b]

Again, if the difference in the weight of bodies is determined by the number of their surfaces,

ments as being formed after the shape of regular solids, which were themselves formed of triangular surfaces in different combinations. A. objects that if the ultimate realities are these triangles, there is no reason why they should always combine edge to edge so as to form pyramids, cubes, etc. They might as easily be piled one on top of the other like a block of note-paper. The Platonic system leaves no room for this contingency.

300 a

ἐπιπέδων, ὥσπερ ἐν τῷ Τιμαίῳ διώρισται, δῆλον
ὡς ἕξει καὶ ἡ γραμμὴ καὶ ἡ στιγμὴ βάρος· ἀνάλογον γὰρ πρὸς ἄλληλα ἔχουσιν, ὥσπερ καὶ πρότερον
εἰρήκαμεν. εἰ δὲ μὴ τοῦτον διαφέρει τὸν τρόπον
ἀλλὰ τῷ τὴν μὲν γῆν εἶναι βαρὺ τὸ δὲ πῦρ κοῦφον,
5 ἔσται καὶ τῶν ἐπιπέδων τὸ μὲν κοῦφον τὸ δὲ βαρύ.
καὶ τῶν γραμμῶν δὴ καὶ τῶν στιγμῶν ὡσαύτως·
τὸ γὰρ τῆς γῆς ἐπίπεδον ἔσται βαρύτερον ἢ τὸ τοῦ
πυρός. ὅλως δὲ συμβαίνει ἢ μηδέν ποτ' εἶναι μέγεθος, ἢ δύνασθαί γε ἀναιρεθῆναι, εἴπερ ὁμοίως
ἔχει στιγμὴ μὲν πρὸς γραμμήν, γραμμὴ δὲ πρὸς
10 ἐπίπεδον, τοῦτο δὲ πρὸς σῶμα· πάντα γὰρ εἰς ἄλληλα ἀναλυόμενα εἰς τὰ πρῶτα ἀναλυθήσεται· ὥστ'
ἐνδέχοιτ' ἂν στιγμὰς μόνον εἶναι, σῶμα δὲ μηθέν.

Πρὸς δὲ τούτοις καὶ εἰ ὁ χρόνος ὁμοίως ἔχει,
ἀναιροῖτ' ἄν ποτε ἢ ἐνδέχοιτ' ἀναιρεθῆναι· τὸ γὰρ
νῦν τὸ ἄτομον οἷον στιγμὴ γραμμῆς ἐστίν.

15 Τὸ δ' αὐτὸ συμβαίνει καὶ τοῖς ἐξ ἀριθμῶν συντι-
θεῖσι τὸν οὐρανόν· ἔνιοι γὰρ τὴν φύσιν ἐξ ἀριθμῶν
συνιστᾶσιν, ὥσπερ τῶν Πυθαγορείων τινές· τὰ μὲν
γὰρ φυσικὰ σώματα φαίνεται βάρος ἔχοντα καὶ
κουφότητα, τὰς δὲ μονάδας οὔτε σῶμα ποιεῖν οἷόν
τε συντιθεμένας οὔτε βάρος ἔχειν.

ᵃ Tim. 56 B. Cf. Cornford, Plato's Cosmology, p. 222,
n. 4.

CHAPTER II

ARGUMENT

1. The elements all have a natural motion. *Motion must
be either natural or enforced, and in fact enforced motion*

as the *Timaeus* affirms,[a] then clearly lines and points will also have weight, since all these stand in a definite ratio to one another, as we have already noted. If on the other hand it is not this which determines the difference but the fact that earth is heavy and fire light, then surfaces too must be light or heavy, and by the same reckoning lines and points ; for the surface which makes earth must be heavier than that of fire. In sum, either there is no magnitude at all on their arguments, or magnitude can be annihilated, once granted that as the point is to the line, so the line is to the surface and the surface to body ; for all can be resolved into one another, and hence can be resolved into the one which is primary, so that it would be possible for there to exist nothing but points, and no body at all.

Besides this, if time is subject to the same arguments, it will be, or at least could be annihilated, for the indivisible " now " corresponds to the point in a line.

There are some, *e.g.* certain Pythagoreans, who construct nature out of numbers. But to construct the world of numbers leads them to the same difficulty, for natural bodies manifestly possess weight and lightness, whereas their monads in combination cannot either produce bodies or possess weight.

CHAPTER II

ARGUMENT (*continued*)

implies natural. Rest is natural when a body has reached the place to which its natural motion tended. It is thus with

the earth's rest at the centre. Were it enforced, then (a) if
that which prevented it moving were itself at rest, we should
only push the fact of natural rest one stage further back, or
else embark on an infinite regress ; (b) if the constraining
body were in motion, we should proceed to the further question : were the constraint removed, where would the earth
go to ? To travel to infinity is impossible, but if it stops at
all, in that place its rest must be natural. The disorderly
motions posited by the atomists and Plato shirk these questions
and others arising out of them (300 a 20—301 a 20).

2. The elements all have weight or lightness. This
follows from the possession of a natural motion. (a) If a
weightless body moves at all, it must traverse a distance pro-

200 a 20 "Ὅτι δ' ἀναγκαῖον ὑπάρχειν κίνησιν τοῖς ἁπλοῖς
σώμασι φύσει τινὰ πᾶσιν, ἐκ τῶνδε δῆλον. ἐπεὶ
γὰρ κινούμενα φαίνεται, κινεῖσθαί γε ἀναγκαῖον
βίᾳ, εἰ μὴ οἰκείαν ἔχει κίνησιν· τὸ δὲ βίᾳ καὶ παρὰ
φύσιν ταὐτόν. ἀλλὰ μὴν εἰ παρὰ φύσιν ἐστί τις
25 κίνησις, ἀνάγκη εἶναι καὶ κατὰ φύσιν, παρ' ἣν
αὕτη· καὶ εἰ πολλαὶ αἱ παρὰ φύσιν, τὴν κατὰ φύσιν
μίαν· κατὰ φύσιν μὲν γὰρ ἁπλῶς, παρὰ φύσιν δ'
ἔχει πολλὰς ἕκαστον.

   "Ἔτι δὲ καὶ ἐκ τῆς ἠρεμίας δῆλον· καὶ γὰρ
ἠρεμεῖν ἀναγκαῖον ἢ βίᾳ ἢ κατὰ φύσιν· βίᾳ δὲ
30 μένει οὗ καὶ φέρεται βίᾳ, καὶ κατὰ φύσιν οὗ κατὰ
φύσιν. ἐπεὶ οὖν φαίνεταί τι μένον ἐπὶ τοῦ μέσου,
εἰ μὲν κατὰ φύσιν, δῆλον ὅτι καὶ ἡ φορὰ ἡ ἐνταῦθα
κατὰ φύσιν αὐτῷ· εἰ δὲ βίᾳ, τί τὸ φέρεσθαι κωλῦον;
εἰ μὲν ἠρεμοῦν, τὸν αὐτὸν κυκλήσομεν λόγον·

---

   [a] If παρὰ φύσιν is taken in its strongest sense, this statement conflicts with the doctrine " one thing one contrary "
enunciated in bk. i. (269 a 10)   But A. allows himself to

portionate to that traversed in the same time by a body possess-
ing weight, i.e. a distance traversed by a body smaller indeed
than that body, but yet possessed of some weight itself. This
is absurd. (b) The motion of a weightless body would have
to be enforced, and by arguments similar to the foregoing it
can be shown that it would have to continue to infinity, which
is impossible (301 a 20–b 16).

3. *Definitions of " nature " and " force " as motive*
causes. Force assists natural motion and is sole cause of
unnatural. Part played by the air (301 b 17–30).

4. *Generation ex* nihilo *is an impossibility, for it demands*
a void to hold previously non-existent bodies, and such a void
has been disproved in earlier treatises (301 b 30—302 a 9).

THAT all the simple bodies must have a certain natural motion can be demonstrated as follows. They
are manifestly in motion, therefore they must be
moved by force unless they have a proper motion of
their own ; and " by force " is the same as " unnaturally." But if there is an unnatural movement, there
must be one according to nature also, from which
the other diverges. And though the unnatural movements may be many, the natural movement is one ;
the natural motion of each body is simple, its unnatural motions are manifold.[a]

It may be proved further from their behaviour at
rest, for rest too must be either enforced or natural,
and where a thing was brought by force, there it
remains by force, where it came naturally there it
remains naturally. Now there is a body which manifestly rests at the centre. If this is natural, then
clearly its motion thither was natural too. If it is
enforced, what is it which prevents it from moving ?
If it is something itself at rest, we shall argue

use it in the weaker sense of μὴ κατὰ φύσιν, as at 269 b 2,
where see note.

271

300 b ἀνάγκη γὰρ ἢ κατὰ φύσιν εἶναι τὸ πρῶτον ἠρεμοῦν
ἢ εἰς ἄπειρον ἰέναι, ὅπερ ἀδύνατον· εἰ δὲ κινούμενον
τὸ κωλῦον φέρεσθαι, καθάπερ φησὶν Ἐμπεδοκλῆς
τὴν γῆν ὑπὸ τῆς δίνης ἠρεμεῖν, ποῦ ἂν ἐφέρετο,
ἐπειδὴ εἰς ἄπειρον ἀδύνατον; οὐθὲν γὰρ γίγνεται
5 ἀδύνατον, τὸ δ' ἄπειρον διελθεῖν ἀδύνατον. ὥστ'
ἀνάγκη στῆναί που τὸ φερόμενον, κἀκεῖ μὴ βίᾳ
μένειν ἀλλὰ κατὰ φύσιν. εἰ δ' ἐστὶν ἠρεμία κατὰ
φύσιν, ἔστι καὶ κίνησις κατὰ φύσιν, ἡ εἰς τοῦτον
τὸν τόπον φορά.

Διὸ καὶ Λευκίππῳ καὶ Δημοκρίτῳ, τοῖς λέγουσιν
10 ἀεὶ κινεῖσθαι τὰ πρῶτα σώματα ἐν τῷ κενῷ καὶ τῷ
ἀπείρῳ, λεκτέον τίνα κίνησιν καὶ τίς ἡ κατὰ φύσιν
αὐτῶν κίνησις. εἰ γὰρ ἄλλο ὑπ' ἄλλου κινεῖται βίᾳ
τῶν στοιχείων, ἀλλὰ καὶ κατὰ φύσιν ἀνάγκη τινὰ
εἶναι κίνησιν ἑκάστου, παρ' ἣν ἡ βίαιός ἐστιν· καὶ
δεῖ τὴν πρώτην κινοῦσαν μὴ βίᾳ κινεῖν, ἀλλὰ κατὰ
15 φύσιν· εἰς ἄπειρον γὰρ εἶσιν, εἰ μή τι ἔσται κατὰ
φύσιν κινοῦν πρῶτον, ἀλλ' ἀεὶ τὸ πρότερον βίᾳ
κινούμενον κινήσει.

Τὸ αὐτὸ δὲ τοῦτο συμβαίνειν ἀναγκαῖον κἂν εἰ
καθάπερ ἐν τῷ Τιμαίῳ γέγραπται, πρὶν γενέσθαι
τὸν κόσμον ἐκινεῖτο τὰ στοιχεῖα ἀτάκτως. ἀνάγκη
γὰρ ἢ βίαιον εἶναι τὴν κίνησιν ἢ κατὰ φύσιν. εἰ
20 δὲ κατὰ φύσιν ἐκινεῖτο, ἀνάγκη κόσμον εἶναι, ἐάν
τις βούληται θεωρεῖν ἐπιστήσας· τό τε γὰρ πρῶτον
κινοῦν ἀνάγκη κινεῖν αὐτό,[1] κινούμενον κατὰ φύσιν,

---

[1] κινεῖν αὐτό. αὐτό FL, Alex., and so Stocks and Allan.
See introd. p. xxi, n. b.

round in a circle: either the first of the bodies at rest must be naturally in that state, or we must carry on to infinity, which is impossible. But perhaps that which prevents it from moving is in motion, like the vortex which Empedocles asserts to be the cause of the earth's immobility. If so, we ask, where would the earth have gone to? It could not go on to infinity. Impossibilities do not happen, and to traverse an infinite distance is impossible. Therefore what moves must somewhere come to a stop, and its rest in that place will be not enforced but natural. But if rest can be natural, motion can also be natural, namely the motion towards the place of rest.

When therefore Leucippus and Democritus speak of the primary bodies as always moving in the infinite void, they ought to say with what motion they move and what is their natural motion. Each of the atoms may be forcibly moved by another, but each one must have some natural motion also, from which the enforced motion diverges. Moreover the original movement cannot act by force, but only naturally. We shall go on to infinity if there is to be no first thing which imparts motion naturally, but always a prior one which moves because itself set in motion by force.

We get the very same difficulty if we accept the account of the *Timaeus*, that before the creation of the cosmos the elements were in disorderly motion. The motion must have been either enforced or natural. But if it was natural, careful consideration will show that there must have been a cosmos. For the first mover must move itself (since its movement must be natural), and

καὶ τὰ κινούμενα μὴ βίᾳ, ἐν τοῖς οἰκείοις ἠρεμοῦντα
τόποις, ποιεῖν ἥνπερ ἔχουσι νῦν τάξιν, τὰ μὲν βάρος
25 ἔχοντα ἐπὶ τὸ μέσον, τὰ δὲ κουφότητα ἀπὸ τοῦ
μέσου· ταύτην δ᾽ ὁ κόσμος ἔχει τὴν διάταξιν.

Ἔτι δὲ τοσοῦτον ἐπανέροιτ᾽ ἄν τις, πότερον δυνατὸν ἢ οὐχ οἷόν τ᾽ ἦν κινούμενα ἀτάκτως καὶ
μίγνυσθαι τοιαύτας μίξεις ἔνια, ἐξ ὧν συνίσταται
τὰ κατὰ φύσιν συνιστάμενα σώματα, λέγω δ᾽ οἷον
ὀστᾶ καὶ σάρκας, καθάπερ Ἐμπεδοκλῆς φησὶ γίνε-
30 σθαι ἐπὶ τῆς φιλότητος· λέγει γὰρ ὡς

πολλαὶ μὲν κόρσαι ἀναύχενες ἐβλάστησαν.

Τοῖς δ᾽ ἄπειρα ἐν ἀπείρῳ τὰ κινούμενα ποιοῦσιν,
εἰ μὲν ἓν τὸ κινοῦν, ἀνάγκη μίαν φέρεσθαι φοράν,
ὥστ᾽ οὐκ ἀτάκτως κινηθήσεται, εἰ δ᾽ ἄπειρα τὰ
801 a κινοῦντα, καὶ τὰς φορὰς ἀναγκαῖον ἀπείρους εἶναι·
εἰ γὰρ πεπερασμέναι, τάξις τις ἔσται· οὐ γὰρ τῷ
μὴ φέρεσθαι εἰς τὸ αὐτὸ ἡ ἀταξία συμβαίνει· οὐδὲ
γὰρ νῦν εἰς τὸ αὐτὸ φέρεται πάντα, ἀλλὰ τὰ συγ-
5 γενῆ μόνον. ἔτι τὸ ἀτάκτως οὐθέν ἐστιν ἕτερον ἢ
τὸ παρὰ φύσιν· ἡ γὰρ τάξις ἡ οἰκεία τῶν αἰσθητῶν
φύσις ἐστίν. ἀλλὰ μὴν καὶ τοῦτο ἄτοπον καὶ ἀδύνατον, τὸ ἄπειρον ἄτακτον ἔχειν κίνησιν· ἔστι γὰρ
ἡ φύσις ἐκείνη τῶν πραγμάτων οἵαν ἔχει τὰ πλείω
καὶ τὸν πλείω χρόνον· συμβαίνει[1] οὖν αὐτοῖς τοὐ-
10 ναντίον τὴν μὲν ἀταξίαν εἶναι κατὰ φύσιν, τὴν δὲ
τάξιν καὶ τὸν κόσμον παρὰ φύσιν· καίτοι οὐδὲν ὡς
ἔτυχε γίγνεται τῶν κατὰ φύσιν. ἔοικε δὲ τοῦτό γε

[1] συμβαίνει FHMJ, Simpl., Stocks, Allan; συμβαίνειν EL,
Bekker.

[a] Diels, *Vors.* 31 [21], B. 57 = Diels-Kranz⁵ i., p. 333.

things whose motion is without constraint must find rest in their proper places and therefore form the same arrangement as they do now, the heavy travelling to the centre, and the light away from the centre. But that is the disposition of the cosmos.

One might ask the further question, whether or not it is possible that with this disorderly motion some of the elements might have united in those combinations which constitute natural bodies like bones or flesh—the sort of thing which happened when Love was prevailing according to Empedocles, who writes :

Many a head grew up without a neck.[a]

As for those who posit an infinite number of entities moving in infinite space, if the moving cause is one, they must all have the same movement and therefore their movement will not be disorderly, but if there is an infinite number of movers, the movements also must be infinite. For if they are finite, order will be introduced : disorder does not consist simply in motion towards different quarters. Even in our cosmos, all things do not move towards the same place, but only those which are of the same kind. Moreover, " disorderly " is nothing else but " unnatural," for nature is the proper order of sensible things. In any case, the very idea of a disorderly motion continuing infinitely is absurd and impossible. The nature of things means the nature which most of them have for the longest time. It falls to these men therefore to maintain a view which is the contrary of that just stated, namely that disorder is natural and orderly arrangement unnatural. Yet no natural event occurs haphazard.

301 a

αὐτὸ καλῶς Ἀναξαγόρας λαβεῖν· ἐξ ἀκινήτων γὰρ
ἄρχεται κοσμοποιεῖν. πειρῶνται δὲ καὶ οἱ ἄλλοι
συγκρίνοντές πως πάλιν κινεῖν καὶ διακρίνειν. ἐκ
15 διεστώτων δὲ καὶ κινουμένων οὐκ εὔλογον ποιεῖν
τὴν γένεσιν. διὸ καὶ Ἐμπεδοκλῆς παραλείπει τὴν
ἐπὶ τῆς φιλότητος· οὐ γὰρ ἂν ἠδύνατο συστῆσαι
τὸν οὐρανὸν ἐκ κεχωρισμένων μὲν κατασκευάζων,
σύγκρισιν δὲ ποιῶν διὰ τὴν φιλότητα· ἐκ διακεκρι-
μένων γὰρ συνέστηκεν ὁ κόσμος τῶν στοιχείων,
20 ὥστ’ ἀναγκαῖον γίνεσθαι ἐξ ἑνὸς καὶ συγκεκριμένου.

Ὅτι μὲν τοίνυν ἐστὶ φυσική τις κίνησις ἑκάστου
τῶν σωμάτων, ἣν οὐ βίᾳ κινοῦνται οὐδὲ παρὰ
φύσιν, φανερὸν ἐκ τούτων· ὅτι δ’ ἔνια ἔχειν ἀναγκαῖον ῥοπὴν βάρους καὶ κουφότητος, ἐκ τῶνδε
δῆλον. κινεῖσθαι μὲν γάρ φαμεν ἀναγκαῖον εἶναι·
25 εἰ δὲ μὴ ἕξει φύσει ῥοπὴν τὸ κινούμενον, ἀδύνατον
κινεῖσθαι ἢ πρὸς τὸ μέσον ἢ ἀπὸ τοῦ μέσου. ἔστω
γὰρ τὸ μὲν ἐφ’ οὗ Α ἀβαρές, τὸ δ’ ἐφ’ οὗ Β βάρος
ἔχον, ἐνηνέχθω δὲ τὸ ἀβαρὲς τὴν ΓΔ, τὸ δὲ Β ἐν
τῷ ἴσῳ χρόνῳ τὴν ΓΕ. μείζω γὰρ οἰσθήσεται τὸ
βάρος ἔχον. ἐὰν δὴ διαιρεθῇ τὸ σῶμα τὸ ἔχον
30 βάρος ὡς ἡ ΓΕ πρὸς τὴν ΓΔ (δυνατὸν γὰρ οὕτως
ἔχειν πρός τι τῶν ἐν αὐτῷ μορίων), εἰ τὸ ὅλον
φέρεται τὴν ὅλην τὴν ΓΕ, τὸ μόριον ἀνάγκη ἐν τῷ
αὐτῷ χρόνῳ τὴν ΓΔ φέρεσθαι, ὥστε ἴσον οἰσθή-
301 b σεται τὸ ἀβαρὲς καὶ τὸ βάρος ἔχον· ὅπερ ἀδύνατον.

276

It is just this point which Anaxagoras seems to have well taken when he starts his cosmogony from immobility, and other philosophers at least imagine things as collected together, and their subsequent motion as at the same time separation. But to make the world-process start from things in motion and separate is irrational. That is why Empedocles passes over the process of formation in the period when Love is prevailing : he could not have built up his universe by making it out of separate elements and combining them by love. The elements of the cosmos *are* in a state of separation, so that its formation must have proceeded from unity and combination.

The foregoing has proved that every body has a natural motion, performed neither under compulsion nor contrary to nature. That some [a] bodies must owe their impulse to weight or lightness can be shown as follows. (i) We agree that they move of necessity. But if that which moves has no natural impulse, it cannot move either towards or away from the centre. Suppose a body A to be weightless, and another body B to have weight, and let the weightless body move a distance CD and the body B move in an equal time CE. (The heavy body will move farther.) Now if the heavy body be divided in the proportion in which CE stands to CD (and it can quite well bear such a relationship to one of its parts), then if the whole traverses the whole distance CE, the part must traverse CD in an equal time. Thus that which has weight will traverse the same distance as that which has none, and this is impossible. The same

[a] All, of course, in the sublunary world. The only exception is the *aither*.

301 b

ὁ δ' αὐτὸς λόγος καὶ ἐπὶ κουφότητος. ἔτι δ' εἰ
ἔσται τι σῶμα κινούμενον μήτε κουφότητα μήτε
βάρος ἔχον, ἀνάγκη τοῦτο βίᾳ κινεῖσθαι, βίᾳ δὲ
κινούμενον ἄπειρον ποιεῖν τὴν κίνησιν. ἐπεὶ γὰρ
5 δύναμίς τις ἡ κινοῦσα, τὸ δ' ἔλαττον καὶ τὸ κουφότερον ὑπὸ τῆς αὐτῆς δυνάμεως πλεῖον κινηθήσεται,
κεκινήσθω τὸ μὲν ἐφ' ᾧ τὸ Α, τὸ ἀβαρές, τὴν ΓΕ,
τὸ δ' ἐφ' ᾧ τὸ Β, τὸ βάρος ἔχον, ἐν τῷ ἴσῳ χρόνῳ
τὴν ΓΔ.   διαιρεθέντος δὴ τοῦ βάρος ἔχοντος
10 σώματος ὡς ἡ ΓΕ πρὸς τὴν ΓΔ, συμβήσεται τὸ
ἀφαιρούμενον ἀπὸ τοῦ βάρος ἔχοντος σώματος τὴν
ΓΕ φέρεσθαι ἐν τῷ ἴσῳ χρόνῳ, ἐπείπερ τὸ ὅλον
ἐφέρετο τὴν ΓΔ.   τὸ γὰρ τάχος ἕξει τὸ τοῦ ἐλάττονος πρὸς τὸ τοῦ μείζονος ὡς τὸ μεῖζον σῶμα
πρὸς τὸ ἔλαττον. ἴσον ἄρα τὸ ἀβαρὲς οἰσθήσεται
σῶμα καὶ τὸ βάρος ἔχον ἐν τῷ αὐτῷ χρόνῳ.   τοῦτο
15 δ' ἀδύνατον· ὥστ' ἐπεὶ παντὸς τοῦ προτεθέντος[1]
μεῖζον κινήσεται διάστημα τὸ ἀβαρές, ἄπειρον ἂν
φέροιτο.   φανερὸν οὖν ὅτι ἀνάγκη πᾶν σῶμα βάρος
ἔχειν ἢ κουφότητα διωρισμένον.[2]

Ἐπεὶ δὲ φύσις μέν ἐστιν ἡ ἐν αὐτῷ ὑπάρχουσα
κινήσεως ἀρχή, δύναμις δ' ἡ ἐν ἄλλῳ ἢ ᾗ[3] ἄλλο,
20 κίνησις δὲ ἡ μὲν κατὰ φύσιν ἡ δὲ βίαιος πᾶσα, τὴν

---

[1] προτεθέντος Stocks and Allan with all mss. but M; προσ-
τεθέντος M, Bekker.
[2] διωρισμένον L and first hand of E, Simpl. and Alex. τὸ
διωρισμένον FHMJ, second hand of E, Bekker (cf. note
a below).
[3] ἢ ᾗ Stocks, adopted by Allan; ᾗ ἡ L, ᾗ with other mss.
Bekker.

---

[a] Simpl. and Alex. take διωρισμένον as agreeing with σῶμα,

278

argument applies to lightness. (ii) Moreover if there is to be a moving body which is neither light nor heavy, its motion must be enforced, and it must perform this enforced motion to infinity. That which moves it is a force, and the smaller, lighter body will be moved farther by the same force. Now suppose A, the weightless body, is moved the distance CE, and B, the heavy body, the distance CD in an equal time. If the heavy body be divided in the proportion in which CE stands to CD, the part cut off from it will as a result be moved CE in an equal time, since the whole was moved CD. For as the greater body is to the less, so will be the speed of the lesser body to that of the greater. Thus a weightless and a heavy body will be moved an equal distance in the same time, and this is impossible. Seeing, therefore, that the weightless body will be moved a greater distance than any other given body, it must travel to infinity. The necessity for every body to have a definite weight or lightness is now clear.[a]

Nature is a cause of movement in the thing itself, force a cause in something else, or in the thing itself regarded as something else.[b] All movement

---

but their explanations seem inadequate. It must of course be so taken if τό is read before διωρισμένον (see critical note 2), but Simpl. does not seem to have this reading, though he does place διωρισμένον immediately after σῶμα.

[b] Stocks's ἢ ᾗ can hardly be questioned. *Cf. Met.* 1019 a 16, 1046 a 11. Simpl. illustrates by the example of the doctor healing himself (*Phys.* ii. 192 b 23, also mentioned at *Met.* 1019 a 16). (If a doctor heals himself, it is only accidental (κατὰ συμβεβηκός) that the force and that which it acts upon are united in the same concrete object. What heals is the physician's art in his mind : what is healed is his body.)

μὲν κατὰ φύσιν, οἷον τῷ λίθῳ τὴν κάτω, θάττω[1]
ποιήσει τὸ κατὰ δύναμιν, τὴν δὲ παρὰ φύσιν ὅλως
αὐτή. πρὸς ἀμφότερα δὲ ὥσπερ ὀργάνῳ χρῆται
τῷ ἀέρι· πέφυκε γὰρ οὗτος καὶ κοῦφος εἶναι καὶ
βαρύς. τὴν μὲν οὖν ἄνω ποιήσει φορὰν ᾗ κοῦφος,
25 ὅταν ὠσθῇ καὶ λάβῃ τὴν ἀρχὴν ἀπὸ τῆς δυνάμεως,
τὴν δὲ κάτω πάλιν ᾗ βαρύς· ὥσπερ γὰρ ἐναφάψασα
παραδίδωσιν ἑκατέρῳ. διὸ καὶ οὐ παρακολου-
θοῦντος τοῦ κινήσαντος φέρεται τὸ βίᾳ κινηθέν. εἰ
γὰρ μὴ τοιοῦτόν τι[2] σῶμα ὑπῆρχεν, οὐκ ἂν ἦν ἡ
βίᾳ κίνησις. καὶ τὴν κατὰ φύσιν δ' ἑκάστου κίνη-
30 σιν συνεπουρίζει τὸν αὐτὸν τρόπον.

Ὅτι μὲν οὖν ἅπαν ἢ κοῦφον ἢ βαρύ, καὶ πῶς αἱ
παρὰ φύσιν ἔχουσι κινήσεις, ἐκ τούτων φανερόν.
ὅτι δ' οὔτε πάντων ἐστὶ γένεσις οὔθ' ἁπλῶς οὐ-
θενός, δῆλον ἐκ τῶν προειρημένων. ἀδύνατον γὰρ
302 a παντὸς σώματος εἶναι γένεσιν, εἰ μὴ καὶ κενὸν
εἶναί τι δυνατὸν κεχωρισμένον· ἐν ᾧ γὰρ ἔσται
τόπῳ τὸ γινόμενον ὅτε ἐγένετο,[3] ἐν τούτῳ πρότερον τὸ κενὸν ἀναγκαῖον εἶναι σώματος μηθενὸς
ὄντος. ἄλλο μὲν γὰρ ἐξ ἄλλου σῶμα γίγνεσθαι
5 δυνατόν, οἷον ἐξ ἀέρος πῦρ, ὅλως δ' ἐκ μηδενὸς
ἄλλου προϋπάρχοντος μεγέθους ἀδύνατον. μάλιστα
μὲν γὰρ ἐκ δυνάμει τινὸς ὄντος σώματος ἐνεργείᾳ
γένοιτ' ἂν σῶμα· ἀλλ' εἰ τὸ δυνάμει ὂν σῶμα

---

[1] θάττω. θᾶττον F, Bekker.
[2] τι. τι τὸ HM, Bekker.
[3] ὅτε ἐγένετο JH and later hand of E, Allan ; εἰ ἐγίγνετο L;

is either natural or enforced, and force accelerates natural motion (*e.g.* that of a stone downwards), and is the sole cause of unnatural. In either case the air is employed as a kind of instrument of the action, since it is the nature of this element to be both light and heavy. In so far as it is light, it produces the upward movement, as the result of being pushed and receiving the impulse from the original force, and in so far as it is heavy the downward. In either case the original force transmits the motion by, so to speak, impressing it on the air. That is the reason why an object set in motion by compulsion continues in motion though the mover does not follow it up. Were it not for a body of the nature of air, there could be no such thing as enforced motion. By the same action it assists the motion of anything moving naturally.

Our discussion has made it clear that everything is either light or heavy, and has explained how unnatural movements take place. That all things are not subject to generation, and that nothing is generated in an absolute sense, follows clearly from previous arguments. Generation of any body is impossible unless we can posit a void free of body ; for the place which has held, since its inception, the thing now in course of generation, must previously have contained only emptiness without any body at all. One body can be generated from another, *e.g.* fire from air, but from no pre-existing magnitude nothing can be generated. The most we can say is that an actual body can be generated from a potential ; but if the body in its potential state is

---

εἰ ἐγίγνετο ὅτε ἐγένετο M, first hand of F ; εἰ ἐγένετο Bekker. Thus Bekker's reading has no MS. authority.

302 a

μηθέν ἐστιν ἄλλο σῶμα ἐνεργείᾳ πρότερον, κενὸν
ἔσται κεχωρισμένον.

CHAPTER III

ARGUMENT

What is meant by an element, and why there must be
elements. *An element is that into which other bodies are
analysed, but which cannot itself be analysed further. The
compounds contain it, it does not contain them—even*

10 Λοιπὸν δ' εἰπεῖν τίνων τέ ἐστι γένεσις σωμάτων,
καὶ διὰ τί ἐστιν. ἐπεὶ οὖν ἐν ἅπασιν ἡ γνῶσις διὰ
τῶν πρώτων, πρῶτα δὲ τῶν ἐνυπαρχόντων τὰ στοιχεῖα, σκεπτέον ποῖα τῶν τοιούτων σωμάτων ἐστὶ
στοιχεῖα, καὶ διὰ τί ἐστιν, ἔπειτα μετὰ ταῦτα πόσα
15 τε καὶ ποῖ' ἄττα. τοῦτο δ' ἔσται φανερὸν ὑποθεμέ-
νοις τίς ἐστιν ἡ τοῦ στοιχείου φύσις. ἔστω δὴ στοιχεῖον τῶν σωμάτων, εἰς ὃ τἆλλα σώματα διαιρεῖται,
ἐνυπάρχον δυνάμει ἢ ἐνεργείᾳ (τοῦτο γὰρ ποτέρως,
ἔτι ἀμφισβητήσιμον), αὐτὸ δ' ἐστὶν ἀδιαίρετον εἰς
ἕτερα τῷ εἴδει· τοιοῦτον γάρ τι τὸ στοιχεῖον
ἅπαντες καὶ ἐν ἅπασι βούλονται λέγειν.

20 Εἰ δὴ τὸ εἰρημένον ἐστὶ στοιχεῖον, ἀνάγκη εἶναι

---

^a The present section proves that generation *ex nihilo*
demands the existence of a " separate " void. In conjunction with " previous arguments," this is sufficient to prove
the impossibility of such generation. The arguments
referred to are those of *Phys.* iv. 6-9, especially ch. viii., where
the possibility of κενὸν κεχωρισμένον is denied. " Separate "
or " bodiless " void means empty space *between* bodies, a
framework in which bodies can move, as opposed to inter-

not already some other body in actuality, there must be a bodiless void.[a]

CHAPTER III

ARGUMENT (continued)

potentially. This would hold good even on a monistic view. It is all a matter of how one regards the process of generation. Views of Anaxagoras and Empedocles contrasted. The existence of simple bodies is argued from the existence of simple motions.

IT remains to decide what bodies are subject to generation, and why. Since, then, knowledge is always to be sought through what is primary, and the primary constituents of bodies are their elements, we must consider which of such bodies are elements, and why, and afterwards how many of them there are and what is their character. The answer will be plain once we have laid down what is the nature of an element. Let us then define the element in bodies as that into which other bodies may be analysed, which is present in them either potentially or actually (which of the two, is a matter for future debate), and which cannot itself be analysed into constituents differing in kind. Some such definition of an element is what all thinkers are aiming at throughout.

Now if this definition is correct, elemental bodies

stitial void, or void existing *within* bodies, and according to some theories a necessary postulate to explain condensation and rarefaction. *Cf. Phys.* iv. again, especially ch. viii. *init.* and ch. ix., 216 b 31 ff.

ἄττα τοιαῦτα τῶν σωμάτων. ἐν μὲν γὰρ σαρκὶ
καὶ ξύλῳ καὶ ἑκάστῳ τῶν τοιούτων ἔνεστι δυνάμει
πῦρ καὶ γῆ· φανερὰ γὰρ ταῦτα ἐξ ἐκείνων ἐκκρινόμενα. ἐν δὲ πυρὶ σὰρξ ἢ ξύλον οὐκ ἐνυπάρχουσιν, οὔτε κατὰ δύναμιν οὔτε κατ' ἐνέργειαν·
25 ἐξεκρίνετο γὰρ ἄν. ὁμοίως δ' οὐδ' εἰ ἕν τι μόνον
εἴη τοιοῦτον, οὐδ' ἐν ἐκείνῳ· οὐ γὰρ εἰ ἔσται
σὰρξ ἢ ὀστοῦν ἢ τῶν ἄλλων ὁτιοῦν, οὔπω φατέον
ἐνυπάρχειν δυνάμει, ἀλλὰ προσθεωρητέον τίς ὁ
τρόπος τῆς γενέσεως.

Ἀναξαγόρας δ' Ἐμπεδοκλεῖ ἐναντίως λέγει περὶ
τῶν στοιχείων. ὁ μὲν γὰρ πῦρ καὶ γῆν καὶ τὰ
30 σύστοιχα τούτοις στοιχεῖά φησιν εἶναι τῶν σωμάτων καὶ συγκεῖσθαι πάντ' ἐκ τούτων, Ἀναξαγόρας δὲ τοὐναντίον· τὰ γὰρ ὁμοιομερῆ στοιχεῖα
(λέγω δ' οἷον σάρκα καὶ ὀστοῦν καὶ τῶν τοιούτων
302 b ἕκαστον), ἀέρα δὲ καὶ πῦρ μῖγμα τούτων καὶ τῶν
ἄλλων σπερμάτων πάντων· εἶναι γὰρ ἑκάτερον αὐτῶν ἐξ ἀοράτων ὁμοιομερῶν πάντων ἠθροισμένων.
διὸ καὶ γίγνεσθαι πάντ' ἐκ τούτων· τὸ γὰρ πῦρ καὶ
5 τὸν αἰθέρα προσαγορεύει ταὐτό. ἐπεὶ δ' ἐστὶ παντὸς φυσικοῦ σώματος κίνησις οἰκεία, τῶν δὲ κινήσεων αἱ μὲν ἁπλαῖ αἱ δὲ μικταί, καὶ αἱ μὲν μικταὶ
τῶν μικτῶν αἱ δὲ ἁπλαῖ τῶν ἁπλῶν εἰσί, φανερὸν

---

[a] If, as the early monistic scientists affirmed, everything
were generated from a single underlying substance, it might
be supposed that the element must have contained the
products no less than the products now contain the element.
But this is only true if we accept the further view of some of
them that the process of generation is nothing more than a
" separating out " (ἔκκρισις). If (with A.) it is assumed to

must exist. In flesh and wood, for instance, and all such substances, fire and earth are potentially present, for they may be separated out and become apparent. But flesh or wood are not present in fire, either potentially or actually ; otherwise they could be separated out. Even if there only existed one single element, they would not be present in it. It may be flesh, bone etc. are to be produced from it, but that does not immediately involve saying that they are potentially present in it. One must also take into consideration the manner of their generation.[a]

Anaxagoras is opposed to Empedocles on the subject of the elements. Empedocles' view is that fire and earth and the other substances of the same order are the elements of bodies, and everything is composed of them. According to Anaxagoras, on the other hand, the homoeomeries are elements (flesh, bone and other substances of that order), whereas air and fire are a mixture of these and all the other seeds, for each consists of an agglomeration of all the homoeomeries in invisible quantities. That is why everything is generated from these two.[b] (He makes no distinction between fire and aither.) But since (i) every natural body has its proper motion, (ii) some motions are simple and others composite, and (iii) simple motions are of simple bodies, composite of composite, it clearly

---

involve actual qualitative change (ἀλλοίωσις), the supposition is untrue.

[b] For the theory of the elements in Anaxagoras see especially F. M. Cornford in *Class. Quart.* xxiv. (1930), pp. 14 ff. and 83 ff., C. Bailey, *The Greek Atomists and Epicurus* (Oxford, 1928) App. i., A. L. Peck in *Class. Quart.* xxv. (1931), pp. 27 ff. and 112 ff.

302 b

ὅτι ἔσται ἄττα σώματα ἁπλᾶ. εἰσὶ γὰρ καὶ κινήσεις ἁπλαῖ. ὥστε δῆλον καὶ ὅτι ἔστι στοιχεῖα καὶ
διὰ τί ἐστιν.

CHAPTER IV

ARGUMENT

There cannot be an infinite number of elements. *Criticism of two theories which posit an infinite number.*

(i) *The theory of Anaxagoras that all homoeomerous
substances are elements (302 b 10—303 a 3).*

(a) *Some homoeomerous substances can be proved to be
composite.*

(b) *His own cosmogony would be possible without the postulate of an infinite number of elements. It is not as if his
postulate enabled him to construct everything out of homogeneous parts : he cannot say that a face is composed of
parts similar to itself.*

(c) *Mathematics teaches the need for economy in first
principles : never an infinite number and always as few as
possible.*

(d) *The specific differentiae of bodies are finite, and this
points to a finite number of elements.*

(ii) *The atomic theory of Leucippus and Democritus
(303 a 3–b 3).*

(a) *This theory is practically the same as the number-
cosmogony of the Pythagoreans (criticized above, 300 a 14).*

10   Πότερον δὲ πεπερασμένα ἢ ἄπειρα, καὶ εἰ πεπερασμένα, πόσα τὸν ἀριθμόν, ἑπόμενον ἂν εἴη
σκοπεῖν. πρῶτον μὲν οὖν ὅτι οὐκ ἔστιν ἄπειρα,
καθάπερ οἴονταί τινες, θεωρητέον, καὶ πρῶτον τοὺς
πάντα τὰ ὁμοιομερῆ στοιχεῖα ποιοῦντας, καθάπερ
Ἀναξαγόρας. οὐθεὶς γὰρ τῶν οὕτως ἀξιούντων

286

follows that certain simple bodies must exist. For
there are simple motions. Thus we see both that
there are elements and why.

CHAPTER IV

ARGUMENT (continued)

(b) *They are vague about the shape of the atoms forming
different bodies, although this is an essential part of their
theory.*

(c) *Criticisms* (b) *and* (d) *of Anaxagoras apply with equal
force to the atomists.*

(d) *Their views conflict with the findings of mathematicians
and other scientists. This has been discussed elsewhere.*

(e) *On their own showing, that the popular elements are
composed of indivisible particles differing in size, their theory
of the generation of these elements into and out of one another
is impossible.*

(f) *The specific differentiae of bodies are reduced by them
to differences of shape. This makes an infinite number of
elements still more obviously superfluous, since all solids can
be analysed into pyramids as their sole element or principle.*

*As a final general argument against an infinite number of
elements, we note that every simple body has a simple motion
of its own, and the number of simple motions is finite* (303 b
4-8)

THE next question that arises is whether they are
finite or infinite in number, and if finite, how many.
First then we must observe that they are not infinite, as some think, and we may begin with those [a]
who, like Anaxagoras, regard all homoeomerous
substances as elements. None of those who hold

---

[a] Anax. was not without his followers. Simpl. mentions
Archelaus.

802 b

15 ὀρθῶς λαμβάνει τὸ στοιχεῖον· ὁρῶμεν γὰρ πολλὰ
καὶ τῶν μικτῶν σωμάτων εἰς ὁμοιομερῆ διαιρού-
μενα, λέγω δ' οἷον σάρκα καὶ ὀστοῦν καὶ ξύλον καὶ
λίθον. ὥστ' εἴπερ τὸ σύνθετον οὐκ ἔστι στοιχεῖον,
οὐχ ἅπαν ἔσται τὸ ὁμοιομερὲς στοιχεῖον, ἀλλὰ τὸ
ἀδιαίρετον εἰς ἕτερα τῷ εἴδει, καθάπερ εἴρηται
20 πρότερον.

Ἔτι δ' οὐδ' οὕτως λαμβάνοντας τὸ στοιχεῖον
ἀνάγκη ποιεῖν ἄπειρα· πάντα γὰρ ταὐτὰ ἀποδοθή-
σεται καὶ πεπερασμένων ὄντων, ἐάν τις λάβῃ· τὸ
αὐτὸ γὰρ ποιήσει, κἂν δύο ἢ τρία μόνον ᾖ τοιαῦτα,
καθάπερ ἐπιχειρεῖ καὶ Ἐμπεδοκλῆς. ἐπεὶ γὰρ καὶ
25 ὡς αὐτοῖς συμβαίνει μὴ πάντα ποιεῖν ἐξ ὁμοιομερῶν (πρόσωπον γὰρ οὐκ ἐκ προσώπων ποιοῦσιν,
οὐδ' ἄλλο τῶν κατὰ φύσιν ἐσχηματισμένων οὐθέν),
φανερὸν ὅτι πολλῷ βέλτιον πεπερασμένας ποιεῖν
τὰς ἀρχάς, καὶ ταύτας ὡς ἐλαχίστας πάντων γε
τῶν αὐτῶν μελλόντων δείκνυσθαι, καθάπερ ἀξιοῦσι
30 καὶ οἱ ἐν τοῖς μαθήμασιν· ἀεὶ γὰρ τὰ πεπερασμένα[1]
λαμβάνουσιν ἀρχὰς ἢ τῷ εἴδει ἢ τῷ ποσῷ.

Ἔτι εἰ σῶμα σώματος ἕτερον λέγεται κατὰ τὰς
οἰκείας διαφοράς, αἱ δὲ τῶν σωμάτων διαφοραὶ
πεπερασμέναι (διαφέρουσι γὰρ τοῖς αἰσθητοῖς,

---

[1] τὰς πεπερασμένας F, Bekker.

---

[a] The distinction between homoeomerous and simple is
this. A homoeomerous body is one which, however far it
is divided by a cutting or breaking process, will reveal only
parts which are similar to themselves and to the whole.
Example : " a piece of wood " (as opposed to " a face ").
A simple body or element is one which, *whatever* process it

288

this opinion have a proper conception of an element, for many composite bodies also can be seen to be divisible into homogeneous parts, *e.g.* flesh, bone, wood, stone. If, then, what is composite is not an element, an element is not any homoeomerous body, but only, as we said before, one which cannot be analysed into constituents differing in kind.[a]

Moreover, even with their conception of an element, it was unnecessary to make them infinite in number, for should a finite number be assumed, it will give all the same results. The same result will be obtained if there are only two or three such bodies, as Empedocles tries to show. Even with an infinite number, they do not succeed in forming everything out of homogeneous parts—they do not construct a face out of faces, nor any other finished products of nature similarly—so that it would clearly be much better to make the principles finite, and indeed as few as possible provided that all the same effects can be demonstrated. Mathematicians are certainly of this opinion : they always take, as principles, data which are limited either in kind or in quantity.

Finally, if bodies are distinguished from one another by their proper differentiae, and bodily differentiae are finite in number (it is in their sensible qualities that they differ, and these are finite,

is subjected to, will not reveal a composite nature. Thus wood, though homoeomerous, is not simple, because, for instance, if two pieces of wood are rubbed together they prove to contain fire in a potential state.

A. has a right to call Anaxagoras mistaken, since he believed to be composite what Anax. thought simple (flesh, wood etc.) and simple what Anax. thought composite (earth, fire). But since in fact Anax. did believe flesh, wood etc. to be simple in the proper sense, the charge of misunderstanding the nature of an element is unjust.

ARISTOTLE

803 a ταῦτα δὲ πεπέρανται· δεῖ δὲ τοῦτο δειχθῆναι),
φανερὸν ὅτι καὶ τὰ στοιχεῖα ἀνάγκη πεπερασμένα
εἶναι.

Ἀλλὰ μὴν οὐδ' ὡς ἕτεροί τινες λέγουσιν, οἷον
Λεύκιππός τε καὶ Δημόκριτος ὁ Ἀβδηρίτης, εὔ-
5 λογα τὰ συμβαίνοντα· φασὶ γὰρ εἶναι τὰ πρῶτα
μεγέθη πλήθει μὲν ἄπειρα μεγέθει δὲ ἀδιαίρετα,
καὶ οὔτ' ἐξ ἑνὸς πολλὰ γίγνεσθαι οὔτε ἐκ πολλῶν
ἕν, ἀλλὰ τῇ τούτων συμπλοκῇ καὶ περιπαλάξει[1]
πάντα γεννᾶσθαι. τρόπον γάρ τινα καὶ οὗτοι πάντα
τὰ ὄντα ποιοῦσιν ἀριθμοὺς καὶ ἐξ ἀριθμῶν· καὶ γὰρ
10 εἰ μὴ σαφῶς δηλοῦσιν, ὅμως τοῦτο βούλονται
λέγειν. καὶ πρὸς τούτοις, ἐπεὶ διαφέρει τὰ σώματα
σχήμασιν, ἄπειρα δὲ τὰ σχήματα, ἄπειρα καὶ τὰ
ἁπλᾶ σώματά φασιν εἶναι. ποῖον δὲ καὶ τί ἑκάστου
τὸ σχῆμα τῶν στοιχείων, οὐθὲν ἐπιδιώρισαν, ἀλλὰ
μόνον τῷ πυρὶ τὴν σφαῖραν ἀπέδωκαν· ἀέρα δὲ καὶ
15 ὕδωρ καὶ τἆλλα μεγέθει καὶ μικρότητι διεῖλον, ὡς
οὖσαν αὐτῶν τὴν φύσιν οἷον πανσπερμίαν πάντων
τῶν στοιχείων.

Πρῶτον μὲν οὖν καὶ τούτοις ταὐτὸν ἁμάρτημα
τὸ μὴ πεπερασμένας λαβεῖν τὰς ἀρχάς, ἐξὸν ἅπαντα

---

[1] περιπλέξει EL, Bekker; ἐπαλλάξει FHMJ. The word
περιπαλάξει was restored by Diels from the evidence of Simpl.,
who (according at least to two mss. of his commentary) read
it here, and who explains it as an Abderite (i.e. Ionian) word
for συμπλοκή. See Diels's arguments in Hermes, 40, p. 306,
and cf. Simpl. In phys. 1318. 33 (Diels, Vors. 68 [55]. A. 58 =
Diels-Kranz[5] ii. 99).

[a] Stocks refers to De sensu 6. 445 b 20 ff. for the proof.
[b] It is a little surprising to find A. ranking Leucippus and

though this is something which awaits demonstration),[a] it is clear that the elements themselves must be finite.

There is another view, championed by Leucippus and Democritus of Abdera, whose conclusions are no more acceptable to reason. According to this view the primary magnitudes are infinite in number and not divisible in magnitude. Generation is neither of many out of one, nor of one out of many, but consists entirely in the combination and entanglement of these bodies. In a way these thinkers too are saying that everything that exists is numbers, or evolved from numbers; they may not show it clearly, but nevertheless that is what they mean.[b] Besides, if shape is the distinguishing feature of bodies, and there is an infinite number of shapes, they are asserting an infinite number of simple bodies. Yet they never went so far as to define or characterize the shape of each element, except to assign the sphere to fire. Air and water and the rest they distinguished by greatness and smallness, as if it were their nature to be a sort of " seed-mixture " of all the elements.

First of all, then, this school makes the same mistake of failing to grasp that the elements are finite in number, though they could have drawn all

Democritus with the Pythagorean number-atomists, since he has just formulated so clearly the natural objection to the latter, namely that they made an unwarrantable transition from weightless, non-physical entities to physical bodies (300 a 16-19). He would not deny that the atoms of L. and D. were bodies. Stocks says " the atom is practically a mathematical unit, out of which bodies are formed by simple addition," and it is true that A. draws an analogy between the two types of atomism in the *Metaphysics* (2. 13. 1039 a 3 ff.).

303 a

ταὐτὰ λέγειν. ἔτι δ' εἰ μὴ ἄπειροι τῶν σωμάτων
αἱ διαφοραί, δῆλον ὅτι οὐκ ἔσται τὰ στοιχεῖα
20 ἄπειρα. πρὸς δὲ τούτοις ἀνάγκη μάχεσθαι ταῖς
μαθηματικαῖς ἐπιστήμαις ἄτομα σώματα λέγοντας,
καὶ πολλὰ τῶν ἐνδόξων καὶ τῶν φαινομένων κατὰ
τὴν αἴσθησιν ἀναιρεῖν, περὶ ὧν εἴρηται πρότερον ἐν
τοῖς περὶ χρόνου καὶ κινήσεως. ἅμα δὲ καὶ ἐναντία
25 λέγειν αὐτοὺς αὑτοῖς ἀνάγκη· ἀδύνατον γὰρ ἀτόμων
ὄντων τῶν στοιχείων μεγέθει καὶ μικρότητι διαφέρειν ἀέρα καὶ γῆν καὶ ὕδωρ· οὐ γὰρ οἷόν τ' ἐξ
ἀλλήλων γίγνεσθαι· ὑπολείψει γὰρ ἀεὶ τὰ μέγιστα
σώματα ἐκκρινόμενα, φασὶ δ' οὕτω γίγνεσθαι ὕδωρ
καὶ ἀέρα καὶ γῆν ἐξ ἀλλήλων. ἔτι οὐδὲ κατὰ τὴν
30 τούτων ὑπόληψιν δόξειεν ἂν ἄπειρα γίγνεσθαι τὰ
στοιχεῖα, εἴπερ τὰ μὲν σώματα διαφέρει σχήμασι,
τὰ δὲ σχήματα πάντα σύγκειται ἐκ πυραμίδων, τὰ
303 b μὲν εὐθύγραμμα ἐξ εὐθυγράμμων, ἡ δὲ σφαῖρα ἐξ
ὀκτὼ μορίων. ἀνάγκη γὰρ εἶναί τινας ἀρχὰς τῶν
σχημάτων. ὥστε εἴτε μία εἴτε δύο εἴτε πλείους,
καὶ τὰ ἁπλᾶ σώματα τοσαῦτα ἔσται τὸ πλῆθος.
5 ἔτι δ' εἰ ἑκάστῳ μὲν τῶν στοιχείων ἐστί τις οἰκεία
κίνησις, καὶ ἡ τοῦ ἁπλοῦ σώματος ἁπλῆ, μή εἰσι
δ' αἱ ἁπλαῖ κινήσεις ἄπειροι διὰ τὸ μήτε τὰς ἁπλᾶς

---

[a] Stocks refers especially to *Phys.* vi. 1-2 (231 a 18 ff.).

[b] If the difference lies in the size of the atoms, and the generation of, say, air from water consists in the separating-out of particles of air-size which the water contained, we shall

the same conclusions. Also, the limitation of bodily differentiae proves that the number of elements must be limited. Moreover by positing indivisible bodies they cannot help coming into conflict with mathematics, and undermining many accepted beliefs and facts of observation. These we have discussed already in the works on time and motion.[a] At the same time they are even forced to contradict themselves, for if the elements are indivisible it is impossible for air and earth and water to be differentiated by greatness and smallness. If they are, they cannot be generated from one another, for the supply of large atoms will fail in the continual separating process by which, according to them, this mutual generation between water and air and earth takes place.[b] Again, even their theory does not seem to demand an infinite number of elements. Bodies, they say, differ on account of differing shapes, but all shapes are constructed out of pyramids, rectilinear from rectilinear and the sphere from its eight parts.[c] Shapes must have certain principles, and whether these are one or two or more, the simple bodies will be of the same number. Finally, every element has its proper motion, and the motion of a simple body is simple. But there is not an infinite number of simple motions, because the directions of

in the end be left with a residue of each element which cannot generate another from itself.

[c] As the triangle is the elementary plane figure (or " principle ") to which all plane figures can be reduced, so the pyramid is the elementary solid. The parts obtained by symmetrical division of a sphere into eight will be pyramids with spherical bases. Since these are not quite properly (κυρίως) pyramids, says Simpl., A. chooses the vague word " parts."

303 b

φορὰς πλείους εἶναι δυοῖν μήτε τοὺς τόπους ἀπείρους, οὐκ ἂν εἴη οὐδ' οὕτως ἄπειρα τὰ στοιχεῖα.

CHAPTER V

ARGUMENT

But there must be more than one.
Criticism of monistic theories.
(a) *Those who choose one of the four " elements " other
than fire as their primary body (303 b 13—304 a 7).*
(i) *Their theory of generation by condensation and rarefaction demands that the finest body be primary. Yet they
usually agree that fire is the finest body.* (ii) *This same
theory of generation in the last resort means assigning
priority to bodies according to the greatness or smallness of
their particles. But greatness and smallness are relative
terms. The same pattern may be repeated on a different
scale, and what is fire relatively to* x *will be air relatively to*
y. *This applies to pluralist theories too, if they make size
the differentiating factor.*
(b) *Those who choose fire as their primary body (304 a 7–
b 22).*
These may be divided into (i) *those who assign a definite
shape (the pyramid) to fire-particles, either because the
pyramid is sharp and piercing or because it is the smallest
solid, and* (ii) *those who simply speak of it as the body composed of the smallest and finest particles. We may consider
them together. They must suppose their primary body to be
either* (α) *atomic or* (β) *divisible.*

9 Ἐπεὶ δ' ἀνάγκη πεπεράνθαι τὰ στοιχεῖα, λοιπὸν
10 σκέψασθαι πότερον πλείω ἔσται ἢ ἕν. ἔνιοι γὰρ
ἓν μόνον ὑποτίθενται, καὶ τοῦτο οἱ μὲν ὕδωρ, οἱ δ'

---

a *i.e.* up and down, because (as Stocks points out) there is
no circular movement below the moon.

movement are limited to two [a] and the places also are limited. On this argument also there cannot be an infinite number of elements.

CHAPTER V

ARGUMENT (*continued*)

(*a*) *Assuming that the ratio of size between homoeomerous substances in the mass is the same as that between their single particles, and finer bodies take up more room than coarse, the atoms of the finest body must be larger than those of the others and divisible.*

(*β*) (i) *Those who speak of fire-particles as pyramidal have no room in their system for parts of pyramids.* (ii) *Those who speak of their size only are faced with an infinity of bodies each prior to the last, if every body is divisible.*

In general, a monistic theory allows of only one natural motion, and in fact there are several.

Note.—*It is difficult to see to whom the theory* (b) (i) *is to be assigned. Not Plato, for although he constructs fire out of pyramids, and apparently for both the reasons given* (Tim. 56 A τὸ μὲν ἔχον ὀλιγίστας βάσεις εὐκινητότατον ἀνάγκη πεφυκέναι, τμητικώτατόν τε καὶ ὀξύτατον ὂν πάντῃ πάντων, ἔτι δὲ ἐλαφρότατον, ἐξ ὀλιγίστων συνεστὸς τῶν αὐτῶν μερῶν), *he regards none of the four popular elements as primary.* (Ib. 48 B λέγομεν ἀρχὰς αὐτὰ (sc. πῦρ καὶ ὕδωρ καὶ ἀὴρ καὶ γῆ) τιθέμενοι στοιχεῖα τοῦ παντός, προσῆκον αὐτοῖς οὐδ᾽ ὡς ἐν συλλαβῆς εἴδεσιν . . . ἀπεικασθῆναι.)

HAVING established that the number of the elements must be limited, it remains for us to consider whether there are more than one. Some philosophers posit one alone, either water [b] or air [c] or

---

[b] Primarily Thales.
[a] Anaximenes and Diogenes of Apollonia.

ARISTOTLE

ἀέρα, οἱ δὲ πῦρ, οἱ δ' ὕδατος μὲν λεπτότερον ἀέρος
δὲ πυκνότερον, ὃ περιέχειν φασὶ πάντας τοὺς
οὐρανοὺς ἄπειρον ὄν.

Ὅσοι μὲν οὖν τὸ ἕν τοῦτο ποιοῦσιν ὕδωρ ἢ ἀέρα
15 ἢ ὕδατος μὲν λεπτότερον ἀέρος δὲ πυκνότερον, εἶτ'
ἐκ τούτου πυκνότητι καὶ μανότητι τἆλλα γεννῶσιν,
οὗτοι λανθάνουσιν αὐτοὶ αὑτοὺς ἄλλο τι πρότερον
τοῦ στοιχείου ποιοῦντες· ἔστι γὰρ ἡ μὲν ἐκ τῶν
στοιχείων γένεσις σύνθεσις, ὥς φασιν, ἡ δ' εἰς τὰ
στοιχεῖα διάλυσις, ὥστ' ἀνάγκη πρότερον εἶναι τῇ
20 φύσει τὸ λεπτομερέστερον. ἐπεὶ οὖν φασι πάντων
τῶν σωμάτων τὸ πῦρ λεπτότατον εἶναι, πρῶτον ἂν
εἴη τῇ φύσει τὸ πῦρ· διαφέρει δ' οὐθέν, ἀνάγκη γὰρ
ἔν τι τῶν ἄλλων εἶναι πρῶτον καὶ μὴ τὸ μέσον.

Ἔτι δὲ τὸ μὲν πυκνότητι καὶ μανότητι τἆλλα
γεννᾶν οὐθὲν διαφέρει ἢ λεπτότητι καὶ παχύτητι· τὸ
25 μὲν γὰρ λεπτὸν μανόν, τὸ δὲ παχὺ βούλονται εἶναι
πυκνόν. πάλιν δὲ τὸ λεπτότητι καὶ παχύτητι ταὐτὸν καὶ τὸ μεγέθει καὶ μικρότητι· λεπτὸν μὲν γὰρ
τὸ μικρομερές, παχὺ δὲ τὸ μεγαλομερές· τὸ γὰρ
ἐπεκτεινόμενον ἐπὶ πολὺ λεπτόν, τοιοῦτον δὲ τὸ
ἐκ μικρῶν μερῶν συνεστός· ὥστ' αὐτοῖς συμβαίνει
30 μεγέθει καὶ μικρότητι διαιρεῖν τὴν τῶν ἄλλων
οὐσίαν. οὕτω δὲ διοριζομένοις ἅπαντα συμβήσεται

ᵃ Primarily Heracleitus.
ᵇ For this substance cf. *Phys.* 203 a 18, 205 a 27, *De gen.
et corr.* 332 a 21, *Met.* 989 a 14. A substance intermediate
between air and *fire* is mentioned at *Phys.* 187 a 14, *De gen.
et corr.* 328 b 35, 332 a 21, *Met.* 988 a 30.   The authorship
of this theory has been much disputed, and the case against

296

fire [a] or a substance rarer than water but denser
than air,[b] and this they say is infinite in extent and
embraces all the worlds.

Now all those who posit as the single element
water or air or the substance intermediate in density
between the two, and generate everything else
from this by a process of condensation and rarefaction, are unwittingly assuming the existence of
a substance more fundamental than their element.
Generation from the elements, they say, is a
synthesis, and back into the elements an analysis.
If so, then the substance with finer particles must
be prior in nature. Since therefore they agree that
fire is the finest of all bodies, fire must be primary
in the order of nature. Whether it is fire or not
does not matter; in any case it must be one of the
others that is primary and not the intermediate.[c]

Secondly, to attribute generation to density or
rarity is the same as attributing it to coarseness
and fineness, for fine is what they mean by rare, and
coarse by dense. To attribute it to coarseness
and fineness is, in its turn, to attribute it to greatness and smallness, for fine = composed of small
parts, coarse = composed of large parts, seeing that
fine means extended over a wide area, and that is
the condition of a body composed of small parts.
In fact, therefore, they are making greatness and
smallness the distinguishing mark of bodies other
than the primary. But on this criterion all the
names which they give must be relative : it cannot

referring it (with most ancient commentators) to Anaximander is very strong. See Ross's discussion in his ed. of
the *Physics*, p. 482.

[c] *i.e.* intermediate in density. Whichever body is finest
or rarest in texture must be primary.

303 b

λέγειν πρός τι, καὶ οὐκ ἔσται ἁπλῶς τὸ μὲν πῦρ τὸ
δ' ὕδωρ τὸ δ' ἀήρ, ἀλλὰ τὸ αὐτὸ πρὸς μὲν τόδε
304 a πῦρ, πρὸς δέ τι ἄλλο ἀήρ, ὅπερ συμβαίνει καὶ τοῖς
πλείω μὲν τὰ στοιχεῖα λέγουσι, μεγέθει δὲ καὶ
μικρότητι διαφέρειν φάσκουσιν· ἐπεὶ γὰρ τῷ ποσῷ
διώρισται ἕκαστον, ἔσται τις λόγος πρὸς ἄλληλα
5 τῶν μεγεθῶν, ὥστε τὰ τοῦτον ἔχοντα τὸν λόγον
πρὸς ἄλληλα ἀνάγκη τὸ μὲν ἀέρα εἶναι τὸ δὲ πῦρ
τὸ δὲ γῆν τὸ δ' ὕδωρ, διὰ τὸ ἐνυπάρχειν ἐν τοῖς
μείζοσι τοὺς τῶν ἐλαττόνων λόγους.

Ὅσοι δὲ πῦρ ὑποτίθενται τὸ στοιχεῖον, τοῦτο μὲν
διαφεύγουσιν, ἄλλα δ' αὐτοῖς ἀναγκαῖον ἄλογα
10 συμβαίνειν. οἱ μὲν γὰρ αὐτῶν σχῆμα περιάπτουσι
τῷ πυρί, καθάπερ οἱ τὴν πυραμίδα ποιοῦντες, καὶ
τούτων οἱ μὲν ἁπλουστέρως λέγοντες ὅτι τῶν μὲν
σχημάτων τμητικώτατον ἡ πυραμίς, τῶν δὲ σωμάτων τὸ πῦρ, οἱ δὲ κομψοτέρως τῷ λόγῳ προσ-
άγοντες ὅτι τὰ μὲν σώματα πάντα σύγκειται ἐκ
15 τοῦ λεπτομερεστάτου, τὰ δὲ σχήματα τὰ στερεὰ
ἐκ τῶν πυραμίδων, ὥστ' ἐπεὶ τῶν μὲν σωμάτων
τὸ πῦρ λεπτότατον, τῶν δὲ σχημάτων ἡ πυραμὶς
μικρομερέστατον καὶ πρῶτον, τὸ δὲ πρῶτον σχῆμα
τοῦ πρώτου σώματος, πυραμὶς ἂν εἴη τὸ πῦρ. οἱ
δὲ περὶ μὲν σχήματος οὐδὲν ἀποφαίνονται, λεπτο-
20 μερέστατον δὲ μόνον ποιοῦσιν, ἔπειτ' ἐκ τούτου
συντιθεμένου φασὶ γίγνεσθαι τἆλλα καθάπερ ἂν
εἰ συμφυσωμένου ψήγματος.

---

^a *i.e.* the atomists, whose elements are, strictly speaking,
the atoms; but A is using the word to mean the four elements
of his own system. *Cf.* 303 a 15, 26 above.

be said simply of one thing that it is fire, of another water, and of another air, but the same body will be fire relatively to this, and air relatively to something else. Those who posit a plurality of elements, but distinguish them by greatness and smallness,[a] are in the same position. For since it is quantity that distinguishes each one, their magnitudes must bear a certain ratio to one another, and hence those which exhibit this ratio must be air, fire, earth and water with respect to each other, seeing that the same ratios may be found among the larger bodies as among the smaller.

As for those who make fire the element, they escape this difficulty, but cannot avoid other absurd consequences. Some fit a shape to fire, e.g. those who make it a pyramid. Among them we find (a) the cruder argument that the pyramid is the sharpest of figures and fire the sharpest of bodies, and (b) the subtler reasoning put forward that all bodies are built up out of the finest body, and solid figures out of pyramids, and that therefore, since fire is the finest of bodies, and the pyramid the finest [b] and the primary among figures, the primary figure belongs to the primary body, therefore fire is pyramidal. Others leave aside the question of shape, and simply postulate it as the finest body, from the agglomeration of which, as of filings blown together, the other bodies are generated.

[b] Whether μικρομερέστατον (FHMJ, Bekker, Prantl, Stocks) or λεπτομερέστατον (EL, Simpl., Allan) be read, the meaning must be, not that the pyramid *has* the smallest parts, but that it *is* the smallest kind of part, *i.e.* that a body constructed of pyramidal atoms would have the smallest parts of any, since the pyramid is the smallest solid. *Cf.* Stocks's note here and on 302 a 31.

Ἀμφοτέροις δὲ ταὐτὰ συμβαίνει δυσχερῆ· εἰ μὲν
γὰρ ἄτομον τὸ πρῶτον σῶμα ποιοῦσι, πάλιν
ἥξουσιν οἱ πρότερον εἰρημένοι λόγοι πρὸς ταύτην
τὴν ὑπόθεσιν. ἔτι οὐκ ἐνδέχεται τοῦτο λέγειν
25 φυσικῶς βουλομένους θεωρεῖν. εἰ γὰρ ἅπαν σῶμα
σώματι συμβλητὸν κατὰ τὸ ποσόν, ἔχει δ' ἀνάλογον τὰ μεγέθη τά τε τῶν ὁμοιομερῶν πρὸς
ἄλληλα καὶ τὰ τῶν στοιχείων (οἷον τὰ τοῦ παντὸς
ὕδατος πρὸς τὸν ἅπαντα ἀέρα καὶ τοῦ στοιχείου
πρὸς τὸ στοιχεῖον, ὁμοίως δὲ καὶ ἐπὶ τῶν ἄλλων),
30 ὁ δ' ἀὴρ πλείων τοῦ ὕδατος καὶ ὅλως τὸ λεπτομερέστερον τοῦ παχυμερεστέρου, φανερὸν ὅτι καὶ
τὸ στοιχεῖον ἔλαττον ἔσται τὸ τοῦ ὕδατος ἢ τὸ τοῦ
ἀέρος. εἰ οὖν τὸ ἔλαττον μέγεθος ἐνυπάρχει τῷ
304 b μείζονι, διαιρετὸν ἂν εἴη τὸ τοῦ ἀέρος στοιχεῖον.
ὡσαύτως δὲ καὶ τὸ τοῦ πυρὸς καὶ ὅλως τῶν
λεπτομερεστέρων. εἰ δὲ διαιρετόν, τοῖς μὲν σχη-
ματίζουσι τὸ πῦρ συμβήσεται μὴ εἶναι τὸ τοῦ πυρὸς μέρος πῦρ διὰ τὸ μὴ συγκεῖσθαι τὴν πυραμίδα
5 ἐκ πυραμίδων, ἔτι δὲ μὴ πᾶν σῶμα εἶναι ἢ στοιχεῖον ἢ ἐκ στοιχείων (τὸ γὰρ μέρος τοῦ πυρὸς οὔτε
πῦρ οὔθ' ἕτερον στοιχεῖον οὐδέν)· τοῖς δὲ τῷ
μεγέθει διορίζουσι πρότερόν τι τοῦ στοιχείου
στοιχεῖον εἶναι, καὶ τοῦτ' εἰς ἄπειρον βαδίζειν,
εἴπερ ἅπαν σῶμα διαιρετὸν καὶ τὸ μικρομερέστατον
10 στοιχεῖον. ἔτι δὲ καὶ τούτοις συμβαίνει λέγειν ὡς

---

a " The ascertained fact on which this argument is based
is that when (e.g.) water turns into air, the volume of the
resultant air is greater than that of the original water. This
increase of volume can only be accounted for (since the
hypothesis of a void has been refuted) by supposing an
increase in the volume of the atom proportionate to the

Both views are open to the same objections. (*a*) If they make the first body indivisible, our former arguments recur to refute their hypothesis. In any case, no one who wishes to look at the matter scientifically can speak as they do. For if all bodies are comparable in respect of size, and the magnitudes of homoeomerous substances stand in the same ratio to one another as do their elements (for instance, as the magnitude of the whole mass of water is to that of the whole mass of air, so that of the element of water is to that of the element of air, and so on), and if, further, air is more widely extended than water, and in general the finer body than the coarser, then clearly the element of water will be smaller than the element of air. If therefore the smaller magnitude is contained in the greater, the element of air must be divisible. The same applies to the element of fire and of the finer bodies in general.[a] (*b*) Suppose on the other hand they make it divisible. Then those who assign a figure to fire will discover that a part of fire is not fire, since a pyramid is not composed of pyramids ; also that not every body is either an element or composed of the elements, for a part of fire will be neither fire nor any other element. Those on the other hand who make size the differentia must admit that there is an element prior to *their* element, and so on to infinity, once granted that every body is divisible and that the finest is the element. Moreover these too are in the position of saying that the same body is fire

observed increase in the volume of the total mass. But the enlarged atom would be divisible, and therefore no atom " (Stocks).

ταὐτὸν πρὸς μὲν τόδε πῦρ ἐστὶ πρὸς ἄλλο δ᾽ ἀήρ,
καὶ πάλιν ὕδωρ καὶ γῆ.

Κοινὸν δὲ πᾶσιν ἁμάρτημα τοῖς ἓν τὸ στοιχεῖον
ὑποτιθεμένοις τὸ μίαν μόνην κίνησιν ποιεῖν
φυσικήν, καὶ πάντων τὴν αὐτήν. ὁρῶμεν γὰρ πᾶν
τὸ φυσικὸν σῶμα κινήσεως ἔχον ἀρχήν. εἰ οὖν
15 ἅπαντα τὰ σώματα ἕν τί ἐστι, πάντων ἂν εἴη μία
κίνησις· καὶ ταύτην ἀναγκαῖον ὅσῳπερ ἂν πλείων
γίγνηται, κινεῖσθαι μᾶλλον, ὥσπερ καὶ τὸ πῦρ
ὅσῳ ἂν πλεῖον γίγνηται, φέρεται θᾶττον ἄνω τὴν
αὑτοῦ φοράν. συμβαίνει δὲ πολλὰ κάτω φέρεσθαι
θᾶττον. ὥστε διά τε ταῦτα, καὶ πρὸς τούτοις
20 ἐπεὶ διώρισται πρότερον ὅτι πλείους αἱ φυσικαὶ
κινήσεις, δῆλον ὅτι ἀδύνατον ἓν εἶναι τὸ στοιχεῖον.
ἐπειδὴ δὲ οὔτε ἄπειρα οὔτε ἕν, πλείω ἀνάγκη εἶναι
καὶ πεπερασμένα.

CHAPTER VI

ARGUMENT

The elements (1) are not eternal, (2) are generated from
each other.

1. *They can be seen in process of dissolution, and this process cannot either (a) be of infinite duration or (b) stop before
the whole of the element has perished.   (a) A second infinity
would be required for the reverse process of synthesis.   (b)
The remnant could not be either* (i) *indissoluble (proved elsewhere) or* (ii) *capable of, but never undergoing, dissolution,*

23 Ἐπισκεπτέον δὲ πρῶτον πότερον ἀΐδιά ἐστιν ἢ

in relation to this and air in relation to that, and again water or earth.

The mistake common to all those who postulate a single element only is that they allow for only one natural motion shared by everything. We know that every natural body contains a principle of motion. If then all bodies are one substance, they must all have the same motion, and they will move the more swiftly with this motion, the more abundantly its source is available, just as with fire, the more of it there is, the faster it performs its proper motion upward. But in fact there are many things which move faster *downward* the more there is of them. For this reason, and taking into account our earlier decision that there are several natural motions, it is clearly impossible that there should be one element only. The elements, then, are neither infinite in number nor reducible to one, and must therefore be (*a*) a plurality but (*b*) a limited number.

CHAPTER VI

ARGUMENT (*continued*)

for the smaller a body the easier its dissolution (304 b 23—305 a 14).
    2. They cannot be generated from anything else, either (a) *incorporeal or* (b) *corporeal.* (a) *involves void as denied in ch. ii.* (b) *If the body from which they are generated has a motion, it will itself be one of the elements. If not, it cannot exist in space at all* (305 a 14-32).

FIRST however we must inquire whether they are

304 b

γινόμενα φθείρεται· τούτου γὰρ δειχθέντος φανερὸν
25 ἔσται καὶ πόσ᾽ ἄττα καὶ ποῖά ἐστιν.

Ἀΐδια μὲν οὖν εἶναι ἀδύνατον· ὁρῶμεν γὰρ καὶ
πῦρ καὶ ὕδωρ καὶ ἕκαστον τῶν ἁπλῶν σωμάτων
διαλυόμενον. ἀνάγκη δὲ ἢ ἄπειρον εἶναι ἢ ἵστασθαι
τὴν διάλυσιν. εἰ μὲν οὖν ἄπειρον, ἔσται καὶ ὁ
χρόνος ὁ τῆς διαλύσεως ἄπειρος, καὶ πάλιν ὁ τῆς
30 συνθέσεως· ἕκαστον γὰρ ἐν ἄλλῳ χρόνῳ διαλύεται
καὶ συντίθεται τῶν μορίων. ὥστε συμβήσεται ἔξω
τοῦ ἀπείρου χρόνου ἄλλον εἶναι ἄπειρον, ὅταν ὅ τε
τῆς συνθέσεως ἄπειρος ᾖ καὶ ἔτι τούτου πρότερος
ὁ τῆς διαλύσεως. ὥστε τοῦ ἀπείρου ἔξω γίγνεται
305 a ἄπειρον· ὅπερ ἀδύνατον. εἰ δὲ στήσεταί που ἡ
διάλυσις, ἤτοι ἄτομον ἔσται τὸ σῶμα ἐν ᾧ ἵσταται,
ἢ διαιρετὸν μὲν οὐ μέντοι διαιρεθησόμενον οὐδέποτε, καθάπερ ἔοικεν Ἐμπεδοκλῆς βούλεσθαι
5 λέγειν. ἄτομον μὲν οὖν οὐκ ἔσται διὰ τοὺς πρότερον εἰρημένους λόγους· ἀλλὰ μὴν οὐδὲ διαιρετὸν
μὲν οὐδέποτε δὲ διαλυθησόμενον. τὸ γὰρ ἔλαττον
σῶμα τοῦ μείζονος εὐφθαρτότερόν ἐστιν. εἴπερ
οὖν καὶ τὸ πολὺ φθείρεται κατὰ ταύτην τὴν
φθοράν, ὥστε διαλύεσθαι εἰς ἐλάττω, ἔτι μᾶλλον
τοῦτο πάσχειν εὔλογον τὸ ἔλαττον. δύο δὲ τρόπους
10 ὁρῶμεν φθειρόμενον τὸ πῦρ· ὑπό τε γὰρ τοῦ ἐναντίου φθείρεται σβεννύμενον, καὶ αὐτὸ ὑφ᾽ αὑτοῦ
μαραινόμενον. τοῦτο δὲ πάσχει τὸ ἔλαττον ὑπὸ
τοῦ πλείονος, καὶ θᾶττον, ὅσῳ ἂν ᾖ ἔλαττον. ὥστ᾽

ᵃ This sentence is so condensed as to cause a slight
obscurity. Understand : " Since the elements can be observed in process of dissolution, therefore, *if they are to be*

304

eternal or come to be and perish ; for a demonstration of this will make clear their number and character as well.

Eternal they cannot be, for both fire and water and indeed each of the simple bodies are observed in process of dissolution. This process must either be infinite or come to a stop.[a] (a) If infinite, the time which it takes will also be infinite, and also the time of the synthesis which follows ; for the dissolution and the synthesis of each part take place successively. Inevitably therefore there will be a second infinite time apart from the first, in every case where the time of synthesis is infinite and the time of dissolution precedes it. Thus we have two infinites side by side, which is impossible. (b) If there is a term to the process of dissolution, the body left when it stops must be either indissoluble or destined never to be dissolved ; the latter is what Empedocles seems to aim at describing. Our previous arguments forbid that it should be indissoluble : nor on the other hand can it be capable of, but destined never to undergo, dissolution. A smaller body is always more perishable than a larger : if therefore the larger body itself submits to destruction by this process of being broken up into smaller parts, it is likely that the smaller will submit to it even more readily. Now fire may be observed to perish in two ways : it may be quenched, *i.e.* destroyed by its opposite, or it may die out, destroyed by its own action. A smaller quantity is acted upon by a greater, and the smaller it is the quicker the effect. The elements

eternal, either the process must never come to an end or it must come to an end *before all of the element has perished.*"

305 a

ἀνάγκη φθαρτὰ καὶ γενητὰ εἶναι τὰ στοιχεῖα τῶν
σωμάτων.

15 Ἐπεὶ δ' ἐστὶ γενητά, ἤτοι ἐξ ἀσωμάτου ἢ ἐκ
σώματος ἔσται ἡ γένεσις, καὶ εἰ ἐκ σώματος, ἤτοι
ἐξ ἄλλου ἢ ἐξ ἀλλήλων. ὁ μὲν οὖν ἐξ ἀσωμάτου
γεννῶν λόγος ποιεῖ ἀφωρισμένον¹ κενόν. πᾶν γὰρ
τὸ γινόμενον ἔν τινι γίνεται, καὶ ἤτοι ἀσώματον
20 ἔσται ἐν ᾧ ἡ γένεσις, ἢ ἕξει σῶμα· καὶ εἰ μὲν ἕξει
σῶμα, δύο ἔσται σώματα ἅμα ἐν τῷ αὐτῷ, τό τε
γιγνόμενον καὶ τὸ προϋπάρχον· εἰ δ' ἀσώματον,
ἀνάγκη κενὸν εἶναι ἀφωρισμένον· τοῦτο δ' ὅτι
ἀδύνατον, δέδεικται καὶ πρότερον. ἀλλὰ μὴν οὐδ'
ἐκ σώματός τινος ἐγχωρεῖ γίνεσθαι τὰ στοιχεῖα·
συμβήσεται γὰρ ἄλλο σῶμα πρότερον εἶναι τῶν
στοιχείων. τοῦτο δ' εἰ μὲν ἔχει βάρος ἢ κου-
25 φότητα, τῶν στοιχείων ἔσται τι, μηδεμίαν δ' ἔχον
ῥοπὴν ἀκίνητον ἔσται καὶ μαθηματικόν· τοιοῦτον
δὲ ὂν οὐκ ἔσται ἐν τόπῳ. ἐν ᾧ γὰρ ἠρεμεῖ, ἐν
τούτῳ καὶ κινεῖσθαι δυνατόν. καὶ εἰ μὲν βίᾳ, παρὰ
φύσιν, εἰ δὲ μὴ βίᾳ, κατὰ φύσιν. εἰ μὲν οὖν ἔσται
ἐν τόπῳ καὶ που, ἔσται τι τῶν στοιχείων· εἰ δὲ
30 μὴ ἐν τόπῳ, οὐδὲν ἐξ αὐτοῦ ἔσται· τὸ γὰρ γινόμενον, καὶ ἐξ οὗ γίγνεται, ἀνάγκη ἅμα εἶναι. ἐπεὶ
δ' οὔτε ἐξ ἀσωμάτου γίγνεσθαι δυνατὸν οὔτ' ἐξ
ἄλλου σώματος, λείπεται ἐξ ἀλλήλων γίγνεσθαι.

---

¹ I have adopted Allan's suggestion of reading ἀφωρισμένον
(as at line 21) for the γεννώμενον of EL, which is printed by
Bekker. Simplicius's text clearly had not γεννώμενον, and
FHMJ have no epithet at all. *Cf.* Stocks's note.

ᵃ *Cf.* note at end of ch. ii. above.

of bodies, therefore, must be subject to destruction and generation.

Since they are generated, their generation must be either from the incorporeal or from the corporeal, and if from the corporeal, either from some extraneous body or from each other. The theory which generates them from the incorporeal involves a void separate from body ; for everything which comes to be comes to be *in* something, and that in which its coming to be takes place must be either incorporeal or corporeal : if corporeal, there will be two bodies in the same place at once, that which is in process of formation and that which was there before : if incorporeal, there must be a separate void. But the impossibility of this has been proved before.[a] On the other hand there is no body from which the elements could be generated, for that would mean that some other body was prior to the elements. If this body has weight or lightness, it will itself be one of the elements : if it has no impulse in any direction, it will be unmoved, *i.e.* a mathematical object. But in that case it will not occupy a place. If it rests in a place, it will be possible for it to move in that place, if by force, then unnaturally, or if not by force, then naturally. If then it occupies a place somewhere, it will be one of the elements. If not, nothing can be generated from it, for that which comes to be and that from which it is generated must be together. Seeing therefore that the elements can neither be generated from the incorporeal nor from an extraneous body, it remains to suppose that they are generated from each other.

ARISTOTLE

CHAPTER VII

ARGUMENT

How does generation take place ? Criticism of previous theories.

1. *The " separation " theory of Empedocles and Demo-critus (305 a 33–b 26).*

(a) *This is a denial of generation in any real sense.*

(b) *How do they account for the gain in weight when, e.g., water is " separated out " from air ?*

(c) *How do they account for the expansion when, e.g., air is separated out from water ? It would in any case require explaining, if separation is the only process involved, but considering that* (i) *there is no such thing as void, and* (ii) *their own theories do not allow for the actual expansion of solid bodies, it becomes impossible.*

(d) *A stage is bound to be reached when all the elements are separated off from one another, and generation will auto-matically cease.*

2. *The theory which explains generation as change of*

Πάλιν οὖν ἐπισκεπτέον τίς ὁ τρόπος τῆς ἐξ ἀλλήλων γενέσεως, πότερον ὡς Ἐμπεδοκλῆς λέγει καὶ Δημόκριτος, ἢ ὡς οἱ εἰς τὰ ἐπίπεδα διαλύοντες, ἢ ἔστιν ἄλλος τις τρόπος παρὰ τούτους.

Οἱ μὲν οὖν περὶ Ἐμπεδοκλέα καὶ Δημόκριτον λανθάνουσιν αὐτοὶ αὑτοὺς οὐ γένεσιν ἐξ ἀλλήλων ποιοῦντες ἀλλὰ φαινομένη γένεσιν· ἐνυπάρχον γὰρ ἕκαστον ἐκκρίνεσθαί φασιν, ὥσπερ ἐξ ἀγγείου τῆς 5 γενέσεως οὔσης ἀλλ' οὐκ ἔκ τινος ὕλης, οὐδὲ γίγνεσθαι μεταβάλλοντος. ἔπειτα κἂν οὕτως οὐδὲν ἧττον ἄλογα τὰ συμβαίνοντα. τὸ γὰρ αὐτὸ μέγεθος οὐ δοκεῖ συμπιληθὲν γίνεσθαι βαρύτερον. ἀνάγκη

CHAPTER VII

ARGUMENT (continued)

shape (305 b 26—306 a 1). *Dismissed as involving the sup-position of indivisible bodies.*

3. *The Platonic theory of generation from triangular sur-faces (306 a 1–b 2).*

(a) *Why make one element (earth) exempt from the general law of mutual transmutation ?*

(b) *The notion of triangles drifting about by themselves in space is absurd.*

(c) *Generation from surfaces is generation of bodies from the incorporeal.*

(d) *Indivisible bodies are a necessary assumption on this theory too.*

Note.—*Simpl. does not know to whom to assign the second theory. He connects it with Plato's simile of the goldsmith (Tim. 50 A), but is aware that this is of course only an illustra-tion of a particular point, and has nothing directly to do with the main theory of triangles.*

WE must now turn to ask what is the manner of this generation out of one another. Is it as de-scribed by Empedocles and Democritus, or by those who analyse bodies into surfaces, or is there some other, different process ?

The followers of Empedocles and Democritus fail to see that their theory produces, not generation, but only the semblance of generation out of one another. They speak of each element "inhering" and "being separated out," as if generation were emergence from a receptacle instead of from a material, and did not involve change in anything. Even granted that it were so, the consequences remain just as absurd. In the first place a body of a certain size is not observed to grow heavier

309

805 b

δὲ τοῦτο λέγειν τοῖς φάσκουσιν ἐκκρίνεσθαι τὸ
10 ὕδωρ ἐκ τοῦ ἀέρος ἐνυπάρχον· ὅταν γὰρ ὕδωρ ἐξ
ἀέρος γένηται, βαρύτερόν ἐστιν. ἔτι δὲ τῶν με-
μιγμένων σωμάτων οὐκ ἀνάγκη χωρισθὲν θάτερον
ἀεὶ πλείω τόπον ἐπέχειν· ὅταν δ' ἐξ ὕδατος ἀὴρ
γένηται, πλείω καταλαμβάνει τόπον· τὸ γὰρ¹
λεπτομερέστερον ἐν πλείονι τόπῳ γίγνεται. (φανερὸν δὲ τοῦτό γε καὶ ἐν τῇ μεταβάσει· διατμιζο-
15 μένου γὰρ καὶ πνευματουμένου τοῦ ὑγροῦ ῥήγνυται
τὰ περιέχοντα τοὺς ὄγκους ἀγγεῖα διὰ τὴν στενοχωρίαν.) ὥστ' εἰ μὲν ὅλως μή ἐστι κενὸν μηδ'
ἐπεκτείνεται τὰ σώματα, καθάπερ φασὶν οἱ ταῦτα
λέγοντες, φανερὸν τὸ ἀδύνατον· εἰ δ' ἔστι κενὸν
καὶ ἐπέκτασις, ἄλογον τὸ ἐξ ἀνάγκης ἀεὶ πλείω
20 τόπον ἐπιλαμβάνειν τὸ χωριζόμενον. ἀλλ' ἀνάγκη
καὶ ὑπολείπειν τὴν ἐξ ἀλλήλων γένεσιν, εἴπερ ἐν
τῷ πεπερασμένῳ μεγέθει μὴ ἐνυπάρχει ἄπειρα
μεγέθη πεπερασμένα. ὅταν γὰρ ἐκ γῆς ὕδωρ
γένηται, ἀφήρηταί τι τῆς γῆς, εἴπερ ἐκκρίσει ἡ
γένεσις· καὶ πάλιν ὅταν ἐκ τῆς ὑπολειπομένης,
25 ὡσαύτως. εἰ μὲν οὖν ἀεὶ τοῦτ' ἔσται, συμβήσεται
ἐν τῷ πεπερασμένῳ ἄπειρα ἐνυπάρχειν· ἐπεὶ δὲ
τοῦτ' ἀδύνατον, οὐκ ἂν ἀεὶ γίγνοιτο ἐξ ἀλλήλων.

Ὅτι μὲν οὖν οὐκ ἔστι τῇ ἐκκρίσει ἡ εἰς ἄλληλα
μετάβασις, εἴρηται. λείπεται δ' εἰς ἄλληλα μεταβάλλοντα γίγνεσθαι. τοῦτο δὲ διχῶς· ἢ γὰρ τῇ
30 μετασχηματίσει, καθάπερ ἐκ τοῦ αὐτοῦ κηροῦ

---

¹ γὰρ EFJ, Simpl., Allan; δὲ HLM, Bekker.

310

by compression. But they are forced to argue
that it does, if they maintain that water inheres
in air, and is separated out from it; for when
from being air it becomes water, it gains in weight.
Secondly, when from a mixture one body is extracted, there is no reason why it should always
extend over a greater area than before. But when
air is formed from water, it does occupy more
space : the finer body takes up more room. (This
can be actually observed in the process of change.
As a liquid turns to steam and vapour vessels containing the substances burst for lack of room.)
If then there is no void at all, and if (as the authors
of the theory affirm) bodies cannot expand, the
impossibility of this happening is obvious. If void
and expansion be granted, it remains unconvincing
that a body should always and of necessity take up
more room as it is separated off. Thirdly, the
process of generation from one another must actually
come to a stop, unless a finite magnitude can have
an infinite number of finite magnitudes within it.
For when water is generated from earth, something
has been taken away from the earth—if generation
is by separation—and so on when more is generated
from the remainder. If therefore the process went
on for ever, it would mean that the finite contained
an infinity ; and since this is impossible, they could
not for ever be generated from one another.

Now that we have determined that the transition from one element into another is not effected
by separation, there remains the alternative that
they are generated by actual transmutation into
one another. Two processes have been suggested :
(a) change of shape, as a sphere and a cube might

305 b

γίγνοιτ' ἂν σφαῖρα καὶ κύβος, ἢ τῇ διαλύσει τῇ εἰς
τὰ ἐπίπεδα, ὥσπερ ἔνιοί φασιν. εἰ μὲν οὖν τῇ
μετασχηματίσει γίνεται, συμβαίνει ἐξ ἀνάγκης
ἄτομα λέγειν τὰ σώματα· διαιρετῶν γὰρ ὄντων
οὐκ ἔσται τὸ τοῦ πυρὸς μέρος πῦρ, οὐδὲ τὸ τῆς γῆς
35 γῆ, διὰ τὸ μὴ εἶναι μήτε τὸ τῆς πυραμίδος μέρος
306 a πάντως πυραμίδα μήτε τὸ τοῦ κύβου κύβον. εἰ
δὲ τῇ τῶν ἐπιπέδων διαλύσει, πρῶτον μὲν ἄτοπον
τὸ μὴ πάντα γεννᾶν ἐξ ἀλλήλων, ὅπερ ἀνάγκη
λέγειν αὐτοῖς, καὶ λέγουσιν. οὔτε γὰρ εὔλογον
5 ἓν μόνον ἄμοιρον γενέσθαι τῆς μεταβάσεως, οὔτε
φαίνεται κατὰ τὴν αἴσθησιν, ἀλλ' ὁμοίως πάντα
μεταβάλλειν εἰς ἄλληλα. συμβαίνει δὲ περὶ τῶν
φαινομένων λέγουσι μὴ ὁμολογούμενα λέγειν τοῖς
φαινομένοις. τούτου δ' αἴτιον τὸ μὴ καλῶς λαβεῖν
τὰς πρώτας ἀρχάς, ἀλλὰ πάντα βούλεσθαι πρός
τινας δόξας ὡρισμένας ἀνάγειν. δεῖ γὰρ ἴσως· τῶν
10 μὲν αἰσθητῶν αἰσθητάς, τῶν δὲ ἀϊδίων ἀϊδίους,
τῶν δὲ φθαρτῶν φθαρτὰς εἶναι τὰς ἀρχάς, ὅλως
δ' ὁμογενεῖς τοῖς ὑποκειμένοις. οἱ δὲ διὰ τὴν

---

^a The exception is earth (306 a 20), which is exempted
from the cycle of change simply as a consequence of assigning it the cubical figure. This means that its elementary

triangle is of a different sort (isosceles) from

those which form the ultimate constituents of the other three

elements (right-angled scalene). *Cf.* Cornford,

be made from the same piece of wax, (b) the analysis into surfaces which some have put forward. (a) Change of shape carries with it the necessary corollary that there are indivisible bodies. Were all bodies divisible, a part of fire would not be fire, nor a part of earth earth, because the part of a pyramid is not always pyramidal nor of a cube cubical. But if (b) the process is one of analysis into surfaces, there is the absurdity of not allowing *all* the elements to be generated from each other.[a] This they must and do uphold. But for one element alone to have no part in the change is neither logical nor apparent to sense : all should change into each other without discrimination. These philosophers find themselves, in a discussion about phenomena, making statements with which the phenomena conflict. This is because they have a wrong conception of primary principles, and try to bring everything into line with hard-and-fast theories. For surely the principles of sensible things are sensible, of eternal things eternal, and of perishable, perishable : put generally, a principle is of the same genus as what falls under it. Yet

Plato's Cosmology, p. 216, and *Tim.* 54 c: " It appeared as though all the four kinds could pass through one another into one another ; but this appearance is delusive ; for the triangles we selected give rise to four types, and whereas three are constructed out of the triangle with unequal sides, the fourth alone is constructed out of the isosceles. Hence it is not possible for all of them to pass into one another by resolution." Also 56 D: " Earth, when it meets with fire and is dissolved by its sharpness, would drift about . . . until its own parts somewhere encounter one another, are fitted together, and again become earth ; for they can never pass into any other kind." (Trans. Cornford.)

τούτων φιλίαν ταὐτὸ ποιεῖν ἐοίκασι τοῖς τὰς θέσεις
ἐν τοῖς λόγοις διαφυλάττουσιν· ἅπαν γὰρ ὑπο-
μένουσι τὸ συμβαῖνον ὡς ἀληθεῖς ἔχοντες ἀρχάς,
15 ὥσπερ οὐκ ἐνίας δέον κρίνειν ἐκ τῶν ἀποβαινόντων,
καὶ μάλιστα ἐκ τοῦ τέλους. τέλος δὲ τῆς μὲν
ποιητικῆς ἐπιστήμης τὸ ἔργον, τῆς δὲ φυσικῆς τὸ
φαινόμενον ἀεὶ κυρίως κατὰ τὴν αἴσθησιν. συμβαίνει δ' αὐτοῖς μάλιστα τὴν γῆν εἶναι στοιχεῖον,
καὶ μόνην ἄφθαρτον, εἴπερ τὸ ἀδιάλυτον ἄφθαρτόν
20 τ' ἐστὶ καὶ στοιχεῖον· ἡ γὰρ γῆ μόνη ἀδιάλυτος εἰς
ἄλλο σῶμα. ἀλλὰ μὴν οὐδ' ἐν τοῖς διαλυομένοις
ἡ τῶν τριγώνων παραιώρησις εὔλογος. συμβαίνει δὲ καὶ τοῦτο ἐν τῇ εἰς ἄλληλα μεταβάσει διὰ
τὸ ἐξ ἀνίσων τῷ πλήθει συνεστάναι τριγώνων. ἔτι
25 δ' ἀνάγκη τοῖς ταῦτα λέγουσιν οὐκ ἐκ σώματος
ποιεῖν γένεσιν· ὅταν γὰρ ἐξ ἐπιπέδων γένηται, οὐκ
ἐκ σώματος ἔσται γεγονός. πρὸς δὲ τούτοις
ἀνάγκη μὴ πᾶν σῶμα λέγειν διαιρετόν, ἀλλὰ
μάχεσθαι ταῖς ἀκριβεστάταις ἐπιστήμαις· αἱ μὲν
γὰρ καὶ τὸ νοητὸν λαμβάνουσι διαιρετόν, αἱ μαθη-
ματικαί, οἱ δὲ οὐδὲ τὸ αἰσθητὸν ἅπαν συγχωροῦσι
30 διὰ τὸ βούλεσθαι σώζειν τὴν ὑπόθεσιν. ἀνάγκη
γὰρ ὅσοι σχῆμα ποιοῦσιν ἑκάστου τῶν στοιχείων
καὶ τούτῳ διορίζουσι τὰς οὐσίας αὐτῶν, ἀδιαίρετα
ποιεῖν αὐτά· τῆς γὰρ πυραμίδος ἢ τῆς σφαίρας

---

[a] Simpl., p. 647. 9 ff. " Since water is composed of
twenty equilateral triangles, and air of eight, whenever
water is resolved into air two particles of air are formed
from the breaking up of one particle of water, and the other
four triangles are left suspended, as one might put it, with
nothing to do." (The element of water is the icosahedron,
of air the octahedron. *Tim.* 56 B.)

out of affection for their fixed ideas these men behave like speakers defending a thesis in debate : they stand on the truth of their premises against all the facts, not admitting that there are premises which ought to be criticized in the light of their consequences, and in particular of the final result of all. Now practical knowledge culminates in the work produced, natural philosophy in the facts as presented consistently and indubitably to sense-perception. Their conclusion must mean that the earth has best right to be called an element, and is alone indestructible, if it is true that what cannot be dissolved is indestructible and an element ; for the earth alone cannot be resolved into any other body. But even in the conception of the bodies which suffer dissolution there is an irrationality, namely the suspension of triangles in space. This is something which occurs in the process of transition owing to the fact that each body is composed of a different number of triangles.[a] Again, according to this theory generation is not from body, for whatever is generated from surfaces cannot be said to have been generated from body. Besides this, they must assert that not every body is divisible, in contradiction to the most accurate of sciences, mathematics. For mathematics conceives even the intelligible as divisible, whereas these theorists, in their eagerness to preserve their hypothesis, deny the property to some of the sensible world. By assigning to each of the elements a geometrical figure, and claiming that this constitutes the essential difference between them, they are committed to making them indivisible ; for a pyramid or sphere can be divided in such a way that there will be a

306 a

διαιρεθείσης πως οὐκ ἔσται τὸ λειπόμενον σφαῖρα
ἢ πυραμίς. ὥστε ἢ τὸ τοῦ πυρὸς μέρος οὐ πῦρ,
306 b ἀλλ' ἔσται τι πρότερον τοῦ στοιχείου, διὰ τὸ πᾶν
εἶναι ἢ στοιχεῖον ἢ ἐκ στοιχείων, ἢ οὐχ ἅπαν
σῶμα διαιρετόν.

---

^a It is difficult to decide just why A. inserted πως, but
Simpl. suggests that it was out of caution because it is
possible to cut a pyramid—though not a sphere—into two
in such a way that both pieces will be pyramids, though no
longer regular as the original fire-particle was.

The mention of the sphere reminds us that this objection

CHAPTER VIII

ARGUMENT

Criticism of the Platonic theory of the elements (continued).

(e) *Some of the figures assigned to elements are such as
cannot be put together without leaving interstices of void*
(306 b 3-9).

(f) *The shape of elements must be determined by that which
contains them, or again we shall have void. In general, it is
the business of elements to be capable of formation, not formed
in themselves* (306 b 9-22).

(g) *Continuity would be impossible if bodies were formed
from Plato's elements* (306 b 22-29).

(h) *The figures are supposed to be responsible for the
natural properties of the bodies to which they are assigned.
To this there are several objections* (306 b 29—307 b 18) :

(i) *In assigning to fire the figures which they considered
most mobile, neither Plato nor Democritus took into account
the upward direction of fire's motion.*

(ii) *According to their theory, the elements ought to change*

316

remainder which is not a sphere or pyramid.[a] Either, therefore, a part of fire is not fire, but there must be something prior to the element [b] (prior, because every body is either an element or composed of elements), or every body cannot be divisible.

applies to Democritus (who made his fire-atoms spherical) as well as to Plato.

[b] This of course is precisely the point which Plato makes, that fire, air, water, and earth, popularly called elements, are not elements at all—" not letters or even syllables " (*Tim.* 48 B). Plato's elements are the triangles, not the solids, and since his triangles *can* be infinitely divided into triangles, A.'s objection here has no force. (*Cf.* Cornford, *Plato's Cosmology*, p. 234.)

CHAPTER VIII

ARGUMENT (*continued*)

their shapes according as they are or are not in their proper places. Earth, e.g., is only immobile in its proper place. Removed from it, it travels rapidly towards it unless prevented.

(iii) If the burning power of fire is to be ascribed to the sharpness of its angles, all the elements must impart heat in varying degrees, for all have angles.

(iv) What is burned is itself turned to fire. This becomes equivalent to saying that the sharp pyramids of fire, or the spheres of Democritus, cut things only into pyramids or spheres—rather as if a knife cut things only into knives!

(v) Division is not the only or even the essential faculty of fire. Yet this theory does not account for its welding power.

(vi) The theory can give no account of coldness. It is the opposite of heat, but a geometrical figure cannot have an opposite. If it is taken into account at all, it is made a question of size, not of shape.

Conclusion.—*The different properties of the elements cannot be dependent on differences of shape in their particles.*

306 b 3 Ὅλως δὲ τὸ πειρᾶσθαι τὰ ἁπλᾶ σώματα σχη-
ματίζειν ἄλογόν ἐστι, πρῶτον μὲν ὅτι συμβήσεται
5 μὴ ἀναπληροῦσθαι τὸ ὅλον· ἐν μὲν γὰρ τοῖς ἐπιπέδοις τρία σχήματα δοκεῖ συμπληροῦν τὸν τόπον,
τρίγωνον καὶ τετράγωνον καὶ ἑξάγωνον, ἐν δὲ τοῖς
στερεοῖς δύο μόνα, πυραμὶς καὶ κύβος· ἀνάγκη δὲ
πλείω τούτων λαμβάνειν διὰ τὸ πλείω τὰ στοιχεῖα
ποιεῖν. ἔπειτα φαίνεται πάντα μὲν τὰ ἁπλᾶ σώ-
10 ματα σχηματιζόμενα τῷ περιέχοντι τόπῳ, μάλιστα
δὲ τὸ ὕδωρ καὶ ὁ ἀήρ. διαμένειν μὲν οὖν τὸ τοῦ
στοιχείου σχῆμα ἀδύνατον· οὐ γὰρ ἂν ἥπτετο
πανταχῇ τοῦ περιέχοντος τὸ ὅλον. ἀλλὰ μὴν εἰ
μεταρρυθμισθήσεται, οὐκέτι ἔσται ὕδωρ, εἴπερ τῷ
σχήματι διέφερεν. ὥστε φανερὸν ὅτι οὐκ ἔστιν
15 ὡρισμένα τὰ σχήματα αὐτῶν.[1] ἀλλ' ἔοικεν ἡ φύσις
αὐτὴ τοῦτο σημαίνειν ἡμῖν, ὃ καὶ κατὰ λόγον ἐστίν·
ὥσπερ γὰρ καὶ ἐν τοῖς ἄλλοις, ἀειδὲς καὶ ἄμορφον
δεῖ τὸ ὑποκείμενον εἶναι· μάλιστα γὰρ ἂν οὕτω
δύναιτο ῥυθμίζεσθαι, καθάπερ ἐν τῷ Τιμαίῳ γέγραπται, τὸ πανδεχές. οὕτω καὶ τὰ στοιχεῖα δεῖ
20 νομίζειν ὥσπερ ὕλην εἶναι τοῖς συνθέτοις· διὸ
καὶ δύναται μεταβάλλειν εἰς ἄλληλα χωριζομένων
τῶν κατὰ πάθη διαφορῶν. πρὸς δὲ τούτοις πῶς

---

[1] αὐτῶν JLM, Simpl., Stocks, Allan: αὐτοῦ EH, Bekker:
τούτων F.

---

[a] *i.e.* which can be fitted together so as to leave no interstices. Regular figures are meant.

The proper method is to concentrate first of all on their pro-
perties as natural bodies—differences of quality and potency
(307 b 18-24).

THIS attempt to assign geometrical figures to the
simple bodies is on all counts irrational. In the
first place, the whole of space will not be filled up.
Among surfaces it is agreed that there are three
figures which fill the place that contains them [a]—
the triangle, the square, and the hexagon : among
solids only two, the pyramid and the cube. But
they need more than these, since they hold that
the elements are more. Secondly, the shape of
all the simple bodies is observed to be determined
by the place in which they are contained, particularly in the case of water and air. The shape of
the element therefore cannot survive, or it would
not be everywhere in contact with that which contains the whole mass. But if its shape is modified,
it will no longer be water, since its shape was the
determining factor. Clearly therefore the shapes
of the elements are not defined. Indeed it seems
as if nature itself here shows us the truth of a
conclusion to which more abstract reasoning also
points. Here, as in everything else, the underlying
matter must be devoid of form or shape, for so, as
is said in the *Timaeus*, the " receiver of all " will
be best able to submit to modification.[b] It is like
this that we must conceive of the elements, as
the matter of their compounds, and this is why
they can change into each other, and lose their
qualitative differences. Thirdly, how is generation

[b] Plato, *Tim.* 57 A.

806 b

ἐνδέχεται γίγνεσθαι σάρκα καὶ ὀστοῦν ἢ ὁτιοῦν
σῶμα τῶν συνεχῶν; οὔτε γὰρ ἐξ αὐτῶν τῶν
στοιχείων ἐγχωρεῖ διὰ τὸ μὴ γίγνεσθαι συνεχὲς ἐκ
25 τῆς συνθέσεως, οὔτ' ἐκ τῶν ἐπιπέδων συντιθεμένων·
τὰ γὰρ στοιχεῖα γεννᾶται τῇ συνθέσει καὶ οὐ τὰ
ἐκ τῶν στοιχείων. ὥστ' ἐάν τις ἀκριβολογεῖσθαι
βούληται καὶ μὴ ἐκ παρόδου τοὺς λόγους ἀπο-
δέχεσθαι τοὺς τοιούτους, ἀναιροῦντας ὄψεται τὴν
γένεσιν ἐκ τῶν ὄντων.

30 Ἀλλὰ μὴν καὶ πρὸς τὰ πάθη τε καὶ τὰς δυνάμεις
καὶ τὰς κινήσεις ἀσύμφωνα τὰ σχήματα τοῖς
σώμασιν, εἰς ἃ μάλιστα βλέψαντες οὕτω διένειμαν.
οἷον ἐπεὶ τὸ πῦρ εὐκίνητόν ἐστι καὶ θερμαντικὸν
καὶ καυστικόν, οἱ μὲν ἐποίησαν αὐτὸ σφαῖραν, οἱ
δὲ πυραμίδα· ταῦτα γὰρ εὐκινητότατα μὲν διὰ τὸ
307 a ἐλαχίστων ἅπτεσθαι καὶ ἥκιστα βεβηκέναι, θερ-
μαντικώτατα δὲ καὶ καυστικώτατα, διότι τὸ μὲν
ὅλον ἐστὶ γωνία, τὸ δὲ ὀξυγωνιώτατον, καίει δὲ
καὶ θερμαίνει ταῖς γωνίαις, ὥς φασιν.

Πρῶτον μὲν οὖν κατὰ τὴν κίνησιν ἀμφότεροι
5 διημαρτήκασιν· εἰ γὰρ καὶ ἔστιν εὐκινητότατα
ταῦτα τῶν σχημάτων, ἀλλ' οὐ τὴν τοῦ πυρὸς
κίνησιν εὐκίνητα· ἡ μὲν γὰρ τοῦ πυρὸς ἄνω καὶ
κατ' εὐθεῖαν, ταῦτα δ' εὐκίνητα κύκλῳ, τὴν
καλουμένην κύλισιν. ἔπειτ' εἰ ἔστιν ἡ γῆ κύβος
διὰ τὸ βεβηκέναι καὶ μένειν, μένει δ' οὐχ οὗ ἔτυχεν
10 ἀλλ' ἐν τῷ αὑτῆς τόπῳ, ἐκ δὲ τοῦ ἀλλοτρίου
φέρεται μὴ κωλυομένη, καὶ τὸ πῦρ δὲ καὶ τὰ ἄλλα

• *Cf.* line 16 below.   b *Tim.* 55 D, E.

320

possible for flesh and bone or any other continuous body ? They cannot be composed of the elements themselves since nothing continuous can result from their collocation, nor of a collocation of the surfaces, since that generates the elements, not their compounds. Hence if one tries to think accurately, instead of giving careless acceptance to theories of this sort, it becomes obvious that they banish generation from the world.

A serious objection is that the geometrical figures do not even suit the properties, powers, and movements of the bodies which they had especially in mind when they allotted them as they did. For instance, because fire is the most mobile, and has the faculty of heating and burning, the one school made it spherical, the other pyramidal. These figures they considered the most mobile, because they have fewest points of contact and are least stable, and the best able to heat and burn, because the one is all angle,^a and the other has the sharpest angles. For the burning and heating properties, they claim, lie in their angles.

In the first place, however, both schools are wrong on the question of motion. Even if these are the most mobile of figures, yet they are not mobile with the motion of fire : the motion of fire is in a straight line upwards, whereas the motion to which these figures are suited is a circular one, namely what we call rolling. Secondly, if the reason for calling earth a cube is its stability and immobility,^b then, since earth is not immobile wherever it happens to be, but only in its proper place, and moves away from anywhere else unless prevented, and the same is true of fire and the other

307 a

ὡσαύτως, δῆλον ὅτι καὶ τὸ πῦρ καὶ ἕκαστον τῶν
στοιχείων ἐν μὲν τῷ ἀλλοτρίῳ τόπῳ σφαῖρα ἔσται
ἢ πυραμίς, ἐν δὲ τῷ οἰκείῳ κύβος. ἔτι δ' εἰ θερμαίνει καὶ καίει τὸ πῦρ διὰ τὰς γωνίας, ἅπαντα
15 ἔσται τὰ στοιχεῖα θερμαντικά, μᾶλλον δ' ἴσως
ἕτερον ἑτέρου· πάντα γὰρ ἔχει γωνίας, οἷον τό
γε ὀκτάεδρον καὶ τὸ δωδεκάεδρον. Δημοκρίτῳ
δὲ καὶ ἡ σφαῖρα ὡς γωνία τις οὖσα τέμνει ὡς
εὐκίνητον. ὥστε διοίσει τῷ μᾶλλον καὶ ἧττον.
20 τοῦτο δ' ὅτι ἔστι ψεῦδος, φανερόν. ἅμα δὲ συμβήσεται καὶ τὰ μαθηματικὰ σώματα καίειν καὶ
θερμαίνειν· ἔχει γὰρ κἀκεῖνα γωνίας, καὶ ἔνεισιν
ἐν αὐτοῖς ἄτομοι καὶ σφαῖραι καὶ πυραμίδες,
ἄλλως τε καὶ εἰ ἔστιν ἄτομα μεγέθη, καθάπερ
φασίν. εἰ γὰρ τὰ μὲν τὰ δὲ μή, λεκτέον τὴν δια-
φοράν, ἀλλ' οὐχ ἁπλῶς οὕτω λεκτέον ὡς λέγουσιν.
25 ἔτι εἰ τὸ καιόμενον πυροῦται, τὸ δὲ πῦρ ἐστι
σφαῖρα ἢ πυραμίς, ἀνάγκη τὸ καιόμενον γίγνεσθαι
σφαίρας ἢ πυραμίδας. τὸ μὲν οὖν τέμνειν καὶ
τὸ διαιρεῖν οὕτως ἔστω κατὰ λόγον συμβαῖνον τῷ
σχήματι· τὸ δ' ἐξ ἀνάγκης τὴν πυραμίδα ποιεῖν
πυραμίδας ἢ τὴν σφαῖραν σφαίρας παντελῶς ἄλο-
30 γον, καὶ ὅμοιον ὥσπερ εἴ τις ἀξιοίη τὴν μάχαιραν
εἰς μαχαίρας διαιρεῖν ἢ τὸν πρίονα εἰς πρίονας.
ἔτι δὲ γελοῖον πρὸς τὸ διαιρεῖν μόνον ἀποδοῦναι
τὸ σχῆμα τῷ πυρί· δοκεῖ γὰρ μᾶλλον συγκρίνειν
καὶ συνορίζειν ἢ διακρίνειν. διακρίνει μὲν γὰρ τὰ
07 b μὴ ὁμόφυλα, συγκρίνει δὲ τὰ ὁμόφυλα· καὶ ἡ μὲν
σύγκρισις καθ' αὑτό ἐστι (τὸ γὰρ συνορίζειν καὶ
ἑνοῦν τοῦ πυρός), ἡ δὲ διάκρισις κατὰ συμβεβηκός·
συγκρῖνον γὰρ τὸ ὁμόφυλον ἐξαιρεῖ τὸ ἀλλότριον.

elements, it clearly follows that fire and each of the elements are spherical or pyrimidal when at a distance from their proper places, and cubical when they reach them. Thirdly, if the power of fire to heat and burn lies in its angles, all the elements will have this power, though perhaps in different degrees ; for they all have angles, *e.g.* the octahedron and dodecahedron. The sphere itself is regarded by Democritus as an angle, which pierces owing to its mobility. The difference therefore will be one of degree, but this is palpably false. Even mathematical bodies will have to heat and burn, for they too have angles, and include indivisible spheres and pyramids—especially if indivisible magnitudes are a reality, as these philosophers affirm. If one class of bodies has the property and another not, they should have stated where the difference lay, not simply asserted the fact as they do. Fourthly, if what is burned is turned to fire, and fire is a sphere or pyramid, the object burned must turn into spheres or pyramids. By all means let us grant that this power of cutting or dividing goes reasonably with the possession of a certain shape ; but to say that a pyramid necessarily cuts into pyramids or a sphere into spheres is as remote from reason as maintaining that a knife cuts things into knives or a saw into saws. Fifthly, it is absurd to assign to fire its shape for the purpose of division only. Fire to all appearance brings together and unifies rather than divides. It divides things of different kinds, but unites things of the same kind. Moreover uniting is essential to it—it is a property of fire to weld together and unify—but division is accidental : in uniting the homogeneous it expels

307 b

5 ὥστ' ἢ πρὸς ἄμφω ἐχρῆν ἀποδοῦναι ἢ μᾶλλον ἐπὶ
τὸ συγκρίνειν. πρὸς δὲ τούτοις, ἐπεὶ τὸ θερμὸν
καὶ τὸ ψυχρὸν ἐναντία τῇ δυνάμει, ἀδύνατον ἀποδοῦναι τῷ ψυχρῷ σχῆμά τι· δεῖ γὰρ ἐναντίον εἶναι
τὸ ἀποδιδόμενον, οὐθὲν δ' ἐναντίον ἐστὶ σχήματι.
10 διὸ καὶ πάντες ἀπολελοίπασι τοῦτο· καίτοι προσ-
ῆκεν ἢ πάντα ἀφορίσαι σχήμασιν ἢ μηδέν. ἔνιοι
δὲ περὶ τῆς δυνάμεως αὐτοῦ πειραθέντες εἰπεῖν
ἐναντία λέγουσιν αὐτοὶ αὑτοῖς. φασὶ γὰρ εἶναι
ψυχρὸν τὸ μεγαλομερὲς διὰ τὸ συνθλίβειν καὶ μὴ
διιέναι διὰ τῶν πόρων. δῆλον τοίνυν ὅτι καὶ τὸ
15 θερμὸν ἂν εἴη τὸ διιόν· τοιοῦτον δ' ἀεὶ τὸ λεπτο-
μερές. ὥστε συμβαίνει μικρότητι καὶ μεγέθει
διαφέρειν τὸ θερμὸν καὶ τὸ ψυχρόν, ἀλλ' οὐ τοῖς
σχήμασιν. ἔτι δ' εἰ ἄνισοι αἱ πυραμίδες, αἱ
μεγάλαι ἂν εἶεν οὐ πῦρ οὐδ' αἴτιον τὸ σχῆμα τοῦ
καίειν, ἀλλὰ τοὐναντίον.

Ὅτι μὲν οὖν οὐ τοῖς σχήμασι διαφέρει τὰ στοι-
20 χεῖα, φανερὸν ἐκ τῶν εἰρημένων· ἐπεὶ δὲ κυριώταται
διαφοραὶ σωμάτων αἵ τε κατὰ τὰ πάθη καὶ τὰ
ἔργα καὶ τὰς δυνάμεις (ἑκάστου γὰρ εἶναί φαμεν
τῶν φύσει καὶ ἔργα καὶ πάθη καὶ δυνάμεις), πρῶτον ἂν εἴη περὶ τούτων λεκτέον, ὅπως θεωρήσαντες
ταῦτα λάβωμεν τὰς ἑκάστου πρὸς ἕκαστον διαφοράς.

---

a Tim. 62 a-b.
b Cf. Tim. 57 c-d.

foreign bodies. Its shape therefore ought to have been devised with an eye to both, or by preference to its unifying power. Sixthly, since hot and cold have opposite effects, it is impossible to assign a shape to the cold, for it would have to be an opposite, but a shape has no opposite. For this reason they have all left out coldness. But they ought to have defined everything by shape or nothing. Some do make an attempt to describe its power, but only to contradict themselves. That which has large parts, they say, is cold, because it clogs and cannot pass through the pores.[a] Well, then, clearly the hot will be that which can pass through, and this cannot but be what has small parts. In effect, therefore, the difference between hot and cold has become a matter of size, not of shape. If, further, the pyramids were of different sizes,[b] the large pyramids would not be fire, and their shape would not cause burning but rather the reverse.

From what has been said it is clear that it is not shape which differentiates the elements from one another. In fact the most essential differences between bodies are differences in properties and functions and powers, for these are what we speak of as pertaining to every natural object. These therefore must claim our attention first, in order that from a consideration of them we may come to grasp the differences between element and element.

Δ

WEIGHT AND LIGHTNESS

CHAPTER I

ARGUMENT

Preliminary definitions. The terms " heavy " and " light "
may be used absolutely as well as relatively. In the former
sense they mean moving naturally to the centre and the cir-

307 b 28 Περὶ δὲ βαρέος καὶ κούφου, τί τ᾽ ἐστὶν ἑκάτερον
καὶ τίς ἡ φύσις αὐτῶν, σκεπτέον, καὶ διὰ τίν᾽
30 αἰτίαν ἔχουσι τὰς δυνάμεις ταύτας. ἔστι γὰρ ἡ
περὶ αὐτῶν θεωρία τοῖς περὶ κινήσεως λόγοις
οἰκεία· βαρὺ γὰρ καὶ κοῦφον τῷ δύνασθαι κινεῖσθαι
φυσικῶς πως λέγομεν. (ταῖς δὲ ἐνεργείαις ὀνόματ᾽
αὐτῶν οὐ κεῖται, πλὴν εἴ τις οἴοιτο τὴν ῥοπὴν εἶναι
308 a τοιοῦτον.) διὰ δὲ τὸ τὴν φυσικὴν μὲν εἶναι πραγμα-
τείαν περὶ κινήσεως, ταῦτα δ᾽ ἔχειν ἐν ἑαυτοῖς οἷον
ζώπυρ᾽ ἄττα κινήσεως, πάντες μὲν χρῶνται ταῖς
δυνάμεσιν αὐτῶν, οὐ μὴν διωρίκασί γε, πλὴν
5 ὀλίγων. ἰδόντες οὖν πρῶτον τὰ παρὰ τῶν ἄλλων
εἰρημένα, καὶ διαπορήσαντες ὅσα πρὸς τὴν σκέψιν
ταύτην διελεῖν ἀναγκαῖον, οὕτω καὶ τὸ φαινόμενον
ἡμῖν εἴπωμεν περὶ αὐτῶν.

326

BOOK IV

WEIGHT AND LIGHTNESS

CHAPTER I

*cumference of the world respectively. If " up " and " down "
are applied to these motions, their use is legitimate, and it is
wrong to deny (with Plato and others) their application to the
world as a whole.*

OUR next topic must be weight and lightness.
What are they, what is their nature, and why have
they their particular powers ? This is an inquiry
relevant to a study of motion, for in calling things
heavy and light we mean that they have a capacity
for a certain natural motion. (There are no names
for the realization of these capacities, unless we
count " momentum " as one.) And because physical
science is concerned with motion, and weight and
lightness contain within themselves, as one might
say, the germs of motion, all investigators have
availed themselves of their powers, but none save
a few have defined them. Let us then first see
what others have said, then state the difficulties
whose recognition is demanded by the subject,
and so reach an explanation of our own view.

808 a

Λέγεται δὴ τὸ μὲν ἁπλῶς βαρὺ καὶ κοῦφον, τὸ
δὲ πρὸς ἕτερον· τῶν γὰρ ἐχόντων βάρος φαμὲν τὸ
μὲν εἶναι κουφότερον τὸ δὲ βαρύτερον, οἷον ξύλου
10 χαλκόν. περὶ μὲν οὖν τῶν ἁπλῶς λεγομένων οὐδὲν
εἴρηται παρὰ τῶν πρότερον, περὶ δὲ τῶν πρὸς
ἕτερον· οὐ γὰρ λέγουσι τί ἐστι τὸ βαρὺ καὶ τί τὸ
κοῦφον, ἀλλὰ τί τὸ βαρύτερον καὶ κουφότερον ἐν
τοῖς ἔχουσι βάρος. μᾶλλον δ' ἔσται δῆλον τὸ
15 λεγόμενον ὧδε. τὰ μὲν γὰρ ἀεὶ πέφυκεν ἀπὸ τοῦ
μέσου φέρεσθαι, τὰ δ' ἀεὶ πρὸς τὸ μέσον. τούτων
δὲ τὸ μὲν ἀπὸ τοῦ μέσου φερόμενον ἄνω λέγω
φέρεσθαι, κάτω δὲ τὸ πρὸς τὸ μέσον. ἄτοπον γὰρ
τὸ μὴ νομίζειν εἶναί τι ἐν τῷ οὐρανῷ τὸ μὲν ἄνω
τὸ δὲ κάτω, καθάπερ τινὲς ἀξιοῦσιν· οὐ γὰρ εἶναι
τὸ μὲν ἄνω τὸ δὲ κάτω φασίν, εἴπερ πάντῃ ὅμοιός
20 ἐστι, καὶ πανταχόθεν ἀντίπους ἔσται πορευόμενος
ἕκαστος αὐτὸς αὑτῷ. ἡμεῖς δὲ τὸ τοῦ παντὸς
ἔσχατον ἄνω λέγομεν, ὃ καὶ κατὰ τὴν θέσιν ἐστὶν
ἄνω καὶ τῇ φύσει πρῶτον· ἐπεὶ δ' ἐστί τι τοῦ
οὐρανοῦ ἔσχατον καὶ μέσον, δῆλον ὅτι ἔσται καὶ
ἄνω καὶ κάτω, ὥσπερ καὶ οἱ πολλοὶ λέγουσι, πλὴν
25 οὐχ ἱκανῶς. τούτου δ' αἴτιον ὅτι νομίζουσιν οὐχ
ὅμοιον εἶναι πάντῃ τὸν οὐρανόν, ἀλλ' ἓν εἶναι μόνον
τὸ ὑπὲρ ἡμᾶς ἡμισφαίριον, ἐπεὶ προσυπολαβόντες
καὶ κύκλῳ τοιοῦτον, καὶ τὸ μέσον ὁμοίως ἔχειν
πρὸς ἅπαν, τὸ μὲν ἄνω φήσουσιν εἶναι, τὸ δὲ μέσον
κάτω. ἁπλῶς μὲν οὖν κοῦφον λέγομεν τὸ ἄνω

ª That it is the earth which the imaginary traveller is
treading does not emerge from A.'s Greek. His sentence
328

Weight and lightness are predicated both absolutely and relatively. That is, of two heavy things, we may say that one is lighter and the other heavier, *e.g.* bronze is heavier than wood. Our predecessors have treated of the relative sense, but not the absolute : they say nothing of the meaning of weight and lightness, but discuss which is the heavier and which the lighter among things possessing weight. Let me make my meaning clearer. There are certain things whose nature it is always to move away from the centre, and others always towards the centre. The first I speak of as moving upwards, the second downwards. Some deny that there is an *up* or *down* in the world, but this is unreasonable. There is no up or down, they say, because it is uniform in all directions, and anyone who walked round the earth [a] would everywhere be standing at his own antipodes. We however apply *up* to the extremity of the world, which is both uppermost in position and primary in nature ; and since the world has both an extremity and a centre, there clearly must be an *up* and *down*. Popular opinion is right in this, though it does not see far enough, for the reason that the heaven is supposed by the ordinary man not to be uniform all round. He thinks that the hemisphere above our heads is the only one, and if he understood that it was the same all round, and that the centre was equably related to every part, he would call the extremity *up* and the centre *down*. " Absolutely light," then, is the name we give to that which moves upwards and towards

is a paraphrase, compressed to the point of obscurity, of *Tim.* 62 D—63 A.

308 a

φερόμενον καὶ πρὸς τὸ ἔσχατον, βαρὺ δὲ τὸ ἁπλῶς
30 κάτω καὶ πρὸς τὸ μέσον· πρὸς ἄλλο δὲ κοῦφον
καὶ κουφότερον, οὗ¹ δυοῖν ἐχόντων βάρος καὶ τὸν
ὄγκον ἴσον κάτω φέρεται θάτερον φύσει θᾶττον.

CHAPTER II

ARGUMENT

Review of previous theories about weight and lightness.
*The common fault of all of them is to offer no explanation
of absolute weight and lightness (308 a 34–b 3).*
   1. *Plato adduces the number of elementary particles in a
body, these being the same for all bodies alike. On this theory
a large quantity of fire would be heavier than a small, and
indeed heavier than a sufficiently small quantity of one of the
heavy elements. Thus absolute lightness is ignored (308 b
3–28).*
   2. *The atomists, recognizing that on any theory similar to
Plato's bulk and weight must increase proportionately, introduced the void. Void enclosed in a body makes it lighter.
But (a) here too absolute lightness is unexplained, and for
practically the same reason. Fire may contain more void
than earth, but a large quantity of fire can contain more solid
body than a small quantity of earth, and this will make it
heavier. Conversely a large quantity of a downward-moving*

34   Τῶν δὴ πρότερον ἐλθόντων ἐπὶ τὴν περὶ τούτων
35 σκέψιν σχεδὸν οἱ πλεῖστοι περὶ τῶν οὕτω βαρέων
καὶ κούφων εἰρήκασι μόνον, ὅσων ἀμφοτέρων
308 b ἐχόντων βάρος θάτερόν ἐστι κουφότερον· οὕτω δὲ

---

¹ οὗ is a conjecture of Prantl, adopted by Stocks and
Allan; Bekker with the mss. has ὅ.

the extremity, " absolutely heavy " to that which
moves downwards and towards the centre. By
" light " and " lighter " in a relative sense we
mean that one of two bodies of the same size, each
possessing weight, whose natural velocity in a
downward direction is exceeded by that of the
other.

CHAPTER II

ARGUMENT (*continued*)

*element can contain more void than a small quantity of fire,
and can therefore be lighter than it. If they argue that it is
the* proportion *of void to solid which matters, how do they
explain the fact that a large quantity of the same substance
performs its natural motion more quickly than a small ?
(b) If void is the cause of motion, the void ought itself to move.
This conception would raise several difficulties, which they
do not discuss* (308 b 28—309 b 28).

*Approaching the matter differently, we may say that all
who assume only one element, or a single pair of opposites,
are in a similar quandary. Monists cannot explain absolute weight and lightness, and a pair of opposites does not
account for the movements of four different bodies—yet that
is a fact demanding notice (this is yet another objection to the
atomists with their void and plenum). A third type of theory,
which makes size the only criterion of distinction between
bodies, is in effect monistic* (309 b 29—310 a 15).

THOSE who up to now have approached these questions have for the most part spoken of weight and
lightness in the relative sense only, as applied to
two bodies, both possessing weight, of which one
is lighter than the other. By this treatment they

διελθόντες οἴονται διωρίσθαι καὶ περὶ τοῦ ἁπλῶς
κούφου καὶ βαρέος· ὁ δὲ λόγος αὐτοῖς οὐκ ἐφαρ-
μόττει. δῆλον δ' ἔσται τοῦτο μᾶλλον προελθοῦσιν.
Λέγουσι γὰρ τὸ κουφότερον καὶ βαρύτερον οἱ
5 μὲν ὥσπερ ἐν τῷ Τιμαίῳ τυγχάνει γεγραμμένον,
βαρύτερον μὲν τὸ ἐκ πλειόνων τῶν αὐτῶν συνεστός,
κουφότερον δὲ τὸ ἐξ ἐλαττόνων, ὥσπερ μολίβδου
μόλιβδος ὁ πλείων βαρύτερος καὶ χαλκοῦ χαλκός.
ὁμοίως δὲ καὶ τῶν ἄλλων τῶν ὁμοειδῶν ἕκαστον·
ἐν ὑπεροχῇ γὰρ τῶν ἴσων μορίων βαρύτερον ἕκα-
10 στόν ἐστιν. τὸν αὐτὸν δὲ τρόπον καὶ ξύλου μόλι-
βδόν φασιν· ἔκ τινων γὰρ τῶν αὐτῶν εἶναι πάντα
τὰ σώματα καὶ μιᾶς ὕλης, ἀλλ' οὐ δοκεῖν. οὕτω
δὴ διωρισμένων οὐκ εἴρηται περὶ τοῦ ἁπλῶς κούφου καὶ βαρέος· νῦν γὰρ τὸ μὲν πῦρ ἀεὶ κοῦφον καὶ
ἄνω φέρεται, ἡ δὲ γῆ καὶ τὰ γεηρὰ πάντα κάτω
15 καὶ πρὸς τὸ μέσον. ὥστ' οὐ δι' ὀλιγότητα τῶν
τριγώνων, ἐξ ὧν συνεστάναι φασὶν ἕκαστον αὐτῶν,
τὸ πῦρ ἄνω φέρεσθαι πέφυκεν· τό τε γὰρ πλεῖον
ἧττον ἂν ἐφέρετο καὶ βαρύτερον ἂν ἦν ἐκ πλειόνων
ὂν τριγώνων. νῦν δὲ φαίνεται τοὐναντίον· ὅσῳ γὰρ
20 ἂν ᾖ πλεῖον, κουφότερόν ἐστι καὶ ἄνω φέρεται
θᾶττον. καὶ ἄνωθεν δὲ κάτω τὸ ὀλίγον οἰσθήσεται
θᾶττον πῦρ, τὸ δὲ πολὺ βραδύτερον. πρὸς δὲ τούτοις, ἐπεὶ τὸ μὲν ἐλάσσω ἔχον τὰ ὁμογενῆ κουφότερον εἶναί φασι, τὸ δὲ πλείω βαρύτερον, ἀέρα
δὲ καὶ ὕδωρ καὶ πῦρ ἐκ τῶν αὐτῶν εἶναι τριγώνων,
25 ἀλλὰ διαφέρειν ὀλιγότητι καὶ πλήθει, διὸ τὸ μὲν

^a 63 c.

imagine that they have adequately explained the terms in their absolute sense also, but their argument cannot be applied to that sense. This will become clear as we proceed.

Some explain relative lightness and weight in the manner which we find described in the *Timaeus*[a] : the heavier is that which is made up of the greater number of identical parts, the lighter that which is made up of fewer, *e.g.* of two pieces of lead or bronze the larger is the heavier. This applies to all homogeneous bodies : relative heaviness consists in an excess of equal parts. Even the fact that lead is heavier than wood is explained by them in the same way, for they argue that, in spite of appearances, all bodies are formed from identical elements, whatever these may be, and from a single matter. Now these definitions tell us nothing about absolute lightness and weight. The fact is that fire is always light and moves upwards, whereas earth and all earthy substances move downwards towards the centre. Therefore the natural upward motion of fire does not depend on the small number of those triangles of which they say every body is composed. If it did, a greater quantity would move less readily and would be heavier, consisting as it does of a larger number of triangles, and this is directly contrary to observation : the greater the quantity of fire, the lighter it is and the quicker it rises, and similarly from above downwards a small quantity can be moved more quickly than a large. Besides, since on their theory that which has fewer similar parts is lighter, and that which has more is heavier, and since air and water and fire are made up of the same triangles, and differ only in the number which

308 b

αὐτῶν εἶναι κουφότερον τὸ δὲ βαρύτερον, ἔσται τι
πλῆθος ἀέρος ὃ βαρύτερον ὕδατος ἔσται. συμβαίνει δὲ πᾶν τοὐναντίον· ἀεί τε γὰρ ὁ πλείων ἀὴρ
ἄνω φέρεται μᾶλλον, καὶ ὅλως ὁτιοῦν μέρος ἀέρος
ἄνω φέρεται ἐκ τοῦ ὕδατος.

Οἱ μὲν οὖν τοῦτον τὸν τρόπον περὶ κούφου καὶ
30 βαρέος διώρισαν· τοῖς δ' οὐχ ἱκανὸν ἔδοξεν οὕτω
διελεῖν, ἀλλὰ καίπερ ὄντες ἀρχαιότεροι τῆς νῦν
ἡλικίας καινοτέρως ἐνόησαν περὶ τῶν νῦν λεχθέν-
των. φαίνεται γὰρ ἔνια τὸν ὄγκον μὲν ἐλάττω
τῶν σωμάτων ὄντα, βαρύτερα δέ. δῆλον οὖν ὡς
οὐχ ἱκανὸν τὸ φάσκειν ἐξ ἴσων συγκεῖσθαι τῶν
35 πρώτων τὰ ἰσοβαρῆ· ἴσα γὰρ ἂν ἦν τὸν ὄγκον.
τὰ δὲ πρῶτα καὶ ἄτομα τοῖς μὲν ἐπίπεδα λέγουσιν
309 a ἐξ ὧν συνέστηκε τὰ βάρος ἔχοντα τῶν σωμάτων,
ἄτοπον τὸ φάναι· τοῖς δὲ στερεὰ μᾶλλον ἐνδέχεται
λέγειν τὸ μεῖζον εἶναι βαρύτερον αὐτῶν. τῶν δὲ
συνθέτων, ἐπειδήπερ οὐ φαίνεται τοῦτον ἔχειν
5 ἕκαστον τὸν τρόπον, ἀλλὰ πολλὰ βαρύτερα ὁρῶμεν
ἐλάττω τὸν ὄγκον ὄντα, καθάπερ ἐρίου χαλκόν,
ἕτερον τὸ αἴτιον οἴονταί τε καὶ λέγουσιν ἔνιοι· τὸ
γὰρ κενὸν ἐμπεριλαμβανόμενον κουφίζειν τὰ σώματά φασι καὶ ποιεῖν ἔστιν ὅτε τὰ μείζω κου-
φότερα· πλεῖον γὰρ ἔχειν κενόν. διὰ τοῦτο γὰρ
καὶ τὸν ὄγκον εἶναι μείζω συγκείμενα πολλάκις
10 ἐξ ἴσων στερεῶν ἢ καὶ ἐλαττόνων. ὅλως δὲ καὶ

ᵃ The suppression of Plato's premises here is extraordinary.
On Plato's definition weight is the natural tendency of bodies
of like nature to come together : a small portion of earth or
fire has an impulse to join the main mass.   On this definition
the upward motion of fire, increasing in velocity in proportion
to the quantity, is explained without recourse to the hypo-

they contain (which thus becomes responsible for making them lighter or heavier), there must be a quantity of air which is heavier than water.[a] But the truth is just the opposite, for the greater a mass of air the easier is its upward motion, and any portion of air whatsoever always rises from water.

That then is one way in which lightness and weight have been defined. But there were others who were not satisfied with the distinction thus drawn. These belonged to an earlier generation than ours, yet their views on our subject were more advanced. It is obvious that there are bodies which are smaller in bulk than others but heavier. Clearly therefore it is insufficient to say that bodies of equal weight contain an equal number of primary parts : otherwise they would have been equal in bulk. The statement is indeed ridiculous from those who postulate surfaces as the primary and indivisible constituents of bodies possessed of weight : those who postulate solids have more right to assert that the larger of them is the heavier. As for compounds, since they obviously do not conform to the rule, but the heavier may often be observed to be smaller (as *e.g.* bronze than wool), a different explanation has been invented and put forward. This is, that bodies are made light by void contained within them,[b] which accounts for the larger bodies sometimes being the lighter—they contain more void. For this reason also they are greater in bulk though they may be composed of the same number of solid particles as another body, or even fewer. In

thesis of absolute lightness, and against it A.'s arguments are pointless.

  [b] For void as the cause of buoyancy *cf. Phys.* iv. 216 b 33 ff.

παντὸς αἴτιον εἶναι τοῦ κουφοτέρου τὸ πλεῖον
ἐνυπάρχειν κενόν. λέγουσι μὲν οὖν τοῦτον τὸν
τρόπον, ἀνάγκη δὲ προσθεῖναι τοῖς οὕτω διορίζουσι μὴ μόνον τὸ κενὸν ἔχειν πλεῖον, ἂν ᾖ κουφότερον, ἀλλὰ καὶ τὸ στερεὸν ἔλαττον· εἰ γὰρ
15 ὑπερέξει τῆς τοιαύτης ἀναλογίας, οὐκ ἔσται κουφότερον. διὰ γὰρ τοῦτο καὶ τὸ πῦρ εἶναί φασι
κουφότατον, ὅτι πλεῖστον ἔχει κενόν. συμβήσεται
οὖν μικροῦ πυρὸς πολὺν χρυσὸν πλεῖον ἔχοντα τὸ
κενὸν εἶναι κουφότερον, εἰ μὴ καὶ στερεὸν ἕξει
πολλαπλάσιον· ὥστε τοῦτο λεκτέον.

Ἔνιοι μὲν οὖν τῶν μὴ φασκόντων εἶναι κενὸν
20 οὐδὲν διώρισαν περὶ κούφου καὶ βαρέος, οἷον
Ἀναξαγόρας καὶ Ἐμπεδοκλῆς· οἱ δὲ διορίσαντες
μέν, οὐ φάσκοντες δὲ εἶναι κενόν, οὐδὲν εἶπον διὰ
τί τὰ μὲν ἁπλῶς κοῦφα τὰ δὲ βαρέα τῶν σωμάτων,
καὶ φέρεται τὰ μὲν ἀεὶ ἄνω τὰ δὲ κάτω. ἔτι δὲ
περὶ τοῦ ἔνια μείζω τὸν ὄγκον ὄντα κουφότερα τῶν
25 ἐλαττόνων εἶναι σωμάτων οὐδὲν ἐπεμνήσθησαν,
οὐδὲ δῆλον πῶς ἐκ τῶν εἰρημένων ὁμολογούμενα
τοῖς φαινομένοις συμβήσεται λέγειν αὐτοῖς. ἀναγκαῖον δὲ καὶ τοῖς περὶ τῆς τοῦ πυρὸς κουφότητος
αἰτιωμένοις τὸ πολὺ κενὸν ἔχειν σχεδὸν ἐν ταῖς
αὐταῖς ἐνέχεσθαι δυσχερείαις. ἔλαττον μὲν γὰρ
30 ἕξει στερεὸν τῶν ἄλλων σωμάτων, καὶ τὸ κενὸν

---

^{a} Stocks translates : " If the ratio of solid to void exceeds
a certain proportion." But the ratio of solid to void has no
place in the argument here, and is introduced as a new consideration at 309 b 8. The only relevant factor at the
moment is the comparative amount of solid in each of two
bodies. " You may say that one has more void than the
other, and is therefore lighter. But the question is, has it

general, the reason for one thing being lighter than another is that there is more void inside it. That is the theory as they put it, but we must add to their explanation that, if the thing is to be lighter, it must contain not only more void but also a smaller quantity of solid body. For if on the latter comparison it is found to exceed,[a] it will not be lighter. For example, they give as the reason for fire being the lightest body, that it contains most void. On this explanation we should find that a large quantity of gold, containing more void than a small quantity of fire, would be lighter—unless we add that it will also contain many times the amount of solid body. This therefore should be stated.

Those therefore who deny the existence of void have either offered no explanation of lightness and weight (*e.g.* Anaxagoras and Empedocles), or, if they did explain them, but clung to the denial of void, have given no reason why bodies should be *absolutely* light or heavy, *i.e.* should always move upwards or downwards respectively. They also neglected the question raised by the existence of bodies greater in bulk than others but lighter than the smaller, and it is hard to tell from what they say how their theories can be reconciled with appearances. Those on the other hand who speak of the lightness of fire as being caused by the larger amount of void in it cannot escape falling into practically the same difficulties. It may contain less solid and more void than other bodies, but

at the same time less solid ? You cannot leave out the other half of the comparison." (*Cf.* lines 30-32 below.) No doubt ἀναλογία means ratio or proportion rather than comparison, but the relation in question is that between the solid in *x* and the solid in *y*, not between the solid and the void in *x* or *y*.

309 a
πλεῖον· ἀλλ' ὅμως ἔσται τι πυρὸς πλῆθος ἐν ᾧ τὸ
στερεὸν καὶ τὸ πλῆρες ὑπερβάλλει τῶν περιεχο-
μένων στερεῶν ἔν τινι μικρῷ πλήθει γῆς. ἐὰν δὲ
φῶσι καὶ τὸ κενόν, πῶς διοριοῦσι τὸ ἁπλῶς βαρύ;
ἢ γὰρ τῷ πλεῖον στερεὸν ἔχειν ἢ τῷ ἔλαττον κενόν.

309 b
εἰ μὲν οὖν τοῦτο φήσουσιν, ἔσται τι πλῆθος γῆς
οὕτως ὀλίγον ἐν ᾧ στερεὸν ἔσται ἔλαττον ἢ ἐν
πολλῷ πλήθει πυρός. ὁμοίως δὲ κἂν τῷ κενῷ
διορίσωσιν, ἔσται τι κουφότερον τοῦ ἁπλῶς κούφου
καὶ φερομένου ἀεὶ ἄνω αὐτὸ φερόμενον ἀεὶ κάτω.
5 τοῦτο δὲ ἀδύνατον· τὸ γὰρ ἁπλῶς κοῦφον ἀεὶ κουφότερον τῶν ἐχόντων βάρος καὶ κάτω φερομένων,
τὸ δὲ κουφότερον οὐκ ἀεὶ κοῦφον διὰ τὸ λέγεσθαι
καὶ ἐν τοῖς ἔχουσι βάρος ἕτερον ἑτέρου κουφότερον,
οἷον γῆς ὕδωρ. ἀλλὰ μὴν οὐδὲ τῷ τὸ κενὸν ἀνάλογον ἔχειν πρὸς τὸ πλῆρες ἱκανὸν λῦσαι τὴν λεγο-
10 μένην νῦν ἀπορίαν. συμβήσεται γὰρ καὶ τοῦτον
τὸν τρόπον λέγουσιν ὡσαύτως τὸ ἀδύνατον. ἐν
γὰρ τῷ πλεῖονι πυρὶ καὶ ἐν τῷ ἐλάττονι τὸν αὐτὸν
ἕξει λόγον τὸ στερεὸν πρὸς τὸ κενόν. φέρεται δέ
γε θᾶττον τὸ πλεῖον ἄνω πῦρ τοῦ ἐλάττονος, καὶ
κάτω δὲ πάλιν ὡσαύτως ὁ πλείων χρυσὸς καὶ ὁ
15 μόλιβδος· ὁμοίως δὲ καὶ τῶν ἄλλων ἕκαστον τῶν
ἐχόντων βάρος. οὐκ ἔδει δὲ τοῦτο συμβαίνειν,
εἴπερ τούτῳ διώρισται τὸ βαρὺ καὶ κοῦφον. ἄτοπον δὲ καὶ εἰ διὰ τὸ κενὸν μὲν ἄνω φέρονται, τὸ
δὲ κενὸν αὐτὸ μή. ἀλλὰ μὴν εἴ γε τὸ μὲν κενὸν
ἄνω πέφυκε φέρεσθαι, κάτω δὲ τὸ πλῆρες, καὶ διὰ

nevertheless there must exist a quantity of fire in which the solid and full portion exceeds the solid parts contained in a given small quantity of earth. If they reply that there is an excess of void also, how are they going to explain absolute weight? It must be due either to excess of solid or to defect of void. If this is their answer, there must exist a quantity of earth so small that it contains less solid than a large quantity of fire. Or similarly if they choose to define it with reference to the void, there will exist a body lighter than that which is absolutely light and always moves upwards, though this body itself move always downwards. But this is impossible. That which is light in the absolute sense must always be lighter than bodies which have weight and move downwards (though that which is relatively light need not be absolutely so, owing to the habit of calling one body lighter than another even among those which have weight, *e.g.* calling water *lighter* than earth). It does not help towards the solution of this difficulty to invoke the ratio between void and solid. Even when they speak in these terms they are faced with the same impossibility. A large and a small quantity of fire will contain void and solid in the same proportions, yet the large quantity moves upwards more quickly than the small. Similarly a larger quantity of gold or lead moves downwards faster than a smaller, and so with all heavy bodies. But this ought not to happen if the difference between heavy and light were what they assert. It is also surprising if void is the cause of upward motion in bodies, but does not move itself. If on the other hand it is the nature of void to move upwards, and of

20 τοῦτο τοῖς ἄλλοις αἴτια τῆς φορᾶς ἑκατέρας, οὐθὲν
περὶ τῶν συνθέτων ἔδει σκοπεῖν διὰ τί τὰ μὲν
κοῦφα τὰ δὲ βαρέα τῶν σωμάτων, ἀλλὰ περὶ τούτων αὐτῶν εἰπεῖν διὰ τί τὸ μὲν κοῦφον, τὸ δ' ἔχει
βάρος, ἔτι δὲ τί τὸ αἴτιον τοῦ μὴ διεστάναι τὸ
πλῆρες καὶ τὸ κενόν. ἄλογον δὲ καὶ τὸ χώραν τῷ
25 κενῷ ποιεῖν, ὥσπερ οὐκ αὐτὸ¹ χώραν τινὰ οὖσαν·
ἀναγκαῖον δ', εἴπερ κινεῖται τὸ κενόν, εἶναι αὐτοῦ
τινὰ τόπον, ἐξ οὗ μεταβάλλει καὶ εἰς ὄν. πρὸς δὲ
τούτοις τί τῆς κινήσεως αἴτιον; οὐ γὰρ δὴ τό γε
κενόν· οὐ γὰρ αὐτὸ κινεῖται μόνον, ἀλλὰ καὶ τὸ
στερεόν.

Ὡσαύτως δὲ συμβαίνει κἄν τις ἄλλως διορίζῃ,
30 μεγέθει καὶ σμικρότητι ποιῶν βαρύτερα καὶ κουφότερα θάτερα τῶν ἑτέρων, καὶ ἄλλον ὀντινοῦν
τρόπον κατασκευάζων, μόνον δὲ τὴν αὐτὴν ὕλην
ἅπασιν ἀποδιδούς, ἢ πλείους μὲν ὑπεναντίας δὲ
μόνον. μιᾶς μὲν γὰρ οὔσης οὐκ ἔσται τὸ ἁπλῶς
βαρὺ καὶ κοῦφον, ὥσπερ τοῖς ἐκ τῶν τριγώνων
310 a συνιστᾶσιν· ἐναντίας δέ, καθάπερ οἱ τὸ κενὸν καὶ
πλῆρες, οὐκ ἔσται τὰ μεταξὺ τῶν ἁπλῶς βαρέων
καὶ κούφων διὰ τίν' αἰτίαν βαρύτερα καὶ κουφότερα
ἀλλήλων καὶ τῶν ἁπλῶν ἐστίν. τὸ δὲ μεγέθει καὶ
5 μικρότητι διορίζειν πεπλασμένῳ μὲν ἔοικε μᾶλλον
τῶν πρότερον, ὅτι δ' ἐνδέχεται καθ' ἕκαστον ποιεῖν

---

¹ αὐτό. So Stocks and Allan, with all mss. but L. αὐτῷ
L, Bekker.

ᵃ i.e. water and air. There are four bodies to be accounted
for (since all show diversity of movement), and a theory which
assumes only a single pair of opposites as elementary cannot
explain the behaviour of more than two.

a plenum to move downwards, and that is why they are respectively the causes of these motions in others, the question demanding attention was not concerned with concrete objects, or the reason why some bodies are light and others heavy, but rather with these two, plenum and void, why one of them should be light and the other possess weight, and why, further, they are not completely separate. Besides, it is illogical to make a space for the void, as if it were not itself a space ; yet if it moves, it must have a place into which and out of which to move. Moreover what would be the general cause of motion ? It certainly cannot be the void, for not only the void is in motion but also the solid.

The same difficulties confront those who draw the distinction differently, attributing the relative weight and lightness of bodies to greatness and smallness, or perhaps accounting for it in some other way, but in any case assuming that there is only one and the same matter for all, or if more than one, then simply a pair of opposites. (a) If the matter is single, as with those who compose things of triangles, there cannot be absolute weight and lightness. (b) If it consists of opposites like void and plenum, there is no reason for the weight and lightness of the bodies intermediate between the absolutely heavy and light *a*—relatively either to each other or to the absolutes themselves. (c) The view which makes greatness and smallness the criterion of distinction *b* is harder to believe in than those we have just mentioned, although it

b This apparently does not refer to Plato's triangles of different sizes, but to theories of condensation and rarefaction. So Simpl.

310 a

διαφορὰν τῶν τεττάρων στοιχείων, ἀσφαλεστέρως
ἔχει πρὸς τὰς ἔμπροσθεν ἀπορίας. τῷ δὲ μίαν
ποιεῖν¹ φύσιν τῶν τῷ μεγέθει διαφερόντων ἀναγκαῖον ταὐτὸν συμβαίνειν τοῖς μίαν ποιοῦσιν ὕλην,
καὶ μήθ᾽ ἁπλῶς εἶναι μηθὲν κοῦφον μήτε φερόμενον
10 ἄνω, ἀλλ᾽ ἢ ὑστερίζον ἢ ἐκθλιβόμενον, καὶ πολλὰ
μικρὰ ὀλίγων μεγάλων βαρύτερα εἶναι. εἰ δὲ
τοῦτο ἔσται, συμβήσεται πολὺν ἀέρα καὶ πολὺ πῦρ
ὕδατος εἶναι βαρύτερα καὶ γῆς ὀλίγης. τοῦτο δ᾽
ἐστὶν ἀδύνατον.

Τὰ μὲν οὖν παρὰ τῶν ἄλλων εἰρημένα ταῦτα,
15 καὶ τοῦτον λέγεται τὸν τρόπον.

¹ τῷ . . . ποιεῖν EL, Prantl, Stocks, Allan; τῷ . . .
ποιοῦντι JHM and later hand of E; τὸ . . . ποιεῖν F, Bekker.
The paraphrase of Simpl. suggests that he read τῷ . . . ποιεῖν.

CHAPTER III

ARGUMENT

The true meaning of weight and lightness.

*Weight and lightness are a tendency exhibited by bodies to
move downwards or upwards respectively. The reason for
this tendency is that each of the four elements has its own
proper place in the world, and therefore a natural tendency to move towards that place. This local motion of the
elements must be defined as analogous to all other kinds of
motion and change, namely as the actualization of a potency
(Phys. viii. 257 b 8). The light and the heavy, as such, do not
exist in actuality (have not fully realized their form) until
they have passed upwards or downwards to their proper
places. In one respect bodies subject only to locomotion seem
to differ from those undergoing other kinds of change, namely*

can distinguish between all four elements and therefore is better safeguarded against those particular
difficulties. But the result of imagining that things
have a single nature, and differ in size, must be to
put one in the same position as those who assume
a single matter : nothing will be absolutely light
nor move upward, except in the sense of being
left behind or by being squeezed out,[a] and many
small bodies will be heavier than a few large. This
means that a large quantity of air or fire will be
heavier than a small quantity of water or earth,
which is impossible.

These, then, are the views of others, and the
terms in which they speak.

[a] In the first case it is illusory—all things are moving
downwards but some more slowly than others—in the
second it is unnatural.

CHAPTER III

ARGUMENT (*continued*)

*that they appear to have the cause of their motion wholly
within themselves. This is because these bodies are more
fully formed than the others—locomotion is the final stage of
actualization. But* (i) *other changing bodies also appear
sometimes to need little or no external stimulation,* (ii) *strictly
speaking there is an external cause for all motion, even that
of the elements, either essential* (*the agent which first made
them heavy or light*) *or accidental* (*the remover of a hindrance
to their natural motion, the surface off which they may re-
bound and so have their direction influenced*). (*For fuller
description and examples of these external causes, see* Phys.
viii. 4, 255 b 24—256 a 3.)

310 a 16 Ἡμεῖς δὲ λέγομεν πρῶτον διορίσαντες περὶ οὗ
μάλιστα ἀποροῦσί τινες, διὰ τί τὰ μὲν ἄνω φέρεται
τὰ δὲ κάτω τῶν σωμάτων ἀεὶ κατὰ φύσιν, τὰ δὲ
καὶ ἄνω καὶ κάτω, μετὰ δὲ ταῦτα περὶ βαρέος καὶ
20 κούφου καὶ τῶν συμβαινόντων περὶ αὐτὰ παθημάτων, διὰ τίν᾽ αἰτίαν ἕκαστον γίνεται.

Περὶ μὲν οὖν τοῦ φέρεσθαι εἰς τὸν αὑτοῦ τόπον
ἕκαστον ὁμοίως ὑποληπτέον ὥσπερ καὶ περὶ τὰς
ἄλλας γενέσεις καὶ μεταβολάς. ἐπεὶ γάρ εἰσι τρεῖς
αἱ κινήσεις, ἡ μὲν κατὰ μέγεθος, ἡ δὲ κατ᾽ εἶδος,
25 ἡ δὲ κατὰ τόπον, ἐν ἑκάστῃ τούτων τὴν μεταβολὴν
ὁρῶμεν γινομένην ἐκ τῶν ἐναντίων εἰς τὰ ἐναντία
καὶ τὰ μεταξύ, καὶ οὐκ εἰς τὸ τυχὸν τῷ τυχόντι
μεταβολὴν οὖσαν· ὁμοίως δὲ οὐδὲ κινητικὸν τὸ
τυχὸν τοῦ τυχόντος, ἀλλ᾽ ὥσπερ τὸ ἀλλοιωτὸν καὶ
τὸ αὐξητὸν ἕτερον, οὕτω καὶ τὸ ἀλλοιωτικὸν καὶ τὸ
30 αὐξητικόν. τὸν αὐτὸν δὴ τρόπον ὑποληπτέον καὶ
τὸ κατὰ τόπον κινητικὸν καὶ κινητὸν οὐ τὸ τυχὸν
εἶναι τοῦ τυχόντος. εἰ οὖν εἰς τὸ ἄνω καὶ τὸ κάτω
κινητικὸν μὲν τὸ βαρυντικὸν καὶ τὸ κουφιστικόν,
κινητὸν δὲ τὸ δυνάμει βαρὺ καὶ κοῦφον, τὸ δ᾽ εἰς
τὸν αὑτοῦ τόπον φέρεσθαι ἕκαστον τὸ εἰς τὸ αὑτοῦ
310 b εἶδός ἐστι φέρεσθαι (καὶ ταύτῃ μᾶλλον ἄν τις ὑπολάβοι ὃ ἔλεγον οἱ ἀρχαῖοι, ὅτι τὸ ὅμοιον φέροιτο
πρὸς τὸ ὅμοιον. τοῦτο γὰρ οὐ συμβαίνει πάντως·
οὐ γὰρ ἐάν τις μεταθῇ τὴν γῆν οὗ νῦν ἡ σελήνη,
οἰσθήσεται τῶν μορίων ἕκαστον πρὸς αὐτήν, ἀλλ᾽

OUR own account starts from the determination
of a question which some thinkers have found
especially baffling, namely, why some bodies always
and naturally move upwards and others downwards,
and others both upwards and downwards, and turns
then to the subject of weight and lightness, the
properties and affections connected with them, and
their several causes.

The motion of a thing towards its proper place
must be regarded as analogous to other forms of
generation and change. There are three forms of
motion, change of size, change of form, and change
of place, and in each one the change may be observed to proceed from opposites to opposites (or
intermediate states). A thing does not change at
random into anything else whatsoever. Similarly, any
and every mover cannot affect any and every object,
but just as what is capable of alteration is different
from what is capable of growth, so is the cause of
alteration different from the cause of growth. In the
same way with locomotion we must suppose that
there is no mere chance relationship between
mover and moved. We may say, then, that the
cause of motion upwards and downwards is equivalent to that which makes heavy or light, and the
object of such motion is the potentially heavy or
light, and motion towards its proper place is for
each thing motion towards its proper form. (This
is the best way of taking the old saying that "like
moves to like," for it is not a statement that is
true in every sense. If the earth were removed
to where the moon is now, separate parts of it
would not move towards the whole, but towards
the place where the whole is now. In general it

5 ὅπου περ καὶ νῦν. ὅλως μὲν οὖν τοῖς ὁμοίοις καὶ
ἀδιαφόροις ὑπὸ τῆς αὐτῆς κινήσεως ἀνάγκη τοῦτο
συμβαίνειν, ὥσθ' ὅπου πέφυκεν ἕν τι φέρεσθαι
μόριον, καὶ τὸ πᾶν. ἐπεὶ δ' ὁ τόπος ἐστὶ τὸ τοῦ
περιέχοντος πέρας, περιέχει δὲ πάντα τὰ κινούμενα
ἄνω καὶ κάτω τό τε ἔσχατον καὶ τὸ μέσον, τοῦτο
10 δὲ τρόπον τινὰ γίγνεται τὸ εἶδος τοῦ περιεχομένου,
τὸ εἰς τὸν αὑτοῦ τόπον φέρεσθαι πρὸς τὸ ὅμοιόν
ἐστι φέρεσθαι· τὰ γὰρ ἐφεξῆς[1] ὅμοιά ἐστιν ἀλλήλοις, οἷον ὕδωρ ἀέρι καὶ ἀὴρ πυρί. ἀνάπαλιν δὲ
λέγειν τοῖς μὲν μέσοις ἔστι, τοῖς δ' ἄκροις οὔ, οἷον
ἀέρα μὲν ὕδατι, ὕδωρ δὲ γῇ· ἀεὶ γὰρ τὸ ἀνώτερον
15 πρὸς τὸ ὑφ' αὑτό, ὡς εἶδος πρὸς ὕλην, οὕτως ἔχει
πρὸς ἄλληλα), τὸ δὲ ζητεῖν διὰ τί φέρεται τὸ πῦρ
ἄνω καὶ ἡ γῆ κάτω, τὸ αὐτό ἐστι καὶ διὰ τί τὸ
ὑγιαστὸν ἂν κινῆται καὶ μεταβάλλῃ ᾗ ὑγιαστόν, εἰς

---

[1] ἐφεξῆς is the reading of all mss. save the first hand of E
(which has ἑξῆς), and also of Simpl. Stocks refers also to
De gen. et corr. 331 b 4, 26, 34. ἑξῆς Bekker.

---

[a] *i.e.* " Though we have just spoken of water as like air,
we may equally well say that air is like water. On the
other hand we must always say ' water is like earth,' not
' earth is like water.' "

[b] Lines 11-15. The thought of this artificial and obscure
addition seems to be this. " Like " is used to mean " given
its form by," as hinted at in the previous sentence. The
extreme bodies, fire and earth, receive their form from the
boundaries which enclose them. Hence movement to their
proper places may be described as movement to their " like."
But what, A. now asks, of the intermediate bodies, air and
water ? These receive their form from the contiguity of fire
and earth, and only indirectly from the " boundaries."
Hence we may say that air is like fire, or water like earth,
but not *vice versa*, because fire and earth do not take their

must be true of bodies which are similar and un-differentiated and subject to the same motion that the place towards which any one part naturally moves is the place for the whole. And since " the place " means the boundary of that which encloses it, and the boundaries of all bodies which move upwards and downwards are the extremity and the centre, which in a way constitute the form of the body they enclose, it follows that to move towards its own place is to move towards its like. For the bodies which lie next to one another are alike, *e.g.* water to air and air to fire. Between the intermediate bodies the relation may be con-verted, but not where the extremes are concerned : air is like water, water like earth.*a* The relation-ship between bodies is that the upper one stands to that which lies under it as form to matter.)*b* It follows therefore that to ask the reason why fire moves upwards and earth downwards is the same as asking why the curable, when moved and changed *qua* curable, progresses towards health and not to-

form from air and water. The last clause is confusing, see-ing that earth, which is lower than water, yet gives it its form. Besides the upward matter-to-form series of water, air, fire, there must also be a downward series of air, water, earth. Alex., taking the last sentence as it stands, supposed water to be formative in relation to earth, but this cannot be A.'s meaning here, since centre and circumference are both stated to be equally formative. Yet the argument is isolated and unsatisfactory, and the clause ἀεὶ γὰρ τὸ ἀνώτερον κτλ. is probably influenced by what was A.'s real belief, that the upper part of the Universe, the region of fire, and, still further up, of *aither*, stood for form, perfection, " honourableness " etc., and the lower part for the reverse. This is borne out by many of his remarks on the first body in book i., and also about fire (*e.g. De gen. et corr.* 335 a 18). *Cf.* esp. the next chapter, 312 a 15 f.

310 b

ὑγίειαν ἔρχεται ἀλλ' οὐκ εἰς λευκότητα. ὁμοίως
20 δὲ καὶ τἆλλα πάντα τὰ ἀλλοιωτά. ἀλλὰ μὴν καὶ
τὸ αὐξητὸν ὅταν μεταβάλλῃ ᾖ αὐξητόν, οὐκ
εἰς ὑγίειαν ἔρχεται ἀλλ' εἰς μεγέθους ὑπεροχήν.
ὁμοίως δὲ καὶ τούτων ἕκαστον τὸ μὲν ἐν τῷ ποιῷ
τὸ δ' ἐν τῷ ποσῷ μεταβάλλει, καὶ ἐν τόπῳ τὰ μὲν
κοῦφα ἄνω τὰ δὲ βαρέα κάτω· πλὴν ὅτι τὰ μὲν ἐν
25 αὑτοῖς δοκεῖ ἔχειν ἀρχὴν τῆς μεταβολῆς (λέγω δὲ
τὸ βαρὺ καὶ τὸ κοῦφον), τὰ δ' οὔ, ἀλλ' ἔξωθεν, οἷον
τὸ ὑγιαστὸν καὶ τὸ αὐξητόν. καίτοι ἐνίοτε καὶ
ταῦτα ἐξ αὑτῶν μεταβάλλει, καὶ μικρᾶς γενομένης
ἐν τοῖς ἔξω κινήσεως τὸ μὲν εἰς ὑγίειαν ἔρχεται τὸ
δ' εἰς αὔξην· καὶ ἐπεὶ ταὐτὸν τὸ ὑγιαστὸν καὶ τὸ
30 νόσου δεκτικόν, ἐὰν μὲν κινηθῇ ᾖ ὑγιαστόν, εἰς
ὑγίειαν φέρεται, ἐὰν δ' ᾖ νοσερόν, εἰς νόσον. μᾶλλον δὲ τὸ βαρὺ καὶ τὸ κοῦφον τούτων ἐν ἑαυτοῖς
ἔχειν φαίνεται τὴν ἀρχὴν διὰ τὸ ἐγγύτατα τῆς
οὐσίας εἶναι τὴν τούτων ὕλην· σημεῖον δ' ὅτι ἡ
φορὰ ἀπολελυμένων ἐστί, καὶ γενέσει ὑστάτη τῶν
311 a κινήσεων, ὥστε πρώτη ἂν εἴη κατὰ τὴν οὐσίαν
αὕτη κίνησις. ὅταν μὲν οὖν γίγνηται ἐξ ὕδατος ἀὴρ
καὶ ἐκ βαρέος κοῦφον, ἔρχεται εἰς τὸ ἄνω. ἅμα δ'
ἐστὶ κοῦφον, καὶ οὐκέτι γίνεται, ἀλλ' ἐκεῖ ἔστιν.[1]
φανερὸν δὴ ὅτι δυνάμει ὄν, εἰς ἐντελέχειαν ἰὸν
5 ἔρχεται ἐκεῖ καὶ εἰς τοσοῦτον καὶ τοιοῦτον, οὗ ἡ
ἐντελέχεια καὶ ὅσου καὶ οἵου [καὶ ὅπου].[2] τὸ δ'
αὐτὸ αἴτιον καὶ τοῦ ἤδη ὑπάρχοντα καὶ ὄντα γῆν

---

[1] ἔστιν Stocks, Allan; ἐστίν with the mss. Bekker.
[2] καὶ ὅπου om. F, Stocks, Allan. The words are only an
unintelligible repetition of οὗ in line 5, of which the paraphrase
of Simpl. naturally shows no trace.

---

[a] A fundamental Aristotelian tenet, often repeated, *e.g.*

wards whiteness. All other subjects of alteration are similarly consistent. Again, whatever is capable of growth, when it changes in virtue of this capacity, progresses not towards health but towards increase of size. So it is with everything : one changes within the category of quality, another in that of quantity, and other things again—to wit, the light and the heavy—in place, moving upwards and downwards respectively. The only difference is that the last-named appear to contain within themselves the principle of change, but the others, such as the curable and the growing, to be changed from outside. Yet on occasion these too change of themselves, and proceed towards health or growth upon a small movement in the outside world. And since the same thing is curable and receptive of disease, it may be moved to health *qua* curable or to disease *qua* susceptible to disease. But the heavy and light seem to contain in a fuller sense than these their own principle of motion because their matter is nearest to perfected being. It is evidence of this that locomotion is a property of independent entities, and comes last of the forms of motion in order of generation. Such motion, therefore, must be primary in order of being.[a] Now whenever air is generated from water, a light thing from a heavy, it progresses to the upper region. Once arrived, it is light—no longer " becomes," but " is." Clearly then it is moving from potentiality to actuality, and that means attaining the place, quantity and quality proper to its actual state. It is for the same reason that

Met. 1050 a 4 τὰ τῇ γενέσει ὕστερα τῷ εἴδει καὶ τῇ οὐσίᾳ πρότερα.

311 a

καὶ πῦρ κινεῖσθαι εἰς τοὺς αὑτῶν τόπους μηδενὸς
ἐμποδίζοντος. καὶ γὰρ ἡ τροφή, ὅταν τὸ κωλῦον,
καὶ τὸ ὑγιαστόν, ὅταν τὸ ἐπίσχον μὴ ᾖ, φέρεται
10 εὐθύς. καὶ κινεῖ δὲ τό τε ἐξ ἀρχῆς ποιῆσαν καὶ τὸ
ὑποσπάσαν ἢ ὅθεν ἀπεπήδησεν, καθάπερ εἴρηται ἐν
τοῖς πρώτοις λόγοις, ἐν οἷς διωρίζομεν ὅτι οὐθὲν
τούτων αὐτὸ ἑαυτὸ κινεῖ.

Διὰ τίνα μὲν οὖν αἰτίαν φέρεται τῶν φερομένων
ἕκαστον, καὶ τὸ φέρεσθαι εἰς τὸν αὑτοῦ τόπον τί
ἐστιν, εἴρηται.

CHAPTER IV

ARGUMENT

The distinctive properties of the four elements, with
reference to weight and lightness.

Definitions.—*Fire and earth are absolutely light and
heavy, which means that nothing naturally rises above fire or
sinks below earth. Air and water are relatively so, being
heavier than fire but lighter than earth, but in relation to each
other are absolutely heavy and light, i.e. a small quantity of
water will always sink through a large quantity of air. The
behaviour of composite bodies is determined by the nature of
their elements* (311 a 15–b 13).

*All philosophers agree on the existence of an absolutely
heavy, but not all admit the existence of an absolutely light
body. Yet this must exist too, if " heavy " means moving to
the centre. The centre is determined, and so therefore must
the outer extremity be. Seeing then that there is a body,
namely fire, which can be observed to rise to the top of everything else, it must be moving towards the extremity, and this
is what is meant by absolutely light. (The determinate nature
of the centre is undoubted because* (a) *no body can continue*

16 Τὰς δὲ διαφορὰς καὶ τὰ συμβαίνοντα περὶ αὐτὰ

what already is and exists as earth or fire moves towards its own place unless something prevents it. So too nutriment and the curable, when there is nothing to clog or hinder, enter at once on their motion. Yet motion is also caused by the primary agent and by that which removed the hindrance or off which the thing rebounded, as was said in our early discussions, where we tried to show that none of these things moves itself.[a]

We have now explained the reason for the movement of each moving body, and what is meant by the movement of a body to its own place.

CHAPTER IV

ARGUMENT (continued)

moving to infinity, (b) falling bodies move towards the earth at similar angles to it.) (311 b 13—312 a 8.)

Just as there is a space between the two opposite boundaries of centre and extremity, which is above the one and below the other, so there is body to fill it which is both heavy and light. This is the explanation of air and water, heavy in relation to fire but light in relation to earth (312 a 8-12).

If we relate the antithesis of light and heavy to the antithesis of form and matter, the lighter, upper body will be more akin to form and the heavier and lower to matter. The same matter may have the potentiality of being both light and heavy, just as the same matter may have the potentiality of health and disease. The two potentialities must be kept logically distinct, as the actualities are in fact distinct (312 a 12-21).

WE must now speak of their individual differences

[a] *Phys.* viii. 4, 254 b 33—256 a 3. The fuller account there given throws light on this compressed sentence.

311 a

νῦν λέγωμεν. πρῶτον μὲν οὖν διωρίσθω, καθάπερ
φαίνεται πᾶσι, βαρὺ μὲν ἁπλῶς τὸ πᾶσιν ὑφιστάμενον, κοῦφον δὲ τὸ πᾶσιν ἐπιπολάζον. ἁπλῶς δὲ
λέγω εἴς τε τὸ γένος βλέπων, καὶ ὅσοις μὴ ἀμ-
20 φότερα ὑπάρχει· οἷον φαίνεται πυρὸς μὲν τὸ τυχὸν
μέγεθος ἄνω φερόμενον, ἐὰν μή τι τύχῃ κωλῦον
ἕτερον, γῆς δὲ κάτω· τὸν αὐτὸν δὲ τρόπον καὶ
θᾶττον τὸ πλεῖον. ἄλλως δὲ βαρὺ καὶ κοῦφον, οἷς
ἀμφότερα ὑπάρχει· καὶ γὰρ ἐπιπολάζουσί τισι καὶ
ὑφίστανται, καθάπερ ἀὴρ καὶ ὕδωρ· ἁπλῶς μὲν γὰρ
25 οὐδέτερον τούτων κοῦφον ἢ βαρύ· γῆς μὲν γὰρ
ἄμφω κουφότερα (ἐπιπολάζει γὰρ αὐτῇ τὸ τυχὸν
αὐτῶν μόριον), πυρὸς δὲ βαρύτερα (ὑφίσταται γὰρ
αὐτῶν ὁπόσον ἂν ᾖ μόριον), πρὸς ἑαυτὰ δὲ ἁπλῶς
τὸ μὲν βαρὺ τὸ δὲ κοῦφον· ἀὴρ μὲν γὰρ ὁπόσος ἂν
ᾖ, ἐπιπολάζει ὕδατι, ὕδωρ δὲ ὁπόσον ἂν ᾖ, ἀέρι
ὑφίσταται.

30 Ἐπεὶ δὲ καὶ τῶν ἄλλων τὰ μὲν ἔχει βάρος τὰ
δὲ κουφότητα, δῆλον ὅτι τούτων μὲν αἰτία πάντων ἡ ἐν τοῖς ἀσυνθέτοις διαφορά· κατὰ γὰρ τὸ
ἐκείνων τετυχηκέναι τοῦ μὲν πλεῖον τοῦ δ' ἔλαττον,
ἔσται τὰ μὲν κοῦφα τὰ δὲ βαρέα τῶν σωμάτων.
ὥστε περὶ ἐκείνων λεκτέον· τἆλλα γὰρ ἀκολουθεῖ
35 τοῖς πρώτοις, ὅπερ ἔφαμεν χρῆναι ποιεῖν καὶ τοὺς
311 b διὰ τὸ πλῆρες τὸ βαρὺ λέγοντας καὶ διὰ τὸ κενὸν
τὸ κοῦφον. συμβαίνει δὴ μὴ πανταχοῦ ταὐτὰ
βαρέα δοκεῖν εἶναι καὶ κοῦφα διὰ τὴν τῶν πρώ-

and the properties which follow from their nature. First then let us state that, as everyone would agree, " absolutely heavy " applies to that which sinks below everything else, " absolutely light " to that which rises to the top of everything else. When I say " absolutely " I am thinking of the nature of the heavy or light as such, and excluding bodies which possess both weight and lightness. For instance, any chance portion of fire moves upwards, and of earth downwards, if nothing else gets in the way, and a larger portion moves more quickly with the same motion. Bodies which possess both contraries are heavy and light in another sense, rising to the top of some and sinking beneath others. Such are air and water, neither of which is absolutely light or heavy. Both are lighter than earth (*i.e.* any portion of them seeks the top of it), but heavier than fire (*i.e.* a portion of them, whatever its size, sinks beneath it). But in relation to each other they are absolutely heavy and light respectively, *i.e.* air, in whatever quantity, rises to the top of water, and water, in whatever quantity, sinks to the bottom of air.

Other bodies too are heavy or light, and it is clear that in every case the cause is a difference in the simple components, *i.e.* bodies will be light or heavy according to the amount of this or that element which they contain. It is to the elements, therefore, that our discussion should be confined, for on these primary bodies the others depend, and should have been made to depend (as we pointed out) in those theories which attribute weight to plenum and lightness to void. Thus the fact that the same bodies do not appear to be heavy (or

τῶν διαφοράν· λέγω δ' οἷον ἐν μὲν ἀέρι βαρύτερον ἔσται ταλαντιαῖον ξύλον μολίβδου μναϊαίου,
5 ἐν δὲ ὕδατι κουφότερον· αἴτιον δ' ὅτι πάντα βάρος
ἔχει πλὴν πυρὸς καὶ κουφότητα πλὴν γῆς. γῆν μὲν
οὖν καὶ ὅσα γῆς ἔχει πλεῖστον, πανταχοῦ βάρος
ἔχειν ἀναγκαῖον, ὕδωρ δὲ πανταχοῦ πλὴν ἐν γῇ,
ἀέρα δὲ πλὴν ἐν ὕδατι καὶ γῇ· ἐν τῇ αὑτοῦ γὰρ
χώρᾳ πάντα βάρος ἔχει πλὴν πυρός, καὶ ὁ ἀήρ.
10 σημεῖον δ' ὅτι ἕλκει πλεῖον ὁ πεφυσημένος ἀσκὸς
τοῦ κενοῦ· ὥστ' εἴ τι ἀέρος ἔχει πλεῖον ἢ γῆς καὶ
ὕδατος, ἐν μὲν ὕδατι ἐνδέχεται κουφότερον εἶναι
τινός, ἐν δὲ ἀέρι βαρύτερον· ἀέρι μὲν γὰρ οὐκ ἐπιπολάζει, τῷ δὲ ὕδατι ἐπιπολάζει.

Ὅτι δ' ἔστι τι ἁπλῶς κοῦφον καὶ ἁπλῶς βαρύ,
15 ἐκ τῶνδ' ἐστὶ φανερόν. λέγω δ' ἁπλῶς κοῦφον ὃ
ἀεὶ ἄνω καὶ βαρὺ ὃ ἀεὶ κάτω πέφυκε φέρεσθαι μὴ
κωλυόμενον· τοιαῦτα γάρ ἐστί τινα, καὶ οὐχ ὥσπερ
οἴονταί τινες πάντ' ἔχειν βάρος· βαρὺ μὲν γὰρ δοκεῖ
τισὶν εἶναι καὶ ἑτέροις, καὶ ἀεὶ φέρεσθαι πρὸς τὸ
μέσον. ἔστι δ' ὁμοίως καὶ τὸ κοῦφον. ὁρῶμεν
20 γάρ, καθάπερ εἴρηται πρότερον, ὅτι τὰ γεηρὰ πᾶσιν
ὑφίσταται καὶ φέρεται πρὸς τὸ μέσον. ἀλλὰ μὴν
ὥρισται τὸ μέσον. εἰ τοίνυν ἔστι τι ὃ πᾶσιν ἐπιπολάζει, καθάπερ φαίνεται τὸ πῦρ καὶ ἐν αὐτῷ τῷ
ἀέρι ἄνω φερόμενον, ὁ δ' ἀὴρ ἡσυχάζων, δῆλον ὅτι

---

^a Sc. and therefore the opposite boundary must be deter-
mined also.

light) in every place is to be explained by differences in the primary bodies. In air, for instance,
a talent of wood is heavier than a mina of lead,
but in water it is lighter. The explanation is that
all bodies possess weight except fire, and all possess
lightness except earth. Earth, therefore, and those
bodies which contain most earth, must everywhere
be heavy, water everywhere save in earth, air save
in water or earth; for in its own place every body
has weight except fire, even air. It is proof of this
that an inflated bladder weighs more than an empty
one, showing that if anything contains more air
than earth and water, it may be lighter than something else in water but heavier in air; for it rises
to the top of water, but not of air.

The existence of an absolutely light and an
absolutely heavy body may be demonstrated as
follows. By these terms I mean a body whose
nature it is to move always upwards, and one whose
nature it is to move always downwards, unless
prevented. There are bodies of both sorts, and
it is not true, as some believe, that all bodies have
weight. Others besides ourselves agree that there
is such a thing as a heavy body, in the sense of one
moving always towards the centre. But there is
similarly a light one also. For we see, as has been
said earlier, that earthy bodies sink to the bottom
of everything else and move towards the centre.
But the centre is determined.[a] If then there is
a body which rises to the top of everything else
(and fire is observed to rise even in air itself, though
the air remain at rest),[b] it is clear that this body

---

[b] *Sc.* and therefore cannot be forcing it upwards in the
manner described by the atomists.

311 b

τοῦτο φέρεται πρὸς τὸ ἔσχατον. ὥστε βάρος οὐδὲν
25 οἷόν τ᾽ ἔχειν αὐτό· ὑφίστατο γὰρ ἂν ἄλλῳ· εἰ δὲ
τοῦτο, εἴη ἄν τι ἕτερον, ὃ φέρεται ἐπὶ τὸ ἔσχατον,
ὃ πᾶσι τοῖς φερομένοις ἐπιπολάζει. νῦν δ᾽ οὐδὲν
φαίνεται. τὸ ἄρα πῦρ οὐδὲν ἔχει βάρος, οὐδὲ ἡ γῆ
κουφότητα οὐδεμίαν, εἴπερ ὑφίσταται πᾶσι καὶ τὸ
ὑφιστάμενον φέρεται ἐπὶ τὸ μέσον. ἀλλὰ μὴν ὅτι
30 γ᾽ ἔστι[1] μέσον πρὸς ὃ ἡ φορὰ τοῖς ἔχουσι βάρος καὶ
ἀφ᾽ οὗ τοῖς κούφοις, δῆλον πολλαχόθεν, πρῶτον μὲν
τῷ εἰς ἄπειρον μὴ ἐνδέχεσθαι φέρεσθαι μηθέν.
ὥσπερ γὰρ οὐκ ἔστιν οὐθὲν ἀδύνατον, οὕτως οὐδὲ
γίγνεται· ἡ δὲ φορὰ γένεσίς ποθέν ποι. ἔπειτα
πρὸς ὁμοίας φαίνεται γωνίας τὸ μὲν πῦρ ἄνω
35 φερόμενθν, ἡ δὲ γῆ κάτω καὶ πᾶν τὸ βάρος ἔχον.
312 a ὥστ᾽ ἀνάγκη φέρεσθαι πρὸς τὸ μέσον. (τοῦτο δὲ
πότερον συμβαίνει πρὸς τὸ τῆς γῆς μέσον ἢ πρὸς
τὸ τοῦ παντός, ἐπεὶ ταὐτόν ἐστιν, ἄλλος λόγος.)
ἐπεὶ δὲ τὸ πᾶσιν ὑφιστάμενον φέρεται πρὸς τὸ
μέσον, ἀνάγκη τὸ πᾶσιν ἐπιπολάζον φέρεσθαι πρὸς
5 τὸ ἔσχατον τῆς χώρας, ἐν ᾗ ποιοῦνται τὴν κίνησιν·
ἐναντίον γὰρ τὸ μὲν μέσον τῷ ἐσχάτῳ, τὸ δὲ
ὑφιστάμενον ἀεὶ τῷ ἐπιπολάζοντι. διὸ καὶ εὐλόγως
τὸ βαρὺ καὶ κοῦφον δύο ἐστίν· καὶ γὰρ οἱ τόποι δύο,
τὸ μέσον καὶ τὸ ἔσχατον. ἔστι δὲ δή τι καὶ τὸ
μεταξὺ τούτων, ὃ πρὸς ἑκάτερον αὐτῶν λέγεται
10 θάτερον· ἔστι γὰρ ὡς ἔσχατον καὶ μέσον ἀμφο-

---

[1] ἔστι Simpl., Stocks, Allan; ἐστὶ with the mss. Bekker.

[a] Cf. i. 7. 274 b 13-18.　　　[b] Cf. ii. 14. 296 b 19.

is moving towards the extremity. It cannot therefore possess weight, for if it did it would sink beneath something, and if that were so, there would be another body moving towards the extremity and rising above all moving bodies. We have no evidence of such a body. Fire therefore has not weight nor earth lightness, since it sinks beneath all bodies and that implies motion towards the centre. That there is a centre, towards which heavy bodies move and from which light bodies recede, can be seen in many ways. First, no body can go on moving to infinity ; for the process leading to an impossibility is as impossible as its actual achievement, and locomotion is a process, of removal from one place to another.[a] Secondly, fire in its upward movement and earth and all heavy bodies in their downward movement, make similar angles.[b] Therefore the movement of the latter must be towards the centre. (Whether it is in fact the centre of the earth or the centre of the Universe to which they move—the two being at the same point—belongs to another inquiry.)[c] But since that which sinks beneath all things is moving towards the centre, that which rises to the top of all must be moving to the extremity of the space in which their motion is performed ; for the centre is the contrary of the extremity, and the constantly falling body of the rising. That there are two kinds of body, the heavy and the light, is thus conformable to reason, for the places are two, centre and extremity. But there is also the space between the two, which bears the opposite name in relation to each, for that which lies between the

[c] ii. 14. 296 b 9 ff.

312 a

τέρων τὸ μεταξύ· διὰ τοῦτο ἔστι τι καὶ ἄλλο βαρὺ καὶ κοῦφον, οἷον ὕδωρ καὶ ἀήρ.

Φαμὲν δὲ τὸ μὲν περιέχον τοῦ εἴδους εἶναι, τὸ δὲ περιεχόμενον τῆς ὕλης. ἔστι δ' ἐν πᾶσι τοῖς γένεσιν αὕτη ἡ διάστασις· καὶ γὰρ ἐν τῷ ποιῷ καὶ
15 ἐν τῷ ποσῷ ἐστὶ τὸ μὲν ὡς εἶδος μᾶλλον, τὸ δ' ὡς ὕλη. καὶ ἐν τοῖς κατὰ τόπον ὡσαύτως τὸ μὲν ἄνω τοῦ ὡρισμένου, τὸ δὲ κάτω τῆς ὕλης. ὥστε καὶ ἐν αὐτῇ τῇ ὕλῃ τῇ τοῦ βαρέος καὶ κούφου, ᾗ μὲν τοιοῦτον δυνάμει, βαρέος ὕλη, ᾗ δὲ τοιοῦτον, κού-
φου· καὶ ἔστι μὲν ἡ αὐτή, τὸ δ' εἶναι οὐ ταὐτόν,
20 ὥσπερ καὶ τὸ νοσερὸν καὶ τὸ ὑγιαστόν. τὸ γὰρ[1] εἶναι οὐ ταὐτόν· διόπερ οὐδὲ τὸ νοσώδει εἶναι ἢ ὑγιεινῷ.

[1] γὰρ EL, Allan; δ' FHMJ, Bekker.

a Cf. note on 310 b 11-15 above.

CHAPTER V

ARGUMENT

The matter of the four elements, how differentiated.
There must be four varieties of matter, in the sense that there must exist the four potentialities exhibited by the elements, heavy and light as they are, two absolutely and two relatively. But in another sense they must all have the same matter, in that they can undergo mutual transformations. One common matter, then, with differences of being. Repetition (cf. 311 b 8) and amplification of the statement that every body save fire has weight in its own place, i.e. sinks to the

two is in a sense both extremity and centre. Owing to this there is something else heavy and light, namely water and air.

We hold further that that which surrounds is on the side of form, that which is surrounded is on the side of matter. This distinction exists in all the categories : in quality as in quantity there is seen a more formal and a more material aspect, and it is the same where place is concerned. That which is above belongs to the determinate, that which is below to matter.[a] Thus in the particular matter of heavy and light, we find according to one of its potentialities the matter of the heavy, and according to the other the matter of the light. It is the same matter, but logically distinguishable, as is the matter of health and disease. Here too there is a logical distinction, which accounts for the distinction between being diseased and being healthy.

CHAPTER V

ARGUMENT (continued)

bottom of that place and to the surface of the body next beneath it (312 a 22–b 19).

Summary refutation of the views which allow only one form of matter or two. The one would allow of only one form of motion, up or down, and the other, while allowing for both these, would fail to account for the motions of the two intermediate bodies. The refutations take the form of showing that on either type of theory a large quantity of a light body will be heavier than a small quantity of a heavy body, or vice versa, which is contrary to observation (312 b 19—313 a 13).

312 a 22 Τὸ μὲν οὖν ἔχον τοιαύτην ὕλην κοῦφον καὶ ἀεὶ
ἄνω, τὸ δὲ τὴν ἐναντίαν βαρὺ καὶ ἀεὶ κάτω· τὸ¹ δ'
ἑτέρας μὲν τούτων, ἐχούσας δ' οὕτω πρὸς ἀλλήλας
25 ὡς αὗται ἁπλῶς, καὶ ἄνω καὶ κάτω φερομένας¹· διὸ
ἀὴρ καὶ ὕδωρ ἔχουσι καὶ κουφότητα καὶ βάρος
ἑκάτερον, καὶ ὕδωρ μὲν πλὴν γῆς πᾶσιν ὑφίσταται,
ἀὴρ δὲ πλὴν πυρὸς πᾶσιν ἐπιπολάζει. ἐπεὶ δ' ἐστὶν
ἓν μόνον ὃ πᾶσιν ἐπιπολάζει καὶ ἓν ὃ πᾶσιν ὑφί-
στατα, ἀνάγκη δύο ἄλλα εἶναι ἃ καὶ ὑφίσταταί τινι
30 καὶ ἐπιπολάζει τινί. ὥστε ἀνάγκη καὶ τὰς ὕλας
εἶναι τοσαύτας ὅσαπερ ταῦτα, τέτταρας, οὕτω δὲ
τέτταρας ὡς μίαν μὲν ἁπάντων τὴν κοινήν, ἄλλως
τε καὶ εἰ γίγνονται ἐξ ἀλλήλων, ἀλλὰ τὸ εἶναι ἕτε-
312 b ρον. οὐδὲν² γὰρ κωλύει τῶν ἐναντίων εἶναι μεταξὺ
καὶ ἓν καὶ πλείω, ὥσπερ ἐν χρώμασιν· πολλαχῶς
γὰρ λέγεται τὸ μεταξὺ καὶ τὸ μέσον.

Ἐν μὲν οὖν τῇ αὑτοῦ χώρᾳ τῶν ἐχόντων καὶ
βάρος καὶ κουφότητα ἕκαστον ἔχει βάρος (ἡ δὲ γῆ
5 ἐν ἅπασιν ἔχει βάρος), κουφότητα δ' οὐκ ἔχει, εἰ μὴ
ἐν οἷς ἐπιπολάζει. διὸ καὶ ὑποσπωμένων μὲν φέρεται εἰς τὸ ἐφεξῆς κάτω, ἀὴρ μὲν εἰς τὴν τοῦ
ὕδατος χώραν, ὕδωρ δὲ εἰς τὴν τῆς γῆς. ἄνω δ'
εἰς τὴν τοῦ πυρός, ἀναιρουμένου τοῦ πυρός, οὐκ
οἰσθήσεται ὁ ἀήρ, ἀλλ' ἢ βίᾳ, ὥσπερ καὶ τὸ ὕδωρ

---

¹ The readings of Bekker here are those of all mss. I have
therefore retained them, although both Stocks and Allan
adopt Prantl's conjectures of τὰ for τὸ in line 23 and φερόμενα
in line 25. Translation is difficult, and the comments of
Simpl. suggest that emendation is needed, but not this
particular emendation.   That A. should refer to air and water
collectively in the singular is not unusual.   Cf. line 11 above.
² οὐδὲν.   Bekker misprints as οὐδὲ.

ᵃ i.e. can refer to a region as well as a point.   Cf. the

THE body therefore which has matter of the one sort is light and always moves upwards, that which has matter of the opposite sort is heavy and always moves downwards. But the material constituents in bodies different from these, but constituted relatively to each other the same as these are absolutely, are subject to both upward and downward motions. Hence air and water each have both lightness and weight, water sinks beneath everything save earth, and air rises to the top of everything save fire. Since there is one body only which rises to the top of everything, and another which sinks beneath everything, there must exist two others which both sink beneath something and rise to the top of something else. The kinds of matter, therefore, must be the same in number as the bodies, namely four, in the sense, however, that there is really one matter common to all (because, for one thing, they are generated out of each other) but logically susceptible to differentiation. There is no reason why there should not be either one or more intermediate stages, as in colours, for " intermediate " and " middle " can have several meanings.[a]

Now each of the bodies possessing both weight and lightness has weight in its own place (whereas earth has weight everywhere), but lightness only among the things in which it rises. Therefore if support is removed, it goes to the body next beneath it, air to the place of water, water to the place of earth. But air will not move upwards into the place of fire, if the fire is removed, except by force

tiresome ambiguity in the sense of μέσον in the first paragraph of bk. i. ch. vi.

312 b

10 σπᾶται, ὅταν γένηται τὸ ἐπίπεδον ἓν καὶ θᾶττον
σπάσῃ τις ἄνω τῆς φορᾶς, ἣν φέρεται τὸ ὕδωρ
κάτω. οὐδὲ τὸ ὕδωρ εἰς τὴν τοῦ ἀέρος, ἀλλ' ἢ ὡς
νῦν εἴρηται. ἡ γῆ δὲ τοῦτο οὐ πάσχει, ὅτι οὐχ ἓν
τὸ ἐπίπεδον. διὸ τὸ μὲν ὕδωρ εἰς τὸ ἀγγεῖον
πυρωθὲν σπᾶται, γῆ δ' οὔ. ὥσπερ δὲ οὐδ' ἡ γῆ
ἄνω, οὐδὲ τὸ πῦρ κάτω εἰσὶν ὑφαιρουμένου τοῦ
15 ἀέρος· οὐδὲν γὰρ ἔχει βάρος οὐδ' ἐν τῇ αὑτοῦ χώρᾳ,
ὥσπερ οὐδ' ἡ γῆ κουφότητα. φέρεται δὲ κάτω τὰ
δύο ὑποσπωμένων, ὅτι τὸ μὲν ἁπλῶς βαρύ ἐστιν ὃ
πᾶσιν ὑφίσταται, τὸ δὲ πρός τι βαρὺ ὂν εἰς τὴν
αὑτοῦ χώραν ἢ οἷς ἐπιπολάζει, δι' ὁμοιότητα
τῆς ὕλης.

20 Ὅτι δ' ἀναγκαῖον ποιεῖν ἴσας τὰς διαφορὰς αὐτοῖς, δῆλον. εἰ μὲν γὰρ μία ὕλη πάντων, οἷον ἢ τὸ
κενὸν ἢ τὸ πλῆρες ἢ τὸ μέγεθος ἢ τὰ τρίγωνα, ἢ
πάντα ἄνω ἢ πάντα κάτω οἰσθήσεται, ἡ δὲ ἑτέρα
φορὰ οὐκέτι ἔσται· ὥστ' ἢ κοῦφον οὐδὲν ἔσται
25 ἁπλῶς, εἰ πάντα ῥέπει μᾶλλον τῷ ἐκ μειζόνων
εἶναι σωμάτων ἢ ἐκ πλειόνων ἢ ὅτι πλήρη (τοῦτο

ᵃ Stocks comments that the admissions in this paragraph
" inflict some damage on the doctrine of ' places '—for where
a body has weight it cannot be said to ' rest naturally ' or
to ' be in its place '—and also on the symmetry of the elements—for if the fire above air were removed the air would
not move upward, but if the earth below water were removed
the water would move downward." But the weight, say, of
water in its natural place persists only to the bottom of that
place and no farther. (*Cf.* εἰς τὴν αὑτοῦ χώραν ἢ οἷς ἐπιπολάζει at 312 b 18 f. I take it that ἀὴρ μὲν εἰς τὴν τοῦ ὕδατος χώραν
κτλ. at 312 b 6 f. means " till it *reaches*, *i.e.* rests on the top
of, the place of water," whereas εἰς τὴν αὑτοῦ χώραν here
means " till it *occupies* its own place." If that is so, the first
objection of Stocks is removed.) It is hardly fair to probe
the consequences of removal of the earth from below water

in the same way as water is drawn up when its surface is amalgamated with that of air and the upward suction acts more swiftly than its own downward tendency. Nor will water move into the place of air, except as just described. And for earth this motion is not possible, for its surface is not capable of amalgamation. For this reason water is drawn up into a heated vessel, but earth is not. And just as earth does not pass upwards, so fire does not pass downwards if the air is removed, for it has no weight even in its own place, just as earth has no lightness. But the other two bodies move downwards when support is taken away, because, whereas the body which sinks beneath all things is absolutely heavy, the others are relatively heavy and sink as far as their own place or as the body in which they rise, owing to similarity of matter.[a]

It is clear that we must posit as many differences of matter as there are bodies. For if there were the same matter for all—void or plenum or size or triangles—either everything would move upwards or everything would move downwards, and the other motion would disappear. Either therefore there would be nothing absolutely light, if the momentum of everything were proportionate to the size or number of its component bodies, or due to its being

on a cosmic scale. Were that to occur, there would no longer be a cosmos and the consequences would be fantastic. A. would have no objection to agreeing that one reason why the centre is not the place of water is that it is the place of earth. Were it not, admittedly the world would not be constructed on A.'s lines. But that is hardly a criticism.

For the last phrase (δι᾽ ὁμοιότητα τῆς ὕλης), cf. the discussion of ὁμοιότης in ch. iii. above.

312 b

δὲ ὁρῶμέν τε, καὶ δέδεικται ὅτι ὁμοίως κάτω τε ἀεὶ
καὶ πανταχοῦ φέρεται καὶ ἄνω)· ἐὰν δὲ τὸ κενὸν ᾖ
τι τοιοῦτον ὃ ἀεὶ ἄνω, οὐκ ἔσται τὸ ἀεὶ κάτω. καὶ
τῶν μεταξὺ δὴ ἔνια ἔσται κάτω θᾶττον γῆς· ἐν γὰρ
30 τῷ πολλῷ ἀέρι τρίγωνα πλείω ἢ τὰ στερεὰ ἢ τὰ
μικρὰ ἔσται. οὐ φαίνεται δ' οὐδὲ ἓν μόριον ἀέρος
κάτω φερόμενον. ὁμοίως δὲ καὶ ἐπὶ τοῦ κούφου,
ἐὰν ἐκεῖνο ποιῇ τις ὑπερέχειν τῇ ὕλῃ.

Ἐὰν δὲ δύο, τὰ μεταξὺ πῶς ἔσται ποιοῦντα ἃ
313 a ποιεῖ ἀήρ τε καὶ ὕδωρ; (οἷον εἴ τις φαίη εἶναι
κενὸν καὶ πλῆρες· τὸ μὲν οὖν πῦρ κενόν, διὸ καὶ
ἄνω, τὴν δὲ γῆν πλῆρες, διὸ καὶ κάτω· ἀέρα δὲ
πλεῖον πυρὸς ἔχειν, ὕδωρ δὲ γῆς.) ἔσται γάρ τι
ὕδωρ ὃ πλεῖον ἕξει πῦρ ὀλίγου ἀέρος, καὶ ἀὴρ
5 πολὺς ὀλίγου ὕδατος γῆν πλείω, ὥστε δεήσει ἀέρος
τι πλῆθος θᾶττον φέρεσθαι κάτω ὕδατος ὀλίγου.
τοῦτο δ' οὐ φαίνεται οὐδαμοῦ οὐδέποτε. ἀνάγκη
τοίνυν, ὥσπερ καὶ τὸ πῦρ ἄνω, ὅτι τοδὶ ἔχει, οἷον
τὸ κενόν, τὰ δ' ἄλλα οὔ, καὶ τὴν γῆν κάτω, ὅτι τὸ
πλῆρες ἔχει, καὶ τὸν ἀέρα εἰς τὸν αὑτοῦ καὶ ἀνώ-
10 τερον τοῦ ὕδατος, ὅτι τοδὶ τι ἔχει, καὶ τὸ ὕδωρ

ᵃ Sc. in earth.

a plenum (and not only can we observe that there is, but it has been proved that just as there are bodies which always and everywhere move downwards, so, similarly, are there upward-moving bodies) ; or, if the movement were due to the void, or anything similar which always moves upwards, there would be nothing moving constantly downwards. Further, there would be bodies of the intermediate sort which moved downwards more quickly than earth, for a large quantity of air would contain more triangles or solids or small parts. But no portion of air is observed to move downwards.[a] The same argument applies to lightness, if it is assumed to be due to excess of the matter.

If on the other hand there are two forms of matter, how account for the existence of intermediate bodies behaving as do air and water ? If the pair suggested are void and plenum, then fire moves upwards because it is void, earth downwards because it is plenum, and air contains a preponderance of fire, water of earth. But there will be a quantity of water containing more fire than a small quantity of air, and a large quantity of air containing more earth than a little water, so that a certain amount of air will necessarily move downwards faster than a little water. This is never in any circumstances observed to happen. The truth therefore must be this : just as fire moves upwards because it possesses a certain characteristic—void perhaps—and no other, and earth moves downwards because it possesses the characteristic of plenitude, so air moves to its own place above water because it possesses a peculiar characteristic and water passes beneath it because it is of

κάτω, ὅτι τοιόνδε τι. εἰ δὲ ἦν ἕν τι ἄμφω ἢ δύο,
ἄμφω δ' ὑπάρξει ταῦτα ἑκατέρῳ, ἔσται τι πλῆθος
ἑκατέρου οὗ ὑπερέξει ὕδωρ τε ἀέρος ὀλίγου τῷ ἄνω
καὶ ἀὴρ ὕδατος τῷ κάτω, καθάπερ εἴρηται πολλάκις.

CHAPTER VI

ARGUMENT

Part played by shape in the motion of bodies. *Shape is
not the cause of the upward or downward motion of bodies,
but may help or hinder that motion. Why do heavy objects
sometimes float if flat and sink if of other shapes ? After
rejecting the answer of Democritus, A. suggests that it is
because flat bodies cover a larger surface of the air or water
containing them, and a large amount of a substance is not so
easily cleft or dispersed as a small. The flat object, being*

14   Τὰ δὲ σχήματα οὐκ αἴτια τοῦ φέρεσθαι ἁπλῶς ἢ
15 κάτω ἢ ἄνω, ἀλλὰ τοῦ θᾶττον ἢ βραδύτερον. δι'
ἃς δ' αἰτίας, οὐ χαλεπὸν ἰδεῖν· ἀπορεῖται γὰρ νῦν
διὰ τί τὰ πλατέα σιδήρια καὶ μόλιβδος ἐπιπλεῖ ἐπὶ
τοῦ ὕδατος, ἄλλα δὲ ἐλάττω καὶ ἧττον βαρέα, ἂν ᾖ
στρογγύλα ἢ μακρά, οἷον βελόνη, κάτω φέρεται,
20 καὶ ὅτι ἔνια διὰ μικρότητα ἐπιπλεῖ, οἷον τὸ ψῆγμα
καὶ ἄλλα γεώδη καὶ κονιορτώδη ἐπὶ τοῦ ἀέρος. περὶ
δὴ τούτων ἁπάντων τὸ μὲν νομίζειν αἴτιον εἶναι
ὥσπερ Δημόκριτος οὐκ ὀρθῶς ἔχει. ἐκεῖνος γάρ
φησι τὰ ἄνω φερόμενα θερμὰ ἐκ τοῦ ὕδατος ἀνακω-
313 b χεύειν τὰ πλατέα τῶν ἐχόντων βάρος, τὰ δὲ στενὰ
διαπίπτειν· ὀλίγα γὰρ εἶναι τὰ ἀντικρούοντα αὐτοῖς. ἔδει δ' ἐν τῷ ἀέρι ἔτι μᾶλλον τοῦτο ποιεῖν,

a certain nature. For if both have one and the
same matter, or if two sorts of matter are to be
shared in by both, there will be a quantity of the
one which can be exceeded by the other, water exceeding a little air in the upward-moving matter,
and air exceeding water in the downward-moving, as
we have often remarked.

CHAPTER VI

ARGUMENT (continued)

*unable to disperse what is beneath, must ride on top of it.
Similarly it is easier for a body to float in water than in air
because air is more fissile (=yielding, " liquid," " buxom ")
than water. The motion of a heavy body is the result of a
conflict between its own weight and the resistance to fission
offered by the continuous surface of the body beneath it.*

THE shapes of bodies are not responsible for the
actual downward or upward direction of their
motion, but for making this motion faster or slower.
It is not hard to see how they do this : the question
at issue is why flat objects of iron or lead float on
water, whereas others, smaller and less heavy, if
they are round or elongated—a needle for instance
—sink ; and why certain bodies float on account of
their smallness, like metal filings and other earthy
or dustlike particles in the air. Concerning all
these instances, it cannot be right to accept the
explanation upheld by Democritus. His statement
is that the heat-particles rising from the water
bear up flat heavy bodies, whereas the narrow fall
through, because only a few of these particles
oppose them. But this ought to happen even more

313 b

ὥσπερ ἐνίσταται κἀκεῖνος αὐτός. ἀλλ' ἐνστὰς λύει
μαλακῶς· φησὶ γὰρ οὐκ εἰς ἓν ὁρμᾶν τὸν σοῦν,
λέγων σοῦν τὴν κίνησιν τῶν ἄνω φερομένων
σωμάτων. ἐπεὶ δ' ἐστὶ τὰ μὲν εὐδιαίρετα τῶν
συνεχῶν τὰ δ' ἧττον, καὶ διαιρετικὰ δὲ τὸν αὐτὸν
τρόπον τὰ μὲν μᾶλλον τὰ δ' ἧττον, ταύτας εἶναι
νομιστέον αἰτίας. εὐδιαίρετον μὲν οὖν τὸ εὐόρι-
στον, καὶ μᾶλλον τὸ μᾶλλον· ἀὴρ δὲ μᾶλλον ὕδατος
10 τοιοῦτον, ὕδωρ δὲ γῆς. καὶ τὸ ἔλαττον δὴ ἐν
ἑκάστῳ γένει εὐδιαιρετώτερον καὶ διασπᾶται ῥᾷον.
τὰ μὲν οὖν ἔχοντα πλάτος διὰ τὸ πολὺ περιλαμβάνειν ἐπιμένει, διὰ τὸ μὴ διασπᾶσθαι τὸ πλεῖον
ῥᾳδίως· τὰ δ' ἐναντίως ἔχοντα τοῖς σχήμασι διὰ τὸ
15 ὀλίγον περιλαμβάνειν φέρεται κάτω, διὰ τὸ διαιρεῖν
ῥᾳδίως. καὶ ἐν ἀέρι πολὺ μᾶλλον, ὅσῳ εὐδιαιρετώ-
τερος ὕδατός ἐστιν. ἐπεὶ δὲ τό τε βάρος ἔχει τινὰ
ἰσχὺν καθ' ἣν φέρεται κάτω, καὶ τὰ συνεχῆ πρὸς
τὸ μὴ διασπᾶσθαι, ταῦτα δεῖ πρὸς ἄλληλα συμβάλ-
λειν· ἐὰν γὰρ ὑπερβάλλῃ ἡ ἰσχὺς ἡ τοῦ βάρους τῆς
20 ἐν τῷ συνεχεῖ πρὸς τὴν διάσπασιν καὶ διαίρεσιν,
βιάσεται κάτω θᾶττον, ἐὰν δὲ ἀσθενεστέρα ᾖ, ἐπι-
πολάσει.

Περὶ μὲν οὖν βαρέος καὶ κούφου καὶ τῶν περὶ
αὐτὰ συμβεβηκότων διωρίσθω τοῦτον ἡμῖν τὸν
τρόπον.

---

a The Greek word quoted from Democritus is a Laconism.
Cf. Plato, *Crat.* 412 в τὴν γὰρ ταχεῖαν ὁρμὴν οἱ Λακεδαιμόνιοι
τοῦτο (*sc.* σοῦς) καλοῦσιν.

b *i.e.* the liquid (τὸ ὑγρόν), so described in *De gen. et corr.*
329 b 30.

easily in air, an objection which is raised by the
author of the view himself. Having raised it,
however, he answers it but feebly. He says that
the " surge " does not work in one direction only—
" surge " [a] being his word for the motion of upward-
moving bodies. But since some continuous bodies
are more easily divided than others, and in the
same way some are more efficient agents of fission
than others, it is here that we must suppose the
causes to lie. Now the fissile is that which is easily
brought within bounds,[b] and fissile in proportion as
it is easily bounded ; and air has this characteristic
to a greater degree than water, water than earth.
Further, in every kind the smaller quantity is more
fissile and more easily cleft. Thus bodies possessed
of breadth stay where they are because they cover
a large quantity, and the larger quantity is not
easily cleft ; but bodies of the contrary shape move
downwards because they only cover a little, and
easily divide it. In air this happens much more
readily than in water, in proportion as it is more
fissile. But since there exist at the same time (a)
the weight possessing a certain strength of downward impulse, and (b) the continuity of the resisting
body working against its cleavage, these two forces
must come into conflict. If the strength exerted by
the weight in the direction of cleavage and division
exceeds the resistance of the continuum, then the
body will force its way so much the more quickly
downwards ; but if it is weaker, it will keep on the
surface.

This then is our manner of describing weight and
lightness and the properties that follow from their
nature.

INDEX

To Introduction, Translation and Notes

1. *English*

371

INDEX

Columbus 255 n.

Complete, meaning of 7 ; no straight line is 15 ; (=perfect) defined 155

Contact, dist. continuity 161 n.; makes each body many 8 f. *and note*; not the result of process 105, 107

Continuous = infinitely divisible 5 ; of two bodies = sharing the same limit 161 n.

Cornford, F. M. 5, 12 n., 70 n., 74 n., 285 n.; *Plato's Cosmology* 99 n., 193 n., 218 n., 220 n., 243 n., 268 n., 313 n., 317 n.

Counter-earth 217

Cyprus 253

Democritus (*see also* Atomic Theory) 67, 70 n., 273, 291, 317 n., 323; explains effect of shape on motion 367 ; on the Earth 227 ; theory of generation 309 f.

Des Places, E. 137

Development in Aristotle's thought xv f., 65 n., 134 n., 149 n.

Diogenes of Apollonia 295 n.

Down, defined 11, 329

Earth ii. 13 and 14 ; is at rest 183, and in centre of Universe 241 ff.; its function in the Cosmos 151 ; natural motion of 231 f., 243 ; not a planet 243 ; shape held to be flat 223 ; shape and position, opinion of Pythagoreans 217 f., of

Plato 221, 241, of Xenophanes 225, of Thales 225, of Anaximenes, Anaxagoras, Democritus 227, of Empedocles 231 ff., of Anaximander 235 f. ; size of 253 f. ; spherical 247 ff.

Eclipses 201 (sun), 221, 253 (moon)

Egypt 253

Egyptians 25 n., 205

Elements (*see also* Simple Bodies), defined 283 ; do not contain their products 285 ; generated from each other iii. 6 ; must be finite in number iii. 4

Elephants 253

Empedocles 97, 225, 231 f., 229 n., 273, 275, 277, 305 ; elements in 285, 289 ; neglected weight and lightness 337 ; theory of generation 309 f. ; vortex 135, 231 ff., 273

Epicurus 79 n.

Er, myth of 192 n.

Experience, evidence of common 24 f.

Falling Bodies, make similar angles with Earth 245, 251, 357

False, dist. impossible 113

Fifth Body (*see also* Aither), divinity of 25 ; eternal and unalterable 21 f. ; existence of, demonstrated 13 ; motion of is circular 13 ; neither heavy nor light 21 ; primacy of 15 f.

Fire (*see also* Atomic Theory)

373

INDEX

Possibility refers to *maximum* attainable 109 f.

Potentiality. Co-existence of opposite potentialities i. 12 (*see esp.* 124 n.) ; equated with matter 127 ; one potentiality of opposite states 127 ; progress from potentiality to actuality 349

Prantl, C. 31 n., 166 n., 235 n., 254 n.

Priority, senses of distinguished 143 *and note*, 349 *and note*

Pythagoreans, assign right and left sides to the heaven 139 ; correlation of dimensions and numbers 6 n. ; number-atomism of 269, 291 n. ; on position of earth 217 f. ; on the Triad 5 ; said motion of fixed stars is to the right 137

Religion, evidence of 25, 133

Rest, natural and enforced 231, 271

Richardson, Hilda 219 n.

Rivaud, A. 137

Ross, Sir W. D. *Aristotle* (Methuen) 253 n. ; Ed. of Aristotle's *Physics* xv n., xvi n., xx n., xxvi, xxvii, xxviii, xxxi, xxxiii, 38 n., 229 n., 297 n.

Schoch, K. 205 n.

Seneca (*Nat. Qu.* ii. 57. 2) 180 n.

Shape of bodies, effect on their motion iv. 6

Sight, explanation of 188 n. ; effect of distance on 187

Simple Bodies, defined 11 f. ; fineness of, increases with distance from centre 163

Soul, considered as mover of the stars xxix ff. ; counteracts natural motions of the elements in living creatures xxxvi n., 64 n., 173 ; in Plato xix n. ; movement of heaven not due to constraint of soul xxxi, xxxvi n., 135

Sound, destructive power of 195

Sphere, how constructed 293; motions proper to spherical bodies 187 ; regarded as an angle by Democritus 323 (*cf.* 321) ; shape least suited to progression 191 ; the primary solid 155 f.

Stars, are alive 207, spherical 187, ii. 11 ; heat and light of, how produced 179 f. ; motion of, how explained in *De philosophia* xxiv, not self-caused ii. 8, 195 ; not made of fire 179 ; no variation in relative positions of fixed stars 173 ; twinkling of 189

Stengel, P. 5

Stocks, J. L. *See notes passim.*

Strato 79 n.

Sun, apparent rotation of 187 ; heat of, how produced 181 ; in eclipse 201 ; shape at horizon 223

INDEX

INDEX

2. Selected Greek Words